European Fascism

European Fascism

Edited by
S. J. Woolf

Random House/New York

FIRST PRINTING

READING UNIVERSITY STUDIES ON
CONTEMPORARY EUROPE
I Studies in Fascism

Library of Congress Catalog Card Number: 69-16434

Contents

European Fascism

1 Introduction

S. J. Woolf

Perhaps the word fascism should be banned, at least temporarily, from our political vocabulary. For like other large words – democracy, reactionary, radical, anarchy – it has been so misused that it has lost its original meaning; or, at least, it has been so overlaid with newer and broader connotations that the narrower, historical sense almost seems to require apologetic inverted commas.

Not that I wish to proclaim a puristic attitude. For in that case, I could point to only one fascism – the original version produced in Italy, which according to its creator was not for export. The word obviously has a far wider significance. It is certainly difficult to define with precision what is fascism; but we should remember that it is no easier to define democracy. The concepts are too broad for the words. It may upset the tidiness of the sociological mind that probably no single historical example could meet the exacting requirements of a carefully constructed 'model' of fascism or democracy. But this does not mean that neither really existed. Historically speaking, fascism was originally understood to describe a particular political – and, to some extent, cultural, economic and social – system of a specific geographical area in a delimited period of time – Europe between the wars. It is open to discussion whether the Japanese régime of the 1930s or Argentina in the 1940s or certain more recent developments in the postwar world can, strictly speaking, be described as fascist. The word, unfortunately, has certain commode-like tendencies – the more you stuff into it, the more it takes. But there can be no doubt

1

about the correctness of its usage for the interwar period in Europe.

Indeed, one of the conclusions which emerges most clearly from the essays in this volume is the difference between fascism and the authoritarian movements which increasingly dominated central and eastern Europe after the first world war. At politically opportune moments, approval might be expressed of fascism as a system of government by Horthy, Dollfuss, Pilsudski or Svinhufvud. But the régimes they controlled, or were trying to create, were not fascist. Any 'real' fascist from Hungary, Austria, Poland or Finland would have told you so. For these fascists claimed they were trying to create something different, to break with the existing structure of power and forge a new, wholly disciplined state which would revive real or mythical glories of a past age or achieve a new pre-eminence for their race. Admittedly, their claims should be examined with a degree of scepticism. For such fascists were, at best, disingenuous in their refusal to recognize how much of fascism actually existed in the authoritarian régimes they were attacking and trying to infiltrate.

In fact, the contrast between ambitions and practice, so evident in Italy and Germany, held true in the central European fascisms as well. Fascist aims everywhere were ambitious, ambiguous, contradictory or simply nebulous. Fascist practice – which only triumphed unquestionably in Italy and Germany – was to be found to some degree in all the right-wing régimes of central Europe, although in no instance was any régime peaceably transformed into a fullblown fascism. It needed Hitler's aggression to achieve such a transformation. Until then – the later 1930s – the native fascists continued to grumble bitterly about the inadequacies of their respective régimes. In a sense, this is understandable. For in Italy and Germany fascist régimes emerged *subsequently* to their period of opposition and striving, so allowing their members time to forget or rationalize (and historians facility to point out) the contradictions between the two separate phases. In Austria, Hungary, Rumania or Poland the two phases were as if partially superimposed: given the

2

existence of certain fascist elements in right-wing authoritarian régimes, it was difficult to be so totally hostile and revolutionary as in western-type parliamentary democracies. These régimes obliged the fascist leaders to be more precise in their ambitions, and by placing these ambitions side by side with certain existing practices may well have rendered the contrast more immediate and frustrating.

Such general remarks touch upon some of the complexities of the fascist phenomenon in Europe. Fascism was strongly nationalist and firmly rooted in the historical development of each country. Yet increasingly it laid claims to its importance as an international system capable of replacing democracy or communism. Fascism developed as a counterpoise to the socialist threat in industrialized countries. Yet fascist movements sprang up like mushrooms in some of the most backward and unlikely countries of Europe. Fascism vaunted the *Führerprinzip*, but in many countries – such as Hungary, Poland, Finland – it failed to produce an outstanding leader. Fascist ideology proclaimed revolutionary changes in a modern society, but its rituals exuded a deep nostalgia for a return to a mythical medieval past. Fascist strength was based on the urban or rural *petite bourgeoisie*, but once in power fascism turned for support to the industrialists and big landowners. These complexities and contradictions cannot be explained in any simple, or single, manner. They can only be studied in their individual manifestations, in terms of their national peculiarities.

But three general distinctions can be made which seem to me to assist one's understanding of European fascism. They are: the difference between fascism in western Europe and fascism in central and eastern Europe; the contrast between early fascist claims and later fascist actions; and the changing character of fascism in the 1920s, 1930s and during the second world war.

The first distinction, between the western and the central and eastern European movements, is extremely broad. Professor George Mosse has pointed to the racialist element as a particular characteristic of central European fascism. This may be so, although French, Spanish and British fascists were also decidedly antisemitic. But the differences between the two areas of fascism seem to me far more wide-ranging.

It is of course possible to find certain general conditions conducive to the rise of a fascist movement common to both western and central Europe. (It should be added that it is also possible to find an exception to almost every such condition.) Strong nationalist feeling is the most obvious example, common to Europe from Portugal to Finland, with the understandable exception of Austria, which had little to be nationalist about after the collapse of the Empire. Anti-socialism is another trait, as even in countries where marxism was not a real threat, the menace of bolshevik Russia offered a convenient whipping-boy. Weak and inefficient parliamentary government was yet another characteristic to be found, to a greater or lesser degree, throughout Europe between the wars. The effects of the Great War, both immediate and long-term, cannot be underestimated as a necessary condition without which it is difficult to imagine the rise of fascist movements and their success. For the war not only brought in its aftermath economic and political disruption to almost all the countries of Europe. It also 'politicized' the peoples of the different countries to a hitherto unknown degree, so encouraging the growth of mass parties. And at the same time it gave the Right its chance to revive its fortunes, and then created vast masses of ex-combatants who were to form the most fertile seedbeds of nascent nationalistic and fascist movements. The future fascist parties in almost all the countries of Europe traced their origins back to the numerous groupings of patriotic associations which emerged or re-emerged in strength after the war.

Yet, if certain 'pre-conditions' of fascism seem common to all the countries, there can be no doubt that central and eastern European fascism remained distinct from that of the west. It is fashionable to explain the success of fascist movements in terms of mass middle-class support in industrialized or industrializing countries. But it should be remembered that fascism emerged as

4

a significant force in a large number of agrarian societies. For it is not inaccurate to include among agrarian societies countries such as Spain, Austria or Finland, where the existence of modern industry and a large working class in a clearly delimited geographical area had as yet made little impact on the *mores* and traditional pattern of rural society. In industrialized countries, such as Germany, northern Italy or France, the emergence of fascism as an organized, articulated party is relatively easy to understand in terms of a political, economic, social and psychological crisis. In agrarian societies, without a large or significant middle class, it is far less easy to understand. It would perhaps be possible to describe the Finnish peasant smallholders as offering a mass base similar to that of the *petite bourgeoisie*, and so explain the support for the Lapua movement. But it is not possible to equate similar social categories with the support given to the Portuguese national syndicalists or the Rumanian Iron Guard. The 'middle class' interpretation of fascism – while perfectly valid for industrialized countries – is, in fact, inadequate as a general explanation, because it fails to account for the significant fascist movements in backward or agrarian societies (of which, after all, there were a considerable number in Europe between the wars). It needs, at least, to be supplemented by other interpretations, some perhaps sociological in character, others far more political.

It would evidently be false to identify western Europe with industrialized countries and central and eastern Europe with agrarian societies. For Spain and Portugal would hardly qualify – although in this sense undoubtedly Germany belongs to western Europe. But nor should one be so crude as to regard all the agrarian societies as basically the same. There were clearly important political and social differences which help to explain why fascist movements should have been particularly important at specific moments in some agrarian societies, but not in others. For example, only in Spain and Portugal did feeling about the monarchy run so deep that the existence of a republic was regarded (by the monarchists naturally) as a national shame to be washed out, if necessary in blood; for in Austria and Hungary

5

the issue was too recent and lacked the historical roots to engender such deep feelings. Similarly, there is a difference between agrarian societies with a relatively advanced degree of political education or respect for law and those with an extremely traditional pattern of society and overwhelming illiteracy. In the former, with a large educated class (not necessarily middle class), such as Finland, specific factors – like the very real threat of bolshevism, weak governments and the world economic crisis – offered an opening for a fascist movement with a strongly defined structure. Even in Norway, at one particular moment, the opportunity seemed there.

✗ Elsewhere in central and eastern Europe – with the curious exception of the self-destructive Rumanian Iron Guard – fascism as an organized and articulated party would not seem to be a characteristic. Why was this so? Political life in such agrarian, sometimes even semi-feudal societies was dominated by conservative or reactionary circles. The Left never represented a threat, as political authority was exercised by the traditional sources of power – the landowners, the Church, perhaps the bankers. In Hungary and Poland, as in Rumania and Yugoslavia, almost the entire political spectrum was composed of the Right. In such political systems, fascism could make little headway as it lacked the necessary freedom to manoeuvre. This was particularly true where a military *coup d'état* had formally consecrated the predominance of the Right. Where no 'bolshevik' threat existed, it was difficult for a fascist movement to act as a rallying-point of reaction – for the space had already been occupied by the politically powerful and socially respectable forces of the Right.

Under authoritarian régimes, in fact, fascism's main hope was to permeate the entire system, and in particular the army. In this – as can be seen in the cases of Hungary or Poland – it was successful, especially after the triumph of nazism. But unless the army was prepared to carry out a specifically fascist *coup*, fascism could only hope to set the tone for the whole régime, not to gain control. A fascist-minded army, which lacked a fascist leader, spelled doom for a fascist takeover – for the

6

Church, for all its sympathy, could hardly (or was reluctant to) provide such a leader.

It is this state of frustration that explains the conspiratorial nature of fascism in central Europe. No doubt an old tradition of conspiracies, a deep and widespread network of freemasonry, lay behind this trait. But in so authoritarian a setting conspiracy offered the main chance of influencing those in control of the political system; conspiracy might even lead to control of the army GHQ. In western Europe, fascism and nazism possessed their private armies – the squads, the SA. In central and eastern Europe, the fascist paramilitary organizations could not hope to rival the army. For fascism in these countries was a movement from above, an attempt to transform an already existing authoritarian régime into a fascist dictatorship from within. It only developed as a spontaneous movement from below if the repercussions of an economic or international crisis were such as to upset the economic-social equilibrium to a degree where enfranchised but apathetic groups of the population blamed the conservative government for being insufficiently radical. By the late 1930s, such repercussions began to be felt under the impact of Nazi expansion. It was, for instance, at this time that racialism began to develop as a prominent feature in Hungary.

Two other features distinguishing western from central European fascism can be noted: the 'socialist' claims of western fascism; and the extreme romanticism of the central European movements.

The socialist or corporativist claims of fascism have often been noted. The Italian revolutionary syndicalists and corporativists, the very name of the German National Socialist Party, the Spanish vertical syndicates, the Portuguese national syndicalists, Mosley's driving concern with the problem of unemployment left contemporaries bewildered and have sometimes made historians uncertain about where to locate fascism in the political spectrum. It is worth remembering that such combinations of socialist ideals and nationalistic feeling predated fascism: in Italy, Germany and Austria nationalistic movements of workers existed at the turn of the century. They were of importance to

7

fascist movements because they offered the hope of mass working-class support. But once this support began to come from the lower bourgeoisie, fascist 'socialism' lost its driving force and increasingly became a façade for the régimes. It was, in any case, a special type of socialism – a socialism of class collaboration, not of class conflict. The German worker was to enjoy a respected, but subordinate place within the strong nation. For the elitist, hierarchical concept of fascism could not conceive of a privileged position for the worker. If any class was to enjoy a privileged place, it was to be the 'small men', the businessmen or farmers, the 'healthy' German middle class, the Italian 'productive bourgeoisie'. It was a socialism without the economic claims of expropriation or the political claims of the dictatorship of the proletariat.

It was, in any case, a socialism of western fascisms, not of those of central or eastern Europe. This is not surprising, given the industrialized character of many western European countries and the presence of large urban masses. If social reform meant anything in central and eastern Europe, it meant agrarian reform; such were the claims of the Hungarian fascists of the 1930s. But, in fact, social reform – whether urban or rural – did not loom large in the fascist programmes of these areas. Its absence offers a more clear-cut version of fascism. Whatever the ambiguity or confusion of western fascism, there can be no doubt about the reactionary character of the central and eastern European examples.

To compensate, however, the romanticism of central European fascism appears far more prominently. The ritualistic preoccupations of fascism are, of course, to be found in all countries, from the French *Cagoulards* to the Hungarian Arrow Cross, from the Rumanian Iron Guard to the Norwegian *Nordisk Folkereisning*. The very hostility of fascism towards freemasonry would, ironically, seem to have encouraged it to cultivate archaic ceremonies. Rites were the exemplification of history. For almost all fascisms – precisely because they were so nationalistic – looked back to the past and desired both to revive some bygone age of glory and to prove their movements to be the culmination of their country's history. The Teutonic master-race, the new Roman empire, the Turanian Hunters, the Nordic tribes were all motifs on the same theme, as was the search for 'precursors' of fascism. In western Europe, this desire for a return to a pre-industrial and pre-French Revolution society, where hierarchy was respected and each was happy in his place, offers yet one more contradiction in movements which claimed to embody the true future, the transcendence of liberal capitalism and marxist expropriation.

In western fascisms the contrast is striking because of the modern nature of fascism as an articulated and often mass movement of reaction. In central European fascisms, as the modernity diminished, the romanticism grew stronger. For it acquired apocalyptic, millenarian overtones. It was not merely a question of a man of destiny. It was a belief so deep that it could even become self-destructive, as in Rumania. It was a belief that fascist success would bring salvation, that all problems would be solved miraculously in the new Kingdom of Heaven. This messianic feeling was far stronger in central and eastern European fascism than in the west. 'National character' is the unenlightening phrase often employed to explain away such differences. But perhaps it was more a consequence of fascism's need in these regions to work within the system, a consequence of its relatively subordinate position, its greater influence as an opposition movement than in the west, but its lesser likelihood of achieving power. Excited by the symbolic use of sword and oath, central European fascists went forth to indulge in the chivalric shedding of blood. If fate proved hostile they yielded to death as true and gallant knights.

The second, and perhaps most obvious distinction in a discussion of European fascism is that between fascism out of power and fascism in power, between ambitions and practice, between the origins of fascism and the régimes. It is not easy to compare fascist régimes as – fortunately for the modern world – so few movements ever achieved full power. There are far more instances of fascisms *manqués*. It is commonplace to point to the

9

contradictions between the revolutionary claims of fascism in opposition and the conservative practices of fascist régimes. In abstract terms, it might be argued that parliamentary leaders who fail to carry out their promises once in power behave in a similar manner. But the fundamental difference is that parliamentary leaders work within the system, whereas fascist leaders were determined to change the system itself (Sir Oswald Mosley is perhaps the sole partial exception).

But the contrast between fascist promises and practice needs to be examined more closely, unless its sole purpose is to serve as a contemptuous expression of dismissal of fascism and hence of its study. For there is some continuity between fascism in opposition and fascism in power, in terms of both personalities and policies. Who were the early leaders who managed to retain positions of influence in the régimes? For Spain the question is perhaps inappropriate, as the leaders were in good part killed in the civil war. But in Italy, Germany and Portugal the left-wing fascist leaders desirous of genuine social change were those who failed to assert themselves, who disappeared or were placed in positions where they were unable to further the causes for which they had once fought. The 'intellectuals' of fascism in opposition, usually closely identified with the movement's most revolutionary claims, proved the victims of the régimes. Strasser or Rosenberg, Massimo Rocca or Panunzio were but typical instances.

Conversely, the policies that were continued were those most concerned with either the permanent conservation of power or the development of the economic and military strength of the state. That such policies should have aroused less opposition from the traditional centres of power than would have attempts totally to subvert the existing structure of society, is evident. But it would be inaccurate to conclude that fascist régimes inevitably compromised and abandoned their revolutionary ambitions. Hitler's control over Germany, his transformation of its economic system – and indeed its 'intellectual' climate – are clear evidence to the contrary. Fascist régimes selected among the various aims they had expressed in their years of opposition.

Indeed, given the eclectic and catholic character of Italian fascist aims before 1922, it would have proved impossible not to select. The important questions are what was selected and why? And to what degree the régimes proved able to implement their selections? The test of the strength of a fascist régime must surely lie in its capacity to direct inevitable compromises in its own favour, to follow through its aims, even if such aims needed to be partially or temporarily modified by the force of external circumstances. Nazism and Salazar's régime emerge sucessfully from such a test, Francoism and Italian fascism failed.

Naturally the whole problem of fascist régimes cannot be summed up in so simplified a manner. It would distort, because of its exclusive concentration on the 'internal' lines of communication of a single régime. The impact on fascist policies of international trends, such as the economic crisis of the early 1930s or the breakdown of the League of Nations, cannot be ignored. The new tensions created by the pursuit of such policies and their effect on the claim to permanency of the régime need to be assessed. But the point of departure – in practical more than ideological terms – remains the link between fascism in opposition and fascism in power. Fascist régimes were conditioned, to a greater or lesser extent, by what they proclaimed and what they represented in their early days.

Perhaps the two most significant aspects of fascist régimes are their method of utilizing the existing machinery of power and their intervention in the economy. No fascist régime seized power with a ready-made blueprint of aims. The structure of the state administration was rapidly changed to ensure the supreme position of the leader and the permanency of the régime. There can be no doubt about the crucial importance of the leader to a fascist movement: no movement without a leader succeeded in establishing itself as a régime. Less important – at least to judge by the examples of Salazar and Franco – were the charismatic qualities of the leader. But the greater part of the old machinery of state continued to be used. Fascist régimes superimposed the party on the existing structure of the state. The party was to serve as the channel of communication between the leader and the masses. Hence the creation of a network of party organs parallel to those of the old state. The result was undoubtedly to create a new political system. The old economic and even cultural centres of power and influence might remain, but a new political class was emerging. The unusually rapid growth in the size of the bureaucracies was an external symptom of this transformation.

But the final result was to create new strains, new tensions. Within the régimes ambiguous dualities of power resulted from this fusion of the new order with the old. In Italy the King remained alongside the Duce; in Portugal the Head of State continues to be chosen from among the army leaders. At lower levels, in Germany and Spain as much as in Italy or Portugal, the militia or SA maintained an equivocal relationship with the army, the Church and its organizations were never absorbed by the régime.

The party inevitably changed in nature from its years of opposition. In Spain and Portugal the small fascist parties which had existed before the military seizure of power drowned within the newly created official parties. But even in Italy and Germany – where the fascists and not the military seized power – the party changed in character. No longer was to be found that dedication so typical of fascist movements in opposition, particularly marked in countries where fascists were in a small minority and rationalized their existence by the cult of the élite, of the 'chosen'. No longer were to be found those characteristically youthful party members and especially young intellectuals, typical of backward societies like Rumania or Portugal where university students enjoyed particular prestige but risked unemployment because of lack of vocational training. The change was inevitable not only because the original members grew old, not only because the 'new waves' of carpet-baggers swelled party numbers, but because the functions of the party changed with the assumption of power. Exclusiveness and dedication were bound to disappear as the party tried to identify itself, sometimes in an almost literal sense, with the nation. Youth could not but suffer as the party crystallized into a bureaucratic instrument.

12

In its new role, the party remained a relatively loose organization, despite the appearance of monolithic unity. Its very looseness served the purposes of the leader as it enabled him to conserve control by fostering rivalry among his immediate subordinates and their organizations. This undoubtedly worked against the formation of a body of party members adequately unified and professional to solve the problem of the succession, to ensure the permanency of the régime after the leader's death. But, in practical and immediate terms, this was hardly the leader's preoccupation. Ultimately, however, this system of departmental and local autonomy led to confusion. Competing agencies created unclear lines of communication, contradictory sources of authority beneath the leader. At its least efficient, chaos and *sottogoverno* resulted – as in Italy and Spain. At its most efficient – in Germany – separate and conflicting policies were pursued by Nazi leaders in rivalry with each other.

Fascist intervention in the economy was an inevitable result of the exaltation of the state. Autarchy, however, whether of the Italian, German or Portuguese variety, needs to be judged against the world trend towards protectionism which rapidly gathered force during the years of the depression. Autarchy was not just a political measure designed to mobilize the economic resources of the country for war. It was also a response to the protectionist policies of non-fascist countries. As a policy, it was more successful in the industrial than in the agricultural sector. For it was easier to persuade the big industrialists of the advantages of a cartel than to satisfy absentee landowners about the benefits of intensive cultivation of crops which the party judged necessary. Moreover, as agriculture formed a major source of domestic taxable income, the régime was probably reluctant to interfere excessively. This explains, at least in part, the failure of the Italian, Spanish and Portuguese régimes to transform the agricultural sector and the structure of landownership.

Intervention in industry proved more effective. It is true that the Nazi development of the chemical industry was a conscious choice, whereas the Italian creation of a state holding company, IRI, was an accidental and traditional result of the State's policy

13

of salvaging sick industries. But in both instances the fascist régime did gain substantial control over industry – at least to the extent that the régimes dragged the industrialists down in their *Götterdämmerung*. Fascist economics may have been improvised, short-sighted, inequitable and erroneous. But they existed.

The final distinction I would make is in the periods of fascism. It is enough to look at the chronological tables in this volume to realize the changes in fascism as a European phenomenon from the 1920s to the 1930s and 1940s.

In the 1920s fascism remained a national characteristic with virtually no international implications. Italian fascism, as the prototype, was clearly a source of interest and admiration for enthusiastic fascists elsewhere (as it was for leading statesmen in western parliamentary democracies). Mussolini's desire to extend his sphere of influence in the Danubian basin also had inevitable repercussions on fascist movements in this area: the Austrian *Heimwehr* is the most obvious example. But fascism as yet did not aspire to a role of universality. Born of nationalistic movements, concerned to vindicate nationalistic aspirations, the very obsession of the various fascisms with their country's past bore witness to their local, limited preoccupations.

By the later 1920s and 1930s, however, fascist leaders all over Europe were explicit about the international implications of their cause, and consciously looked towards Italy or (increasingly) Germany as a model to be imitated once power had been won. The still-born 'fascist international' was merely the outward manifestation of this growing internationalism. Such a development was perhaps inevitable, for if fascism stood for social stability at home, it signified subversion abroad. There can be no doubt about the immense importance of the Nazi seizure of power in this period: 1933 saw the emergence of a new fascist Mecca which rapidly supplanted the old shrine at Rome. As Nazi influence spread, fascism became more extremist and racialist. The year 1936 and the Spanish civil war marked another major development, as international fascism felt called upon to challenge international bolshevism.

14

But a basic contradiction existed between the deep-rooted nationalistic character of all fascisms and their international aspirations. Even in the 1930s a national fascism, such as the Finnish Lapua movement, could lose popular support because of its imitation of foreign (Nazi) ideology and practices. When war broke out, this contradiction emerged with force in the frustrations of fascist régimes set up in the wake of Nazi conquest. But it can be seen as clearly in the discussions about the New Order, to be established after an Axis victory.

In their varying and discordant statements about the New Order the 1940s' vintage of fascist leaders were, logically enough, stating their faith in the new international system which they hoped would prevail. Yet the very contradictions of these statements reflected not merely the incoherencies of the concept of the New Order as expressed in Nazi Germany, but the effective tensions within, and limitations of, international fascism. The future relationship of the Teutons and the Latins was never overtly faced, at least in concrete terms. The French fascists might hope for a partnership. At the other end of Europe, the Finns – although not aryan – might calculate on finding a place in the sun at the expense of the Russians. But what hope existed for Polish fascists in the event of a Nazi victory? And where would the other Slav fascists find themselves? The Hungarian fascists, by the end, were in good part hostile to the Germans. With reason, for the Austrian fascists, although they had hoped to be the dominant influence in the Balkans and northern Italy, had already paid the price for their internationalism – the end of their national identity. For movements born of exacerbated nationalistic feeling and nurtured on the exaltation of war and the bloody suppression of the weak, fascist internationalism was a contradiction in terms. Even if race hatred had somehow been attenuated, geographical space did not exist to requite the demands of all. The New Order meant the triumph of select fascist movements over the others and the Nazis made no attempt to hide this. Its interest today lies not in any concrete proposals it contained, but as a symbol of the illogicality of an internationalized fascist movement as it emerged in

15

its final phase. So long as fascism developed separately in individual countries, related to and concerned with national developments, this illogicality did not appear. But, increasingly, as its exponents proclaimed a *Weltanschauung* capable of transforming the world, the implausibility of the claim became apparent. Fascism, a fundamentally nationalistic movement, could not offer a viable alternative to the more genuinely international pretensions of capitalist democracy or communism.

What of fascism since 1945? In Spain and Portugal it survived the shock of the war, more through the isolation of these countries than through the merits of the régimes. In other countries fascist movements have started up once more. Yet it seems unlikely that fascism – in its prewar form – could re-emerge as a major threat in western Europe. The conditions which assisted fascism after 1918 no longer hold true, or exist in attenuated form. Socialism is no longer a bogey-man in western European countries, while anti-bolshevism has been so internationalized by the Cold War that it can hardly be monopolized by any single national movement. Weak parliamentary government has not disappeared, but at the national level there is a greater respect for the law (perhaps due to the extension of the power of the state), possibly reinforced by the growth of international organisms. Irredentism and the desire for the liberation of ethnic brothers from foreign rule, while still existing, is no longer in the forefront of national and international politics, as the horizon has broadened to an inevitable consideration of world problems. Imperialism can hardly offer the basis for a popular appeal, as the problems of decolonization emerge with increasing force. Anti-capitalism is less plausible, as capitalism in the postwar period has shown its ability to avoid the debilitating international crises of the prewar years. Moreover, the very identification of capitalism with the struggle against communism makes it a less easy object to attack. Finally, the end of the war and transition to peace did not produce the same shock and repercussions throughout society in 1945 as occurred after 1918: the shock was cushioned by American aid.

16

But if fascism of the old variety does not seem likely to re-emerge, this does not mean that its place might not be taken by a new version, a new-style mass movement of reaction. Neither western democracy nor capitalism is so impregnable and perfect that the threat can be dismissed. Indeed, the elements are already there. Fascism, after all, need not necessarily begin from outside the existing system: it can also work from within. Some political commentators, looking at the power of the church or the army in the world today, would even say that it has already begun.

The present collection of essays originated in a series of lectures and seminars held by the Graduate School of Contemporary European Studies and the Centre for the Advanced Study of Italian Society of the University of Reading in 1966-7. The series of lectures laid no greater claim to comprehensiveness than does the present volume. Studies of fascism in Greece, Belgium, Czechoslovakia or Estonia, to mention some omissions, would have proved valuable. But I believe that the range and scope of these essays is already sufficiently wide to draw valid conclusions and to act as a stimulus to further research. The chronological tables and bibliographies have been compiled by the authors.

2 The Phenomenon of Fascism

H. R. Trevor-Roper

The public appearance of fascism as a dominant force in Europe is the phenomenon of a few years only. It can be precisely dated. It began in 1922–3, with the emergence of the Italian fascist party which Mussolini led to power in the famous, or mythical, 'march on Rome' of 1922, which was followed, next year, by Hitler's abortive Munich *putsch*. It came of age in the 1930s when 'fascist' parties sprang up throughout Europe and were brought to power, sometimes by conspiracy, sometimes by civil war, but always under the patronage of Hitler and Mussolini, bound together, as a force in European politics, by the 'Pact of Steel' of 1936. It ended in 1945 with the defeat and death of the two dictators, the collapse or scurry of their European clients. Of course there were 'precursors' of fascism before 1922, whom it is easy, and fashionable, now to discover. But in the public history of that time they had no place, and a historian writing in 1920 would probably not even have noticed them: at most, he would have dismissed them as separate, parochial figures. Equally, since 1945, there have been movements on which the uncritical dogmatists of the Left have been quick to fasten the name of fascist. But these are but the ghosts of the true fascist movement which threatened and dominated the Europe of the 1930s. The great age of fascism, the period when it seemed an international movement, capable – however violently – of solving the problems of the world, was a brief and distinctive period in European history. It is inseparable from the special experience of one generation: the generation which flourished – or failed to flourish – between the two world wars.

Nevertheless, when we have said this, how grossly we have simplified the phenomenon! Fascism may be limited in time and place, it may have a clear beginning and a clear end in public history, it may seem easily defined; but this unity, this definition, was artificially imposed upon it. Behind the one name lie a hundred forms. The abstraction, so convenient as a term of abuse, is singularly unhelpful as a means of definition. By comparison, communism, its ideological antithesis, though also a term of abuse, is clear and definite. Communism leads us back, past all its heresies and deviations, to a single intellectual source. It has a doctrine, or a dogma, which can be stated and whose identity is proclaimed by all its adherents throughout the world. Fascism has no such intellectual rigour, no agreed prophets. Its origins are plural, divergent, imprecise. If it acquired, in the 1930s, an apparent unity, that was simply because Hitler and Mussolini, in their years of power, imposed a uniform colour upon an ill-assorted hodge-podge of ideas whose origins, from country to country, are very diverse.

How diverse those origins are is obvious once we look at the different 'national' forms of fascism. Behind the disciplined Germanized movements of the 1930s with their common features of authoritarianism, nationalism, militarism, anti-semitism, we discover the ultra-conservative, secularized, Catholic French nationalism of the *Action Française*; the pan-German, anti-semitic Catholic socialism of Karl Lueger and Georg Schönerer in Vienna; the electoral rodomontade of d'Annunzio and the mechanics of Giolitti in Italy; the century-old tradition of rural *caciquismo* and military *pronunciamientos* in Spain. And farther back still, to our surprise, among the prophets of fascism, we can discern those former liberal heroes of the nineteenth century, Giuseppe Mazzini with his 'Young Italy', whom time has changed from the idol of Victorian drawing-rooms into the forerunner of Mussolini, with his *Giovinezza*, and those 'good Germans' of the Frankfurt Parliament whose slogan of *Einheit, Freiheit und Macht* would not have been disavowed by Hitler. These men would no doubt have been shocked had they seen the last form of the movement

19

to which they had contributed their ideas, just as Burke and Carlyle would also have been shocked at their contribution; but to these, as to those, the line of descent can nevertheless be traced.

This is not to say that fascism has no distinctive, positive content, that it is merely a congeries of disparate national movements, artificially drawn or forced together by German power in the 1930s. There were some common features even in the early formative years, and afterwards, in the years of power, the various national movements, though independent in origin, borrowed ideas from each other and so helped to build up, retrospectively, a common ideology. But it is important to realize that fascism, by its very nature, being a movement of aggressive nationalism, began in a more disorderly fashion than communism, and preserved that disorderly quality to the end. Communism is an international doctrine which has gradually been adjusted to differing national circumstances. Fascism is the exact opposite: a series of non-intellectual, even anti-intellectual national reactions artificially united and transformed into an international doctrine by the facts of power. And the history of fascism, as an ideology, is largely the history of this transformation.

Let us consider how this transformation came about. To do so, we must begin by looking back, far beyond the public emergence of fascism, to the mid-nineteenth century, the period of what we may call the liberal breakthrough. For the triumph of free capitalism in the nineteenth century, which provoked, directly, the new movements of socialism and communism, provoked also, indirectly, the other authoritarian movement which was to appear as their antidote. Or at least, to be more precise, it generated some of the intellectual raw material out of which fascism would, long afterwards, be compounded. This raw material consisted of ideas which, at the time, were purely conservative. Only later, in the very different circumstances of the twentieth century, would they become radical.

For the liberal breakthrough of the last century was not achieved painlessly. In England indeed, thanks to constant economic expansion and an elastic political system, the shock was cushioned. But on the continent of Europe it was not. In France the 'bourgeois' victory was achieved only through a series of revolutions. In Germany and Italy it was inseparable from a struggle for national unity which, at times, was a civil war. In such a civil war there were victims as well as victors, and the victims did not surrender quietly. The old élite of Europe, the aristocracy, the landlords, the established churches, and their theorists, nursed their wounds and meditated revenge on the upstart bourgeoisie which seemed everywhere to have triumphed over them. It was out of these disgruntled meditations in manor-houses and vicarages that some of the first fascist fantasies were born.

Of course, many of them were absurd archaisms, the agonized myths of a defeated class. Karl Marx made heavy, Germanic mirth at the antics of the Young England group in Britain: 'feudal' aristocrats presenting themselves as the champions of the working class against the new materialist tyranny. Liberals everywhere poured scorn on the 'Vaticanism' of Pope Pius IX: his wholesale ideological condemnation of the whole philosophy of 'liberal' progress. The antisemitic myth elaborated by over-heated French clergymen passed unnoticed in the educated world. And who, outside Wilhelmian Germany, could take seriously the rhetorical theories of the faded French aristocrat, the comte de Gobineau, who sought to save the hierarchical principle by associating it with a Teutonic 'master-race'? In the days of liberal triumph, of that 'leaping and bounding prosperity' which Gladstonian England seemed to promise, in perpetuity, to all who would imitate it, such follies were dismissed out of hand. They seemed ridiculous: the last convulsions of a dying *ancien régime*, twilight phantoms, unworthy of serious attention by the complacent masters of the new day.

Indeed, in their own right, as ideas, they were ridiculous. The nineteenth-century prophets of fascism, or those who now seem to be their prophets, were often phantom figures. They were the idiot-fringe of defeated conservatism. Their eyes were turned back to the past. They looked away in disgust from the liberal triumph; they had no understanding of the future, no interest

21

in it; and they took refuge in a world of illusion. But for all that they have their significance. History teaches us that even the most tenuous phantoms can come to life if objective circumstances change. The fantasies of one generation can provide the mental furniture, even the life-blood, of another. Nobody could have predicted that the heraldic archaisms of Young England, the hierarchical clericalism of Pius ix, the antisemitism of Gougenot des Mousseaux, the racialism of Gobineau would become part of a twentieth-century myth which would nearly conquer the world. And yet this is what would happen. It would happen not because these ideas themselves had any validity, but because objective circumstances would change. The bourgeois triumph would become a bourgeois retreat; and that same European bourgeoisie, which had been liberal in its days of triumph, would, in its days of retreat, borrow and reanimate these phantoms generated by the retreating forces of an older régime.

Some political thinkers did indeed foresee the future, at least in general terms. In England, Lord Acton insisted that the organic structure of society would not tolerate the insult of continuous *laissez-faire*. In Switzerland Jacob Burckhardt – like Acton an aristocrat and a pressimist – was more precise. The liberal, democratic juggernaut, he declared, was heading for disaster, and in the end would be taken over by very illiberal, undemocratic drivers who alone would be able to steer it. And these new masters would not be the old ruling dynasties, tamed by defeat and too 'soft-hearted' for so stern a task. They would be *Gewaltmenschen*, men of power, *'terribles simplificateurs'*, who would 'rule with utter brutality'. By 'a presentiment that may now seem completely mad, but yet will not leave me', Burckhardt suggested that this fearful tyranny of the future would be first established in industrial Germany.

In the 1890s, when it was uttered, Burckhardt's prophecy might indeed seem 'mad'. Europe was still prosperous and liberalism still seemed to offer continuing prosperity. Even the defeated old order found it more profitable, in general, to invest in the new world than to denounce it. The European aristocracy became industrialized, the landed classes *embourgeoisées*. Even the new industrial working classes hoped to benefit by the liberal system – or at least they saw no practical alternative to it. In the generation before the first world war, the intellectual position of liberalism might be frayed at the periphery but its economic power remained strong. Even where it was weak, as in central Europe, its weakness was ascribed rather to the survival of older patterns of organization than to any inherent defect in the liberal order. Where liberalism did not prosper it was, said the liberals, because there was not enough of it. The remedy was to have more. And this remained the remedy even at the end of the first world war. In 1918, after all, it was the liberal, Western powers that were the victors. Did not their very victory prove the claims of the liberal system? Therefore liberalism must be exported everywhere. Parliamentary democracy and economic *laissez-faire* was the gospel which, as preached by President Wilson, was now to save the whole world.

And yet already, by that time, the economic foundations of liberalism had begun to crack. The victory of 1918 did not in fact usher in a new era of general prosperity. The physical damage done by the war was too great. Recovery was difficult and slow. And in the meantime, while the West was preaching the saving virtues of liberalism, voices from the East were offering, to the hungry working classes of central Europe, a new means of salvation. In 1917 the Russian Revolution had broken out, and from 1917 to 1923 the Russian Communists preached not socialism in one country but world revolution. This was the catalytic force which gathered up the intellectual *detritus* of the Gobineaus and the Gougenots and rearranged it in a new, dynamic pattern. Faced by the terrible threat of bolshevism, the European middle classes, recently so confident, took fright. And in their fright they found themselves crouching in the same postures and adopting some of the ideas which they had once ridiculed in their own previous victims.

For fascism, as an effective movement, was born of fear. It might have independent intellectual roots; it might owe its form, here and there, to independent national or personal freaks; but its force, its dynamism, sprang from the fear of a new, and this time a 'proletarian' revolution. As long as 'liberal' economics had worked, as long as *laissez-faire* had led to economic expansion, with adequate benefits for the working classes, the middle classes had felt safe. But once the economy began to contract, and liberal economics left the proletariat no cushion between unemployment and starvation, no remedy except the revolution to which they were now summoned by Russia, the nemesis foreseen by the nineteenth-century conservatives seemed to have arrived. So each stage in the rise of European fascism can be related to a moment of middle-class panic caused either by economic crisis or by its consequence, the threat of socialist revolution. It was after the great success of the socialists in the Italian elections of 1919 that Italian fascism became a political force. Hitler's first bid for power in Germany – the Munich *putsch* of 1923 – came in the year of the great inflation, when the communists reckoned on seizing power in Berlin. His rise to power in the state followed the world depression of 1929–32. The Spanish Falange was the response to Spanish anarchism, Franco's *coup* the response to the electoral victory of the Popular Front.

European fascism, then, is the political response of the European bourgeoisie to the economic recession after 1918 – or rather, more directly, to the political fear caused by that recession. Before all else, it was anti-communist. It lived and throve on anti-communism, and its anti-communist virtue, which made it international, covered a multitude of sins. But apart from its social base and its anti-communist spirit, it had little else to unite it. It was a heterogeneous movement which varied greatly from country to country. For this there were two obvious reasons: one historical, the other structural. Historically, fascism was essentially, nationalist. Structurally, it was never simple: it was always something of a coalition.

The nationalism of the various fascist parties was inseparable from history. In the days of its advance, the European bourgeoisie, like the Asiatic and African bourgeoisie of today, had always been nationalist. It had been particularly nationalist in the two countries where national unification had been a condition of its power: Italy and Germany. Now, in the days of its retreat, its nationalism remained constant, easily inflamed. But nationalism, which draws upon and exaggerates the differences of national character, necessarily varies from country to country. Consequently fascism reflected this variety. Italian fascism and German fascism were necessarily more distinct than Italian communism and German communism would be.

Secondly, behind the vague term of 'fascism' there lie, in fact, two distinct social and political systems which the opportunism of politicians and the muddled thinking of journalists have constantly confused. These two systems are both ideologically based. Both are authoritarian, opposed to parliamentary liberalism. But they are different; and the confusion between these essentially different systems is an essential factor in the history of fascism. They can be conveniently described as 'clerical conservatism' and 'dynamic fascism'. Almost every fascist movement has been compounded of both these elements, but in varying proportions; and the variety of the proportions bears some relation to the class structure of the society concerned. It is therefore important to distinguish between these two ingredients in the mixture.

Clerical conservatism is the direct heir of the aristocratic conservatism over which the liberal bourgeoisie triumphed in the second half of the nineteenth century. Driven into postures of absurd reaction in the days of Pius IX, it was modernized in form, and given a more respectable political philosophy, in the reign of his successor Leo XIII, whose encyclical *Rerum Novarum* of 1891 remains its charter. For the next thirty years, while liberal movements rose and fell in Europe, the Catholic Church continued to preach its alternative gospel; and with the crisis of liberalism in the 1920s, it believed that its hour had come. Liberalism, the anti-clerical bourgeois nostrum of the nineteenth century, had failed. Socialism, the anti-clerical workers' doctrine of the twentieth century, which had revealed its true character in Russia, must not be allowed to succeed. So the Church everywhere sought to resist socialism – which, on the Continent, was everywhere, at least theoretically, marxist – and those political parties which seemed to compromise with it, even if, like the 'Christian Democrats' they were not anti-clerical. Instead, it offered the conservative ideal of the 1890s: an ordered, hierarchical, undemocratic, 'corporative' state.

That was all very well in countries in which the social structure had not changed, or had not changed too much, since the 1890s: countries like Spain, Portugal, rural Austria, Hungary. But what of those societies which had been radically transformed by industrialism: societies in which the middle class, in its crisis, was not only frightened and radical – that might be true anywhere – but powerful? In the highly industrialized countries the middle class was not only the effective ruling class: it had also absorbed large sections of the other classes in society. It had transformed the landed classes into its tributaries, so that they no longer represented an independent interest. It had imposed its values upon them. Even more important, it had drawn to it, often out of the working class, a large 'lower middle class' of artisans, shopkeepers, petty civil servants, skilled workers, who had also accepted 'bourgeois' ideas, and who, as the most exposed members of the middle class, were the most zealous defenders of its status. This 'lower middle class' provided the social force of 'dynamic fascism'.

It is easy to see how this could happen. In times of economic crisis, landlords, capitalists, professional men, might feel themselves sinking within their class; but less-secure members of the middle class might well feel themselves falling out of it. Their social betters might cushion their decline, or sense of it, by reserves of property, or education. These had little of either, and they felt themselves betrayed. By practising the 'bourgeois' virtues of industry and thrift they had risen from the proletariat, which they therefore felt entitled to despise. Now, thanks to an impersonal crisis for which they were not responsible, they were in danger of being thrown back into it, or subjected to its mercy. With the fanaticism of the frontiersman, they would fight in defence of their status. They would be the front-fighters, the storm-troopers, even the pace-makers of the 'bourgeois' resistance.

Only, in their keeping, the philosophy of the bourgeoisie would no longer be liberal. Liberalism was a luxury which they, of all men, could least afford. They would believe in hierarchy, even in an aristocratic hierarchy – up to a point: for a hierarchy above them, provided it did not betray them, was some guarantee of a hierarchy below. But 'liberalism', to them, was a purely relative concept. It might have served its turn in the past, but now circumstances had changed. Besides, the liberal ideals – indeed, all political ideals – had been devalued. A new cult had arisen, for their benefit: the cult of force.

Once again we are taken back to the 1890s – that incubatory period of fascism. It was then that the old world began to crack, even if the cracks were invisible to the natural eye. It was then also that the new doctrines began to take form. Already Marx had declared that all political ideals were relative, mere rationalizations of the interest of struggling classes. Now Freud carried the same process farther, arguing that motives are different, often fundamentally different, from the professions in which the human mind instinctively clothes them. Once such devaluation of ideas was accepted, it was natural to draw certain consequences. If political ideals were merely a smoke-screen, concealing the struggle for power, why should we not cut out the hypocrisy, recognize that the political world is a jungle, and fight openly for power? The socialists had already drawn some of those consequences; why should not their adversaries do so too? So, while conservatives defended the social hierarchy by appeals to religious or political ideals, more radical men, repudiating all such ideals – or using them cynically as mere means of propaganda – defended it by quite different arguments. Georges Sorel wrote of the illusions of progress, the necessity of violence, the utility of the 'myth'; Vilfredo Pareto of the iron law of oligarchy, the perpetuation of the élite; Nietzsche of the superman, who is a law to himself. These writers were largely unnoticed by the established prophets of conservatism – though it was in dialogue with Nietzsche that Burckhardt made his notable prophecy. They were to be the teachers of the new generation of fascists – who also – often, grossly perverted their teaching.

27

Thus fascism proper, what I have called 'dynamic fascism' – the cult of force, contemptuous of religious and traditional ideas, the self-assertion of an inflamed lower middle class in a weakened industrial society – is radically different from ideological conservatism, the traditional 'clerical conservatism' of the older régime, modified and brought up to date for the twentieth century. Both were authoritarian. Both defended social hierarchy. But the difference between them is as great as that between the divinely consecrated absolutism of the Stuart Kings and the naked, unconsecrated absolutism of Hobbes. Nevertheless these two different political forms are constantly confused. They were confused in fact – for both were brought together by common fear of communist socialism in the 1920s. They were confused by design: in order to attain power, 'fascists', like Hitler, would pose as conservatives, and 'conservatives', like Franco, would pose as fascists. This confusion was sometimes justified by tactical success. But in a cheating match, the tactical success of one party is the tactical defeat of another, and it also led to disappointment and recrimination. The German conservatives were to find that, instead of a docile tool, they had raised up a Frankenstein monster who detested the Church and whose last ambition was to liquidate the European aristocracy. Hitler, in his turn, was to complain that he had poured out blood and treasure to establish Franco in power in Spain, only to find that he had raised up a contemptible creature of dukes and priests. The two forms were also confused in the vocabulary of the Left. Socialists, hating both, easily treated them as one, and denounced the rule of Dollfuss in Austria, or Franco in Spain, or Horthy in Hungary, as 'fascist'. This was excusable in the 1930s when the confusion was general and politics required opposition to both. It is less excusable now, when fascism is dead and our need is not to oppose but to understand.

In order to see how this confusion was exploited by the dictators we may look at the rise to power of both Hitler and Mussolini. The pattern of events is remarkably similar. In each case the Catholic Church played a significant and positive role;

and it did so because – with the conservative classes generally – it supposed that 'dynamic fascism' could be used as the instrument of 'clerical conservatism'. In each case the calculation proved wrong: the Church, by its opportunism, gave itself not a tool but a master.

First, let us take Mussolini, the founder of political fascism. Mussolini's later history has made him appear a mere windbag, a flatulent demagogue who was allowed to flourish, for a time, by the craven inactivity of the Western powers. Certainly this is the character which he wears in that revealing document, the diary of his Foreign Secretary and son-in-law, Count Ciano. And yet Mussolini cannot be entirely deflated. He was, after all, the founder of a formidable political movement, and but for him history would have been very different. Hitler himself, who would be very critical of Mussolini at times, nevertheless paid constant tribute to his achievement. In 1924, in *Mein Kampf*, written when Mussolini's power was still a recent growth, he wrote firmly that Mussolini was 'in the front rank of world statesmen' because he had shown, in a yielding time, that the drift towards communism could be stopped and society be set firmly on another base. Later, in his wartime *Table Talk*, Hitler reiterated his admiration. If it had not been for the example of Mussolini, he said, he doubted whether he would have had the courage, the conviction, to embark on his own quest of power: he would not have believed that any human effort could have turned the tide. And at the very end, when he at last recognized defeat and, seeking the cause of it, blamed 'my fatal friendship with Mussolini', he nevertheless paid tribute to Mussolini himself as indisputably the greatest of his contemporaries, 'almost equal to myself'. There can be no question that Hitler's admiration for Mussolini, though somewhat oppressive, was genuine. He showed it in the truest possible way: by imitation.

Consider how Mussolini came to power. He himself was an ex-socialist demagogue who had transferred his radicalism from the socialist to the nationalist cause. Both as a socialist and as a nationalist he was, in Italian circumstances, anti-clerical: his early writings included works entitled 'There is no God' and

'The Cardinal's mistress'. He was thus, at first sight, an unnatural ally for the old conservative classes who, by definition and in natural opposition to anti-clerical liberalism, were clerical. But the conservative, clerical classes were conscious of their need. They might have social strength. They might have a respectable doctrine: the doctrine of the 'corporative' state. But in an industrial society they lacked mass support. The *Popolari*, or 'Christian Democrats', seemed too radical. Therefore, when this new lower middle-class movement presented itself, they did not look too critically at it. Provided it was anti-socialist, they were prepared to overlook its anti-clericalism. On their side, the new 'fascist' ideologues, though themselves essentially atheist, were prepared to use religion as a convenient 'myth'. Thus in France Charles Maurras, the founder of the *Action Française*, was himself an atheist, but regarded Catholicism as a political necessity, and on this basis had been courted by Pope Pius x, who did not hesitate to condemn a genuine Catholic party, the French Christian Democrats. On the same basis, Pius xi decided to invest in the atheist Mussolini rather than in the Italian Christian Democrats or *Popolari*. In 1922, on the eve of Mussolini's 'march on Rome', the Pope ordered all priests to withdraw from politics and thus, at a critical moment, hamstrung the *Popolari*. Next year, he demanded the resignation of Don Luigi Sturzo, their Secretary-General. Finally, in 1924, after the murder by the fascists of the socialist leader Matteotti, the Pope condemned the *Popolari* and ordered all priests to resign from their party. By these successive acts the Papacy destroyed the only popular movement which might have outbidden Mussolini. It did so – it seems clear – for two reasons. First, it distrusted the whole parliamentary system as incapable of resisting the growth of socialism. Secondly, it believed that the new, authoritarian, 'fascist' movement, in spite of its overt 'atheism', would accept the social necessity of Catholicism and make a satisfactory concordat with the Church; which is precisely what Mussolini then did (1925–9), although the Pope would afterwords complain, in his encyclical *Quadragesimo Anno*, that he did not honour all the terms of the concordat.

Ten years later, exactly the same pattern of events was repeated in Germany. The Papacy was obsessed by fear of communism, and saw Italy and Germany as the bastion of the Church, and of society, in Europe. But Pius XI had no more confidence in the Catholic Centre Party, which ruled in republican Germany, than in the Italian Christian Democrats, who might have ruled in Italy. In the years of economic crisis, the Centre Party seemed unable to check the rise of communism. It also ruled through a parliament, the Reichstag, in which the Protestant and socialist members were always able to prevent a concordat with the Catholic Church. The Pope was therefore ready, at the crucial moment, to switch his support from the Catholic Centre Party to the Nazi Party, on the assumption that the latter, though openly anti-religious – indeed, condemned as such by the German hierarchy – would provide mass support for a conservative régime which, being independent of parliamentary parties, would make a satisfactory concordat with the Church. This, once again, is precisely what happened. Evidently on advice from Rome, Mgr Kaas, the leader of the Centre Party, advised his supporters to vote for the Enabling Act which legalized Hitler's dictatorship. Having done so, Kaas himself appeared in Rome to work out the details of the concordat. Once again, as in Italy, the Pope would afterwards complain, in his encyclical *Mit brennender Sorge*, that the terms of the concordat were not honoured; but he did not denounce either the concordat or the Nazi government of Germany.

Thus both in Italy and in Germany the fascist party moved into power through a similar door. That door was held open for it by the Catholic Church. Of course it was not only the Catholic Church which was responsible. The Church, in this, acted as the representative of conservative society. It intervened, at a crucial moment, to give its ideological blessing to the surrender of conservative society: a surrender already made, not only by conservative politicians, but deep in the body of society. And so it was not only the Church which was deceived by the result. Like the Church, the conservative classes in both Italy and Germany supposed that, by patronizing Mussolini and Hitler, they had

31

enlisted mass support for a conservative programme. These vulgar demagogues, they thought, could be used to destroy 'socialism' at the grass-roots, or rather, in the streets. Then they could be discarded. In fact, the reverse happened. It was the conservative patrons and their ideas that were discarded, the vulgar demagogues that survived.

How did this happen? It happened, I suggest, for two main reasons. First, neither Hitler nor Mussolini was interested in being a 'conservative' ruler: both were revolutionaries who saw and relished the possibility of radical power. Secondly, in both Germany and Italy, they saw a basis for that power: a lower middle class made radical by social fear. Themselves familiar with this class, its fears and aspirations, they believed that they could mobilize it as a dynamic force in the state and thereby realize ambitions unattainable by mere conservative support.

Clerical conservatives assumed a stable or at least a static society. Hitler and Mussolini saw that so negative a philosophy could have no appeal to their supporters. They undertook to ensure the prosperity and the self-respect of the frightened middle classes. But they also went further. Unlike the conservatives, who represented only the possessing classes, and the socialists, who represented only the working classes, they undertook to defend the interests of the lower middle classes without disturbing the existing social hierachy. Repudiating the suicidal doctrine of class war, they emphasized the organic unity of the nation in its natural hierarchy. But that hierarchy was to be preserved at all levels, not merely at the summit of society: indeed, the conservative classes must pay for their privileges by defending those of their inferiors. And if the lower middle classes were thus to be guaranteed in their status, the working classes must not feel neglected in theirs. They too must be economically secured and made to share in national identity, national glory. Thus, from the basis of the lower middle class, Hitler and Mussolini preached a doctrine which could attract both conservatives, whose own ideology lacked dynamism, and socialists, whose aims had been discredited and whose policies had failed. They were also able to enlist the idealism of men who were weary of class interests and economic claims.

But how was such dynamism to be realized? Claiming to represent the nation, not a mere class, the dictators could not, like the socialists, advocate an internal redistribution of resources. Some improvements could be made by greater efficiency: by the use of power to eliminate waste and increase production; by more energetic marketing, fiscal devices, currency control. But equally – and the gospels of nationalism, force and racial superiority would naturally encourage this – they could be gained by internal or foreign aggression: the spoliation of a social 'out-group' at home or the conquest of 'inferior' races abroad. An upper class which lacked ideas or ideals of its own, which had already lost the initiative when it accepted nihilist demagogues as its protectors, was not likely to make a solid front in defence of Jews or foreigners, provided its interests were spared. Industrialists were prepared to pay something towards the cost of a dictatorship which controlled their workers, prevented strikes, and might ultimately widen markets and increase profits. So, little by little, the conservative classes who had brought the fascist dictators to power found themselves the prisoners of that power. They were imprisoned because that power, in a highly industrialized society, had another, and wider base.

Thus the dynamism of fascism depends directly on the existence of a strong industrial middle class – and on the *malaise* of that class. Germany was more highly industrialized than Italy, and it was in Germany that the 'fascist' dictatorship was most complete. In 1934 Hitler seemed the tool of the German conservatives. They had brought him to power. They stood by while he murdered the radicals on his Left. But by 1936 he was independent of them and could begin to subdue the Right. By 1944 German conservatives were in the mood to murder him, and failed. In Italy no such complete dictatorship was possible. Though he often raged at them, Mussolini was never able to destroy either the Papacy or the monarchy (Hitler was fortunate in having no such permanent institutions in his way), and ultimately the monarchy was the means of his overthrow. To the end, Italian fascism was unable to dominate Italian society as German Nazism dominated German society. In the early years, the years of internal violence, the *fascisti* had beaten up Italian Jews; but in the years of war, when antisemitism again became the rule in Italy, it could not be enforced. Society was stronger than government, and the Jews were safer in Italy than anywhere else in Axis-dominated Europe.

At the opposite end of the scale from Germany is Spain. In 1936-9, when civil war raged in Spain, the rest of Europe saw the struggle as a war between 'fascism' and 'communism'. This was not entirely untrue. While the struggle lasted, German and Italian patronage of one side, Russian patronage of the other, did indeed encourage the ascendancy of the 'fascist' Falange as against Franco here, the communists as against the Republicans and anarchists there. But it was a temporary truth only. Once the struggle was over, the native Spanish pattern re-asserted itself. The explanation is clear enough. In Spain there had been no such industrial development as in Germany or Italy. The bourgeoisie had been too weak to make, far less to maintain, an effective 'liberal' régime; and there was no social basis for 'dynamic fascism'. The attempted *coup d'état* of General Franco, like that of General Carmona in Portugal ten years earlier, was a conservative *pronunciamiento*. Carmona had entrusted political power to a professional economist, Dr Salazar, who established an efficient mercantile dictatorship with nothing specifically 'fascist' in it. Franco ruled in Spain as the regent of a conservative monarchy, like Admiral Horthy in Hungary. Both Franco and Salazar – in differing degrees – were allies of the Catholic Church. Their government was 'corporative': its philosophy that of Leo XIII. The Papacy would have its little quarrels with both of them in time to come, but it was never disappointed in their system of government: an unparliamentary, conservative, clerical police state.

It is true, there was in Spain an authentic 'fascist' party. The Falange, founded by Jose António Primo de Rivera, was a native party, and it had all the marks of true 'dynamic' fascism. It was nationalist, idealist, aggressive, based on the urban lower middle class. But that class, so formidable in industrial Germany, was feeble in agrarian Spain, and a number of accidents – regional rivalry, the failure to control Madrid and Barcelona during the war – made it feebler still. During the civil war, in order to humour his fascist backers, Franco uttered fascist slogans and played up the Falange. But at best he was half-hearted, as the German ambassador repeatedly complained. Even had he been serious, it is doubtful – given the limited success even of Mussolini – whether he could really have made the Falange an instrument of radical power. And after 1942, when he had broken with Hitler, he ceased even to pretend. The Falange subsided. It dropped its radical gestures. It became a mere freemasonry of job-hunters. And Franco subsided too. He allowed himself to be absorbed into the conservative society of which he was really the champion. He abated his imperialist claims, forgot *Hispanidad*, and became the caretaker of the authoritarian 'kingdom' of Spain. His fascism, always factitious, simply withered away.

Much of the 'fascism' of the interwar years was factitious: an artificial 'fascist' colour temporarily imposed on native conservative movements by the example or domination of Germany and Italy. In the late 1930s almost every 'conservative' movement in continental Europe borrowed a 'fascist' colour and during the second world war many 'fascist' movements were artificially created in conquered countries for which there was no native social base. Right-wing authoritarian rulers, like Marshal Pétain or Admiral Horthy, yielded gradually and reluctantly to the 'fascist' policies which German patronage forced upon them. Clerical bosses like the Catholic priests Fr Hlinka and Fr Tiso in Slovakia converted themselves into 'fascist' rulers. Dr Salazar in Portugal, like General Franco in Spain, took on a temporary fascist hue. He accepted the advice of Himmler in order to reorganize the Portuguese police, and set up the Greenshirts to keep up with the Italian Blackshirts and the German Brownshirts; which afterwards, like the Spanish Blueshirts, declined into a mere boy-scout organization. Fascist 'movements', esoteric and ridiculous, were hatched, by the warm sun of Rome and Berlin, out of the most unpromising matter even in stable industrial societies like Britain and Belgium, or were created as mere subsidized instruments of German power, as in Norway. Such movements were almost entirely derivative. Who would have heard of the Iron Guard in Rumania, or the Arrow Cross in Hungary, if it had not been for the sustaining power of Germany? No doubt they had a base in their own countries, just as the Falange had a base in Spain. But in those rural societies, it was a narrow base, and without the German example, and German support, they would have remained impotent pressure-groups on the fringe of politics; just as the Rumanian and Hungarian communist parties would have been impotent without the support of Russian power.

The extent to which 'international fascism' was really a generalization of the German model by means of German power is illustrated by the racialism and antisemitism which is often regarded as an essential feature of it. The doctrine of race was published by a Frenchman, the comte de Gobineau, and an Englishman, Houston Stewart Chamberlain; but both Gobineau and Chamberlain were repudiated by their own countries and accepted only in Germany. It was the Germans who, having annexed Strasbourg from France in 1870, enriched it with the Gobineau Museum, to advertise the French prophet whom they had also annexed; and Chamberlain, who lived in Germany, was one of Hitler's earliest supporters. Antisemitism has been endemic in Europe for centuries, but from the 1920s it was only in Germany that it assumed a rabid form, only there that society was willing to tolerate systematic persecution. The independent national conservative movements were, in general, quite untainted by it. Italian society, which tolerated fascism, would not tolerate antisemitism. General Franco, since the war, has openly sought to woo the small Jewish communities of Spain. Marshal Pétain in France, Admiral Horthy in Hungary, resisted and sought to limit the persecution of the Jews which was imposed upon them by Germany. In fact, we may say that, in this respect, 'fascism' was simply the means of generalizing, in a reluctant

Europe, the pathological attitudes of German society. Without German power there would no doubt have been occasional pogroms in Eastern Europe, but the systematic destruction of the Jews, even by native 'fascist' governments, is unthinkable.

But indeed 'international fascism' itself is unthinkable without Germany. Remove nazism from the Europe of the 1930s, and what would have happened? In every country we can see the rudiments of a national conservatism, sometimes traditional, sometimes radical. In every country this national conservatism was inflamed by the economic crises of the 1920s and the threat of communist revolution – which was real enough: we should not forget the communist régime of Bela Kun in Hungary, overthrown by Admiral Horthy in 1920, or the communist hopes in Germany, culminating in 1923. But in every country which was affected by these fears, the form of resistance was different. Only in industrial countries with a radical, organized working class was there a native base for dynamic 'fascism'; and even here there were notable differences from country to country. Who can tell how Italian fascism would have developed had it not been for the fatal dependence on Nazi Germany? Mussolini might even have subsided, like Franco, into a mere Latin dictator, preserved in power (if at all) by electoral manipulation and diversionary rhetoric – 'Nice, Savoy, Tunis, Malta' serving the one as Gibraltar serves the other. 'Fascism' would then have a different definition, without racialism, without public atheism, without Nordic nonsense or German *Schadenfreude*. It was German power, and that alone, which gave a hideous similarity to national anti-communist movements, so that the party of Flemish autonomy could be tainted with Nazi colours and local tensions in the Balkans could be inflamed by the irrelevant fantasies of Teutonic pedants.

Conversely, with the collapse of German power, the unifying force has dissolved and today it is impossible to speak any longer of 'fascism' in a significant sense. It is not merely that the ideas and the gestures are discredited by defeat. The essential conditions of fascism are absent: the economic crisis, the danger of proletarian revolution, the unifying patronage of a dominant industrial power. Behind these accidental circumstances there are, of course, certain permanent attitudes which were incorporated in fascism, and should those circumstances recur, a 'dynamic fascism' might incorporate them again. But the pattern would be different, and it would be safest not to use the old word: a word which, by now, is either precisely dated or a meaningless term of abuse.

3 Italy

S. J. Woolf

With the 'march on Rome' in late October 1922, fascism came to power in Italy. In immediately practical terms, the 'march' of the fascist squads was unnecessary, as Mussolini was called to power in a more or less constitutional manner by the king. But psychologically it was of importance, as it gave the impression of a violent seizure of power. This combination of violence and legality reflected at least one of the contradictory aspects of fascism, which so bewildered contemporaries and led to superficial or erroneous assessments of the significance and strength of fascism, which in turn weakened the tactical measures adopted by the anti-fascist militants. Even twenty years after the fall of the régime, it is easy to be misled by the wild incoherencies of particularly the early movement, and the apparently monolithic structure of the régime in power. There is frequently a tendency to underestimate or ignore changes or developments during the quarter of a century of the movement's existence. At the same time, the study of Italian fascism presents certain methodological problems. For it was the first fascist régime, and remained virtually alone for half its period of power. During the last decade of its existence, when other fascist régimes arose with increasing frequency, the Italian example undoubtedly served in many respects as a model. But at the same time the younger fascisms – and particularly German Nazism – influenced the development of this original model. In this latter period, there is thus a double perspective constantly to be borne in mind, of the extent to which the development of Italian fascism was conditioned by its emergence from a position of isolation among the

39

'normal' patterns of government current in Europe to one where it represented the father-figure, but only a single instance of a more general, new type of state structure.

It is hardly surprising that the foreign statesmen and journalists of western European countries did not judge the fascist seizure of power to be a particularly threatening event. If not a Balkan-type military *coup*, it remained remote, a matter concerning Italy, which could not repeat itself even in neighbouring countries, as the official French press congratulated itself. Even more, it was easy to regard fascism as another product of the confusing postwar situation. At worst, Mussolini would prove as weak as his predecessors. At best, it seemed possible that he would finally offer Italy strong government and strengthen the anti-bolshevik forces. If it was difficult to approve of the violence of some of his supporters, one needed to remember that the Italian case was a special one, because of the total breakdown of the authority of the state and the need to resist the violence of the bolshevists.

So benevolent an attitude was strongly encouraged by fascist propaganda. Mussolini's acute sensitivity to foreign opinion led to the immediate creation of a widespread network of propaganda, with carefully chosen representatives sent abroad. The basic success of this policy can be easily judged by the willing acceptance of the fascist viewpoint put forward in England by Luigi Villari, son of a famous historian and an English mother. The authoritative French newspaper *Le Temps* could theorize at the beginning of 1924 that fascist rule would slowly transform the parliamentary system along the lines of the English two-party system, with the fascists as tories and their right-wing liberal supporters as a whig coalition. Even the murder of a leading member of the parliamentary opposition, Matteotti, in June 1924 could hardly shake the optimism of conservative circles. For fascism represented primarily anti-bolshevism and the rule of order and strong government.

The extent to which this view had permeated even apolitical strata of the population can be illustrated in the following quotation from a public school story published in *Boys Own Paper* in 1924:

'Now, I'm all for rags that are cheery rags, but I bar dirty tricks and rebellion of the proletariat. So I mean to start a company of Fascisti to counteract the deplorable laxity of the present age.'

'Company of what?' asked Johns.

'Fascisti – like that Italian bloke who got fed-up with excessive rags and organized a counter-party of orderly creatures. My notion is to start an unofficial league of half-a-dozen or so – a secret society – to stop this sort of thing, etc.'

In liberal and conservative circles, not until the invasion of Abyssinia in 1936, and then almost entirely because of the dangerous nature of fascist foreign policy, did a partial revision of this superficial assessment of fascism begin.

At the other end of the political spectrum, judgments of fascism were equally out of focus. Early communist interpretations at least attempted to analyse the social significance of fascism, but were hampered by the rigidity of their overall analysis of world politics. In 1922 the Communist International regarded fascism as no more than the 'white terror' of a bourgeoisie no longer able to control the proletariat by legal methods; it was a sign of the final crisis of capitalism, when the class struggle grew most acute, and would be followed inevitably by the successful proletarian revolution. Although it was recognized that fascism had gained widespread support among the small bourgeoisie and even sectors of the peasantry and working class, this was regarded as the result of social demagogy and the disorientation created by the collaborationist tactics of the social democrats; fascism, in fact, with no programme of its own, was the instrument of imperialist capitalism. By mid-1923, the fact that fascism was not merely a bourgeois terrorist militarist movement, but was supported by popular masses, began to be acknowledged. By 1928 the sixth Congress of the Comintern finally judged fascism worthy of detailed analysis, and recognized in what ways it differed from the pattern of bourgeois parliamentary democracy: according to the Comintern, fascism created a dictatorship disguised by appeals to the national spirit, with its own particular

41

type of social demagogy (antisemitism, anti-parliamentarianism, attacks on usury capitalism, etc.); it was characterized by its demagogy, its corruption, its terrorism, its imperial aggressiveness, and (except in moments of crisis) its defence of big capital. But even in this analysis the old polemic continued against the social democrats, the 'social fascists', as they were called, responsible for weakening the class consciousness of the working class and so sabotaging the revolutionary movement not only in 1914, but in the objectively favourable conditions that existed immediately after the war. Not until the mid-1930s did a realization of the extent and permanency of the threat of fascism permit the dying down of this old polemic and the creation of the popular front.

These assessments from Right and Left contain elements of truth but remain partial and unsatisfactory, not so much because of inadequate information as because of the ideological blinkers through which Italian fascism was viewed. Foreign observers saw in fascism what they wanted to see, judging it according to the relationship they thought it bore to their own more immediate problems and to their *Weltanschauung*. For the same reasons most Italian politicians offered equally partial assessments and did not begin to realize the fundamental break with the past that fascism represented until the murder of Matteotti and the fascist laws of 1925 left them no alternative.

There can be little doubt that it was the inability of the opposition parties to think other than in terms of the old pattern of politics that convinced them for so long that fascism was no more than a parenthesis, a transient interruption of the 'normal' course of politics. In no other way is it possible to explain the persistent adoption of tactics aimed at denouncing before public opinion the illegality of fascist measures and the corruption of its government. The communists alone stood outside this framework, but were restricted for their part by their more or less general acceptance of the analysis of the Communist International.

Given these premises, it is not surprising that the detailed discussions of fascism, which emerged with increasing frequency from 1921, either concentrated on a single element or aspect of the new movement, or else listed its component parts and concluded that fascism was too contradictory to last. On the liberal side, one of the most acute critics, Luigi Salvatorelli, explained fascism in terms of an aggressive nationalist mythology which had contaminated the lower middle classes in the war; such feeling was exacerbated by petty bourgeois hatred of the anti-patriotic socialists and by fears of the decline of their own economic and social position, threatened by inflation and the rise of mass parties. The communists regarded the agrarian terrorism of fascism as incompatible with rational bourgeois capitalism. Not only the communists, but the social democrats and even some progressive liberals like Amendola analysed a conflict of interests between lower middle-class and capitalist support of fascism, and saw in the discontent of the former an element which would bring fascism to a rapid end. The anarchist Luigi Fabbri judged fascism to be a preventive counter-revolution of all the forces of social conservation. The mixed support of left-wing revolutionary syndicalists and ex-combatants, of lower middle-class, and extremely youthful elements, of the landowners of the Po valley and the industrialists of the North were all noted and judged to be as incompatible and contradictory as the sources of fascist ideology or the succession of fascist programmes.

Not that fascism itself was much clearer. In Mussolini's words: it was 'a new principle in the world, the clear, final and categorical antithesis of democracy, plutocracy, freemasonry, and the immortal principles of 1789'. For the 'ideals of democracy are exploded, beginning with that of "progress". Ours is an aristocratic century: The State of all will end by becoming the State of the few.' Indeed, 'democracy has taken away the sense of style from the life of the people. Fascism brings back a sense of style to the life of the people, that is, a line of conduct, colour, force, the picturesque, the unexpected, the mystic; in short, all those things that count in the spirit of the masses. We play the lyre on all its strings: from violence to religion, from art to politics.' For, 'fascism is a desire for action, and *is* action; it is

43

not party, but anti-party and movement.' The future Duce explained further: 'For we do not believe in dogmatic programmes . . . we permit ourselves the luxury of being aristocratic and democratic, conservative and progressive, reactionary and revolutionary, legalists and illegalists, according to the circumstances of the moment, the place and the environment.'

In the words of one of the leading fascist historians, Francesco Ercole, 'the advent of Fascism signified the return to the values of the spirit in the political consciousness of Italians'. Although, to achieve this metamorphosis of base materialism into the ether of the spiritual world, as Mussolini explained in a speech to his 'squads of action', 'however much one may deplore violence, it is clear that to make our ideas penetrate peoples' minds, we have to play upon refractory skulls to the sound of cudgel blows'. And who more fitted to carry out this gentle work of persuasion than the fascist *Ardito*, whose physical characteristics are: '(1) a lively, genial head with thick unruly hair; (2) glowing, fierce, ingenuous eyes, not unaware of irony; (3) a sensual and energetic mouth, ready to kiss with fury, to sing with sweetness, and to command imperiously; (4) elasticity of hard muscles, irradiated by groups of ultra-sensitive nerves; (5) a heart like a dynamo, pneumatic lungs, the guts of a leopard; (6) legs like a squirrel, to jump up all peaks and stride over all abysses; (7) a sober, virile, sporting elegance, permissive of running, fighting and disengaging, dancing and haranguing a crowd.' And who more fitting to lead these supermen than the Duce? For, in the words of one, not untypical adulator, Ottavio Dinale, 'his name was Benito Mussolini, but in fact he was Alexander the Great and Caesar, Socrates and Plato, Virgil and Lucretius, Horace and Tacitus, Kant and Nietzsche, Marx and Sorel, Machiavelli and Napoleon, Garibaldi and the Unknown Soldier'.

This, of course, was mere rhetoric, a camouflage to mystify not only opponents, but fascist supporters themselves. But in its early period (and to some extent throughout its existence) fascism was indeed contradictory and the social groups it represented were indeed incompatible. It defied the normal principles of social explanation, and in some respects its success cannot be accounted for simply in social terms. For the characteristics of early Italian fascism (until the mid-1920s) derived in good part from the manner in which it was conditioned by the peculiar historical development of Italy. It is here that one must look as much as, or more than, at the general historical climate of the early twentieth century. It is here that one may hope to find the explanation of many of its contradictions.

The two most fundamental and consistent characteristics of Italian fascism were its nature as a mass party, and the employment of its power in the interests of both social and economic conservation, in the interests of bourgeois capitalism. Despite the existence of a left-wing fringe and the vociferousness of its social demagogy, it would be sophistic to pretend that Italian fascism was other than a mass party of reaction. It is evident that these characteristics apply to most fascisms. But the way in which Italian fascism acquired these characteristics is peculiar to Italy, as (to a lesser extent) is the imprint these birthmarks left on certain of the developments of the régime.

The late development from the 1880s of an industrial economy in Italy is a well-established fact, as is the unbalanced nature of this process of industrialization, limited geographically to a small area of the north, characterized by a strong interdependence between banks and industry and concentrating qualitatively on certain heavy industries which relied in fair part on government protection and orders. With the war the close relationship between large-scale industry and the government developed rapidly, as the process of industrial mobilization accelerated the creation of cartels, increased out of all proportion the number and size of state orders and subventions, limited the right of collective negotiations of workers in the so-called 'auxiliary' industries and assisted the creation of a new bureaucratic class, free of parliamentary control through the widespread use of decree-laws, and working close to the new centres of decision represented by the small group of industrialists and bankers. The effect of the war, in short, had been to create a new level of the somewhat abnormal pre-existing relationship

45

between state and industry. On the one hand, the state had found itself obliged to move far from its traditional *laissez-faire* attitudes and to intervene in vast sectors of the life of the country; on the other hand, industry gained an enormous degree of autonomy and annexed to itself many of the decisional powers formerly vested in the state. In the postwar economic crisis the state found itself unable, even if willing, to break these links because of the threat to certain of the major banks, too heavily involved in industry. Control had been lost. It may be excessive to assert – as has an Italian historian, Giuliano Procacci, recently – that the state had been taken over by industrial satrapies and proconsuls. But there can be little doubt that from about the time of the Libyan war in 1912 until after the first world war the power and freedom from control of the heavy industrial sector increased in a dramatic manner.

Early support for fascism did not come from the traditional industrial establishment of shipbuilders, steelmasters or automobile manufacturers. It tended to come far more and earlier from the wartime profiteers, fearful of punitive taxation or confiscation, and from the small local entrepreneurs of agriculturally-based industries. The very strength of early fascism in certain regions could perhaps be explained partly in terms of the importance of specific agricultural industries (such as sugar-beet in Emilia), which drew together landowners and local entrepreneurs. But given the relationship between heavy industry and the state, it was inevitable that, once fascism had shown its power to seize control of the state, support would also come from the industrial establishment. Nevertheless, this support would be given from a position of strength, and we shall need to return to the implications of this later. For the moment, it is enough to note that fascism undoubtedly represented the interests of Italian capitalism, although the contemporary Communist International analysis of it as the 'white guard' of capitalism was too loose and too restrictive.

For fascism was a mass party, representing primarily the middle and lower bourgeoisie, the white-collar employees, the army officers and NCOs, the small landed proprietors and

46

richer peasants, the provincial intelligentsia. Its ability to mobilize this support was, and for a long time remained, the key to its success, the reason why the collapse of liberal parliamentary government ended in this type of solution rather than in some other manner, such as the rule of the mass popular parties of the socialists or catholics. How it achieved this support is a matter of some importance. The various answers to the question reflect situations, attitudes or methods in part common to other European countries, particularly of the postwar period, in part peculiar to Italy.

Fascism's exploitation of nationalist ideology, its consistent attack on bolshevik saboteurs, neutralist during the war and subversive since its end, are of course elements to be found in other extreme right-wing or fascist movements. In Italy they gained particular strength because of Mussolini's personal break with the socialists over the issue of intervention in the war in 1914–5, and because of the deep split caused by the war in the only country where the socialists had refused to abandon their internationalism for the sake of bourgeois patriotism, a refusal they never failed to proclaim even after the victory. Nevertheless, the trumpeting of antibolshevism and nationalist myths in the form of the 'mutilated' victory – whose fruits were to be seen in D'Annunzio's occupation of Fiume in 1919 – would not have been adequate. After all, the nationalist party stood for the same ideals – far more coherently than the fascists – but remained an élite group with little popular support. Fascism was able to achieve more because of the unexpected changes wrought by the war, and because of its own words and, even more, actions.

It is difficult, in fact, to conceive of fascism achieving mass support without the new sense of political consciousness which existed in Italy after 1918. The war had had the effect of arousing in the nation for the first time an awareness of the state, a sense of belonging to the country shared by the millions who had participated in the exhausting struggle. That the peasants who had formed the mass of the army, and who had suffered nearly 1,500,000 dead or wounded, should have felt differently about the state from their officers is natural enough. But vast strata of the population, of the middle classes involved directly or indirectly in the war, remained infected by the nationalist spirit – in Italy as in France or in all the other countries involved in the struggle – and were ready to respond to a lead.

This lead was offered by the fascists, organizing punitive squads to destroy socialist, communist and catholic party cells, trade union and co-operative centres. It was the activism of fascism which, as Mussolini and so many fascist leaders boasted then and later, preceded any ideology or theoretical programme. Although less 'noble' than the occupation of Fiume, the fascist squadrist attacks against for the most part defenceless socialist organizations offered the same sense of comradeship, of *camera-derie*, as had been experienced in the trenches – or, as the disproportionate number of students too young to have participated in the war would have liked to believe, existed in the trenches. It was an activism against the theorizing of normal 'old-fashioned' parties which attracted the left-wing syndicalists as much as the landed proprietors. It was through these terrorist activities that fascism not only mobilized widespread support in central and northern Italy but created a private army, which differentiated it from all other parties, and which (although it would almost certainly never have been able to resist a straight trial of strength with the army) enabled it to maintain power in the early uncertain period of the régime.

Thus, through its patriotism, its antisocialism and its terrorism, fascism was able to gain strength in Italy, as later in other countries. At the same time, it was able to attract support from two other sectors of the population: from certain groups of the working class and from the conservative wing of the middle class liberals. In both cases it exploited the reaction against nineteenth century ideals which developed in so many countries from the 1880s, a reaction both intellectual and emotional, philosophical and jurisprudential, scientific and literary, political and artistic. The antidemocratic nature of these attacks on individualism and bourgeois values offered common ground to both Right and Left. On the left wing fascism gained some, though limited, support from syndicalist followers of the Sorelian theory of violence, who believed in the overthrow of bourgeois parliamentary democracy and the creation of a new proletarian state by the employment of trade unions for political purposes, by the proclamation of the general strike. The revolutionary syndicalists had already merged with Mussolini over the issue of intervention in 1915. The effect of the war had been to transform syndicalism, to imbue it with nationalist rhetoric. Patriotism, contempt for parliamentary democracy and the cult of direct action combined to convince syndicalist leaders like Panunzio and Rocca of the relevance and possibilities of the fascist cause. But the weakness of the syndicalists was that they failed to mobilize genuine mass working-class support for fascism. After the early 1920s their importance diminished, and ultimately, as corporativists, they served primarily demagogic purposes.

At the same time, Mussolini's violently anti-parliamentary attitude appealed to certain intellectuals. Some were already convinced by the elitist theories of Mosca and Pareto. Others were dissatisfied with the clumsy system of territorial representation offered by the existing parliamentary system and looked for alternatives – as did their counterparts in other western European countries – favouring a system of representation by economic groupings or functions. These were the intellectuals later to be found in the so-called fascist 'groups of competence' or 'technical councils' which came to an inglorious end by 1924.

On the right wing, fascism's promise of stability and order appealed to conservative liberals worried by the emergence of mass parties, and nostalgic for a tradition of 'strong government', for a 'return to the Statute' of 1849, with its guarantee of ample powers reserved to the Crown, so reminiscent of the English eighteenth century parliamentary system. Mussolini could win their support by claiming his historical descent from the Risorgimento. He pointed to the tradition of Risorgimento values embodied first in the 'historic Right' of the immediate post-unitarian period and then in Spaventa and Crispi. At the same time, his anti-clericalism – another Risorgimento tradition

– attracted the support of some intellectuals, especially when combined with promises of educational reform.

In this manner, through its demagogy and actions, fascism claimed support from disparate and contradictory sectors of the population and emerged as a mass party of reaction. To some extent, these means of gaining support were common to other fascist movements. But Italian fascism managed so successfully to appear all things to all men in a particular manner peculiar to Italy.

Italian political life until and indeed after the first world war was characterized by the predominance of regional, municipalistic or local interests and rivalries. Party structures in a modern sense did not exist in the Centre and Right; even on the Left, where the mass parties of the socialists and catholics were emerging, personal and local factors remained of prime importance. Thus, in fair part throughout the system parliamentary parties consisted of local personalistic groupings, in which the power of the leader was dependent on the local support he was able to control. In such a system, where politics were dominated not by national party programmes, but by traditional local rivalries going back to the Risorgimento (and sometimes earlier) or the early period of unification, the structure of the fascist movement presented distinct advantages over the old parties. For fascism had arisen as a mass movement on a local basis, by the creation of local *fasci*, without even the etiquette of a party title, offering membership to all who wished to follow its aims irrespective of party allegiance (except, of course, for socialists).

It is difficult not to believe that great care was taken in the very choice of the word *fascio*. In origin, this was no rhetorical appeal to the fasces of the Roman republic, although the advantages of such an association were soon noted. It was an emotive word, consciously chosen because of the sentimental overtones it had acquired in the previous generation: from the revolt of the Sicilian *fasci* of workers in 1892 to the democratic *fascio* organized against an authoritan *coup* at the end of the century, from the interventionist *fascio* of 1914–5 to the *fascio* of national defence organized after the defeat of Caporetto in 1917. It

50

implied extra-parliamentary activities, through despair of and contempt for the normal constitutional paths. But because of its early use by the left-wing it also carried the implication of a revolutionary end. Finally, it denied the creation of an organization with a formal and more or less rigid structure, but implied a looser association outside and above parties, a grouping of men with frequently differing viewpoints for a specific end. With these connotations, the *fascio* could exploit the existing political situation in a novel manner.

Because of their autonomy, the *fasci* were able to graft themselves on to local traditions, to exploit local rivalries, to appear republican, syndicalist, nationalist, according to the strength of the local social groupings and political traditions. In the Romagna the fascists could win the support of the republicans because of their traditional hostility to the socialists; in the lower Po Valley they could appear as syndicalists and win the peasants after destroying the Catholic trade union organizations; in the Alto Adige they could exploit the reactionary form of irredentism; in the Mezzogiorno, after the 'march on Rome', they could pre-empt the nationalists by allying themselves with the local notables. Fascism became a mass party because of the very looseness of its structure, which enabled it to exploit local rivalries. But, at a second stage, this autonomy had repercussions on the development of the movement, for it gave the local leaders or 'ras' excessive influence in the direction of the party and enabled them to defy the leadership of Mussolini. Even after the successive purges of the early 1920s control of the party remained uncertain. Conflict in the different regions and at the different hierarchical levels remained a characteristic of Italian fascism, part of its original inheritance as much as of successive developments.

If we turn from the origins of fascism to the years of the régime, even the new developments remain to some extent conditioned by the early characteristics. Fascism claimed to have constructed a new state structure. At the same time it pronounced that it was the heir and culmination of the national tradition, and belched forth confused and increasingly sickly rhetoric in defence of its claim. By the time of its collapse it could indeed boast that it formed part of the national tradition – not in any philosophical or historical sense, but, ironically, in the sense that it failed to remove effective power from the hands of economic or local groups.

The question whether or not Italian fascism was a truly totalitarian state can be left to political scientists. But it is as well to bear in mind that only for a limited period – from about 1925 to 1932 – did fascism consciously attempt to create an organic state, in which all political, social, economic and cultural forces would be subordinated to the state, the expression and symbol of the nation. Later, its interests turned elsewhere, increasingly towards an aggressively imperialist foreign policy. The acceptance of a nationalist ideology by fascism has often been noted. The union of the two parties in 1923 was regarded at the time by Salvatorelli as the conquest of the fascist Goliath by the nationalist David. There can be little doubt that the amorphous character of fascist ideology facilitated the infiltration of the compactly organized nationalist group, which provided fascism with four keepers of the seal and a large proportion of the top hierarchy and bureaucracy. From 1926 to 1929, with Alfredo Rocco and Luigi Federzoni in the government, there was a fully conscious attempt to break down the entire structure of the old individualist liberal state and create a new order of society in which all human activities were to be embraced by the state. Even in later years, when the nationalist élite had lost its predominant position, Federzoni remained an important figure in the 'moderate' fascist bloc of Balbo and Grandi. But even in their years of real power, Rocco and Federzoni met with continuous opposition from right-wing constitutionalist supporters and independent-minded industrialists as much as from left-wing syndicalists dreaming of a new popular state organized from the base according to economic functions.

Rocco's ideas were rigidly coherent. He, more than the philosopher Gentile, was the true ideologist of the régime. And the structure he tried to create differed in fundamental aspects from that of the Nazis, because of its subordination of all elements – including the fascist party – to the state. It was to be a new integralist ideology in total antithesis to the individualist ideology which had emerged from the French Revolution. In Rocco's words, 'all the social sciences, from history to political economy, from demography to the science of finances, from social psychology to jurisprudence, will emerge transformed.' Its basis was to be found in the German legal concept that individual liberties did not exist before the state, but that the state limited its own power in order to strengthen itself by conceding individual liberties.

The consequences which derived from this were clear. All private freedom, whether of individuals or associations, were only acceptable if approved of by the state. The marxist concept of the social function of property was turned on its head: private property was to be protected in the social interest, as the proprietor was an organ of the state. Class conflict weakened the community, and the private settlement of industrial disputes by the parties concerned could no longer be permitted: hence the creation of an obligatory labour tribunal. At the same time, the existence of mass organizations could not be ignored or denied, but could be turned to good use to strengthen the state by the embodiment of the trade unions within the state: hence the creation of corporations, which were to consist of both workers and employees in the interests of social co-operation, irrespective of the offence this might give to the ILO at Geneva. Logically, the corporations were to possess no autonomy, as the syndicalists wanted and even the industrialists supported, but were to be tightly controlled by the state. Analogously, the party was to be subordinated to, and integrated within the state by its legal recognition as a public organ, exemplified supremely in the creation of the Grand Council of Fascism and in the utilization of the party's various bodies, developed systematically in order to indoctrinate all branches of society. On the one hand, rule by decree and the virtual elimination of the legislature were justified on the grounds that only a strong executive could avoid weakening disputes and achieve true efficiency. On the other hand, the militia and the security laws were necessary in order to protect the state against internal subversion.

But at the same time this strong state was to be a modern state, accepting the developments of capitalism in both the economic and the social sphere. The tendency of capitalism towards monopolies was to be encouraged, because it increased productivity and so the strength of the state. Thus cartels were to be built up, while the new state was to shape the entire commonweal on the hierarchical model of capitalism. By the subordination of all the élites of modern society – industrial enterprises, trade unions, the party, the bureaucracy – under the authoritarian control of the state, no ruling classes could be formed outside the system. Finally, in this rigidly hierarchical society, mass support was to be ensured, on the one hand by high wages (along the lines of Henry Ford's philosophy), and on the other hand by the creation of 'direct' channels of communication between the masses and the leaders through the party.

Rocco's vision was certainly powerful, and together with Federzoni he succeeded in creating the basic structure of an authoritarian reactionary state. But for many reasons he succeeded only in part. The very logic of his ambitions, the determination to achieve a comprehensive and internally coherent system, made him lose touch with reality. How could such rigid centralized discipline be achieved in a society noted of old for its anarchical and centrifugal tendencies – especially as the party which was meant to carry out this transformation included among its leaders so many ex-syndicalist anarchists? How unrealistic to believe it possible to create and maintain clear lines of communication throughout this society by the sole means of the party – a party which would inevitably lose its purity as it extended its numbers, organs and competence. How wilfully short-sighted to believe it possible to offer high wages, given the structure and state of the Italian economy – even in the years of relative boom of the mid-1920s.

But Rocco's fascist state did not fail solely because of its visionary character. It failed because of the resistance of forces both within and outside fascism and because of the incapacity of this self-contained national entity to resist the impact of outside forces, both political and economic, beyond its control. Even during his years of power, Rocco's was only one of various alternatives apparently open to fascism and put forward by fascist leaders. Italo Balbo, the *ras* of Ferrara, was preoccupied about the dangers of leaving fascism without mediating forces between itself and the monarchy. For the régime's inability to abolish the monarchy and so ensure the total loyalty of the army (and indeed of some of the fascist leaders themselves) left a permanent threat – which finally proved reality – of a confrontation between the two. For Balbo, it was crucial not only to preserve the militia as a trustworthy military force, but to maintain the political prerogatives of parliament so as to avoid a further strengthening of the monarchy.

Balbo thought and wrote in extremely practical terms. Perhaps the hopes of Catholic fascists such as Giuseppe Bottai of gaining mass Catholic support for the régime by the formal pacification of Church and state with the Concordat, were less realistic. But even the nationalist ideas which lay at the base of Rocco's plans could offer divergent alternatives. The 'productive bourgeoisie' was an old nationalist idea, dear to Corradini. But in the writings of Nello Quilici and of some of the syndicalists who became supporters of the corporativist idea, it emerged as a vision of a technocratic society of producers, capable of and with power to regulate their own affairs in a co-operative manner within the state. Self-government of producers was a far cry from Rocco's hierarchical capitalist society.

We may seem to have dedicated too much space to a discussion of the years between 1925 and 1932. But these were the crucial years of Italian fascism. The years 1926 to 1929 witnessed Rocco's attempt to create a truly authoritarian state and society; 1929 to 1932 showed up its failures and its inability to overcome both active and passive resistances. The Concordat of 1929 tore an irreparable rent in the fabric Rocco had so laboriously woven because of the concessions it made to the Church in educational matters and over the autonomy of Catholic Action from the authority of the state. The ideology of the Church was established alongside that of the monarchy, despite the contradiction between both and Rocco's fascist ideology. The corporativist system was mistrusted not only by the masses, but also by the industrialists, who were fearful of restrictions on their autonomy by the extension of state authority, and by the possibilities implicit in the corporations – and periodically resuscitated by the syndicalists and fascist left-wing – of creating an anti-individualist form of bourgeois integralism. Nor indeed could the corporations serve the purpose Rocco had envisaged for them – to maintain mass support by high wages – as the world economic depression, precipitated in Italy by the revaluation of the lira at 'quota 90', led almost immediately after their creation to savage cuts in wages. The corporations emerged as places of negotiations with employers sitting on both sides of the table (in Salvemini's phrase), with the obligatory labour tribunal – however impartial its few independent decisions – acting inevitably as an instrument of reaction. Even the creation of the mass party did not have the desired effect of opening up direct channels of communication between the masses and the state, but tended to lead to the loss of a whole range of powers, in practice annexed by the peripheral party representatives and their entourages, so confirming the continued existence of decentralized practical decision-making by *sottogoverno*. Only the rhetoric and demagogy of mass meetings remained as a channel between the hierarchy and the base.

The nationalist ideology of a totalitarian, organic state-society, in fact, never became the sole, or even the predominant characteristic, because it was never widely accepted by Italian fascism. Loyalty to the monarchy and the somewhat bedraggled Statute remained an important element even among the former nationalist leaders of the party and for a flash reasserted itself victoriously in the momentous meeting of 25 July 1943 in the central organ of the régime, the Grand Council of Fascism, when it voted Mussolini out of power. The atheistic exigencies of the totalitarian state were refuted by the clerical wing of fascism and by Mussolini himself, who judged the support of the Church in practical terms – perhaps not so incorrectly – as of greater importance in an almost wholly Catholic society. The syndicalists, who had lost all practical importance by the late 1920s, periodically reasserted their protests – particularly on the occasion of the new corporativist law of 1934 – that fascism's function was to create a new state based on social justice, and finally offered a parody of their vociferations in the fascist republic of Salò under Nazi protection.

But opposition from outside fascism was probably even more important as an explanation of Rocco's failure. The industrialists were fully aware of their strong position and forced a hard bargain with the régime. They protested over the corporativist policy, and opposed the creation of obligatory consortia to hold prices and build new industrial plant as attacks on private initiative. But in the early years they gained the adoption of a classic free-enterprise economy combined with state salvaging of bankrupt industries, and in the following decade tariff protection, the provision of a reserve labour force by the prohibition of emigration, reductions in wages faster than of prices, and the accentuation of pre-existing monopolistic tendencies, which offered concrete advantages in an economy whose productivity and rate of growth were rising more slowly than those of other European countries. These were the practical results of 'fascist economics'. Fascist economic policy was born with the régime, but in the early years its choices were remarkably similar to those of traditional *laissez-faire* capitalism. With the world economic crisis, attempts were made to accentuate its individuality: 'fascist economics' became anti-capitalist, as capitalism had demonstrated its failure. It was up to fascism to show the new path. But, in practice, 'fascist economics' remained strongly conditioned by world trends and in many ways imitative of the protective practices of the capitalist countries it derided. The creation of IRI, formed in 1933 to prop up the tottering edifice of a fragile private sector shaken by the economic crisis, may have been on a large scale, but did not differ in kind from the American Reconstruction Finance Corporation and similar salvaging policies in England and France. The acceptance of cartels and customs protection was common to most Western countries, as a measure of defence against the crisis. Prohibition of emigration might be claimed as coherent with the fascist policy of a strong nation, but it was also the inevitable result of the barriers against immigration imposed by other countries faced with their own unemployment problems. Only the corporative policy was unique to Italian fascism, and even this in practice was never fully enacted, and failed to live up to its claims of creating a new basis of society for the new state.

Thus in its middle phase Italian fascism offered a curious combination of new and old characteristics. A conscious attempt had been made to create a mass-based totalitarian state. But the active opposition of elements within the régime, the inert deadweight represented by centrifugal forces and pressure groups within Italian society, the unfortunate synchronization with the worst economic crisis capitalism had experienced, combined to abort the attempt. In its final decade, the characteristics of the régime changed again. It is in this period, as Nazism seized power and new fascist movements arose, that Italian fascism was modified by outside influences.

The change could be seen already by the time of the *decennale*, the much publicized tenth anniversary of the 'march on Rome' celebrated by the grandiose Exhibition of the Fascist Revolution. Many of the original inner group of fascism no longer held positions of influence. Gentile had come into his own as the régime's philosopher, as had Starace as party leader. But besides Rocco, the quadrumvir Balbo had withdrawn from active politics and both the former party secretary Giuriati and the syndicalist leader Rossoni had lost their influence (although the latter's power revived in 1938–9). It has been suggested that the fall of these leaders marked the failure of the attempt to create a 'national' ruling class above the party. Certainly this final decade saw an accentuation of factions within the party, while the centrifugal forces of an undisciplined, municipalistic-minded society reasserted themselves. Italian fascism was increasingly a dictatorship and ruled in a void by a particularly impressionable dictator. At the top it became increasingly difficult to maintain tight and efficient control because of the concentration of so many ministries in Mussolini's person. No preconstituted ruling class, no cohesive force existed capable of carrying out the dictator's orders, such as the Prussian *Junkertum* in Germany. The enormous growth of the bureaucracy impeded the execution of swift and firm decisions, and encouraged the revival of clientelistic tendencies in an agglomeration of local groupings. An undergrowth of personalistic relationships flourished. In these circumstances, the influence of the Church increased and its final withdrawal of support in the years of racism and war marked the isolation of the régime.

But by then the original optimism surrounding fascism, the hopes that it might create a new society, had vanished. If political régimes justify themselves in the rationalizations offered by the intellectuals who support them, then Italian fascism failed miserably. For if few intellectuals of stature had supported the régime in the early years, now Italian culture became increasingly antifascist, or – in small part – joined the ranks of the discontented fascist left wing. Now only professional hack-writers remained, who could assert the masculinity of the Italian revolution compared to the feminine French and Russian revolutions, or who could dismiss the English as of little danger in the general decline of the West as a people who ate five meals a day. An inquiry into fascist propaganda abroad would show the fall in quality from the early years.

What was left? A régime which concentrated its energies increasingly on propaganda and foreign affairs. The choices were not casual. Propaganda, particularly about the corporativist system, was necessary to camouflage Italy's lethargy in recovering from the world economic crisis. Foreign policy played a prominent part in the Duce's preoccupations because of the rapidity with which the European situation changed after Hitler's seizure of power. Italy was too small to stand still: unless she moved rapidly, she would be too late. It is against this background that the Austrian crisis of 1934 and even the Abyssinian war of 1936 need to be judged. An aggressive foreign policy undoubtedly formed a consistent and permanent element of Italian fascism. But only under the example of Hitler did this imperialism turn wholly irresponsible. The pro-Axis and anti-semitic group around Farinacci and Preziosi grew in influence as Mussolini, impressed by the efficiency and success of the Nazi régime, began to grow drunk on his own propaganda and planned the realization of his dreams of imperial glory. It was Mussolini who launched Italy on the last colonial war of conquest by a Western power. It was Mussolini who – disregarding the limited economic capacity of the country and reversing his earlier assertions about the non-exportability of Italian fascism (already contradicted by his attempts to create a Black International in 1923) – intervened in the Spanish civil war and, finally, in the second world war. It was Mussolini who – overriding the hostility of many of his close collaborators – tried to introduce a racist policy into one of the few countries where antisemitism did not exist.

This last phase of fascism is no longer characterized by the attempt to create a totalitarian régime. It is a phase dominated by an uncontrolled and intermittent exercise of personal power, a would-be imitation of Hitlerian Nazism. But it is also a phase characterized by the general impotence of this personal power, unable to assert itself over the incompetence and corruption of its own régime or over the re-emergence of centrifugal local forces which it had proclaimed it would eradicate. Only at the end did the régime assert itself. Then, by its entry into the second world war, fascism dragged down almost all the forces of Italian society in a final act of immolation.

4 Germany

A. J. Nicholls

The belief that there is something inherently autocratic, aggressive and militaristic in the German character is one which dies hard and has certainly not died yet. Historical myths built up about the German nation in one world war were reinforced by the experience of a second. Our understanding of the Nazi Party has suffered as a result.

The tendency to over-stress the significance of real or imaginary national characteristics has been aided by the fact that the Nazis themselves wished to emphasize these for their own benefit. In this as in other matters, their propaganda has been picked up and exploited by Germany's critics. The interpretations of Germany's past by friends and foes of the Third Reich exhibit remarkable similarities. Both wish to demonstrate that Germany's national history contained the seeds of Hitlerism and that great names in German philosophy, religion and culture were forerunners of the Nazi era.

Needless to say, this kind of interpretation – which sees the Third Reich as a logical culmination of Germany's national development – has found many critics. Professor Gerhard Ritter, for example, pointed out that on the Continent of Europe between the world wars dictatorship was the rule rather than the exception and that Germany was actually the last state where an important dictatorship was established. 'The Germans themselves', he claimed, 'were more surprised than anyone else by the rapid rise of the National Socialist Party to a position in which overall power in the state was at its disposal.' Fascism was to be seen as a European rather than a German phenomenon

61

– the product of tendencies common to many countries in which there were urban populations bereft of a ruling class and deprived of the Christian religion. Totalitarian tyranny grew, he wrote, 'where the great socially disorganized, intellectually uniform masses in the modern city awaken to political consciousness, and where the former public authorities with their roots in the dim past (monarchy or parliamentary government) are destroyed or discredited'. This association of national socialism with the newly awakened and the politically uneducated has a good deal to recommend it, but it can lead to misunderstanding. It might be taken to imply that Nazism is the product of urbanization and democracy – a belief which has some validity in the purely chronological sense, but which masks the true nature of Hitler's appeal and of the social groups from which he mainly drew his support. In particular it seems to link his party with Soviet communism, and indeed the apparent similarity of these 'totalitarian' movements has sometimes been remarked upon. Yet it would be wrong to seek the explanation for Hitler's success in a proletarian mass eager for social revolution. There was a great deal that was revolutionary about National Socialism from a political viewpoint, and its leaders were certainly unknown and politically inexperienced men. But their appeal was not mainly directed at the lowest stratum of society and their most important objectives were not socially revolutionary.

If one looks at the programme of the National Socialist Party, adopted in February 1920 and declared immutable by Hitler six years later, one sees at once that this is the policy of a political group aiming at national self-assertion rather than social revolution. The fact that the Nazis called themselves a 'socialist' workers' party has obscured the special meaning given to socialism by Hitler's supporters. This confusion was increased by the Nazi tendency to talk of a 'National Revolution' with which they would sweep away the aberrations of the Weimar Republic. Their revolution was to be very different from that envisaged by Communists or even Social Democrats. What Hitler understood by socialism was perhaps best explained by his reported exclamation: 'Why need we trouble to socialize banks and factories? We socialize human beings.' The National Socialist worker wanted a strong German nation within which he should have an honoured, but subordinate, place. This was the sense in which Anton Drexler first founded his German Workers' Party. It was the defeatism of his working class colleagues in a Munich railway works which had spurred Drexler into action, not their inferior position within Germany's social structure.

This attitude towards the workers did not change, even after Hitler had taken the party in hand and given it mass appeal. The workers themselves might be flattered by the Nazi claims that only they and not the aging bourgeoisie were capable of asserting Germany's position in the world; they might have their social ambitions stimulated by Goebbels' insistence that the term proletariat was a degrading Jewish invention, and that in National Socialist Germany they would receive the recognition due to them as a creative work force, but status promotion of this kind did not imply a major economic reorganization for the benefit of the industrial working class.

In fact, the 25-point Nazi programme was quite clear in its references to social policy. Point 16 demanded the creation of a healthy middle class and its protection by the state. The nature of this middle class was made evident by a reference to the immediate communalization of department stores and their rental at low rates to small businessmen. By the same token, point 13 required that all trusts and large-scale companies should be nationalized. The purpose here was not to place the means of production in the hands of the working class, but to uphold the principle that the independent businessman, directing his own factory or commercial undertaking, should be preferred to the anonymous corporation, whose shareholders had no function in the direction of the business. Basic to these superficially socialist principles was the belief that a distinction could be drawn between parasitic capital – the capital of the broker and the stock exchange dealer – and so-called creative capital invested and administered by the individual farmer or works proprietor for the benefit of his own concern. This was the principle enunciated by the party's so-called economic expert, Gottfried Feder. He described it as destroying the thraldom of interest. It would liberate Germany's constructive middle-class element from the chains of a legal and financial system beneficial only to international financiers and Jews. Feder himself, whose sincerity is not open to doubt, vehemently denied any intention of interfering with the savings or investments of Germany's struggling middle class. The declared purpose of Nazi economic policy was to defend the property of the small businessman, the shopkeeper, the farmer and the craftsman against marxist expropriation on the one hand and subjection to parasitic capitalists on the other.

This is not to say that there were not many in the National Socialist movement who harboured bitter resentments against Germany's wealthier classes, and others who genuinely hoped that Nazi domination would lead to a complete social change. But the resentments found other, more easily destructible targets, and the social reformers saw their hopes dashed in practice. The major social changes which have occurred in twentieth-century Germany were caused not so much by the Third Reich as by the war which it began and the defeat which ensued.

The fact was that the whole concept of class was regarded by the Nazis as a Jewish invention designed to set Germans against one another. The real purpose of the movement was to evade social friction by denying the validity of class differences and channelling social energy into national expansion. Most of the National Socialist programme was concerned with this.

First of all came the demand for a greater Germany whose frontiers should include all German-speaking people. Then came claims for equality with other powers, and the acquisition of land for food supplies and settlement areas for excess population. Steps were to be taken to preserve the racial purity of the German population. Only those of German blood were to count themselves citizens of the German state and aliens were to be either expelled or treated as underprivileged persons. Alien influences were also to be eliminated from the press, a people's army was to be set up, public health safeguarded, and religious freedom protected so long as it did not endanger the interests of the state or the German race. There was to be a strong central government. This was not a programme which seemed to have much relevance to a twentieth century industrial society. Its most suitable testing ground might have been the state of Sparta.

The extent to which nationalism of the most extreme and even biological kind dominated the programme is in contrast to the official policy of the Fascist Party in Italy, whose leader had, after all, been a celebrated socialist. How was it that Hitler's party came to adopt this programme, and how far did it respond to genuine impulses within Germany in 1920?

There is no easy answer to this question and even an approximation must contain enormous over-simplifications. But it is perhaps no coincidence that we can group the answers under two headings; the first national, the second social. The national aspect goes back to 1866, when the Prussian victory over Austria ensured that German unification would be under the aegis of Prussia and would exclude the German-speaking lands of the Habsburg Empire. This meant that the most ambitious plans of German nationalists were thwarted. Bismarck's alliances with Vienna – perpetuated by his successors – seemed to deny any hope that all Germans might one day enjoy a common frontier. In addition there was a certain feeling of disillusionment abroad in Germany in the decades before the Great War. Unification had not brought quite the golden era some enthusiasts had expected. Romantic urges to purify or perfect the German nation manifested themselves widely, especially among 'middle class youth'.

Unification had brought social change with it – or had at least accelerated changes already in progress. With the introduction of freer trade and careers open to talent many industrious but inflexible individuals were left behind in the race for prosperity. Craftsmen found their businesses threatened by factory production. Shopkeepers and merchants were faced with

65

large-scale competitors – department stores and the like – which introduced a new element in their own struggle for profits. Capitalist techniques in agriculture meant that many small farmers could not face the competition of more efficient food producers in their own country, while free trade cut food prices by bringing in cheap grain from abroad. There was nothing very unusual in these developments – they were taking place all over western and central Europe – but it does seem that Germany possessed elements capable of reacting more powerfully against the liberal wave than was the case in either Britain or France. For one thing, liberalism had not conquered political power in Germany, despite the Empire's apparently advanced consitution. The old ruling groups – the nobility, the landowners, the higher civil service and the army – had never relinquished their control over the political executive.

When, in the 1880s, the economic boom which followed Germany's unification fell away into a depression, when European agriculture began to face one of the most serious crises in its history, and when political influence was taken from liberal groups and put in the hands of more conservative forces, the opposition to liberal ideals became more pronounced. Many of the beliefs which characterized national socialism were to enter the political vocabulary of Germany and other parts of central Europe in the last two decades of the nineteenth century.

These might be roughly summed up as follows. At the root of the liberal view of society lies the belief that social groups are the sum of a number of individuals each of whom shares the same basic rights as a human being. This atomistic view was deeply resented by those who pictured the community as an organic institution, in which status and its accompanying duties were pre-ordained by God and nature. On a slightly less exalted plane, those who could make a success out of individual rights and freedoms were opposed by others who feared for their security in a genuinely free society. One symptom of this was the widespread hostility towards Roman law to be found among conservative and nationalist groups towards the end of the nineteenth century. Roman law was seen as a foreign importation beneficial only to the rich man and his paid lackey – the lawyer. Traditional or common law – rooted in custom – was the only real safeguard for honest men. It comes as no surprise to notice that point 19 of the National Socialist programme was the abolition of Roman law – which 'served a materialist world order' – and its replacement by 'Germanic law'.

Similarly consitutions and parliamentary government, and particularly parliamentary parties, were regarded with suspicion or contempt. These were artificial, corrupt constructions, designed to enable clever but unscrupulous individuals to better themselves at the expense of the community. However, the aim was not the destruction of freedom, but the creation of a truly German freedom which would somehow be purer than that of the West.

Fundamental to these views were three major propositions; first, that political equality was a bad, unnatural thing, and that man should be content to obey those set apart by nature to rule him; secondly, that urban life was less valuable to a nation than rural life; and thirdly, that the backbone of the nation was to be found in what was called the *Mittelstand*, loosely translated as the middle class, but signifying a very different group from Marx's class of capitalists and entrepreneurs. In the mouths of German nationalists, *Mittelstand* was supposed to mean that hard-working, creative stratum of the community set above the unskilled mob at the bottom and more modest than the parasitic aristocrats at the top of the social scale. These were the farmers, the businessmen, the craftsmen, the officials. The ideas I have been describing amounted to a rejection of the enlightenment of the eighteenth century on the political plane and the industrialization of the nineteenth century on the economic plane.

This did not mean that their proponents believed that they were backward-looking. On the contrary, they were able to pervert some of the scientific developments of the nineteenth century to support their own political beliefs. The Darwinian concept of survival of the fittest was used to give the old arguments against natural equality a new vigour. Racial theories which seemed to be scientific could justify intolerance towards foreigners. Above all, the old Christian suspicion of Jewry was reinforced by this pseudo-scientific approach.

Hostility to urban life and to Jews was associated with a romantic yearning for a mythical past, in which heroic and racially pure Germans lived together without class bitterness or exploitation in what was described as a *Volksgemeinschaft* or Folk association. *Völkisch* ideology as it developed in the decades before the first world war was a mixture of mythical history – in which the German race was extolled as the foundation of true culture and civilization – and mythical science – in which biological theories about the survival of the fittest were exploited to demonstrate that the German race was biologically superior to others. This did not exclude a mystical element in *völkisch* thought, and, indeed, the use of reason and experimental method to arrive at truth was scorned as unnatural or even un-German. Many of the sects which propagated such views were wild and woolly in the extreme. Sun-worshippers, nudists and disciples of Wotan probably did not have much impact on German society as a whole. They were the lunatic fringe of an already irrational movement. But *völkisch* ideas did penetrate a wide section of Germany's middle class in the Wilhelmine period. Novels, *völkisch*-minded school-masters, and a youth movement in which *völkisch* attitudes – and particularly anti-semitism – were not uncommon, helped to make such concepts familiar to romantically inclined German youth. On the political plane a number of right-wing organizations made some of the general assumptions upon which *völkisch* ideology was based seem respectable to people who would have rejected the cruder antisemitic political parties which made their appearance in Germany during the 1880s. For example, one organization which attracted many respectable Germans was the Pan-German League. Originally established in 1890 to protest against the surrender of German claims over Zanzibar to the British, it had as its purpose 'the animation of a German-national state of mind, in particular the awakening and cultivation of the awareness of the racial and cultural solidarity of all German peoples'. Although the pan-Germans were not officially anti-semitic, many of their leaders accepted antisemitic views. By the same token most of the antisemitic and *völkisch* groups accepted the extreme nationalism current among the pan-Germans. In 1914 it seemed that these political elements, despite their social influence, were waging a losing battle against liberalism and social democracy. Before the outbreak of war they themselves were on the defensive against an expanding and politically organized working class, and a confident belief that parliamentary power would be expanded in Germany to liberalize the Empire politically as well as economically.

The Right radical element in Germany regarded the outbreak of the first world war as a blessing and a challenge. It created an atmosphere of communal effort overcoming class divisions, and focused national energies on winning glory for the Reich. At the same time it required unwavering resolution from the German people. When reformist elements began to question the policy of the Imperial Government, and to demand political changes which would give the Reich parliament more power, they encountered furious hostility on the Right. A lot of public servants and army officers came to associate liberalism in politics with defeatism and even treachery. Many soldiers who had first begun to think politically as the result of their experiences in the war came to agree with this judgment. Hitler later boasted that the men who died for Germany did so with *Deutschland, Deutschland über Alles* on their lips and not 'universal and secret suffrage'. Like most of his utterances this was a gross over-simplification; many front soldiers were Social Democrats or Progressives and many later welcomed the revolution. But Professor Ernest Nolte is surely right when he refers to the support Hitler was able to find among the politically virgin elements in Germany who were provoked into political activity for the first time by the war and its aftermath.

With German defeat in the war the pessimistic predictions of the anti-semites and pan-Germans about Germany's future if total victory was not attained apparently came true. Germany was completely liberalized, with an undeniably democratic constitution and a government coalition of parties representing the old left-wing reformist opposition in the Wilhelmine empire. At the same time Germany was humbled by her enemies and threatened with economic chaos and political disorder at home. Looked at from the Right, the strongest social force in her Republic seemed to be a working class addicted to an internationalist marxist ideology. When national shame and political defeat were compounded by financial losses of a truly staggering character – such as those suffered by many Germans as the result of the disastrous inflation in the early 1920s – it is not surprising that a lot of people were willing to accept an oversimplified explanation of Germany's problems. It should also be pointed out that, whereas under the empire of Wilhelm II most of the nationalist critics of the German government had loudly proclaimed their loyalty to the dynasty and the state, they felt no such need to bend the knee before the new Republic. Indeed true patriotism involved complete rejection of all that German democracy stood for.

This is not to say that most German judges, professors, teachers, officers, farmers and civil servants became national socialists or anti-semites with the collapse of the German empire. But many such people did sincerely doubt whether the Weimar Republic was compatible with German greatness, and as that Republic developed they seemed to see their suspicions confirmed.

In the early years of the Weimar Republic there was violence on Germany's eastern frontier and civil disturbance at home. This contributed to the formation of militarized organizations – most of which had originally been supported by the state to provide armed forces at a time when the army was in disintegration. These volunteer formations were overwhelmingly nationalist and anti-republican in character, and their members, who were often ex-servicemen disillusioned with the prospect of a return to civilian life, blamed the Republic for Germany's defeat in the war. Politics in Germany took on a pseudo-military character in that nationalist elements were fond of parades, marches, uniforms and the like. Violence was not uncommon.

But after the failure of the Kapp *putsch* in March 1920 the volunteer formations did not usurp the function of the state. They never made themselves masters of towns or provinces. Instead they looked to the army or state authorities for approval and even financial support.

At the same time a number of extreme nationalist and specifically *völkisch* parties established themselves in various parts of Germany. Some, like the German Socialist Party, made a direct appeal to the working classes. Anton Drexler's German Workers' Party in Munich fitted this category, although it received discreet support from a socially superior group – the mysterious *Thule Gesellschaft*, a racialist order established in Munich during the war.

Drexler's party did not attract much attention and precious few workers made their way to it. What changed its fortunes was the Munich Soviet Republic in April 1919. The shock which this communist-led enterprise administered to the middle classes of that and other Bavarian cities was severe. Officials and army leaders made up their minds that nothing like it should ever happen again, and they deliberately encouraged political movements which seemed likely to combat bolshevism. As is well known, one of the Army's political education lecturers was Adolf Hitler, and as an agent for the Bavarian military he was sent to investigate the German Workers' Party. Hitler's arrival ensured that this insignificant group would not only survive, but grow and prosper.

Little mention has so far been made of Hitler because it was necessary to stress the extent to which National Socialist ideas and a *völkisch* state of mind existed in Germany before him. In the realm of general theory Hitler was not very important for the development of German fascism, although it has been claimed that he produced a more compelling amalgam of *völkisch* ideas than any previously available.

When he first joined the Nazi Party – it look its name and programme in 1920 – Hitler had no official position. He was simply a valuable speaker and a link with the Bavarian Army, a man who had brought with him a number of recruits from military circles. Hitler made himself indispensable to the party by exploiting these two personal advantages. Like all such bodies the party was short of money and members; Hitler improved its fortunes by organizing more and better publicized meetings, and by rousing the participants in such meetings with his own oratory. At the same time his connection with the army brought him financial support – some of which, for example, was used to buy the party paper the *Völkische Beobachter* – and the benevolent neutrality of the police authorities even when his followers were rowdy or violent.

Hitler's technique as a speaker was to play upon antagonisms and fears already present in his audience, to simplify these and take them to their utmost extremity. He did not excel in argument, and very soon strong-arm men at his meetings made any discussion impossible. He pictured the German nation as surrounded by mortal enemies, the victor powers in the war, the bolsheviks and the Jews. He always associated social democracy of any kind with bolshevism under the general umbrella of marxism – a habit which found a ready echo in Bavaria, where the mild coalition government in Berlin was seen by many as an agent of Red revolution. By organizing his own para-military formation – the SA – Hitler conformed to the increasing militarization of the extreme nationalists in Bavaria at this time, and also made his movement more attractive to frustrated ex-army men. The SA paraded in style, carrying banners and wearing swastika arm-bands. But they never approached the achievements of the Italian fascist squads in preparing the ground for Hitler's march to power. Opposition parties on the Left might find themselves involved in an occasional street battle with the SA, but on the whole they had more to fear from the Bavarian government. Even later on in 1932, when the SA had 400,000 members, it was used mainly to overawe, to impress and to frighten the public, and as a useful bargaining lever in political deals. Only after Hitler had come to power did provincial Germany feel the real might of the SA, and even then its reign of violence was cut short within eighteen months.

On the organizational level Hitler established himself as a

dictator within his party, and was able to maintain this position even when the party had been eclipsed after the abortive Beer Hall coup in November 1923. This was a very important fact, because, although the *völkisch* opposition to the Weimar Republic was disunited, the Nazi Party itself was to be the means to final victory. Without this party base Hitler could not have attained power. Despite their military trappings, and their denial of any relationship to the corrupt political parties of the Weimar Republic, the Nazis were organized as a political party, with membership dues, meetings and a party press. Hitler laboured to build up this party's strength on the ground in Munich and its environs, and here he gained an advantage over all other *völkisch* rivals. They were mostly generals without armies, seeking to create an umbrella movement to cover the whole of the German-speaking continent. Hitler avoided this mistake. His party could boast six thousand members in 1921, and he resisted attempts to subordinate it to other groups. When Drexler and some committee members tried to oppose this policy, Hitler faced them with an ultimatum and was accorded dictatorial powers. The party could not afford to let him go. The movement soon became the most powerful *völkisch* political organization in southern Germany. Many of the men Hitler recruited at that stage were to lead the party until its final collapse in 1945.

Dictatorial organization – and deliberate worship of the *Führerprinzip* – became a feature of the Nazi movement. Originally this was not true of the party, some of whose members, such as Rosenberg, spoke of traditional German democracy – by which they referred to tribal elections in a mythical past and not to the type of electoral activity represented by modern liberalism. But within the framework of German nationalist movements as a whole there had always been a tendency to equate obedience to a leader and discipline with German – and therefore desirable – attitudes of mind.

This dictatorial power was exercised in a personal way and did not necessarily involve ideological uniformity along the lines made familiar among communists in the Third International.

73

So long as Hitler was sure of the personal loyalty of a local party organizer he was content. If differences over policy threatened to weaken the unity of the party Hitler would often proceed by inserting rival groups to compete against possible dissidents, as he did in the case of the Strasser brothers who, for a long time, ran their own publishing house in Berlin. They were finally undermined by the activities of Goebbels – Hitler's protégé. This system of controlled autonomy and fostered rivalry persisted in Nazi practice into the Third Reich.

One other characteristic emerged from the early years of the Nazi Party, and that was the predominantly middle-class nature of its appeal. Despite the word 'workers' in the title its membership never displayed an overwhelmingly working-class character and the percentage of workers among its leading functionaries was small. Its prosperity depended on support from decidedly non-proletarian sources – including respectable families like the Bechsteins, White Russian émigrés, and even – so it is claimed – the Spanish royal house. In disputes on policy which involved class conflict Hitler usually steered his party away from proletarian paths. In 1922 he refused to let his followers participate in a widely supported Munich rail strike. He rejected support for a campaign to expropriate the property of German royal houses. He prevented more openly socialistic elements in the north German sections of his party from changing the party's programme in a sense more frightening to capitalist elements in society. He never missed an opportunity to impress the business community of the respect his party had for Germany's captains of industry, and when he came to power he made no attempt to remove these men from their role as the backbone of Germany's economic system.

Hitler was never, of course, the tool of heavy industry or of any other capitalist group. Among the seventeen million people who voted for him in 1933 there were many in the working class. But the backbone of his support was the provincial *Mittelstand* in Protestant Germany.

In 1930 came the breakthrough for the Nazi Party. It received nearly six and a half million votes and 107 seats in the German

Parliament. Two years later this figure had risen to 13·7 million, a total never approached by any other political party in the history of the Republic. Hitler himself never regarded the parliamentary activities of his party as anything but a means of exerting pressure on the republican system so that it might be eventually smashed. He did not become a member of the Reichstag until March 1933, by which time he was already Reich Chancellor.

These were the slump years and there is no doubt that the economic depression was an immediate cause of the crisis which undermined German democracy. But mass unemployment alone did not lead to the victory of Nazism. Generally speaking, the unemployed tended to stay loyal to their marxist party allegiance – many of them apparently leaving the ranks of the SPD (German Socialist Party) for the more radical Communist Party. What the crisis did was to renew the feelings of fear and antipathy latent among wide circles of the German population since the beginning of the Republic. It also brought with it severe economic problems for the middle class – bankruptcy for farmers and businessmen, fear of worklessness for skilled workers and clerical staff who were usually immune to such threats, restricted opportunities and prospects for professional people.

The Nazi Party was in a unique position to exploit this situation. For years it had been harping on the evils of the Weimar Republic. It had never been compromised by collaboration with the régime. Its leaders were new men not obviously representative of any class or economic interest: its appeal was classless. Above all it – like the German Communist Party – was a party of youth. Its leaders were young men, most of whom had fought – or even been too young to fight – in the war. It is sometimes suggested that the Nazi voter was not conscious of any material reason to vote for the National Socialist Party, but that he was overwhelmed by a dazzling system of propaganda. This is quite untrue. Nazi propaganda was only effective among those already receptive to its message. The printed word, for example, was never handled well by the Nazis. *Mein Kampf* –

Hitler's political testament – was a symbol of loyalty rather than a genuine source of instruction to those who bought it. As for the party press, its journalism was of very low standard and its circulation derisory. It has been estimated that in 1932 the Nazis had more party members than people buying their newspapers. The most damaging attacks on the Weimar Republic came from other sections of the right-wing bourgeois press – the most obvious example being the Hugenburg concern.

Once a general disenchantment with German parliamentary democracy had established itself the Nazis were able to exploit the fact that they were the most persistent, reckless and flamboyant precursors of a new order. They also had the advantage that they did not promise any steps in Germany which might really frighten any major sector of the population. Only the Jews, Social Democrats and Communists had anything to fear from a Nazi victory. The more genuinely revolutionary aspects of Nazi policy, for example their contempt for legal processes and their hostility to the Christian religion, were not clear to most voters. The party could thus appeal to those who wanted to see a stronger, authoritarian state, and those who wished to see a transformation in German life which might offer them something better than the austerities and uncertainties of that critical era.

For these people the party's propaganda machine was well designed to impress: parades, mass meetings lit by searchlights and torches, speeches at which applause was carefully regulated and opposition absolutely forbidden, posters screaming hostility to Germany's enemies abroad who were bleeding her to death and her enemies at home who were betraying the nation for their own personal gain. Above all, literally as well as metaphorically, there was Adolf Hitler, flying from city to city in Germany with electoral energy that none of his opponents could match. The Nazis, whatever may be said against them, did possess more dynamic party activists – and more of them – than any other party.

Hitler never received a majority of the votes at a general election. He was called to power as the result of a presidential decision. It is, however, fair to point out that as leader of the largest German party he had some right to demand that power should be entrusted to him.

Once he had achieved office he soon demonstrated that the spirit, and in some cases even the letter of a parliamentary constitution had little significance for him.

It has often been remarked upon that the doctrine of National Socialism as set out by the party's theorists did not coincide with the administrative practice of the Third Reich. In the social sphere the reverse of what the Nazis promised sometimes seemed to be happening. For example, the Nazis claimed to favour rural life as against urbanization. They required more land for the settlement of German farmers. They were supposedly supporters of an independent peasantry, and in the breakthrough of 1930 many of their early successes came in rural areas such as Schleswig-Holstein where small farmers were faced with bankruptcy. Yet in the Third Reich the drift from the country to the town increased rather than diminished. Within three years the public works programme, with its emphasis on military expenditure, created a serious and quite unexpected shortage of labour, especially skilled labour. Production costs for farmers rose faster than the prices of their produce. As for the settlement of new peasant communities, the Weimar Republic did more to settle townsmen on the land than the Third Reich.

Then again the independent businessman and craftsman, for whom Nazi propaganda expressed concern, was by the nature of things less able to profit by the large-scale contracts offered by the government in its public works programme than the big business enterprises for whom Nazi ideologists evidently had less sympathy. The expansion and concentration of great industrial enterprises was not checked by the advent of fascism in Germany; on the contrary, the pressure of the government's economic programme hastened this development.

Even the status of women, and it was a *völkisch* maxim that their place was in the home, could not be entirely safeguarded by the new régime. At first it was easy to alleviate unemployment by removing women from the labour market, but such idealism

77

was less easy to sustain when an acute labour shortage developed, and when conscription compounded other demands on the male labour force.

It also became clear that many of the figures most closely associated with ideology in the party were not going to make a great impact on their country's political life. Gottfried Feder, the economic expert, was given a state secretaryship in the Ministry of Economics but was rapidly ejected from this position by a completely orthodox, if ingenious banker-economist, Dr Hjalmar Schacht. He ended his career as a professor of economics in the Berlin Technical University. Alfred Rosenberg, the party's leading specialist on racial questions and metaphysics, was not able to impose a new Germanic religion on the nation. For many years his foreign policy section of the Nazi Party did not seem to exercise much influence, and when in the war he was appointed Minister for the Occupied Eastern Territories, he was unable to compete with the authority of Himmler's ss in the framing of policy towards subject populations. Another theorist, this time in the field of law, Hans Frank, was never able to persuade Hitler to draw up a new legal code to fulfil the party's promise to support German common law. Hitler had no taste for laws of any kind; they might be used to restrict his power. Frank, who had defended Hitler at his trial in Munich in 1924, was not made Minister of Justice as he might have expected. This post was held until 1942 by Gürtner, a member of the German National People's Party.

Coupled with this apparent disregard for dogma in practice was the evident disinterest shown by many of the leaders in doctrinal subjects. Hitler himself is reported to have told Hermann Rauschning that the Nazi Party's social programme was a 'great landscape painted on the background of our stage'. It was for the masses. 'It points the direction of some of our endeavours, neither more nor less. It is like the dogma of the Church.' This latter comment was scarcely reassuring, since Hitler only admired organized religion for its techniques of mass manipulation; never for its Christian message.

Yet when all these points have been taken into account it does

78

not seem reasonable to ignore the extent to which the Nazis did achieve the ideological goals which they had set themselves during their thirteen years in opposition. The first part of their programme, the union of all Germans and the equality of Germany with other powers, was virtually a reality by the summer of 1939. Certainly the Nazi Party had gone farther towards realizing pan-German dreams than any other form of German leadership in modern times. The German army had been reorganized and vastly expanded. The German population was protected from the so-called Jewish danger by the Nuremberg laws, and Germans of Jewish racial origin were being treated as inferior citizens.

As for social policy, there had been setbacks, but there had been attempts to realize the Nazi programme, and there had been successes too. A number of measures taken at the beginning of the Nazi era were designed to strengthen the small businessman and farmer against big business competitors. Restrictions and taxes were imposed on department stores, the training and qualification of skilled artisans were made more rigorous, and early public works schemes were designed mainly to benefit smaller contractors, though as the economy developed and rearmament became a more pressing question so the advantages of large industrial enterprises became more obvious. As for farmers, they were organized into a grandiose-sounding, nationally directed agrarian estate – the *Nährstand*, or community of food producers. Small farmers received a moratorium on rural debts and a new inheritance law which secured their lands in their own family. Food prices were held up by restricting imports, and although the real problems of the farmers – irrational land distribution and uneconomical size of holdings, lack of capital and lack of technical education on the land – were scarcely touched at all, the status and security which many farmers felt were lacking under the Weimar Republic seemed to have been restored under the Third Reich.

Big business certainly profited more from Nazi economic programmes than did the farmers or the small retailers or craftsmen. But the wealth reaped from rearmament contracts

79

was paid for by the need to acquiesce in interference by the government in the fields of investment, overseas trade and finally labour policy. Big business prospered, but its real independence had been far greater under the Weimar Republic which many of its leaders had purported to despise.

Even the industrial working class, whose political organizations were very quickly crushed by the Nazis and whose political leaders had been liquidated, imprisoned or driven abroad, could feel in 1939 that the Nazi promises about a *Volksgemeinschaft* had not been entirely without foundation. The National Socialist State was not their state, but it took a lot more notice of them than ever the old German Empire had done. To be a worker was no longer to be a member of a dangerous, alienated group, creating his own sense of community within the Social Democratic or Communist Party. It was to be a member of the Labour Front, to be flattered in the press, to be offered mass jollity in the form of *Kampf Durch Freude* and government-sponsored benevolence on the part of employers competing for Nazi industrial honours as leaders of the *Volksgemeinschaft*. Above all, there was work, even if real wages were low. The Third Reich was not a workers' state, but it at least gave higher status to working men than the empire of Wilhelm II had done.

Of course the achievements of the Third Reich had been gained at terrible cost. On the domestic front this meant a concentration of power in the hands of the Nazi leadership. This is connected in the public mind with the well-known expression *Gleichschaltung*, 'co-ordination'. The impression is sometimes given that fascism in Germany established an all-pervasive – or totalitarian – system which had been carefully planned to the last detail before Hitler became Chancellor. It is certainly true that within eighteen months of being given the leadership of a coalition government Hitler had destroyed all political opposition, rendered parliament a cipher, subjected the means of public expression to his party's control and neutralized or liquidated possibly dangerous interest groups such as the trade unions (abolished) or the employers' associations (co-ordinated). It is also true that before the Nazis came into office they had set up planning organizations designed to facilitate National Socialist policies once they had achieved power. But, although there is no doubt that the will to power existed everywhere in Hitler's party, the beginnings of the Third Reich were marked by a great deal of improvization. Hitler's method was to give his subordinates in various spheres the opportunity to establish themselves as best they could. If, like Göring, Goebbels and Himmler they succeeded, well and good – if, like Feder, their programmes proved impracticable and aroused too much opposition from powerful social groups they were dropped.

The Third Reich was characterized by tendencies rather than systems. For example there was never any systematic constitutional reform which established a new order in Germany. The Weimar constitution was simply undermined by a series of arbitrary acts thinly camouflaged as emergency legislation. The most important of these were the decree 'to protect the people and the state', issued on 28 February 1933 after – though not simply as a result of – the Reichstag fire, and the Enabling Act passed by the Reich parliament on 23 March 1933. The first enabled the police authorities to imprison persons suspected of treasonable activity or intentions. Established as a short-term emergency act to combat a supposed communist conspiracy, it continued in force for twelve years. The second enabled Hitler to promulgate laws as decrees without reference to parliament. Once again this was presented as a temporary measure, but the power put into Hitler's hands was never relinquished until he designated Admiral Dönitz President of the Reich on 29 April 1945.

Despite talk of a national revolution when the Nazis came to power there was no major purge of the civil service, nor did the professional party men necessarily find themselves entrusted with administrative authority. The most obvious cause of this was the fate of the SA. Attempts by its leader to press the government to incorporate his forces into the regular army finally led to his destruction in the purge of 30 June 1934. The army remained free from party interference in the sense that it retained its military and apolitical character; it did not escape

81

from Hitler's control. Soldiers took a personal oath to Hitler in 1934, and in February 1938 he became their commander-in-chief.

In the civil service a number of officials of obviously republican sympathies were dismissed and Jewish officials were progressively eliminated. But in the central administration there was no great purge. Instead, there was an influx of professional men into the Nazi movement. Between January and April 1933 tens of thousands of officials and teachers joined the party. This did not mean that a career in the bureaucracy was impossible without a party card. Roughly half of the central administration's officials were not party members. Only in new organizations – like Goebbels' propaganda ministry or the Labour Front – did party membership alone offer a great deal of scope for professional advancement. The most powerful force to grow up within the Third Reich – Himmler's SS – was also a purely party-oriented organization, but its members showed a higher standard of professional qualification and even social status than was normal in the party as a whole, and particularly in the relatively plebeian SA.

For most of his period of rule Hitler utilized the old machinery of the German state but subjected the most important sectors of it to his will by placing them under the control of men personally loyal to him. When Himmler became head of the German criminal and political police in 1936 he ran affairs from his own headquarters and his main assistants – like Heydrich – were loyal SS men. Foreign affairs were conducted mainly by officials and diplomats who had served their country under Ebert and probably Wilhelm II. But many major steps in diplomacy ran counter to the instincts of the old-line Foreign Office men, and they were frequently by-passed in important matters. Ribbentrop's Party Bureau on Foreign Affairs was a jealous rival of the old Foreign Office, and was able to trade on Hitler's dislike of upper class diplomats. This illuminates a characteristic of Nazi rule – the tendency to run competing agencies in harness so that a number of choices remained open to the leadership in any field of policy. Of course, this also strengthened the position of Hitler *vis-à-vis* obstructive elements within both party and state administrative machines.

These overlapping and often apparently contradictory elements in Nazi administration made it – and still make it – difficult to assess where power lay in Nazi Germany, and to what end policy was being directed. It is obvious that Hitler was able – by his refusal to formalize arrangements within the power structure, and his preference for arbitrary acts or *ad hoc* decisions – to keep the direction of foreign and military policy very much in his own hands. (This was not so obvious at the time – witness the widespread belief outside Germany that Hitler was the pawn of capitalists or military men.) The use to which he intended to put this position is not always so easy to determine, but there is no good reason to suppose that he ever relinquished the utopian fantasies of Germanic power which had borne him along during his years of struggle in the 1920s.

There were, however, periods of quiet. To an outside observer in the autumn of 1934, Germany might have seemed to be through the most extreme phase of National Socialist revolution and entering upon an era of stability. The most socially disaffected element in the Nazi movement, the SA, had been effectively neutralized by the Röhm purge at the end of July. This series of gangster-type killings without any legal justification was greeted by conservative Germans with relief as heralding a return to normal methods of government. Hitler was able to brush aside the implications of his crime in a way which Mussolini might have envied had he possessed foreknowledge of it at the time of Matteotti's murder. In foreign affairs a crude Nazi attempt to subvert a foreign government – that of Dollfuss in Vienna – met with failure. It was again made clear that Nazis could not expect success without state assistance.

The elimination of the SA as a serious factor in German political life also coincided with a modification in the campaign of terror waged against Hitler's political opponents under the emergency decrees. The eclipse of the SA assisted an already established tendency to abolish many of the semi-official concentration camps and torture centres set up by the SA and

SS during the early months of Hitler's rule. The whole concentration camp system was originally a haphazard growth, resulting from a combination of political venom among the paramilitary elements in the Nazi Party and a serious over-crowding of normal prisons as the result of police arrests under the emergency laws. The fact that the SA and SS were classed as police auxiliaries exemplified the manner in which the normal apparatus of the state and the political armies of the party were intermingled at an early stage of the Third Reich's development. In 1934 the number of camps was reduced and their organization regularized.

On the face of it, Germany had survived a violent political upheaval – in which parliament, parties, unions and politically organized interest groups had been destroyed or neutralized – without serious social difficulties. The civil service and the army were still much as they had been. Business was still conducted in the old way. There had been no damage to property except that belonging to left wing political parties or Jews.

But the nature of Hitler's movement had not changed. It was consolidating itself after a series of rapid advances. On the home front for instance – and I use the word front advisedly, since the Nazi Party always spoke and often acted as though it were at war in peacetime – arbitrary arrests continued, though less frequently. The political police, now under the control of Himmler and being co-ordinated with the SS, was still perverting the course of justice by arresting politically undesirable people without respect for the law courts. The legal theory enunciated to support such measures was the claim that Hitler's will was the expression of the nation's will and must be treated as law. This was not only a far cry from Frank's projected code of Germanic common law; it was at variance with all other legal traditions. Attempts by the Ministry of Justice to resist Himmler usually failed because Hitler supported his party colleague. Hitler was not interested in justice, and the SS was a loyal instrument of power.

Similarly the changes in concentration camp administration regularized these institutions and made them part of German life. Within a very few years they were again to be expanded.

Even before the second world war the organization of terror represented by the Gestapo and the concentration camps was on the upswing, keeping pace with the increasingly aggressive tone of German propaganda, with the rising crescendo of Germany's four-year plan and the successively more radical demands of her foreign policy. Here again there was no real break in policy, although it is not necessary to believe in deliberately framed plans of aggression brought painstakingly to maturity.

The fact is that Hitler and his colleagues stated from the outset of their period in office that it was their intention to rearm Germany. They did this at great speed. To do it they broke international agreements in a manner alarming to professional diplomats, they took strategic risks which alarmed their military advisers, and they placed great strains on the economy which led to the resignation of their most intelligent economic expert – Hjalmar Schacht. At the end of this process there occurred a war. It was perhaps not the war which Hitler had always intended. For one thing it lasted much too long. For another Germany lost it. But it is difficult to imagine that the feverish energies unleashed in an advanced industrial state like Germany in the 1930s could have gone on being whipped up along Nazi lines without military conflict. Had foreign responses to Nazism been different Hitler might indeed have hesitated before risking war, but in that case the whole momentum of his movement would have been checked, and it is likely that the latent social and political rivalries within the Third Reich would have caused its whole system to crumble.

The war itself, when it came, undoubtedly radicalized Nazi policy, since it released it from the need to fear either foreign opinion or the remnants of opposition at home. With Germany at war the most extreme *völkisch* objectives could be pursued both internally and against enemies abroad. The most obvious example of this new opportunity being grasped is to be seen in the administration of occupied eastern territories. This gave the Nazis an opportunity to implement their theories of German colonization, territorial expansion and racial supremacy unhampered by the need to conform to existing patterns of society or administration. A conciliatory policy towards Russian populations, in particular, might have won the Nazis considerable support, but they preferred to treat the Slavs as biologically inferior specimens and the Russian nation – quite apart from its bolshevik government – as a threat to German security.

The most obviously extreme but logical development of Nazi theories was of course the elimination of the Jews. Here again, the war had the result of releasing Hitler from all restraints, and he could pass from the phase of treating the Jews as aliens to the one in which they could be totally liquidated. It was a result quite consistent with the objectives the Nazis had always set out for themselves. But it was a good deal more than most Germans expected when they voted for the Nazis in 1933.

To sum up, German fascism was characterized by a romantic desire to create a new form of political organization which would avoid the conflicts common to industrialized societies. At the same time this organization should exploit the most modern techniques in war, politics and domestic economy in order to develop its power. Here German fascism exhibited a parallel with Germany's own social development, in which backward political forms and nostalgia for a mythical past were combined with extremely rapid technical progress. The theories which underlay German fascism were already current, though not predominant, among discontented middle class elements in Germany before the first world war. They were openly irrational and laid great stress on the racial unity of the Germans. They sought to reform society by stressing that unity and defending it against the supposed assaults of socialism and World Jewry. The war itself sharpened the differences within Germany over the future of the Reich and mobilized support for *völkisch* ideas. The defeat which followed increased the receptiveness with which many middle-class Germans viewed these concepts. In Hitler the Nazis found a man capable of expressing the hopes and resentments of this movement with unexampled clarity and of endowing it with an unflinching will to power. Once in possession of that power German fascism utilized but did not seek to strengthen the apparatus of the state. Instead a multiplicity of agencies – some state, some party and some a mixture of both – enabled the Nazi leaders to impose their will on the nation. The result was administrative chaos which would only avoid serious rupture by a policy of action. That policy brought German fascism initial successes and final disaster.

Had Hitler won the war it is not entirely clear what form his New Order in fascist Europe would have taken. One thing is certain; the Germans would have wielded the power and other peoples would have been their slaves or satellites. Although Himmler's *Waffen-SS* contained many non-German units, the Germans gave little genuine encouragement to nationalist allies in neighbouring states. Hitler obviously had a vision of a Europe colonized by Germany, with perhaps the western and northern countries having a separate but subordinate existence. Smaller nations would be blotted out. In discussions about other nationalities he did indicate certain general and rather obvious preferences – the Slavs and the Greeks were going to fare worse than the Scandinavians, for example – but national co-existence or collaboration were alien concepts to him. He was interested in power for Germany alone.

5 Austria

K. R. Stadler

Austrian fascist movements, inspired and financed from abroad, played a fateful part in the history of the First Republic (1918–1938): one wing undermining and eventually overthrowing the parliamentary democratic system, in 1934; the other seizing this opportunity and paving the way for the German invasion and the temporary extinction of the Austrian state. The latter was the Austrian branch of Hitler's NSDAP (National Socialist Party), orientated towards Germany and often unfavourably compared with the 'pro-Austrian, patriotic' *Heimwehr* movement which, though orientated towards Italy, is represented as the valiant defender of Austrian independence. This view is at best a misleading over-simplification; for even though many *Heimwehr* men fought the Nazi danger in the last phase, neither movement was patriotic in the sense that it wished to defend Austrian independence; it was simply a choice between vassalage under German or Italian rule.

At various times, and on various issues, these two strands of Austrian fascism met, intermingled, borrowed from each other, combined or fought each other. Both showed certain national, i.e. Austrian, characteristics which makes it difficult to be certain of the degree of 'patriotism' in each. It is commonly assumed, for instance, that Austrian Nazis desired only to be Germans. But this was true neither of the respectable, 'legal' section of the party (typified by Seyss-Inquart), nor necessarily of the underground militants many of whom resented the complete disappearance of Austrian traditions and institutions after the German take-over, as we know from the captured German documents. On the other hand we have evidence of Austrian *Heimwehr* men learning Italian and visiting Italy for a first-hand experience of their fascist ideals – and this at a time when the oppression of the South Tyrolese moved the sympathies of the whole civilized world. Both movements had their political ancestors in the Habsburg monarchy, both derived from social and national forces operating in the heartland of the Empire, and both found their *raison d'être* in the Peace of St Germain and the Austrian state it produced. It is therefore necessary for an understanding of Austrian fascism to sketch in its historical background.

The Historical and Political Setting

The roots of Austrian fascism lie in the multi-national Empire with its incessant nationality struggles and in the profound economic changes which, in the last decades of the nineteenth century, produced great social tensions leading to the formation of the popular mass parties of the Left – the Social Democrats – and of the Right – Schönerer's Pan-German Party in the Sudetens, and Lueger's Christian Social Party in Vienna. The right-wing parties contained many features which impressed the young Hitler, as he acknowledged in *Mein Kampf*; his ideological debt was almost entirely to Schönerer, while in Lueger he saw the ideal modern mass leader. Yet no greater contrast could be imagined than between the plebeian Austrian, clerical and demagogic, and the aristocratic pan-German with his anticlerical, anti-Czech and antisemitic obsessions: an early example of the eclecticism which was such an important element in Hitler's mental make-up.

While Schönerer and Lueger, each in his own way, prepared the ground, it is in the period of the First Republic that we see the growth of what must properly be called fascism – national socialism on the one hand, and 'clerico-fascism' (Gulick) or 'Austro-fascism' (Eichstädt) on the other. For they represented, in Ernst Nolte's definition of fascism, 'the most successful branch of right-wing extremism' and combined, 'in varying proportions, a reactionary ideology and a modern mass organization' (H. Seton-Watson). They were activists without a coherent philosophy or ideology, anti-revolutionaries with a nostalgia for the past: the monarchists looking back to the glories of the old Empire, the national socialists an even longer way to the origins of a teutonic master race. They were all ex-soldiers – veterans of the Habsburg armies or of the German free corps, Kapp *putschists* and soldiers of fortune. At first they were without political influence, an irritant rather than a factor in Austrian politics. The crisis of July 1927 marked the turning point when the Christian Social Party 'adopted' the *Heimwehr*, a decision which led inexorably to civil war in February 1934 and the extinction of parliamentary democracy. In that period even the Austrian NSDAP managed to increase its membership from a mere four-and-a-half thousand in 1928 to forty-three thousand in 1933. However, as a rival to the *Heimwehr*, and because it engaged in terrorist activities, the Nazi Party was banned in 1933, and after the unsuccessful *putsch* in 1934 in which Dollfuss was killed and Mussolini rushed troops to the Brenner, its fortunes reached a very low ebb. (It was then that Hitler decided on an 'evolutionary' way to settle the Austrian question; but this is another story.)

The last phase of independent Austria, the 'Christian Corporate State' period from 1934 to 1938, opened quietly enough: with the Socialists and the Nazis driven underground, Schuschnigg's 'Fatherland Front' organization was in sole control of the country's destinies. With the dismissal from the government of Prince Starhemberg, the *Heimwehr* leader whose political (and private) peccadilloes had become intolerable, and the absorption of his organization in the Federal Army, it seemed that the merely authoritarian wing of the conservative camp had won the struggle against the fascist wing. But this victory was short-lived; in the same year – 1936 – Schuschnigg concluded the notorious 'July Agreement' with Hitler which provided for the penetration of the 'Fatherland Front' by Nazi and pro-Nazi elements and for the peaceful *Gleichschaltung* of Austria. After the Berchtesgaden meeting with Hitler, into which he had been tricked by Papen, Schuschnigg at last realized the danger Austria was in, but being rebuffed by Mussolini gave in without a fight. The German invasion on 11 March 1938 was the result of authoritarian policies enforced by fascist methods; Austro-fascism had paved the way for Nazi fascism.

This was the historical and political setting in which Austrian fascism developed and operated. If we now examine its nature we notice immediately that, apart from tactics or symbols, its characteristics are in no way peculiarly Austrian, but are of the kind we meet in several, or all, fascist movements in Europe. Following George Mosse's classification of fascist characteristics, in which he discovers significant differences between west European and central and east European movements, we find Austria with a foot in each camp: her fascism is predominantly bourgeois, and the *Heimwehr* espoused the corporate state idea, both typical of 'western' fascism. The racism and anti-semitism of the NSDAP, however, is a characteristic of the central European tradition of race-orientated nationalism. In this essay I intend to examine the nature of Austrian fascism under the following five headings:

(1) attitudes to socialism
(2) anti-democratic ideology
(3) anti-semitism
(4) nationalism and revisionism
(5) attitudes to Germany.

1 Anti-Socialism

As a reactionary, anti-revolutionary movement Austrian fascism met with complete rejection from the Left, on matters of principle as well as on particular political issues. This was true not only of the more bourgeois *Heimwehr*, but also of the Nazis in spite of the misappropriation of the word 'socialism' in their party's name; and it may explain why neither branch ever succeeded in making any significant inroads into the ranks of organized labour. Thus the circle closes: the social background of the founders of fascism determines the social composition of the movement a generation later.

Admittedly, the anti-socialism of the nationalists had a working-class background when, in the eighteen-eighties, the first *deutschnationale* workers' and journeymen's clubs were founded in Bohemia and spread to Moravia and Silesia. Originally neither trade unions nor of a political character, they developed into a form of protective association against the flood of cheap Czech labour which was attracted by the process of industrialization. Their political influence was slight even when their 'Association of German Journeymen' had become the 'German Workers' Party' in 1903: they had three seats in the *Reichsrat*, and three in the Moravian Diet, before the Great War. Their 'socialism', based on the writings of Rudolf Jung, was an amalgam of reformist – and even marxist – ideas and racist-nationalistic slogans. With the growth of the Social Democratic Party and genuine trade unions they became increasingly isolated, appealing more to white-collar workers, shop assistants and clerks and pandering to their snobbish convictions that they were superior to the 'proletarians' who allowed themselves to be exploited by Jewish leaders. They opposed socialist ideas of the class struggle, workers' solidarity and internationalism with fancy notions of the 'people's community' and the superiority of German over Slav. The separation of the Sudeten lands from Austria made matters even worse after 1918, for the loss of however slight a working-class element isolated the Austrian NSDAP still farther from the common people. A party whose 'ideological basis' was described by one of its historians as a mixture of Jung's social reformism, Riehl's ideas on land reform and profit-sharing, Gottfried Feder's monetary reform scheme and Hitler's anti-parliamentarism, overlaid with antisemitism and borrowings from Italian fascism, was not likely to make much impression in post-revolutionary Austria.

The anti-socialism of the Catholics was of a different kind. Buttressed by a papal interdict on membership of socialist organizations, and with a respectable record of social-reformist teaching (notably the work of Vogelsang who had inspired Lueger), Austrian conservatism presented a more plausible alternative to marxist socialism than national socialism ever did. It had a genuine working-class following, small but loyal, which supported the authoritarian policies of Dollfuss and Schuschnigg but held aloof from the extremism of the *Heimwehr* fascists. And it is the latter we are principally concerned with, and their backers – the Christian Social leadership and the Church.

In a different context F.R.Allemann has remarked that 'for the Right the fear of socialism (or of what it takes for socialism) is an even stronger activating force than nationalism itself'. This was true of the Austria of the twenties where the *Heimwehr* represented the extra-parliamentary arm of the bourgeois parties and was used to shore up their tiny majority over the socialists, to defend the urban bourgeoisie against the proletariat and the conservative countryside against the socialist towns. That the Church should have lent its support to such dangerous policies was due not only to the general 'ambivalence' of organized Christianity towards fascism which Ernst Nolte notes, but to the situation in Austria of which Hugh Seton-Watson writes:

Austrian Catholicism abandoned oligarchic for demagogic procedures with the rise of Karl Lueger's movement, yet can hardly be said to have much modified its reactionary political outlook.

Whatever we may think in retrospect of the character and achievements of the Austrian revolution of 1918, to contemporaries it seemed a genuinely revolutionary situation with all the opportunities and dangers this implied. To the socialists it was a time when the collapse of the old order presented them with the chance to nationalize key industries and services, to introduce long-delayed social reforms and to establish strong bastions of working-class influence and control. Their radical language and behaviour, which prevented the growth of an influential communist movement, frightened the bourgeois groups which found themselves threatened politically and economically. The aftermath of war – radicalized soldiers returning home from the war fronts, marauding bands of hungry townspeople, the state of lawlessness and violence – led

93

to the formation of volunteer defence corps as guards for homes and farms in the country districts, and workers' and factory guards for similar purposes in the towns. The former were controlled by right-wing leaders, the latter by socialists, and both were in possession of arms that had belonged to the imperial forces. The Allied demand for the surrender of these arms was sabotaged as there was still fighting to be done: notably in Carinthia against the Yugoslavs, and in the east against Hungarian free corps seeking to deny to Austria the province of Burgenland.

Unlike the *Republikanischer Schutzbund*, the defence corps of the social democrats which was a highly centralized organization, the *Heimwehr* was in effect a federation of provincial associations, each mirroring the characteristics and political conditions of its *Land*. In consequence, it lacked any central authority or leadership. Its *Bundesführer* was little more than *primus inter pares* and each provincial leader was free to pursue his own policies and offer his services to the highest bidder. (Inevitably, this led to frequent quarrels which revealed the jealousies among the would-be saviours of Austria; but while this is common to all fascist movements, it must be stated that similar divisions in the Austrian Nazi camp never revealed quite such unsavoury conditions – German headquarters were able to impose closer control and stricter discipline.) The result was that in eastern Austria the *Heimwehr* tended towards the Christian Socials, whereas in provinces like Styria, with a strong pan-German tradition, the nationalist element prevailed. This latter influence was further reinforced in the western provinces by the close contacts with German right-wing organizations whose force Ludwig Jedlicka acknowledges:

... the sequel to the use of these voluntary formations was the first big expansion of the *Heimwehr*. It developed into a para-military organization for the defence of Austria against foreign enemies, but also against 'marxism' as the foe within, and this, in its turn, led to significant political, military and ideological relationships with similar movements in Germany.

On these relationships the German archives which have been

available to researchers since the second world war have shed a great deal of light. We now know not only of unofficial links between military leaders and political conspirators on both sides of the frontier, but also of official funds – including German Foreign Office subsidies – finding their way into the coffers of fascist units in Austria.

In the meantime, Hungarian archives have also yielded interesting material: they prove not merely extensive transfers of Hungarian money to the Styrian *Heimwehr*, but eventually even to the central leadership of the Christian Social Party in Vienna which pledged itself to remove the socialists from the government, to reduce their influence in the country, and to seek a peaceful solution of the Burgenland issue with Hungary. Early on in these negotiations contact was made with Bavarian terrorist organizations like that of Orgesch who provided money, arms and leadership for the struggle against the 'Reds'. As it happened, the coalition government in Vienna broke up in November 1920, but the *Heimwehr*, the monarchist *Front-kämpfer* and – less important – the Nazi *Vaterländischer Schutzbund* continued as the strong arm of the bourgeois parties against the socialists, now in opposition. Their opportunity came when, on 15 July 1927, Viennese workers clashed with the police in the course of a demonstration. Bitter street fighting developed, with over a hundred demonstrators killed and many more wounded; and although the Social Democratic Party bore no responsibility for the course the demonstration took, the crisis provided the fascists with a cause and a slogan.

It is worthy of note that these events coincided with renewed Hungarian intrigues against the Little Entente and attempts to disturb the good relations between Austria and Czechoslovakia. At Easter 1928 Premier Bethlen discussed plans with Mussolini for a *Heimwehr putsch* in Austria, and the Duce offered one million lire and arms to foist a government upon Austria that would take the country into the Italian-Hungarian revisionist block. But no amount of foreign money could compensate for the basic weakness of a movement that was unpopular and riven by fierce rivalries, until Mgr Seipel, a Catholic prelate and

95

Federal Chancellor, gave it official recognition and public respectability. Under constant pressure from Mussolini to 'settle accounts' with the Austrian socialists who were the last remaining obstacle to a fascist-dominated central Europe, successive chancellors moved ever nearer to the brink of the abyss, and in February 1934, with Chancellor Dollfuss providentially (or intentionally?) away in Budapest, the *Heimwehr* laid its plans for the overthrow of democracy. For the next four years the socialists – who had represented forty-two per cent of the electorate – existed as an underground movement under conditions of harsh illegality; but even at the height of the crisis before the German invasion, when Schuschnigg consented to talk to their spokesmen about a common front for Austrian independence, it was at the request of the democratic wing of the conservatives and against the advice of the fascist elements. Their anti-socialism proved stronger than their patriotism.

2 The Struggle against Democracy

Since fascism represents the most reactionary and obscurantist ideology in the first half of the twentieth century, it goes without saying that it was irrevocably opposed to any form of democracy. In Austria this meant opposition to the parliamentary democracy which was established in 1918 on the ruins of the Habsburg monarchy and which had made possible the rise of the labour movement to a position of strength in the state. In the beginning fascist organizations of all kinds had argued fiercely among themselves whether or not to boycott elections and thereby demonstrate their contempt for democracy; or else simply to conceal the ludicrously small support they enjoyed in the country.

Since the Austrian Nazi Party in the early nineteen-twenties had become a branch of the German party, its anti-democratic ideology needs no further examination. But the *Heimwehr* movement is rather more interesting because of the thin mantle of ideological respectability provided by the universalist philosophy and *Ständestaat* theories of Othmar Spann, professor of sociology at Vienna University. This Catholic neo-romantic set out to oppose the teachings of Adam Smith and Ricardo with his own vision of the 'true state', in which the individual only counted as part of the whole and where *Formaldemokratie* was replaced by 'corporate (*ständische*) democracy'. This attack on liberal and socialist concepts appealed to both the conservative and the nationalist camp where it was accepted as the ideological justification for their anti-marxism. The Nazis soon lost interest in Spann's ideas, however, because they conflicted with the totalitarian claims of Party and Leader; but the *Ständestaat* became the political goal of the *Heimwehr* and eventually of the Fatherland Front, and in fact provided the name for the pathetic constitutional structure which Dollfuss established in 1934.

However, what historical interest the *Heimwehr* has does not derive from its ideological pretensions but from the role it played in Austrian politics – with the active support, be it noted, of the conservative leadership:

> Since the state authorities have proved too weak, and the parliamentary system unworkable, we shall have to consider ... extra-parliamentary means to cut the Gordian knot. If necessary, by brute force ...

as their journal *Die Heimwehr* wrote on 10 August 1928. Their attitude was stated clearly in the 'Oath of Korneuburg', the political and ideological platform of the movement, adopted at a rally on 18 May 1930:

> ... We repudiate western parliamentary democracy and the party state!
> We are determined to replace them with government by corporations [*Stände*] and by a strong national leadership which will consist, not of the representatives of parties, but of the leaders of the principal *Stände* and of the ablest and most reliable leaders of our movement.
> We are fighting against the subversion of our *Volk* by marxist class struggle and liberal and capitalist economics.
> We are determined to bring about an independent development of the economy on a corporate basis. We shall overcome the class struggle and replace it by dignity and justice throughout society ...

This programme was meant – and admitted – to be completely fascist in conception. What its implementation would have

97

meant was spelled out by Field Marshal Bardolff as president of the *Deutsche Klub* in Vienna, after a series of lectures by Spann, *Heimwehr* leaders, a representative of the German *Stahlhelm* and other reactionaries: the *Volksstaat* of the *Heimwehr* would change the constitution radically, make extensive use of plebiscites, reorganize parliament, simplify (and thereby effect savings in) the administration, change the franchise and the press laws, take the Federal Army out of politics, etc.

Bardolff, however, as befitted his military status, was opposed to the idea of a *Heimwehr putsch* and any activity that would lead to armed conflict with the state executive; but this was before the Korneuburg rally. His associates were anti-parliamentarian not only in words. In September 1931 the Styrian *Heimwehr* under Dr Pfrimer attempted its own 'march on Vienna' which inevitably failed; the time was not yet ripe. But their conservative protectors saw to it that Pfrimer and his eight associates were acquitted by a jury in the subsequent trial at Graz. After all, the Government had known of Pfrimer's plans, and while hoping that he would desist had been toying with the idea of a constitutional *coup* themselves if the general elections failed to result in a two-thirds majority for the bourgeois parties. They were bitterly disappointed, for the elections confirmed the Social Democrats as the strongest single party in parliament, while the 'irresistible people's movement' of the *Heimwehr* polled less than a quarter of a million votes and returned eight members in a house of one hundred and sixty-five, most of them at the expense of the Christian Socials.

> Parliament is no longer the centre of political gravity. We are the ones who make decisions now, we – the storm battalions of the *Heimwehr*. The time for talking politics is past!

Thus Prince Starhemberg, leader of the *Heimwehr* and – Minister of the Interior! But worse was to come: the great depression shook the Austrian economy to its very foundations; and at the same time, in the rivalry between fascist groups, the one least inhibited and most irresponsible was bound to win the race. In the *Land* elections of April 1932 Nazi candidates were returned for the provincial diets of Lower Austria, Salzburg, Carinthia, Styria and Vienna, a success which was due to mass desertions of voters from the small bourgeois parties, and to a lesser degree even from the Christian Socials. Part of the *Heimwehr* – as for example the whole of the Styrian organization – got on the bandwagon and fused with the NSDAP, the rest, under Starhemberg and Fey, allied themselves with Chancellor Dollfuss whose bourgeois coalition rested on a majority of one in the federal parliament. This did not stop their intrigues, however. We now know of a secret meeting, on 24 June 1932, between Starhemberg, Pabst (military adviser of the *Heimwehr*, after an earlier career on the German general staff, involvement in the murder of Rosa Luxemburg and in the Kapp *putsch*), the Italian *chargé d'affaires* and the Secretary of the Hungarian legation in Vienna. The subject of their deliberations was no less than a *coup d'état* against Dollfuss: a violent one if Dollfuss formed a coalition with the socialists, and a more gradualist one if he did not. Pabst claimed that he had the approval of the German NSDAP for a joint *Heimwehr*-Nazi move, while Starhemberg counted on further support from Mussolini to consist of both money and arms. *129216*

If this plot against Dollfuss seems to bear out the assertion that 'he had no intention of becoming a dictator' (Jedlicka), we must at the same time bear in mind the extent to which Dollfuss had become dependent on Mussolini and the promises he had made to his protector about the destruction of the Social Democratic Party, the abolition of parliamentary democracy and the establishment of a corporate state system. These facts have been known since 1948 when the 'secret correspondence between Mussolini and Dollfuss' was published in London. It was a triangular struggle for power in Austria; in addition to the Nazis, there was the Starhemberg wing of the *Heimwehr* aiming at an openly pro-Italian fascist solution, while Dollfuss preferred the refinement of corporate state ideas based on the papal encyclical *Quadragesimo Anno*. The effect was the same, and in order to keep his agreement with the Duce (and to steal the Nazis' clothes?) Dollfuss repudiated not only 'marxist socialism', but also the democratic and liberal ideologies of the past. Seizing the opportunity of a deadlock in parliament in March 1933, Dollfuss started on the road to an authoritarian régime which might well have come about peacefully if some socialist activists had not been provoked into armed resistance by the *Heimwehr* in February 1934.

As a postscript on Starhemberg, who may be said to have personified the nature of Austro-fascism, it should be noted that at a time when he was already receiving aid from Italy and was urging the Chancellor to adopt a firm line against socialists *and Nazis*, allegedly to protect Austrian independence, he also negotiated with the German NSDAP and was even received by Hitler in February 1932. The documents published by Kerekes merely confirm, in this respect, what Starhemberg, that soldier of fortune, had disarmingly confessed, years earlier, in his 'memoirs'. After his brief period of stardom (1933–6) he was dismissed by Schuschnigg and retired sulking to his tent. The crisis of February 1938 presented him with his last opportunity: he offered himself to Hitler as a worthy alternative to Schuschnigg – an offer, however, which was not accepted. Having been let down by Mussolini, and rejected by Hitler, he next embraced the cause of western democracy and was seen for a while in the uniform of the Free French Air force, until he decided to quit Europe. The end of the war saw him return to claim his property – one of many similar 'victims' of Nazi aggression.

3 Anti-Semitism

Anti-semitism, writes P. G. J. Pulzer, the historian of its political consequences in Germany and Austria, was

a 'spontaneous' product, arising out of a particular situation, not a creed foisted on the public from above by an unscrupulous ruling class.

We have encountered its first stirrings in the pan-German movement in the Sudeten lands, which were paralleled on the conservative side in the demagogic opportunist utterances of Lueger ('*I* decide who is a Jew'). It had its roots in the all-pervading nationality struggles of the monarchy, in the social structure of its bourgeoisie, and – last but not least – in the traditional religious antisemitism of the Catholic Church. The only consistently philo-semitic party after the decline of liberalism, the Social Democrats, tended to dismiss antisemitism, perhaps too lightly, in Bebel's (or Kronawetter's?) words as 'Sozialismus der dummen Kerle'. For bourgeois parties a measure of antisemitism was almost obligatory; in their manifesto of 1918 the Christian Socials proclaimed:

The corruption and power-mania of Jewish circles ... forces the Christian Social Party to call on the German-Austrian people for a most severe defensive struggle against the Jewish peril. Recognized as a separate nation, the Jews shall be granted self-determination; they shall never be the masters of the German people.

And hardly less vicious was the Pan-German Party:

The party ... is in favour of a campaign of enlightenment about the corrupting influence of the Jewish spirit and the racial antisemitism necessitated thereby. It will combat Jewish influence in all areas of public and private life.

Before long the antisemitism of the Christian Social Party was moderated and remained an undercurrent rather than avowed policy. This may well have been due, in part, to the fact that the party attracted a number of very rich Jews who, as bankers and industrialists, sought protection against the policies of the socialists.

But the situation changed with the growth of national socialism in Austria and the obvious appeal of its anti-Jewish propaganda: and rather than oppose it, the conservatives preferred to cash in on this sentiment.

We Germans gladly encounter the Jewish people and its national religion with full respect; we wish to see them protected, but also to protect ourselves ...
In future [the Jews] will have to leave us to ourselves in our own concerns ... in our national culture they will not be allowed to have their say except as guests ...
The religious German must decisively reject baptism as an 'entrance ticket' for the Jews.

Thus Emmerich Czermak, chairman of the Christian Social Party, in 1933; and it is worthy of note that while the language is moderate, at any rate compared with contemporary Nazi statements, the opposition to the Jews is based *on race*, which even baptism cannot change. In the period of the corporate state, campaigns copied from Germany under the motto 'Germans, do not buy from Jews!' were conducted by prominent officials of the 'Fatherland Front', Jews were expelled from various organizations, and it required some courage publicly to oppose this new trend; at any rate, there is no record of a single prominent conservative protesting against this revival of antisemitism in the Catholic camp. On the contrary: even the Catholic labour leader Leopold Kunschak, a hard fighter and basically a decent man who was then at odds with Schuschnigg and strenuously opposed the fascist *Heimwehr*, is now known to have accepted financial aid from the Reich for his *Freiheitsbund*. According to Papen, Hitler's ambassador in Vienna, the result was a strengthening of the antisemitic line pursued by Kunschak's group.

In all this, the ambivalence of the Church towards fascist ideologies again played its part, some dignitaries coming out with openly antisemitic statements, others remaining silent when they should have spoken out. When challenged on the un-Christian nature of antisemitism, Catholic apologists sometimes contended that they were not opposed to Jews, but to 'Jewish' materialism, atheism, marxism; and some bright publicist coined the term 'Anti-Judaism' as the Christian version of antisemitism. It was difficult to decide in March 1938, and made little difference to the Jews anyway, whether the perpetrators of pogroms acted on grounds of antisemitism or of anti-Judaism.

4 Nationalism and Revisionism

This aspect of the characteristics of Austrian fascism is rather more complex, and it is necessary to distinguish between the nationalist revisionism of the Nazis and the purely political revisionism of the *Heimwehr*. The position of the Austrian NSDAP was fairly clear: it considered Austria and its people an inalienable part of the German race and Reich; its revisionism embraced the lifting of the ban on the *Anschluss*, the recovery of the lost borderlands, and the acquisition of additional living-space. As well as generally xenophobic, it was particularly anti-semitic in Vienna, anti-Yugoslav in Carinthia and Styria, anti-Czech in Lower and Upper Austria, although, not surprisingly, it dropped its earlier anti-Italian line on orders from Berlin, which did not do it much good in the Tyrol!

In contrast to the Nazis, the Austro-fascists were anything but nationalists. They were nurtured in the Habsburg tradition in which, theoretically at least, there were no conflicting national interests because all nations were equal in the eyes of the Dynasty. German-speaking Austrians therefore became pan-German nationalists with Schönerer, socialist internationalists with Victor Adler, or else remained loyal subjects of the Kaiser with a belief in the supranational mission of the monarchy; but there were no Austrian nationalists then. Nor could these same people develop a spirit of Austrian nationalism after the collapse of the Empire: either because they rejected the Republic altogether and hoped for the restoration of the Habsburgs, as did the monarchists; or because they dreamed of a Catholic federation embracing Bavaria, Austria and Hungary, the hope of reactionary romantics in the Christian Social Party; or simply because they desired a fascist *Mitteleuropa* in which they would provide the missing link in Mussolini's Rome-Budapest axis. This, of course, was the attitude of the dominant section of the *Heimwehr*, whose substitute nationalism was revisionism and who resented the *parvenu* nations that had grown up around them and which, with the aid of the Little Entente, prevented the realization of their hopes. Never before has the venality of small men with delusions of grandeur been quite so pathetically revealed as in Kerekes' book; and neither have the machinations of successive Hungarian governments, the intrigues against their neighbours and their interference in Austrian affairs been so well documented.

Like the national socialists, the *Heimwehr* was selective in its likes and dislikes; we have already noted the ambiguous position its leaders adopted in the Burgenland question when they first conspired with Budapest. Similarly, where Italy was concerned, the South Tyrol issue became an absolute taboo once Mussolini had committed himelf to massive support of Austro-fascism. Oddly enough, it was the Duce who first broached the subject to Count Bethlen at Easter 1928, when he offered the *Heimwehr* one million lire and arms provided it was willing to seize power in the near future: 'When this has been done, I am prepared to negotiate with the new government improvements in the situation of the German minority in South Tyrol.' On Grandi's advice this was specified to mean a government in which Steidle would have the decisive voice, provided the latter gave a written undertaking never to raise the issue in public, officially or otherwise. Steidle – Tyrolese himself – readily pledged his word; and it was not for want of trying that his pledge was never put to the test.

The Nazis on the other hand were bound by party discipline to obey Hitler's decision that a relatively small issue like South Tyrol must not be allowed to damage the good relations between the two fascist nations. Nevertheless, there were rumblings of anti-Italian sentiment thoughout the period, and they almost reached crisis proportions in 1939 when Hitler 'liquidated' the South Tyrol problem by means of a transfer of population to the Reich. Even the Tyrolese *Gauleiter* himself, according to a 'situation report' of Himmler's SD, had some harsh words for his fascist allies:

If there are still people in Italy who believe they need not be satisfied with the frontier on the Brenner pass and talk about a frontier in the Karwendel mountains, it might likewise occur to us to speak of a frontier at Salurn [Salorno].

However, the odd indiscretion or violation of discipline apart, both the Nazi and Austro-fascist leadership proved repeatedly that their nationalism and their revisionism were extremely elastic concepts and more useful as demogagic slogans than as precepts for practical politics. In any case they were totally irrelevant to Austria's real interests; to define and reach general agreement on these, however, would have required a measure of national consciousness and patriotism which was sadly lacking on all sides, a lack which may well have been the result of the ambivalence of most Austrians towards Germany.

Yet mention must be made of one manifestation of a genuinely Austrian national conviction shared by both fascist movements: it related to Austria's 'mission' in the *Donauraum*. Whereas other fascist movements produced visions of a remoulding of Europe on racial or corporate authoritarian lines, or even of a completely 'new order' for Europe, the provincialism of Austrian fascism never raised its sights above and beyond the old Habsburg Monarchy, that is to say toward the South-East and towards northern Italy. Reference has already been made to the monarchist hopes of a Habsburg restoration and the romantic dream of a Catholic federation of Bavaria, Austria and Hungary. After 1933 a number of Catholic writers who were forced to flee Germany settled in Vienna, and their experiences lent urgency to the speculations about an alternative to the pagan Nazi Reich. This was found in an almost metaphysical concept of a new Reich, Catholic, mildly reformist, and based on the alleged traditional virtues of Austria in the ordering of relations among different nationalities, but without reference to such mundane matters as political realities, frontiers or constitutional arrangements. Now these men were by no means fascists themselves, but their acceptance of the *Ständestaat* turned them objectively into allies of the Austro-fascists and with their woolly philosophy provided the educated element in the *Heimwehr* with the ideology which the Starhembergs were incapable of producing.

The special skill in diplomacy which Austrians have always prided themselves on played its part in the thought-processes of Austrian Nazis, too. There are several references to it in Hitler's *Table Talks*, ranging from grudging admiration for the Habsburgs to praise for Seyss-Inquart's rule in Holland. In 1940 Neubacher, first Nazi Mayor of Vienna, was sent to the Balkans as ambassador extraordinary 'because he was an Austrian', and the *Südost-Europa Gesellschaft* in Vienna became the focal point for the Reich's penetration of the South-East. And after Badoglio's 'betrayal' of the Axis, in September 1943, Hitler was persuaded to agree to the extension of the Reich to the borders of 'Austrian Venetia' (the province itself to become a German satellite), while Goebbels noted in his diary how the annexationist appetite of the Austrian *Gauleiters* grew as the situation in Italy deteriorated. Both contemporary utterances and post-war apologetics suggest that the more imaginative and articulate among the Austrian Nazis did have a vision of a 'new order' in south-east Europe which the Reich was to impose, and they were to have been its planners and leaders. It was not the least of their complaints that Hitler did not give them enough scope – or enough time.

5 Austria and Germany

When the Austrian National Assembly in November 1918 unanimously declared, 'German-Austria is a constituent part of the German Republic', it did so because it could see no future for the small and impoverished remnant of the old Empire. Since this was the hour of triumph for nationalism, and German Austrians could expect little sympathy from the former subject races, it is not surprising that they, too, should seek safety with the German people, as well as economic viability. But the *Anschluss* they envisaged was not the unconditional surrender of 1938, but a fraternal union in a federal state. Once this was ruled out by decision of the Allies, and the League of Nations had provided a financial basis for the new state, the demand for an *Anschluss* became, as Renner once put it, 'an academic question'.

The Social Democrats at the time saw in the *Anschluss* the fulfilment of the liberal democratic hopes of 1848, the coming together of the Austrian and German working classes in a great social republic set on a socialist course. Developments in the Weimar Republic soon disillusioned them, and without any hesitation they dropped the *Anschluss* clause from their party programme when Hitler came to power. The Christian Socials, too, who had been much more divided over this question, were not prepared to complicate relations with the Allies, on whose good will the very survival of Austria depended, by insisting on a measure about which they had reservations of their own. After all, to most Catholics 'Germany' was a great Protestant power, fashioned, led and officered by 'Prussians', and memories of 1866 still rankled with them. By inclination and by tradition they were anti-German rather than pro-German; they had accepted the *Anschluss* idea as a way out for Austria and they continued to pay lip-service to it, but it was a real issue only for the *Grossdeutsche Volkspartei*, the pan-German bourgeois splinter group which was eventually swallowed up in the rising tide of national socialism. Yet, for reasons that are difficult to gauge, every single party to the right of the socialists included racial, nationalist elements in its programme and terminology, insisted on its *Deutschtum* and on Austria being a branch of the German *Volk* – Nazis as well as monarchists, urban conservatives as well as anti-clerical farmers' leagues. This national line was used not merely 'for the record', but also as a stick with which to beat the unpatriotic internationalist socialists, and it is not surprising that it should have become an element in Austrian fascism, with disastrous consequences for the country's future.

The pro-German attitude of the national socialists needs no further stressing; it was the Austrian Nazi party's *raison d'être* to work for the absorption of their country in the Reich – with themselves in positions of power and control, of course. We have already noted their disappointment when the *Anschluss* was followed by the appointment of large numbers of Reich-Germans to key posts in the party and the state. What is rather more baffling is the inability of Austro-fascists and authoritarians to understand that their ritual protestations that Austria was but part of the *Deutschtum* were eroding what little national consciousness existed. It began in 1920 with the *Frontkämpfer* Association defining its nature and aims:

... It is aryan in character, stands outside party politics, and has no truck with international subversive elements such as social democrats and communists.
Its ideal is the unification of the entire German *Volk*.

Similarly, the *Heimwehr* leader Steidle explained in 1928 why his organization refused to recognize the twelfth of November, the date of the proclamation of the Republic and Austria's national holiday: it had been celebrated by Austro-marxists and by

the enemies of the German people, when they had trampled underfoot the Germans and prevented their unification. . . . We do not reject the state; on the contrary, we accept it because we want to imbue it with our spirit, rebuild it in accordance with our ideas, and reconquer it for the German *Volkstum*. On this piece of earth where we happen to live we shall have to prove whether this part of the German *Volk* is still viable or whether it will have to perish like a dead branch. Fate has endowed us members of a great and richly talented nation with . . . a territory of our own where we can prepare for our high mission. . . . Our mission may well be that Providence has appointed the *Südmark* [of the Reich] to determine the future and the fate of the nation, just as on a previous occasion the *Nordmark* did, when the German *Volk* had been forced on its knees . . .

And the 'Oath of Korneuburg', which we have already quoted, spoke of the determination of the *Heimwehr* 'to serve the whole community of the German *Volk*' and asked each member 'to realize and to proclaim that he is one of the bearers of a new German national outlook'. This, of course, was the time when Starhemberg negotiated a pact with Gregor Strasser of the German Nazi Party who offered him financial support for a 'national front' in Austria consisting of NSDAP and *Heimwehr* – an offer which the Prince describes at length in his memoirs. Two years later in Berlin, in a lecture to the 'National Club', he still avowed his pan-German conviction: 'Repeatedly and with heavy emphasis he stressed the *Deutschbewusstsein* of the *Heimwehr*, but at the same time tried to impress on his audience that the citizens of an independent Austria could also be very good Germans' (Kerekes).

The same ambivalence, only less excusably, governed the actions of the conservative authoritarians. Schuschnigg's comment on Dollfuss – 'a catholic pan-German' – applied with equal force to himself and characterized his policies in those fateful years. While it may be understandable that in his search for a more broadly based coalition against the socialists Dollfuss in May 1933 authorized negotiations with two Nazi leaders, and inserted in the programme of the 'Fatherland Front' the ominous words of Austria's mission in central Europe 'for the future good of every German', it must be remembered that within fourteen months he paid with his life for his folly; what is rationally inexplicable is the subsequent behaviour of his successor, Schuschnigg. It had never been fully realized that the 'July Agreement' of 1936 between Hitler and Schuschnigg, which provided for the inclusion of several Nazis in the Cabinet and defined Austria as a *deutscher Staat*, was not forced upon Schuschnigg but represented his own idea of a solution, as we now know from the published German documents. It was in April 1936 that he first mentioned the possibility of recognizing the 'national opposition' in a closed circle of friends (one of whom immediately informed Papen), and asked his chief of cabinet for a list of suitable names. One can imagine the delight in Berlin; Hitler even offered to meet Schuschnigg and others if this were desired, but it proved unnecessary: Schuschnigg needed no further prompting, and fate took its course.

Even the 'leftist' labour wing of the 'Fatherland Front' proved no wiser than its university-trained leaders. We have already noted how Papen succeeded in making political capital out of its antisemitism; under his influence – and that of Nazis who had infiltrated into prominent positions – it even committed itself to a pro-Nazi, pan-German policy, thus reversing the process which Pulzer noted, according to which pan-Germanism was 'the ideology which increasingly provided the impulse to political antisemitism'. Points for a political platform at a May Day rally included '*rapprochement* with the Reich' and an 'understanding with the Austrian national socialists on the basis of Austrian independence'. In May Papen was able to report to Hitler that the leaders of the *Freiheitsbund* 'are completely following our line'. Staud, its leader, is said to have refused Czech money offered on condition that his organization 'adopt an anti-German attitude'; Papen comments:

This further shows the necessity of our continuing, as before, to support this movement financially. ... Our connection with the *Freiheitsbund*, especially with its leader, *Staud*, is already so intimate

109

that I have been asked which personalities would be desired by the German Government in the event of ministers from the national opposition being included in the Cabinet.

Even allowing for the fact that Papen is not the most reliable of witnesses, and that Kunschak and Staud – like Schuschnigg – were at no time crypto-Nazis, but patriots of sorts and according to their lights, the evidence of their shortsightedness is nevertheless damning. Their hostility to socialism was greater even than their love of country, and rather than work for reconciliation on the basis of a democratic *Staatsidee* they all engaged in intrigues with one or both of the would-be rulers of Austria. Even within hours of the German invasion, in March 1938, Austrians were asked in Schuschnigg's ill-fated plebiscite, to vote for an Austria 'free *and German*, independent and social, Christian and united'.

The leaders of the 'Fatherland Front' paid dearly for their mistakes in German jails and concentration camps, which they shared with socialists and communists. It was this experience which produced the unity and national consciousness of the Second Austrian Republic.

6 Hungary

J. Erös

1 The Characteristics of the Horthy Régime

Two popular views are current about the character of the Horthy régime which dominated Hungary from 1919 to 1944. On the one hand, it is regarded as an old-fashioned, conservative or even reactionary régime, dominated by landed aristocrats and titled bureaucrats – a suitable ally for Hitler's Germany or Mussolini's Italy, but internally a non-fascist and non-Nazi régime of traditionalist Christian gentlemen who may have been 'wrong' but were 'romantic'. On the other hand, the Horthy period is seen as constituting the first fascist-racialist régime in central Europe, whose founders – Admiral Horthy and his terrorist-propagandist officers and journalists – invented Nazism or were at least the pioneers of fascism and of that new European order which Hitler and Mussolini were later to establish. Is it not true that for these two men of destiny Horthy was an irreplaceable pillar of the new European order? Hitler himself spoke of the 'Horthy myth' which he, Hitler, wanted to preserve at all costs. Even more: Horthy's long-time political associate and prime minister of the early 30s, General Gömbös, was the first central European politician to predict, seven years before it emerged, the formation of the Rome-Berlin axis which was to dominate 'the new map of Europe'. So how can one talk of an anti-fascist Horthy régime?

Reality is of course much more complex. Neither of these extreme and over-simplified judgments will do. The Horthy régime had from beginning to end a *dual character*, and all its important institutions and ruling groups were divided between

111

a fascist and a conservative wing, not to speak of the floating groups in the middle. This was true of the members of parliament who, from 1922 to 1944, formed the unified government party. It was true of the civil service, the army, the various powerful armed security services, and the 'patriotic associations', as well as of the nerve centre of the régime, the secret societies. The history of the régime is the history of the struggles between these two wings in the various institutions – struggles which usually ended in compromises, continuously made and unmade, compromises which are only partially revealed by the changing composition of the cabinets and the personalities of the prime ministers, for the cabinet was by no means the only government of the country. The army, which escaped civilian control, was the instrument of the Regent, Admiral Horthy, whose position in turn depended on the support of the army. The Regent, manoeuvring between the military and civilian centres of power, was the decisive political force, through his ability to balance one wing against the other and keep a foot in both camps. Horthy himself was a counter-revolutionary officer of 1919 vintage and a member of the more well-to-do section of the landed nobility, connected by ties of friendship and later by marriage to the landed aristocracy. Hence both camps hoped he would be *their* leader and only the extremist groups – the revolutionary national socialists on the right, the republicans and socialists on the left and the most militant monarchists in the middle – were from time to time in conflict with him and his régime. Yet they all attempted to influence him time and again.

Miklós de Horthy, one-time member of Francis Joseph's military cabinet and the last commander-in-chief of the Austro-Hungarian navy, was a fairly realistic man with an international outlook. He knew that as Head of State of a small and economically weak country he had to obtain the support of the dominant European powers. Hence, he was not impervious to foreign pressures and advice. Until 1930 he listened (up to a point) to the Western democracies; from then onwards it was fascist Italy and Nazi Germany which had to be placated and won to the cause of Hungary, as seen by Horthy. Finally, by

1943 it was again the Western democracies and even the Soviet Union which had to be appeased. But that was to be the end. The system, as sensitive to events as a seismograph, was finally shattered and destroyed by the earthquake which swept over the Danubian plain in 1944.

The dual character of the régime can be traced to its origins. Many of its most characteristic institutions, leaders, and dominant ideologies emerged already during the summer of 1919 in the provincial capital of south-east Hungary, Szeged. The region was protected from the Red Army of the communist-socialist coalition government of Budapest by a buffer of French occupation forces. But the various anti-communist and anti-democratic groups who gathered in Szeged to prepare for the re-conquest of Hungary were far from united. The three most important groups were the ex-officers of the Austro-Hungarian army, the aristocratic landowners and the unemployed civil servants of old Hungary. The former officers had shared the same experiences of war service, followed by humiliating and stringent economic difficulties, to which had been added perse-cution at the hands of rebellious soldiers and revolutionary workers and intellectuals. The aristocratic landowners had shared some of these experiences, but they did not have the same background of professional humiliation. Indeed, these men seldom suffered economic hardship. Finally, unlike the ex-officers, they could look forward to prosperity and economic security once the 'sanctity of private property' – a favourite slogan among the landowners – was restored. The civil servants, escaping from Red Budapest or from the vast territories de-tached from the kingdom of Hungary by the Paris peace con-ference, had by training a more legalistic outlook than the officers, and hence in their political attitudes were nearer to the group of aristocratic landowners. On the other hand, the econ-omic insecurity of some of the civil servants made them sensitive to the extreme ideas of the military. Significantly, Admiral Horthy, Minister of Defence in the new 'national' government and soon Commander-in-Chief of the slowly emerging new 'national army', was on equally good terms with both the aristocratic politicians in Szeged – such as Counts Paul Teleki and Gyula Károlyi – and the less socially prominent officers, such as Captain Gömbös, Secretary of State for Defence, and Captain Paul de Prónay, the commander and organizer of Special Squads.

These squads were formed exclusively from politically reliable officers with the task of fighting the opponents of the Szeged groups by direct action methods, that is by kidnapping and secret or public executions, always without appeal to 'clumsy' legal methods and courts. It is wholly legitimate to call these men professional right-wing conspirators, because they had spent most of their time since the collapse of the old Army in conspiratorial political activities against the succession of democratic, socialist and communist-led governments in Budapest. When they formed their squads in Szeged, the members were selected on the basis of political skills, which included abilities as propagandists and security agents. These squads worked more or less harmoniously at this stage with the aristocratic ministers and their associates. Their main protectors and political inspirers were Admiral Horthy, Captain Gömbös and the Chief-of-Staff, General K. Soós de Bádok. It was the latter who gave the order to Captain Prónay to create a *tabula rasa* in all towns and villages which his men were to occupy. This unwritten order implied swift execution of all supporters of the Red régimes. As the leading cadres of the Communist Party had fled to Austria during the first days of August, it was mainly workers, peasants, social democrats and radicals who were exposed without defence to this wholesale slaughter.

The right-wing officers and politicians who had gained control of the Szeged power machine soon found allies in all Hungarian cities. The natural allies of the more radical wing were the middle-class groups, especially those who had suffered economic deprivation. The allies of the conservative politicians were the big and medium landowners, including the clergy, and certain bankers and industrialists, driven by the excesses of the revolutionaries toward the conservative Right. Some of these were gathering in Vienna, where Count István Bethlen, their future protector, was organizing the anti-revolutionary forces. Thus the distinctive outlines of both the more cautiously conservative and the adventurous extreme-right wing of the counter-revolutionary movement were already taking shape in the decisive months of the tragic year of 1919.

The picture was complicated by the fact that the conservative wing was divided between the royalists (or 'legitimists' as they were called), and the opponents of the Habsburg dynasty. At this stage the legitimists had some support among the officers. The division between legitimists and their opponents corresponded roughly to the division of the old Hungarian ruling classes into a West-Hungarian (usually Catholic) and an East-Hungarian (mostly Protestant) group. Count Bethlen, a Protestant aristocrat from the east (Transylvania), was a moderate anti-legitimist; Captain Gömbös, the Lutheran military politician, was an extreme nationalistic opponent of the Habsburgs, now the leader of the most intransigent section of the anti-legitimists. Admiral Horthy befriended them both. He also trusted another Transylvanian aristocrat, Count Paul Teleki, who shared – although with certain reservations – most of Count Bethlen's conservative-nationalist ideas. It was these three men who forged the so-called 'Unified' governing party out of the political groups emerging from the elections of 1920, notably the Christian National and Smallholders Parties. The Unified Party 'governed' from 1922 to 1944; that is, most of the time it supported the prime minister and party leader chosen for it by the Regent. Nevertheless, its members were politically not without power and in their parliamentary groupings reflected the division of the régime into moderate conservatism and fascistic, racialist, dictatorial extremism. But in spite of serious disagreements on social and constitutional issues, the leaders of both wings of the party upheld the same ideology, or rather the same political formula – the 'Christian-national' principle.

The slogan of 'Christian-national' politics goes back to the early months of 1919 when, in opposition to the republican régime of Mihály Károlyi, Count Bethlen founded the first

'Christian national' party to counteract the international principles and 'materialistic' outlook of those left-wing social democrats and trade unionists who then dominated the government. The slogan 'Christian' as used in Hungary also suggested racialism. The German term *völkisch* is untranslatable. There was an undoubted influx of German and Austrian *völkisch* ideas in 1919, mainly through the agency of the half-assimilated German minority, living in Hungarian towns and penetrating its army as well as the professions and civil service.

The leaders of both wings of the Horthy régime interpreted these principles as implying the rejection not only of left-wing socialism and communism but also of liberal democracy. Pacifism and anti-militarism was another enemy and was identified with freemasonry on the one hand, and the international labour movement on the other. Yet whilst the conservatives were apologetic about their moderate antisemitism and upheld the principles of parliamentary rule and respect of individual rights, the extremists declared themselves intransigent racialists and enemies of the rule of a 'liberalistic' parliament. They were willing – as events soon showed – to form alliances with the German racialist and dictatorial groups emerging in Berlin and Munich, whose long-term aims were inconsistent with Hungarian national interests. They also preferred violent action against both the internal and external enemy. The conservatives, in contrast – once the dirty work had been carried out efficiently by the officer squads and their civilian counterparts, the patriotic strong-arm groups – preferred to return to the traditional Hungarian policy of cautious authoritarianism. This policy was compatible with the existence of a tamed parliament, such as emerged from partially controlled elections. The conservatives wished to defend the régime by drastic legislation, a strong police force and efficient civil servants rather than by the uniformed or non-uniformed rowdies who had helped them suppress the socialists and democrats.

Lastly, a 'national' policy was equated by all supporters and leaders of the counter-revolutionary régime, as well as by its opposition on the extreme right, with the restoration of Hungary

116

to the old, pre-1918 frontiers. The officers, the conservatives and the racialists alike accepted as the final and supreme aim of Hungarian foreign policy the restoration of the thousand-year-old Hungary in its integrity. This irredentist propaganda had a decidedly millenarian overtone and promised both social and economic salvation for the Hungarian masses. Thus, it played a similar role to the social-imperialist propaganda of the precursors of fascism in Italy and of Hitlerism in Germany – even if the territorial objective was less ambitious. But an empire it was to be, or as the Hungarian Catholics preferred to call it, a 'realm' – the realm of St Stephen, first king of Hungary.

The various groups and wings of the counter-revolutionary movement were united not only by the same, albeit ambiguous, ideological formula, but also by a variety of common organizations. These organizations showed many original traits and characteristics – traits which are decidedly 'modern' and not simply inherited from traditional monarchical-bureaucratic absolutism. At the same time one needs to notice that these forms of organization were not yet fully fledged, mature, fascist or Hitlerite forms of political organization and leadership. The totalitarian system of single-party government dominated by the messianic-demagogic leader could never establish itself in Hungary (unless one wished to describe in this manner the short-lived Szálasi régime, which was nothing but a façade for direct German military rule). The Horthy régime began and until its end functioned as a pluralistic system of competing groups and organizations forming an uneasy coalition, yet at the same time engaged in non-violent struggles with each other.

2 The White Terror

The atmosphere of conspiracy surrounding many of the important organizations of the régime is a most odd characteristic. The historian could find two reasons for this preference of clandestine work among both the civilian and military leaders

117

of the organizational structure. First, the founders of these organizations originally entered into politics as members of small conspiratorial groups, preparing armed insurrections against the leftist régimes. Secondly, they had fantastic notions about the political and social power of freemasonry under liberal or radical democratic régimes, which they believed needed to be combated by similar methods.

Hence, already in Szeged, a small circle of military conspirators and some civilian collaborators decided to set up an 'antimasonic' secret society, which would have its tentacles in all important public and private organizations. The initiators of this plan were members of a small group of military conspirators known as the circle of the twelve captains. Its most prominent members were Captain Marton, Captain Kozma and Captain Gömbös. The circle started its activity as early as the beginning of 1919 in Budapest, where it successfully infiltrated a legal and seemingly loyal organization of republican officers. In January 1919 it succeeded in making Captain Gömbös president of the association, the so-called MOVE (Hungarian National Defence Association). Gömbös and his friends turned this organization into a centre of anti-government activity, so that it was soon suppressed. The twelve captains then dispersed to organize underground movements, finally to emerge together in Szeged during the decisive weeks. There they were connected with the revival of the MOVE – now also open to civilians with the right qualifications – and with the setting-up of such semi-secret societies as the Blood Brotherhood of the Double Cross and the more important EKSZ. The latter was a mock-revival of Hungarian tribal society, run by a committee of seven 'tribal chiefs' – the most important of whom, at a later stage, was Captain Gömbös. The EKSZ was formally established in November 1919, after the entry of Admiral Horthy and his army into Budapest. The immediate task of this secret society would seem to have been to influence the parliamentary elections in such a way as to assure a majority in support of Horthy's candidature for the post of regent. And assured it was, thanks to the organizing activities of Captain M. Kozma, chief of the propaganda department of

118

Horthy's High Command, who directed the intervention of the military during the election period to influence the selection of candidates, especially in the county constituencies. Even the relatively moderate Christian socialist Prime Minister, K. Huszár – accepted by all parties as a constitutionally minded man – was induced to declare that 'Bolshevism was the offspring of radicalism and social democracy'. Hence, the leftist candidates could be freely persecuted, as responsible for bolshevism. (This was the period when train-loads of political undesirables left Budapest for the provincial internment camps.) Not surprisingly, the majority of the first Hungarian parliament to be elected by secret universal suffrage was reliably right-wing. Whether it was also solidly behind Horthy we shall never know, as Prime Minister Huszár frankly told the parliamentary leaders that Horthy had to be elected to the regency or else parliament would be dispersed by the military.

The secret societies and patriotic associations gave loyal support to their 'invisible leader' and protector, the Regent, for years to come. Yet, in day-to-day administration, the influence of Gömbös became stronger as time passed. He made effective instruments out of the proliferating para-military associations, which were co-ordinated by the secret societies, capable not only of harassing the enemies of the régime (including the legitimists) but also of mobilizing popular support for himself once his ambitions to become leader of the régime emerged. The strong-arm squads raided social democratic and liberal newspaper offices, clubs and trade unions in the early stages of the Horthy régime. But they were also used to organize popular demonstrations in support of their favourite leader, Gömbös, who, during his premiership, addressed them from a balcony in the style of Mussolini. The political career of Gömbös was cut short by his premature death in the autumn of 1936. From then on the secret societies and para-military associations became a fighting ground between those more or less moderate ruling statesmen, who had the confidence of the Regent, and the friends and pupils of Gömbös, who made feeble attempts to revitalize these organizations, in order to establish that one-party state and right-wing

119

dictatorship which had been the final aim of Gömbös. But during this struggle the MOVE was disarmed and the EKSZ became paralysed. Consequently the organizational centre of rightist dynamism shifted elsewhere. By 1937 it could be found in the ranks of the right-wing of the government party. But the right-wing members of parliament did not have enough political weight without the support of the right-wing of the army, which, during the premiership of Gömbös, became a decisive political force. At the same time the influence of Germany began to increase. So the pressure began to come simultaneously from the army, from the extreme right, both inside and outside the government party, and last but not least from Berlin. After the occupation of Austria this last influence loomed especially large.

Thus we see the emergence of definite periods in the evolution of the Horthy régime. The first period can be described as the period of the white terror – when the prime ministers (István Friedrich, K. Huszár and finally S. Simonyi-Semadam) were unable to control the activities of the irregular sections of the army or of the secret political branches of the regular army. In the second period Prime Minister Teleki began the process of 'consolidation'.

The period between July 1920, when Count Paul Teleki became Prime Minister, and May 1922, when Count István Bethlen organized an election managed by a conservative administration, can be described as the period of transition from the era of white terror to the age of consolidation and the rule of law – Hungarian style. Already in this period of transition the alliance of the Regent and his more moderate generals with the anti-legitimist wing of the aristocracy began to take shape as the decisive force. Teleki initiated the policy of resisting both the extreme right and the militant legitimists, without relaxing pressure against the extreme left. Not without assistance from courageous liberal members of parliament and from the press, Count Teleki began to restore the ascendancy of the civilian authorities over the officer detachments and racialist associations. This process was completed by Count Bethlen.

3 The Bethlen Era

The greatest danger to their policy was represented by the special squads of the army which were well armed and expanding in numbers. These organizations, however, had inner weaknesses which made the victory of the Regent and his conservative prime ministers inevitable. There was, first of all, the fact that not only the lunatic fringe of the detachments but their psychopathic centre could justly be accused of pursuing their own economic interests with methods more appropriate to a protection racket and criminal gang than to a 'unit of the reserve of the gendarmerie', as these semi-military squads were now called. Secondly, the leadership of the detachments was deeply divided between legitimists and anti-legitimists, between friends and enemies of Gömbös, so that many were deprived of the most effective defence: the support of the *apparat* of Captain Gömbös. Finally, their addiction to violence and direct action was regarded as dangerous both by the aristocratic politicians and by Horthy. The latter realized by now that the abolition of parliament and a take-over by the commanders of the squads might precipitate military intervention by Hungary's suspicious neighbours. Moreover, the foreign policy of the extreme right was immediate invasion of Czechoslovakia and armed intervention in Austria; Horthy and his advisers realized that this was dangerous and 'premature'. The political line on which Horthy, the regular army officers, the aristocrats and the political leaders of the Christian National Union and the Smallholders Party agreed was that there would be *neither restoration of the Habsburgs nor dictatorship by the extreme right*. Hence, the leaders of the special detachments who wanted either one or the other of these solutions had to go. It was a line which was particularly attractive to the members of the Smallholders Party, who were sworn enemies of the Habsburg solution.

Until summer 1923 Gömbös himself supported this political line. Only then did he realize that Bethlen, whom he had helped to win the elections in 1922, was much too liberal and too conservative for him. Yet, he had only to stay for five years in the political wilderness. Gömbös and his friends proved politically more adroit than the commanders of the special squads: they remained 'respectable' and socially acceptable reserve forces of the régime, holding the key positions in the secret societies, in the patriotic associations and also in certain sections of the army. However, when Gömbös formed his own parliamentary group of seven 'racialists', he exposed himself, at the next election, to political defeat and isolation, which forced him to change his tactics and return to the government party. Thus until 1931 Count Bethlen and his conservative friends stole the limelight, having built up a remarkably stable political system.

Under this system there existed a curious relationship between the politically powerful governing groups and the economically leading social classes. The Bethlen group successfully claimed the right for the 'historical classes' to monopolize power. By 'historical classes' they meant the strongly nationalistic and anti-Habsburg wing of the landed aristocracy and their allies: the lesser nobility who, either as civil servants or as owners of middle-sized estates, guaranteed the success of Bethlen's 'united' government party at election time and upheld social order between elections. This dedication to the conservation of social order at home was paradoxically combined with a policy of subversion of the international order. No direct actions were planned but contacts with Mussolini were established and his support was assured for plans of territorial revision. At the same time groups hostile to the established frontiers were financed in the neighbouring countries and money was forged in great quantities to provide the funds.

The Catholic, legitimist aristocracy and the mainly Jewish industrial and banking circles accepted the claim of the 'historical classes' to lead and rule. In exchange, they were consulted on matters of financial and economic policy and enjoyed the unchallenged right to run the large estates and industrial enterprises as seemed to them most profitable. They also obtained protective tariffs, price subventions and, not least, protection against demands for radical agrarian reform and industrial unrest. A stable currency and a balanced budget were established with the assistance of the League of Nations and of the financial centres of Europe and the USA. All this fully satisfied the otherwise powerless monarchical aristocrats and liberal industrialists. On the other hand, one should not forget that both these groups had great influence on the daily press and on the cultural life of the country, besides possessing of course their own powerful professional organizations.

In a sense the Catholic high clergy was itself a section of the big landowner class, for ecclesiastical property constituted an important part of the Hungarian system of big estates. Not unlike the Catholic aristocrats, the bishops were often ardent legitimists. Under the Bethlen system they enjoyed – like their lay counterparts – economic power and cultural influence, but very slight political power. The Catholic-inspired political parties were small and divided between principled legitimists, taking up postures of opposition, and flexible Christian socialists (or, as they were called, members of the Christian Economic Party) who supported Bethlen and his successors 'from the outside'. Some sections of political Catholicism even operated *within* the government party. Catholic groups enjoyed decisive political control only on the local government level, notably in Budapest. It is not surprising that when the struggle between conservatism and national socialism became more acute, most of the Catholic leaders supported the conservative front, whilst their mass base was being undermined by national socialist propaganda. But that was only to happen at the end of the thirties. During the Bethlen régime political Catholicism and the Catholic-dominated sections of the education system greatly contributed to the stability of the structure established by the Calvinist politician Count Bethlen.

This structure, however, was stable only on the surface. Once the European agrarian and financial crisis brought wheat prices down and blocked the source of new international credits, the Bethlen régime was bound to collapse. The suppressed political and social dissatisfaction made the return of the extreme right to power, even if not to total power, inevitable. C. A. Macartney,

123

whose book on Hungary – *October Fifteenth* – must be regarded as a classic whether one likes it or not, has analysed this process in detail and convincingly.

However, a word of caution must be added, lest one assume, from reading the summary review of these events, that the men of the extreme right who assisted General Gömbös to become premier in 1932 were socially more advanced than the conservatives who resisted their bid for power. One has to remember certain historical facts in order to realize that those who worked for a transformation of Hungary into a fascist and racialist country were not enlightened and principled crusaders for social justice; nor were their conservative and liberal opponents such anti-social reactionaries as they were depicted in the German and the Hungarian Nazi press. One should not forget that it was Count Bethlen who restored to the industrial workers the right to establish trade unions and to obtain, within certain limits, political representation. Industrial workers' wages went up during the Bethlen régime, to a normal central European level, whereas during the white terror they had fallen deeply. Unemployment figures also fell, thanks to the economic and financial reforms introduced by Bethlen, who had systematically attracted foreign capital to finance the expansion of industry. Only in the field of agrarian reform were Bethlen and his friends ultra-conservative. But in the same field Gömbös and his friends were pretty vague and some of Gömbös' chief lieutenants were landowners with a very anti-social and money-grabbing reputation. The more extremist, 'revolutionary' national socialist leaders of the post-Gömbös era were of course more radical in their promises of agrarian reform. Yet their practical understanding of the problem was seriously limited by their romantic, mythological and pathological manner of thinking. What they had in mind was the establishment of a military-peasant 'estate' or 'corporation'. Nevertheless, they too relied on the support of certain 'anti-social' minded landowners and county administrators who started their careers in Gömbös' circle, and they too had to rely on Hitler in order to obtain power. And Hitler was a staunch supporter of the principle of productive and mechanized

124

large estates, producing a substantial surplus, to feed his cities and armies.

Yet, a serious weakness of the Bethlen system was created by the prohibition on state employees and agricultural workers to organize freely. They were at the mercy of the official, government-sponsored 'nationalist' unions and many developed into secret supporters of the more extreme national socialist groups.

Of course, the policy of industrialization as practised by Bethlen before 1931 had advantages for the class of big landowners, as it absorbed more and more of the propertyless farmers and agricultural labourers into industry. Hence, it eased the pressure for land in the countryside. In practice, the *absolute* number of Hungarians engaged in the agricultural sector did not decrease during the rule of Bethlen and his successors, but the *percentage* of Hungarians engaged in agriculture fell from 56 to 50 per cent between 1930 and 1937. So the pressure on the big estates during this period did not increase, even if it did not fall. This was particularly important once the pre-war road of emigration to the USA had been blocked. But no land-reform policy could have abolished agricultural over-population and under-employment unless it had been combined with a much more energetic and systematic long-term policy of planned industrialization. The conditions outside and inside Hungary were not favourable for such a policy.

In defence of Bethlen's policy one must add that he did not neglect the development of social services in town and country, concentrating mainly on education and health. Several measures of social policy favouring employees, workers and farmers, which were enacted during the 1930s, were prepared during the last years of the Bethlen era, or framed by conservative politicians who survived their mentor politically, such as F. Keresztes-Fischer and Paul Teleki.

The great scandal of the Horthy régime was that no provisions were made for the unemployed, except organized charity. But the measure to abolish unemployment benefits was introduced before the rise of Bethlen and was not remedied by his successors. All in all, it can be said that whilst the Bethlenites and their allies

125

were moving towards a policy of rational economic advance in the framework of an internationalist economic system, their right-wing rivals were hankering after distorted medieval ideas such as privileged 'estates', economic autarky and a pseudo-tribal organization of social life. Behind all this mumbo jumbo there were, however, two realities guiding most leaders of the Right: subservience to the economic and military needs of Nazi Germany; and demands for economic privileges for themselves and their supporters – not the voters, of course, but the members of the party militia and related organizations. Events showed that in Hungary it was not the cultured upper-middle class and the aristocracy which worshipped the most reactionary ideas, but the alienated sections of the middle classes and of the lower nobility, whether in or out of uniform.

4 The Years of Gömbös

There was just enough social dissatisfaction and political unrest in Hungary during the years of the world economic crisis of the 1930s to undermine the authority of the Bethlenites and induce the Regent to promote General Gömbös from Minister of Defence to the rank of Prime Minister in 1932. With Gömbös some of the men and organizations connected with the first, violent, crusading epoch of the régime were swept into power, although enough conservatism survived in the system to prevent them from gaining *unlimited* power.

The most important factor in the new situation was the personality of the new prime minister. Although now a moderate about the racial question, and fairly cautious in economic policy, he had unlimited personal ambitions. Soon anyone with ears could realize that he wanted to establish a single-party state with himself as all-powerful, infallible leader and dictator. He was of course often clumsy and sometimes even ridiculous when he made his bid for absolute power – as, for instance, when he stated that 'it is enough if there is only one clever man in the country'. He also complained bitterly in public that 'there are powerful leaders elsewhere', only he was not permitted to become one, which he seemed to find both unjust and inexplicable. But there was a simple explanation: his power base was too narrow! Sandwiched between a jealous head of state and a parliamentary party built up by Bethlen, he appealed in vain to the patriotic associations, to the dissatisfied middle classes, to the masses. His programme of social, political and racial reforms was just not radical enough. And his appeals to the workers to become 'nationalist' and discard their freely elected leaders fell on deaf ears. In order to build up popular support and a power machine, Gömbös authorized his old fellow-conspirator Captain Marton to organize a nation-wide 'movement'. Its local organizers were dubbed 'vanguard fighters' by Gömbös, which contributed to the general hilarity surrounding this experiment of building a revolutionary mass movement from above, assisted by well-paid bureaucrats and respectable landowners. The racialist dynamism and anti-Red fury of the early counter-revolutionary movement were missing.

It is a curious thing that Gömbös, who was a racialist till 1928, became so moderate in this respect by 1932. The explanation lies in the fact that in 1928 Bethlen concluded a treaty of friendship with Mussolini. From then onwards the Duce became the source of inspiration for Gömbös. But he rediscovered racialism later, when he established close contacts with the victorious German National Socialist leaders. Gömbös and his political friends had to make paradoxical manoeuvres in order to remain 'defenders of the Hungarian race' without indulging in antisemitism, German style. The records of the cabinet meetings and the official papers of the Gömbös era show pathetic and dangerous attempts by the Hungarian leaders, including Horthy himself, to re-interpret fashionable racialism in an innocuous and 'positive' way. Racial defence in Hungary was to mean improving the health of the Hungarian race by making marriages dependent on medical certificates. Plans to sterilize the sick were also discussed, but not pursued. What these men of power, discussing a policy of racial hygiene, did not realize was that if one starts with 'positive' proposals to strengthen the race, as the highest value, then the door is opened to a more radical interpretation

127

of the same principle which leads directly to the policy of racial discrimination. From this point, as events were soon to show, it was only one more step to the policy of deportations and extermination.

Supporters of Gömbös later suggested that if he had survived as leader of a national socialist Hungary into the war years, he would have prevented the spread of German methods of racial defence to Hungary. But the evolution of his idol, Mussolini, seems to disprove this hypothesis. Furthermore, one should not forget his increasing infatuation with the leaders of Nazi Germany. Gömbös visited Hitler for the first time in June 1933. (Gömbös was the first prime minister of any country to visit the dictator of Nazi Germany.) He demanded markets for Hungarian products from Hitler and discussed foreign policy. Impressed but dissatisfied, Gömbös had to turn for help towards Mussolini, who was then in his anti-Hitlerite phase. But by May 1936 the gulf between Budapest and Berlin had been bridged. Gömbös concluded a secret agreement with Goering, agreeing upon political and military co-operation, and in which Gömbös promised to establish within two years a system in Hungary similar to that which Hitler had established in Germany.

This agreement was never accepted by the Regent or the cabinet, so that when Gömbös died in October 1936 the agreement lost all political significance. On the surface Gömbös' policy failed. Nevertheless, he succeeded in modifying the balance of power in Hungarian politics in such a way that German influence could be effectively exercised in Hungary in the future. Gömbös had established strong economic and political ties between Budapest and Berlin and these were not dismantled by his successors. One of his most fatal moves was to make a colonel of the General Staff, D.Sztojay, Hungarian Minister in Berlin. Furthermore, thanks to the purge of the higher echelons of the army and to the energetic management of the 1935 elections by two members of the circle of twelve captains (B.Marton, now general secretary of the government party and M.Kozma, now Minister of the Interior), right-wing, pro-German elements dominated both the army and the government party. The same was true of the gendarmerie, but less true of the police and of the civil service in general. Gömbös' friends could thus attempt to revive his policy with a certain optimism, even if the extra-parliamentary single-party movement had to be dismantled.

The year 1936 was the turning point in the evolution of the Horthy régime. Seventeen years of its existence were over, two-thirds of its total existence. Eight were still to come. By 1937 the character of the régime was there for all to see. The original leaders of both the conservative and the fascist wings were out of the way: Gömbös was dead and Bethlen had lost the leadership of his party for good. But these groups were still dominated by the pupils and successors of the once powerful leaders. From now on for the remaining years of the régime the two camps engaged in hostile co-operation, interrupted by non-violent struggles. Horthy's power was in the ascendant, both legally and politically. It was he who survived Gömbös and Bethlen, it was he who chose their successors and directed their policies – Hitler permitting. But there was another factor, apart from increasing German pressure, which the Regent had to take into consideration more than the mood of parliament or public opinion. This was the leadership of the army. The army by now was increasingly radical and leaned towards national socialist solutions in both internal and external policies. The main aims of the army were rearmament and close military-political co-operation with Germany, sugar-coated with social and racialist reforms. Prime Minister Darányi, Gömbös' first successor, and incidentally one of the 'tribal leaders' of the top secret society, gave in to army pressure and in spring 1938 announced a programme of massive rearmament, to be financed by taxation levied on big business. The army, it would seem, was now anti-capitalist! The same prime minister also introduced the first legislative measures establishing racial discrimination in the professions and in economic life. These measures were continued and developed even further by his successor B.Imrédy. The latter, both as a financial expert with a European horizon and as a statesman who claimed to follow a Catholic political philosophy, was regarded as more moderate or more conservative than the man whose place he took at the Regent's wish. But the high hopes which the conservatives and liberals attached to this change were dashed by Imrédy, who took a strictly pro-German line when – just after the Munich conference – the first Vienna award expanded Hungarian territory at the expense of Slovakia. He also revived Gömbös' experiments to base the prime minister's power on a party of militant but respectable fascists and racialists and thus establish a dictatorship. This was to be his undoing and the real reason for his fall, not the tragicomic disclosures concerning his alleged Jewish ancestry. The text of the memorandum which the Conservatives and Smallholders, led by Bethlen, submitted to the Regent in January 1939 is clear evidence of the hostility to this attempted new development and the reason for Imrédy's fall.

A reliable conservative and principled Hungarian patriot was to take Imrédy's place. This man was Count Paul Teleki. On the surface his premiership was successful – a third of Transylvania was allotted by the Axis leaders to Hungary in the second Vienna award. But his power was undermined by the manoeuvres of the army leaders, especially by the Chief of Staff, Henrik Werth. Horthy either would not, or could not, defend his prime minister against the fatal coalition of the Germans, the Hungarian army leaders and the right wing of the cabinet, which pressed for intervention in the war on the side of Germany.

5 The Army

The army thus represented a strong political force already during the premiership of Teleki. Under Teleki's successor, L.Bárdossy, much less energetic and clearly anti-western minded, the army became even more powerful. From 1941 onwards, the institution of labour squads for politically and racially unreliable people was misused by the army to deport and decimate tens of thousands of racially or politically undesirable elements, including – besides Jews – social democrat shop-stewards, anti-German journalists and young Hungarian poets. Many thousands perished during the death marches or were starved to death or simply executed by non-commissioned officers, on the instructions of their superiors in the chain of command.

But early in 1942 the military overreached themselves when they organized mass executions in Yugoslav territories occupied by the forces of the Hungarian army and gendarmerie. Two months later the Regent again chose a Bethlen supporter as prime minister, both to put the army in its place and to open the way for armistice negotiations with the Western democracies. This man was the true-born Hungarian nobleman and wealthy landowner Miklós Kállay. Under his premiership the excesses of the army were slowly but effectively eliminated and the censorship of the press was somewhat relaxed. His efforts to obtain an armistice – after the victory of the Allies in North Africa and after Stalingrad – became frantic and were interrupted only by the invasion of Hungary by Hitler's troops on 18 March 1944.

A right-wing government was now imposed on Horthy and the Hungarian people by Hitler. It included a few conservatives tolerable to the Germans, but the bulk of the cabinet was reliably pro-German. The right-wing of the old government party shared the most important jobs with the leaders of the new party of Imrédy and of the smaller national socialist groups, such as the gendarmerie officer L. Baky or the local official and organizer of 'scientific' research into racial conditions, L. Endre. The cabinet was headed by D. Sztojay, the former colonel of the General Staff and Hungarian Minister in Berlin. These men presided over the surrender of anti-German politicians and half a million 'racially unreliable' elements to the ss and Gestapo. The process of total nazification was only interrupted in July 1944, when Horthy, with the help of the reliable sections of his army, turned upon Endre, Baky and their gendarmerie and interrupted the deportations and expropriations. Step by step the Regent, listening to the advice of Bethlen, rid himself of the majority of the pro-German politicians and

131

started secret armistice negotiations with the Russians. Not surprisingly Horthy was arrested by German troops, striking on 15 October on Hitler's orders, against the nerve centres of the Hungarian capital. Endre and Baky, together with the Arrow Cross men, now served as top administrators for the Germans, who in fact controlled those parts of Hungary not yet occupied by the Russian army. The success of the German operation was greatly facilitated by the fact that in the decisive hours the bulk of the Hungarian officers deserted their supreme commander, the Regent, and went over to the Germans. Perhaps the Regent demanded too much of them – after all, they were only acting in accordance with their deep-seated convictions.

The reader may ask himself how it happened that the officers of the national army were so thoroughly indoctrinated by an extremist political ideology. The answer can be found in the peculiarities of the Hungarian army. Many officers were members of secret societies permeated by racialism and hatred of the democratic labour movement. Moreover, the system of officers' training was given an ideological twist by instructors infected by Nazi ideas. Thus General Beregffy, one of the members of Szálasi's right extremist cabinet in 1944, was for many years commander of the 'Ludovika' military academy. Finally, one must remember the influence of the Hungarian right-wing press, which enjoyed powerful financial support from the Hungarian or German authorities or from both. However, influential as the army leaders may have been, they were never able to establish that dictatorship which they often admitted to be their final goal. Thus they were obliged to act indirectly and put pressure on the Regent and his cabinet in order to implement their extremist policies.

More and more documentary evidence has been unearthed since the end of the war confirming the strength of army pressure and throwing light on the spirit of the officer corps, or at least of its powerful 'right-wing'. First of all we have the memorandum drawn up by General Soós de Bádok, one of the 1919 organizers in Szeged of the national army and special terrorist detachments.

The memorandum was submitted to the Regent in January 1938, after consultation with a great number of officers, of whom the most important was General Jenó Rátz, Chief of Staff and a figure trusted by the right wing of the army. According to this document (published by C. A. Macartney in his *OctoberFifteenth*, vol. 1, page 213), the army demanded measures to reduce Jewish influence in the press, in cultural life and in economic activities. In the last field, 'Christian' activities were to be strongly supported. The memorandum also demanded increased taxation and control of the big firms (by the army?). Employment was to be given to students who successfully completed their studies at university. 'All Left-wing agitation' was to be mercilessly persecuted. But this measure, oddly enough, was to be coupled, according to the memorandum, with a 'juster distribution of land' and measures intended to protect the poorer classes.

The author of the memorandum added that only 'a government resting on an autocratic basis' could carry out these reforms speedily. Hence the Regent should run the country without parliament or at least with a parliament which had a strong right-wing majority. Consequently there should be freedom of organization for the forces of the Right, including Szálasi's group.

A memorandum containing similar demands was submitted to Prime Minister Darányi at the same time by General Rátz. This memorandum was more clearly aimed at a massive rearmament programme. Darányi accepted it, without committing himself to a clear-cut system of dictatorship. Soon after, he was succeeded by another partisan of the two measures demanded by the army, B. Imrédy.

By early 1939, when Count Paul Teleki replaced him, Imrédy, together with his Minister of Defence Jenö Rátz, was working actively to build up a single-party state. With Teleki's succession, it seemed reasonable to believe that the drift to the Right would be stopped. But this is not the impression one gets by studying the new Prime Minister's memoranda submitted to the Regent in the autumn of the same year. (The documents were published in a somewhat ambiguous English translation by M. Szinai and

L. Szücs in Budapest in 1965 in the volume entitled *The Confidential Papers of Admiral Horthy*.) Prime Minister Teleki complained that 'in certain respects we have departed from a legal basis and begun to slip over to a certain military dictatorship, which, however, is exercised from below rather than from above'. He added that during his period of office he was made aware that there were 'two governmental machineries and two governmental systems' in Hungary, a legal one and a 'military régime spreading to practically all branches of civil administration, whose functions the lawful governmental system is unable to supervise and control.' He reminded the Regent that the participation of military persons in civil administration started in the days of the premiership of Gömbös. An untenable situation had been created by new powers of this kind given to 'military delegates' in civilian departments. Furthermore, the army was conducting commercial negotiations with Germany and also interfered in the process of foreign policy-making and negotiations. On the one hand, the generals demanded excessive sums for cars – sums which could be used to solve the most urgent social problems of Hungary; on the other hand, they incited the workers and interfered in the process of social policy-making in a demagogic way. He also complained about the interference of the army in the training of students at secondary schools and universities. The military spread an anti-Christian spirit and attempted to introduce 'the use of teenagers for a counter-intelligence service within the school, and even in their families'. Teleki claimed that these were 'symptoms of muddle-headed Arrow Cross ideas' which the officers were attempting to introduce into the education of youth. He added that a 'spirit has evolved in the body of officers, and especially in the General Staff, that is apt to impair the relations between the Army and civilian society. This spirit is even today to some extent of Arrow Cross inclination, manifesting itself in a less overt form, yet existing in the way of thinking.' Finally, the Prime Minister explained that the principle of ministerial responsibility had been systematically violated because measures were being taken which affected government departments without the ministers'

134

participation. Today, 'two parallel administrations' are 'hampering one another both in small and great matters'.

He concluded by demanding an assurance from the Regent that 'with respect to political activities' at home, 'or, more important, in foreign politics', the army and general staff 'should be subordinated to the prime minister' and the army should not 'interfere in departmental duties'.

On 3 April 1941, Paul Teleki committed suicide. His gesture was intended as a protest against the decision of the Regent to give way to the combined pressure of the Germans, his own generals and the right-wing of the cabinet: the transit of German forces was to be permitted through Hungarian territory in their attack on Yugoslavia; Hungarian forces were to be mobilized and allowed to occupy northern Yugoslav territory. No logic-chopping about the timing and legal character of military intervention by the Hungarian army in the war can explain away this basic fact. Teleki's policy of neutrality towards the West and friendship with Yugoslavia had failed – after it had been undermined by the manoeuvres of the same military leadership about whose political influence he had complained so bitterly a few months earlier. It is a historical fact that the Germans used their contacts with the Hungarian army leaders 'to put into motion political leadership' – as General Halder put it when he imposed pressure on Hungary to participate in the war against the Soviet Union. (See the diary of the German general attached to the High Command of the Hungarian army, quoted in Admiral Horthy's *Confidential Papers*, p. 183.)

6 The Fascist Groups

Important as the collusion between the right-wing of the government party and the army leadership may have been, this was only one of the characteristics of the Hungarian political scene after the death of Gömbös. Another was the emergence of new, demagogic, plebeian, extremist national socialist movements. It was a new phenomenon, for both leaders and followers adopted an extremely anti-liberal attitude, not because of memories of the 'sins' committed by left-wing parties and governments, nor because of the hardships connected with the post-war inflation, but because they suffered social frustrations and economic insecurity in a deflationary crisis which they blamed on the conservative wing of the Horthy régime and on the 'racial enemy'. More important perhaps even than frustration and insecurity was the inspiring example of the triumphant German national socialist movement. Inspiration was followed by material incentives, in the form of financial and political assistance from Berlin, culminating in 1944 in the distribution of arms to the storm troopers of the Hungarian extremist movements by the German authorities. Besides these new Nazi features, these Hungarian national socialist groups also showed a few typically Hungarian features, already visible during the white terror; in particular, personal and organizational divisions and disagreements which split the extreme right into many groups.

There were three main groups which operated to the right of the right-wing of the government party. The most 'moderate' and 'gentlemanly' group was led by Imrédy and General Rátz. This group lacked mass support. It obtained thirty seats during the elections of 1939, but only thanks to the official support its members enjoyed in the safe constituencies of the government party. They only left that party in October 1940 to form an energetic opposition against the liberal-conservative and truly national policies of Teleki and M. Kállay.

The second group was led among others by L. Baky. L. Baky had been a leading terrorist at Horthy's headquarters in Transdanubia in 1919; he was promoted to chief of the special branch of the Hungarian gendarmerie and entered politics in 1937 in the national socialist movement, as a retired major. But he remained on good terms with his former fellow officers in the gendarmerie, and was also well-connected in Berlin, especially to Himmler. Being more demagogic than Imrédy, Baky and his group enjoyed some popular support – they obtained eleven seats in 1939 when the elections were secret and they had perhaps a hundred thousand party members in the autumn of 1944.

But the mass basis of the third group – the Arrow Cross Party – was more substantial. According to István Deák its membership fluctuated widely. The party had perhaps twenty thousand members in 1937; more than one hundred thousand at the end of 1940; and perhaps half a million in September 1944. But in between, especially in 1943 and early 1944, its membership was much lower. The reasons for the spectacular rise of the membership between spring and autumn 1944 can be found in the fact that the Germans and the Sztojay government brutally suppressed all Left opposition groups, but treated the Arrow Cross with kid-gloves, leaving it in a monopolistic position as the organizer of the opposition.

Looking at the social composition of Arrow Cross membership, it is surprising to find that the peasantry was under-represented, with only 13 per cent of the membership in 1940. The middle classes were over-represented with 36 per cent – nearly half being army officers! Also over-represented were the workers, but it is fair to assume that these were mainly un-skilled, unemployed or unorganized workers. The workers in the big industries of the Budapest region took an anti-fascist line in 1944: they boycotted the elections to fascist-type nationalistic works' councils in summer 1944 and later resisted the orders of the national socialist authorities to evacuate their factories and move into western Hungary. In 1939 thousands of communist sympathizers must have voted for the Arrow Cross; in 1944 they showed their true colours. The composition of the top leadership of the Arrow Cross was dominated by professional counter-revolutionaries of lower-middle class origin, many of them ex-officers. This may explain the dominant role which the army played in the ideology and utopia of Szálasi. His dream-world Hungary which he dubbed the 'Danubian-Carpathian Great Fatherland' was to be held together by the army, to whom all resources of the nation were to be subordinated.

The social background of the Arrow Cross leader had a certain similarity to that of Adolf Hitler. His father was a non-commissioned officer. Szálasi himself became a professional officer, fought at the front during the first world war and served under the Republican and perhaps also under the 'Red' régime in 1918 and 1919. Going through the staff college of the Horthy army, he served in the counter-intelligence department of the General Staff. It was in the course of these activities that he realized that he was predestined to become the saviour of Hungary and of Europe. This fanatical conviction enabled him to take risks which his more cautious rivals avoided: he organized secret sections of his party, which armed themselves; he was uninhibited in his political, racial and social propaganda. Most of all he demanded total power for himself and his movement and was not afraid of risking lengthy prison sentences. Facing journalists who questioned his qualifications to be a political leader, he answered them by claiming that politics is the art of organization, an art which he had learnt thoroughly on the General Staff of the army. His lieutenants were also adepts of that art, although they learnt it elsewhere, probably in Nazi Germany. One of his main lieutenants was, for instance, a white terrorist officer, Emil Kovarcz, who took part early in 1920 in the kidnapping and murder of two prominent social-democratic journalists – B.Somogyi and B.Bacsó. (This was Hungary's Matteotti affair.) After a period as a teacher at the 'Ludovika' military academy in the early thirties, Kovarez became an Arrow Cross deputy. Prosecuted for organizing bomb outrages, he escaped to Germany in 1940. In October 1944 – following the instructions of the ss – he organized an Arrow Cross rising in Budapest. After this he became 'Minister of Total Mobilization' in Szálasi's so-called government. Another organizer of armed party activities was K.Wirth, a renegade leader of a Christian-socialist trade union. A newcomer to the ranks of the Arrow Cross organizers in autumn 1944 was Colonel Paul de Prónay, whom we met earlier as the most prominent leader of special detachments in the first phase of the white régime. All these men and their less famous associates were now freely applying their various talents as organizers, murderers and extortionists. So the white régime ended – as it had begun – 'dans le sang et dans la boue'.

The period of German occupation, which began in March

1944 and ended – with the exception of western Hungary – early in 1945, gave various opportunities at different times to all three extreme right-wing groups to participate in power – if not in decision making, at least in the execution of policies framed by the Germans. At the same time they were engaged in a fierce fight with each other. It was only during the last months of 1944 that, under German pressure, they began to combine their forces. But by then it was too late. 'Total power' was never enjoyed by Szálasi nor by Baky or Imrédy or their various helpers who were all dreaming of 'leadership' in a national socialist Hungary.

All this again shows the failure of the fascist forces to achieve unity and establish a mature, totalitarian fascist political system. Hungarian fascism remained divided and was only partially successful. Yet it was operating in a pluralist system which did not quite exclude it from power. Hence, its impact on Hungarian politics and society was destructive and effective to a degree which is difficult to assess. The Horthy régime was certainly pluralistic, but hardly a liberal system. This is obvious from the fact that fascist forces operated so freely within a system which was built on an ideologically and politically corrupted army and gendarmerie, both of which were commanded by officers trained in the spirit of the white terror. Hungarian fascism was less 'mature', less 'modern' and less plebeian than fascism in Italy and Germany – just as Hungarian parliamentarism was less modern and less democratic than its German or Italian counterparts. Hungarian fascism may have been backward, semi-feudal, and militaristic, but nevertheless it was an extremist, racialist fascism. Those who did not feel its destructive fury may deny this fact – those who experienced it have to go on testifying to this truth as long as they live. It is historically undeniable that during the Horthy régime fascism and racialism were strong political forces, contained from time to time, only to be unleashed at intervals. These destructive forces could be camouflaged, but never destroyed, as long as the régime existed.

The miscarriage of totalitarian fascism in Hungary was due to the fact that Gömbös, who was in his element in conspiratorial small groups, conspicuously failed when he attempted to act as a charismatic leader of a nation-wide mass movement. Szálasi was more successful in the 'second phase' of fascism, but was incapable of getting himself accepted by the Hungarian establishment as prime minister – a necessary step to transform his mass movement into an all-powerful governing party. Horthy adamantly resisted all attempts to force him to play the role of a Hindenburg. Hence, fascist tendencies in Hungary had to ally themselves with the army in order to attain their goals at least partially. Thus, Hungarian fascism which started as a military conspiracy ended as a militaristic mass-movement.

Finally, we must ask the question: did Hungary produce that type of fascist movement which turned against Hitlerism and defended national interests against plans of German domination? Latin countries did produce such movements and in this respect Hungary was nearer to the Latin countries than to the Slav ones in which the resistance to Nazism seldom took fascist and racialist forms. Reviewing anti-Germanic Hungarian fascist thought one must first of all mention the mediocre novelist and brilliant propagandist Dezsö Szabó. He started his career as a minor member of the pro-French school of progressive Hungarian literature, but his choice of French models and inspirers was rather unusual for that circle of radical democratic intellectuals. His idols were Barrès and Péguy and probably Bergson and Maurras. By the time the left-wing revolution swept over Hungary, he had produced a novel in which he defended the true-born rural Hungarian, peasant or poet, against the forces of capitalism and urbanism. Hailed by the communists, he turned against them and switched from anti-capitalism to antisemitism. He could have been the poet laureate of the Horthy régime, but very quickly he turned against the new 'establishment'. Szabó was deeply suspicious of both the conservatives and the Gömbös followers, the former as the opponents of the land reform he demanded, the latter as the conscious or unconscious tools of German racial imperialism. He was extremely vicious in his attacks on General Gömbös, deriding his claim to become 'leader' of a reborn nationalist Hungary. Szabó's one-man magazine was avidly read by Hungarian nationalist intellectuals and also by some of the more cultured members of the officers' corps. The seeds of a right-wing anti-German movement were sown by Dezsö Szabó, who also had a definite influence – not always a favourable one – on a new, rising generation of Hungarian populist poets, novelists and journalists. Whilst he mercilessly lampooned Gömbös and his friends as comic figures, he shuddered with horror when he described the rise of Szálasi and his men. He called the Arrow Cross movement 'the Hungarian variant of death'. By this he meant two things: first, that the establishment of a pro-German Arrow Cross régime would represent a mortal danger to the survival of the Hungarian race; secondly, that Szálasi and his men personified the Hungarian manifestation of that 'death-principle' which the black uniformed ss squads represented in Germany.

Szabó was not a practical politician and could not organize a political movement. Yet his influence, especially in undermining the authority of Gömbös and mobilizing anti-German instincts in young men on the Right, should not be under-rated. The attempts by more practical minded right-wing politicians to mobilize anti-German racialist sentiment were only more effective on paper. There was, first of all, the so-called 'Order of the Brave' established by Horthy on the advice of his military chief of cabinet, Captain Magasházi, in 1920. (The *chef de cabinet* in question was, not surprisingly, a member of the group of the twelve captains.) The members of the Order of the Brave were recruited from the veterans of the first world war, and also from those who played an honourable part in the various irredentist risings and later in the second world war. They had to possess a gold medal of bravery and had to be men loyal to Horthy, ready to fight any internal or external enemy of his régime. Apart from the inheritable title of 'brave' (*Vitéz*), they received an unalienable plot of land which amounted to forty holds in the case of an officer but only to eight holds in the case of a non-commissioned officer (1 hold = 1·43 acres). The former gift did

141

not satisfy the social ambitions of the officers, the latter grant
was not enough to live on, but too much for dying. More substantial were the advantages which the members of the order
enjoyed as active officers, civil servants or politicians. But special
qualifications were needed for such careers – to be brave was not
enough. In the end the order proved a broken reed – it was unable
and perhaps unwilling to support Horthy against Hitler when
the chips were down.

Another organization of the Right which had anti-German
tendencies was composed of shooting clubs and was called the
Association of Turanian Hunters. The name itself shows that an
effort was made to create a racialist ideology which would infuse
'fascist dynamism' into this para-military organization. The
word Turanian hints at the racial origin of the ancestors of the
Hungarians and carries at the same time an anti-German con-
notation, for the Nazis claimed to be Aryans and – as all students
of mythology know – Aryans and Turanians were fighting epic
battles in legendary times. But nothing like this was to happen in
the prosaic twentieth century. Under the premiership of Miklós
Kállay the Turanian Hunters were especially favoured by the
authorities and their membership reached probably several
hundred thousand. The authorities hoped that the Turanians
would use their weapons – if the call to arms came – against the
Hungarian Nazis or the Reds or even against the invading
German army. But the call to arms never came – Horthy and
his advisers decided in March 1944 to yield to the Germans
without armed resistance. Kállay went into hiding, and the new
pro-German government dissolved the Turanians and reorganized the Order of the Brave and similar right-wing anti-German
organizations. All these movements ceased to count because
Horthy never uttered the call to arms. That came from elsewhere, at a later date, from the leader of a military resistance
movement which emerged in the autumn of 1944. His name was
Endre Bajesy-Zsilinszky. To mention him among the anti-
German racialist and right-wing leaders may seem paradoxical,
but the life history of this hero of the resistance justifies it. After
fighting in the first world war as a courageous officer at the front,

he joined the circle of racialist officers surrounding Admiral Horthy in the first phase of the counter-revolution. Elected member of parliament, he joined the Racial Defence Party of Captain Gömbös. As he took both his Magyar nationalism and his social reform principles seriously, he did not follow Gömbös into the government party, nor did he join the new national socialist movements. Instead he founded his own party, the National Radical Party and demanded a radical agrarian reform as well as a democratic electoral law. In the late thirties he became a member of the Smallholders Party and was the leader of its left-wing during the war years. By now he was a national democrat of deep convictions and fought the army and gendarmerie when it attempted to implement genocide by direct action. He also attacked the foreign policy which led to Hungary's entry into the war on the side of Germany and was especially powerful in his attacks on the demands of the German minority for power. When the Gestapo raided his flat, on 18 March 1944, he received them with revolver shots. Wounded, he was taken to prison and liberated only in mid-October 1944. When the armistice policy of Horthy misfired and the Germans took over power for themselves (assisted by Szálasi's storm-troopers and by Baky's gendarmes) he began to organize the anti-German groups of the Hungarian army, preparing an armed rising. Betrayed, he was again arrested and brought before Baky's officers to be investigated. Finally, he and three of his fellow-officers were executed.

At the time of his martydom German-occupied Budapest witnessed the emergence of a resistance movement inspired by Bajcsy and Szabó; the young officers, students and professional men co-operated with groups of workers who were organized by the parties of the left, united in a popular front. Soon various military objectives, used by the German army, went up in flames. One of the objects to be blown up was the statue of General Gömbös, which his friends had erected in white marble on the banks of the Danube, in memory of his contributions to the creation of a right-wing Hungary. By now that creation was going up in flames.

It may be understandable if the author of this essay ends by reporting his personal observations while working (from 1931 to 1944) at a Budapest institute for popular education. Here the employees had the status of civil servants; half of them were university graduates, the other half had only secondary school education. The graduates were supposed to be actively interested in educational, scientific and cultural matters and usually were; the non-graduates performed important but less glamorous tasks in the clerical and administrative fields. The university graduates were as a whole – with one or two exceptions – ardent Hungarian patriots, who became more and more bitterly opposed to the policies of Nazi Germany during the war years. The *majority* of these graduates had a Catholic outlook and probably voted for the lists of the Christian Economic Party, which supported the more conservative wing of the government. The *minority* was composed of Protestants and persons with a secularist outlook, vaguely 'populist' in politics. 'Populist' included both partisans of the budding democratic Peasant Party and men with a Hungarian racialist or even 'Turanian' outlook. Remarkably enough, some members of this group risked their lives and liberty during the last months of the German occupation in order to engage in underground resistance activities.

On 15 October 1944 the non-graduate clerical staff showed its true colours. Many of them (not including the strictly non-political women and again with one or two exceptions) had been for years secret members of the Arrow Cross Party. Interestingly enough, these men were generally disliked by the students and other members of the general public who came into contact with them; they were regarded as anti-social and narrow-minded. This seems to prove that a revolutionary movement can be rooted in social envy, without producing a sensitive social conscience in its supporters.

Finally, there were also 'uneducated helpers' employed in the institutions. Nobody seemed to care what their political opinions were. In fact they had none, apart from an instinctive and diffuse suspicion of the Germans as well as of the Russians.

Most of them were of peasant origin and were intellectually formed by the Hungarian village and accepted the peasant belief that 'politics is the game of gentlemanly tricksters'. I would be surprised if they would have changed their attitudes since 1945.

Similar observations undertaken among the conscripts of the army in 1944 confirmed the impression that the bulk of the masses of Hungary was untouched by the inhuman ideologies which were proclaimed so loudly in their name. They seem – thanks to their ideological immunity – to survive all ideological dictatorships, just as they have survived the rule of the 'historical' classes.

7 Rumania

Z. Barbu

'Le Roumain est un animal nationaliste', writes the playwright
Eugen Ionesco who once suffered at the hands of Rumanian
fascists. This is obviously an over-dramatization of his own
experience as well as a common form of fallacy based on over-
generalization. Such, or similar, statements may, however,
appear to be true in more than one sense. There is first of all the
language. Though it would be an exaggeration to maintain that
the Rumanian 'nationalistic' vocabulary is richer or more
colourful than that of most other European languages, it is
nevertheless true that Rumanians seem to have special inclinations towards using it. Antisemitic expressions, for instance, are
so deeply ingrained in the language that even Rumanian Jews
often refer to each other by the obviously pejorative term *Jzdan*.
One can, admittedly, take this as an adjustment symptom,
as an identification with the oppressor, as B. Bettelheim would
have it, but before doing so it is useful to bear in mind that
the question of the relationship between prejudiced language
and prejudiced behaviour is by no means a simple one. Many
Rumanians may be guilty of the former, but not of the
latter.

The second sense in which Ionesco's opinion may appear to be
true is more directly connected with the so-called Rumanian
character. Like most peoples who lived for a long period in a
colonial or semi-colonial state, the Rumanians suffer from a
strong feeling of inferiority. Mainly because of this they tend to
establish their self-identity as individuals or as an ethnic group
by strong negative references. In their behaviour, verbal or

otherwise, they make it crystal clear that they do not like to be confounded with their neighbours, Hungarians, Bulgarians, Poles. .... At this very moment their supreme endeavour is to demonstrate to the world that they are not Russians. This implicitly leads to a strong positive self-reference in their search for their identity. In the past, there were three main ways in which they inflated their self-consciousness as a nation, by stressing their latinity, their Christianity and their traditional rural way of life. This demonstrative self-assertion should not be taken to mean that Rumanians hate foreigners, any more than most other nations. It is only that they lack confidence in their dealings with foreigners, and, because of this, fall easily into the extremes either of deference and respect or of rejection. In their contacts with foreigners the Rumanians start from an attitude, or rather a feeling of suspicion. This is, however, often no more than a working hypothesis by which they test differences and similarities with the final purpose of ensuring that they are accepted or acceptable.

Since this sheds direct light on one important aspect of anti-semitism, it seems relevant to mention a frequently voiced opinion, shared by the writer, that the Rumanians did not hate the Jews because they were Jews, but mainly because they were so 'different', because, in Rumania, the Jews were less assimilated than they were in Germany, for instance, or in many other European countries. As will be shown later, Rumanian anti-semitism was to a great extent a behavioural symptom characteristic of a non-differentiated society, of a homogeneous and closed traditional community in which a highly differentiated category of people is normally perceived as an out-group. To understand this, it is enough to mention that in Rumania the Jews were not only racially and culturally different: throughout the modern period, they became more and more identified with the commercial and urban section of society, i.e., with a group and way of life for which there was little if any room in a traditional peasant community. Thus, a great deal of antisemitic feeling in Rumania was generated by a conflict between tradition and modernity. In Rumania, more than in most other European countries, the image of the Jew was closely associated with the image of the middle classes.

There is yet another point which explains, though it does not justify, Ionesco's dictum. This is the westernization of Rumania, which began in the upper strata towards the beginning of the last century and has been growing steadily since. As this is a kind of socio-cultural process which is better known in its Russian version, it is helpful to bear in mind that, in Rumania, it followed approximately the same course and had similar results. The modern intelligentsia of Rumania were a product of westernization and, similar to the Russian intelligentsia, disclosed in their development all the main symptoms of a marginal group. Until the last decades of the nineteenth century the Rumanian intelligentsia saw themselves as a progressive group whose mission was to transform a backward traditional community into a modern society on the model of France. This led, of course, to their gradual alienation from the native culture. Thus, already towards the end of the nineteenth century, one could see the first signs of marginality among Rumanian intellectuals who became aware that they belonged neither to the West because of their origin, nor to their native culture and society because of their education. The crisis was solved in a manner which has by now become a well-known phenomenon. Many Rumanian intellectuals began to reidentify with the people, with their traditional way of life and culture. This started off an intense process of revival, reappraisal and indeed exaggeration of native, hence specifically Rumanian traditions, values, and, generally speaking, Rumanian ways of life. The village and the peasant became symbols of honesty, sanity and primeval purity, the strongholds of national life. Christianity itself became a Rumanian virtue. From the beginning of the century, up to the second world war, the Rumanian cultural scene was dominated by 'populist' movements, literary, political and religious, so many hot-beds of nationalism and antisemitism.

But, needless to say, neither nationalism nor antisemitism should necessarily lead to fascism, a much more complex phenomenon, which can perhaps be defined as follows. It is first of all a type of social-political movement developing within a nationalistic, and often populist, climate of opinion. If a social movement is defined as a collective reaction to a 'problem', then the specific problem of fascism consists of a crisis of social solidarity and identity normally attributed to the decline of the traditional and ethnic characteristics of the community. Secondly, as a political movement fascism displays strong tendencies towards an authoritarian and para-military type of organization. Thirdly, it contains visible totalitarian elements in that the movement, or party, constitutes a concrete model, indeed, an archetype of society as a whole. Fourthly, as a model of society, fascism includes emotional revivalist and, on the whole, regressive forms of social organization. It is backward looking in that it uses traditional and often primeval symbols of social solidarity. The image of a primary group constitutes a central motivational force among the members of such a movement.

Now if the above definition is borne in mind, there was only one movement and one party in Rumania to which the term 'fascist' can be applied. This had various names corresponding to various stages in its development, but it was generally known as the 'Iron Guard'. It is, therefore, the Iron Guard that constitutes the basis of my present considerations of Rumanian fascism. Following the general theme of these essays I should like to make a twofold approach to the subject, a descriptive and an analytical one, thus preparing the ground for the central question with which this study is concerned – the national characteristics of Rumanian fascism. Before I do so, however, it is necessary to say a word about my sources and above all to complain about the difficulty encountered in this respect. Particularly scarce are the sources concerning the social composition of the Iron Guard in its various stages of development. For this reason it was necessary to lean, sometimes heavily, on data presented and often interpreted in previous studies of Rumanian fascism, and particularly those of E. Weber. Among Rumanian publications on the subject, L. Patrascanu's *Under Three Dictatorships* deserves particular mention. Though this study has a limited interpretative value, it has the merit of having been written by someone who witnessed most of the events to which it refers. From time to time in the course of this essay I have had to rely on my personal contact with and recollections of events. The re-reading of the political and autobiographical works of the leaders of the Iron Guard, Codreanu and Motsa, added considerably to my understanding of some of the most characteristic traits of Rumanian fascism. As far as primary sources are concerned, however, it must be said that most of the studies published so far, in Rumanian or other languages, are on the whole under-documented.

The origins of Rumanian fascism can be traced back to 1919, and generally speaking to the period of social turmoil following the first world war. The first thing to be mentioned, however, is that Rumania was not a defeated country. Nor was she disappointed and frustrated as was Italy. On the contrary, by a stroke of luck, Rumania came out of the war somehow dizzy with her success: as the result of the peace treaty of Versailles all the provinces in which the Rumanians constituted a majority – Transylvania, Bucovina and Bessarabia – were united in a new Rumanian national state with a population of over seventeen millions. Thus, Rumanian fascism was not the outcome of national defeat. This does not mean, however, that Rumanian fascism was in no way the child of collective confusion and anxiety. As recent studies of mental disorders and of suicide in particular have shown, sudden riches and sudden poverty produce similar results. If the analogy can be stretched so far, Rumania found herself in the position of the *nouveau riche*, with a territory five times bigger than that of the Old Kingdom, and with a population not only considerably larger, but also highly heterogeneous in traditions and ways of life. The problem, therefore, was one of organization and unity. What were the unifying factors, and what was the basis for consensus and solidarity in the new community? Questions such as these aroused considerable anxiety. This was reflected in the political situation of the country which was marked by vague democratic populist ideologies and even vaguer democratic reforms – with one exception, the extension of electoral rights to all males over the age of 21. The spectrum of political parties was rich, colourful and highly changeable. One structural feature, however, seemed to be constant: an almost empty 'centre', with the large traditional political parties to the Right, and a very small Social Democratic and even smaller Communist Party to the Left. Electorally, there was no sign of political radicalization.

That the birthplace of the Iron Guard was Moldavia has its own significance. Ever since the creation of the first independent Rumanian state (1859) with its capital in Bucharest, the Moldavians have given signs of wounded pride. One way in which they showed this was by a retreat into provincialism and by slightly demonstrative nationalism. Even more significant is the fact that, at this period, Moldavia had a relatively large Jewish population, larger than that of any other Rumanian province. And last but not least was its geographical position adjoining Bessarabia, recently incorporated in the Rumanian state, and thus highly aware of, and sensitive to the threat of communism. As will be seen later, communism as an idea and a threat from outside played a considerable part in the rise and development of Rumanian fascism, despite the fact that – unlike Germany or Italy – she never had a strong marxist party.

Historical circumstances apart, the Iron Guard owed its existence to one man who had been its indisputable leader for almost twenty years. This was Corneliu Zelia Codreanu. Though retrospective interpretations should always be taken with a grain of salt, there is hardly anything in Codreanu's biographical background which can throw serious doubts on the assumption that he had strong authoritarian traits in his personality. His father, a schoolteacher in a provincial town of Moldavia who became a well-known political figure, throughout his life gave unmistakable signs of strong disciplinarian impulses and heroic fantasies wrapped up in bombastic nationalistic language. The relationship between father and son is best illustrated by an incident which is often mentioned by the latter in his autobiographical writings. At the beginning of the first world war the father, despite his advanced age, volunteered for the army. This was a signal for the son, then a schoolboy, to leave home and wander for a few weeks from one military unit to another offering his services. He was refused and so returned home. Thus his first heroic 'flight' ended in disappointment. In this context, it is worth mentioning that before going to university he studied at the military school of Manastirea Dealul.

Though relatively little is known about Codreanu's relationship with his mother, one fact deserves special mention. She was of German origin, and this certainly had something to do with his demonstrative nationalism. As has often been suggested, his need for achievement coupled with a mystic faith in human will may also have come from her. One hastens to add, however, that Codreanu was not a 'voluntarist' in the sense in which Hitler was. If one wanted to size up his personality in a formula, one would say that he was a sentimental and mystic authoritarian. The paranoid streak in his personality reached theomanic proportions and the basic motif of his life was *Imitatio Christi*. Thus it was not the need for action that dominated his conception of the world and of man, but rather the need for faith and sacrifice. His image of Christ, which he avowedly took as the model of his life, was the Christ of *Theologia Crucis* rather than that of *Theologia Gloriae*. This reveals a characteristic aspect of the cultural background of Rumanian fascism.

Considerably more significant is the cultural environment of the formative years of Codreanu and the Iron Guard. In 1919, Codreanu started his student life in Jassy, the capital of Moldavia. From the start his cultural and political development was deeply influenced by Professor A. I. Cuza, a sort of Rumanian Julius Strasser, obsessed by the Jewish threat to the purity of Christian girls. Cuza was also a skilled demagogue and the inspirer and leader of a small political organization which consisted at the time mainly of students. The programme of the organization was nationalistic-racist and was centred around three main points: (1) The unity of all Rumanians in an ethnic national state from which foreigners were to be eliminated or where they would be deprived of positions of social and political responsibility; (2) the emancipation of the peasants, not so much through economic reforms, badly needed at the time, as through political education; (3) by far the best known point of the programme: the solution of the 'Jewish Problem'. In this context Cuza advocated the complete segregation of the Jews and antisemitic violence as a means to this end.

Cuza was Codreanu's mentor of the Right, but nothing that Codreanu learned from him was strikingly new. Cuza served mainly as a catalyst for his nationalism and antisemitism. There was, however, in Jassy at that time, another political mentor, a much more interesting figure towards whom Codreanu throughout his life conserved a warm feeling of respect and admiration. This was a certain Constantin Pancu, a manual worker with intellectual and political aspirations, who managed to organize around himself a small group consisting of one lawyer, one priest, one student and about thirty skilled manual workers. To the extent that Pancu's group possessed any political programme, it can be described as a vague version of national socialism, with a strong emphasis on the first term. At any rate, what held the group together was an obsession, a sort of action-anxiety – the defeat and final destruction of the communist organizations which were apparently gaining ground in many local industrial enterprises. 'Apparently' is a key word here for, according to some views, communism – or rather the threat of communism – did not play any considerable part in the rise of Rumanian fascism. This may be so, but it is worth recording that Codreanu speaks about thousand-strong communist crowds demonstrating on the streets of Jassy. Though of short duration, Codreanu's membership of Pascu's group provided him with an excellent opportunity to learn and rehearse a role for which he soon became famous. It gave him his first opportunity to organize people and lead them into action, which in this case consisted of street demonstrations and fights. But above all he learned one thing which became a basic tactical principle of the Iron Guard, namely, that violence, organized and sustained violence, pays rich political dividends. Pascu's group specialized in strike-breaking activities and Codreanu excelled in this.

With this brief background, we can turn now to the rise and development of the Iron Guard. In a more detailed treatment of the history of this political movement it would be necessary to distinguish between its private and its public face, between the internal organization of the movement and the political programmes and electoral successes of the party. I should like, however, at least for the time being, to keep these two aspects together, not only because they are in reality closely interconnected but also because this leads me more directly to the main question – the particular characteristics of the Iron Guard. The main points in its history are as follows:

Between 1920 and 1923 the Iron Guard consisted of student groups organized outside the official unions, first in Jassy and then in the other three universities of the country, Czernovitz, Bucharest and Cluj. There was only a small minority in each university but all three were well-organized and ready to use threats and other terrorist methods, so that they became an awkward and often dominant group at many student meetings. Their programme can be summed up in two points, violent antisemitism demanding the application of a *numerus clausus* for the admission of Jews, and a vague Christian reformism. Much more important than their programme, however, was their way of life as individuals and as a group – their dedication, discipline and readiness for action.

The period between 1923 and 1927 can in many ways be considered as the period of political consolidation. In 1923, Codreanu and Cuza together formed a political party, the League of National Christian Defence, which, in 1926, won six seats in the Rumanian Parliament. Two events of this period are particularly relevant for the understanding of Rumanian fascism. The first full proof of its violent nature and terrorist methods was given in 1923, when a student, a follower and friend of Codreanu, murdered a member of the organization on the assumption that he had contacts with the police. This brought to light the essential organizational and ethical features of the movement. For it appeared that the victim was previously tried and sentenced by the 'secret tribunal' of the organization, which

154

also designated the executioner.* Expressions such as 'traitors' and 'heroes' as well as the 'blood baptism of the Guard' were used in this context. Public opinion was certainly horrified, but also slightly mystified and fascinated by such language and behaviour. So were the authorities who dealt with the events in what may be described as a paternalistic manner. The students involved in the murder, including Codreanu, were arrested, tried and finally sentenced. However, all this was done in a climate of empathetic excitement so that nothing prevented the offenders from posing as victims and even as heroes. This should be stressed because it played an important part in the formative years of the Iron Guard, and nothing can account for it but the prestige which intellectuals and students in particular enjoyed in the Rumanian society of the time.

The second event relates to Codreanu's life. During a short term of imprisonment, in 1923, he had his first vision: the Archangel Michael came to him and urged him to dedicate his life to God as revealed by the Rumanian Christian tradition.† A few years later (1927) he founded the 'Brotherhood of the Cross', an élitist body, which he placed at the centre of his party. To indicate the nature of this organization it is necessary to mention that, apart from the Archangel's revelation, Codreanu was inspired by an old Rumanian tradition. Such forms of privileged and mystic associations, or rather communions, between two or more people existed and maybe still exist among Rumanian peasants. The association is highly ritualized and often those entering upon it have to taste each other's blood in order to become brothers, 'unto life and death'. The Brotherhood of the Cross conformed in many ways to this pattern of human relations in which the primary ties of blood are symbolically resurrected. The Brotherhood of the Cross was the

---

* This was Ion Motsa, the son of an orthodox priest from Transylvania, famous for his nationalistic activities. Motsa had just returned from France where he was a member of Action Française, and soon became a great figure in the movement, normally referred to as 'the saint'. He died in 1936 in the Spanish war. He was the first translator in Rumania of the *Protocols of the Elders of Zion* in 1923.

† In 1926 Codreanu murdered the prefect of Galatsi, Manciu.

mystic body of the Iron Guard, open only to the few and the elect. Those worthy of membership had to undergo a primitive ceremony, a *rite de passage*. They were summoned to a secret place, and after an incantational ritual which took place at a late hour of the night they made a formal vow pledging their life to the cause and the 'Captain'.

In 1926, as a result of a quarrel between Codreanu and Cuza, the League of National Christian Defence was dissolved, and in 1927 there came into being the first independent political organization of Codreanu's movement, the Legion of the Archangel Michael. This was a prototype of fascist organization. To start with, it had no political programme. 'The country is dying for lack of men and not for lack of programmes' were the words used by Codreanu at the foundation meeting of the Legion. If I may advance an idea, the *legionari* constituted a psychological rather than a political group: the basic trait of their organization was a state of mind. The main points in their programme were, 'Faith in God', 'Faith in the Mission' and 'Love for each other'. All these were 'cultist' in character, and required specific tests and trials and particularly specific states of mind. This is even more clearly revealed by the fourth point in their programme; 'Love of songs'. We shall return to this shortly, but for the moment it is enough to mention that music, vocal music above all, was a basic element of the *legionaris'* way of life. All their meetings started and ended in incantational rituals of song and often dance.

The Legion had a conspiratorial type of organization. The basic unit was the 'nest', a small group consisting of seven, rising to a maximum of twelve members, who called each other *camarazi*, a term which was used not by the Rumanian communists (who called themselves *tovaresi*), but by the Rumanian army. Above the level of the 'nests', the Legion consisted of a semi-military and semi-mystical organization with a rigid hierarchy. At the top was the 'Captain' and a small number of 'great commanders of the Legion'.

The 'nest' as the structural unit of the party was a model of totalitarian groups. Even the name was chosen to appeal to the needs of dependence and security of the young. In it, the *legionari* received their basic training, which consisted of some knowledge of the history and martyrology of the Guard, instructions about rules of conduct expected of them, and above all unconditional obedience to the Leader. The 'nest' had a monolithic internal organization, with all decisions made unanimously. Though in principle and overtly Codreanu was not against democracy in the same sense as Hitler, on the question of leadership he had always held extreme authoritarian views. 'I was a leader from the beginning', he often said, meaning that a leader should have obvious and compelling qualities which make election and, on the whole, formal delegation of authority unnecessary. Consequently the leaders of the 'nests' emerged eruptively, as Max Weber would put it; they were the obvious choice. Since Weber has been mentioned, it would be interesting to raise the question of the specific nature of their charisma. It was certainly not physical power, nor knowledge or organizational skill, but rather loyalty to the cause and a highly sublimated aggression, the aggression of Christ chasing the traders out of the Temple. They were eminently religious people with a Manichean vision of the world in which – following the example of their patron, Saint Michael – they were the angels of light. Since the mission of the *legionari* was nothing less than the moral regeneration of the nation, the distinctive mark of their leaders was a high sense of mission and martyrdom.

This throws light on one of the most characteristic organizational and psychological features of the Iron Guard. I know of no other fascist movement which inculcated in its members a deeper sense of personal dedication and sacrifice. To start with, one of the main élite groups within the Iron Guard was the so-called 'death team', consisting of young fanatics ready to kill and be killed. Their status and mission were highly institutionalized, or rather ritualized. It was said that they used to wear around their necks a tiny bag of Rumanian soil and that there was nothing in the world which they would not do at the sight of it. There were also other less magic expressions of their sense of sacrifice. Most outstanding in this respect were their songs with the mystique of death as the basic motif. Here are a few examples:

> Legionari do not fear
> That you will die young
>
> For you die to be reborn
> And are born to die
>
> For we are the death team
> That must win or die
>
> Death, only the legionari death
> Is a gladsome wedding for us.

Two powerful motifs of the mystique of death inflamed the mind of the legionari. One, explicitly stated in the last quotation, is traditional-native, consituting the central theme in one of the best known Rumanian ballads, Mioritsa, where the hero threatened with imminent death overcomes his fear by comparing death to a wedding, the bridegroom being himself and nature his bride. It was often said that this was the 'typical' Rumanian attitude to death. Even more powerful is the other motif, the Christian mythology of resurrection and victory through death.

While the main slogan of the legionari was 'victory or death', this religious formula seems to reveal more adequately the deep motivation of their behaviour. The more and the heavier they had to pay for their murderous violence, the more they practised it. These are a few figures illustrating this tight chain of action which can be formulated either as 'kill and be killed', or 'kill to be killed'. Between 1924 and 1937 they commited eleven murders – mainly of important political personalities. During this period, however, over 500 legionari were killed, mainly by the police. Between April and December 1939, the year of martyrdom, some 1200 legionari were arrested, imprisoned and exterminated. To this, one should add another point, the significance of which can hardly be overestimated. In the summer of 1936, in one of Bucharest's hospitals, there took place an event which cannot be described otherwise than as ritual killing. It concerns Stelescu, a prominent *legionari* leader who had just left the Iron Guard and joined another nationalist organization. While he was lying in bed, a group of four *legionari* broke in and fired 120 shots at him. After that, they chopped his body in small pieces, danced around it and kissed each other.

How can one understand such a destructive and at the same time ritualized aggression? Professor E.Weber puts forward two interpretative hypotheses. The first refers to the autocratic and terrorist methods used by the Rumanian government and by King Carol in particular against the Iron Guard and against any radical non-conformist political organization. He compares the Rumanian régime of the period to that of pre-revolutionary Russia. Since terror normally breeds greater terror, the legionary violence was a reaction, perhaps an over-reaction, to the violence of authority. While not wholly denying the usefulness of such a hypothesis, in this particular case it raises two points of difficulty As mentioned earlier, Rumanian authorities did not always use harsh methods in their dealings with the Iron Guard. This is particularly true with regard to the early stage of the movement. The second point is more specific and refers to the difficulty of defining and testing 'provoked' behaviour. As far as my personal experience and observation goes, I find no conclusive evidence that the legionaries were provoked to violence. On the contrary, at any student meeting I attended in which *legionari* were present – and there were many such meetings – I could not help noticing that they formed a solid and visible group highly skilled in terrorist method. They provoked long before they were provoked. It is significant to note that they normally described their opponents, passive or active, as 'cowards'.

The second hypothesis put forward by Weber refers to the nature and meaning of legionary violence. The *legionari* were, admittedly, violent but – he is inclined to think – they were not bad people. A certain amount of evidence for this can be derived from Codreanu's writings and particularly from his paternal advice to his followers, where he urges them to use the 'right means' in their struggle against their opponents. Moreover, he praises and stimulates in them virtues such as honesty, integrity, purity, work and Christian faith. This is obviously so, but all this has to be seen in the right context. Leaving aside the more general question regarding the discrepancy between 'ideal' and 'real' behaviour, the first point to be noticed is that expressions such as 'purity of conscience', 'integrity', and 'righteousness' are the staple food of sectarians and authoritarians: this is the normal manner in which they rationalize their violence. As for the meaning and content of the concept of 'right means', it would be enough to note here that in all Codreanu's writings, the enemy – and this included everybody outside the Iron Guard – is described as 'corrupted' and 'doomed'. What the 'right means' can mean, in this context, is easy to guess. In fact Codreanu had a sectarian concept of morality, and the Legion can in many ways be described as a messianic salvationist movement. Its morality was that of a closed group: 'good', 'right', 'honest' were terms which it applied to whatever and whomsoever supported its cause.

It is now time to return to the political activities and success of the Iron Guard. As already mentioned, the League of National Christian Defence won six parliamentary seats in the election of 1926. This represented 120,000 votes. In 1931, the Legion of the Archangel Michael won less than two per cent of the electorate and according to the Rumanian consititution this meant no representation in parliament. One year later, however, it won five seats. This was the first serious warning of its political potential and the government reacted swiftly by dissolving the Legion as a political party. This allowed the legionaries to pose once more as victims. The proof is that, in 1937, when they were recognized again as a political party under the name 'All for the Fatherland' they gained sixty seats, representing more than sixteen per cent of the electorate. This placed the Iron Guard in the second place – after the National Peasant Party – among the political parties of the country. In 1938, the organization was dissolved once more and its leadership decimated by the dictatorial régime of King Carol. Between April and December 1939, more than 1200 legionaries, including Codreanu, were arrested and lost their lives in circumstances which have remained to a great extent obscure. The official version was that they were shot while trying to escape. Although it never recovered from this blow, the Iron Guard appeared once more in the political arena. This was in 1940–1 when Rumania had for the first time a *legionari* government. It was in fact a coalition government of the military group of General Antonescu and the surviving elements of the Iron Guard under the leadership of Horea Sima. The coalition did not work, and after an abortive *putsch* and revolution, in early 1941, the legionaries were eliminated from the government and their leadership was again decimated.

The political career of the Iron Guard can be summed up in two points. First, between 1931 and 1940 it increasingly became one of the most important political forces in Rumania. Second, with the exception of Italian fascism and German Nazism, it was one of the few wholly fascist movements to come to power and form a government. How can one explain this success?

In answering such a question, it is useful to recall one of the best known interpretative models of sociological studies of fascism. According to this model, fascism is a middle-class phenomenon expressing the interests of either the upper middle class, i.e. their expansionist-imperialistic aspirations as well as their apprehensions about the economic implications of liberal democracy, or the specific interests of the lower middle classes in their struggle against 'big capital'. Sometimes these two hypotheses are combined, and the interpretative model is amplified with other variables, such as the level of industrialization of the community as a whole, and the degree of politicization of the masses and of the working classes in particular. The difficulty about applying such interpretative models to Rumania of the inter-war period is that the middle classes were numerically small, as well as ideologically, politically and socio-culturally ill-defined. Something like eighty per cent of the population were peasants while the industrial workers constituted a tiny and poorly organized minority. The difficulty is increased when one takes into account the ideology of the Iron Guard with its systematic attack on urban bourgeois values and ways of life.

161

All this makes it necessary to abandon for Rumania, at least for the moment, the theoretical hypothesis regarding the middle-class character of fascism and to look more closely at the social composition of the Iron Guard at the levels of leadership, party membership and electoral support. Naturally it must be borne in mind that one is dealing here with an authoritarian organization; hence the level which counts most is that of leadership.

From the very beginning, the leadership was dominated by two categories of people, intellectuals and youth. For lack of more adequate documentation, the best one can do to illustrate this point is to refer to the data offered by Weber from the analysis of two groups in terms of their occupation and age. The first consists of 251 legionaries interned in Buchenwald between 1942 and 1944, the second of 32 legionaries executed at Vaslui in September 1939. Though for obvious reasons these cannot be considered as representative samples, the following figures seem to be indicative of both the composition of the leadership and the membership of the organization as a whole. Taking the two groups together, intellectuals represented between forty and fifty per cent, including students who alone represented almost thirty per cent, professions and public servants. The average age in the first group was 27·4. Particularly young was the top leadership. For instance, in 1931 Codreanu was thirty-two, Motsa twenty-nine, Marin twenty-seven and Stelescu twenty-four.

The question of the social origins of the Legion's leadership and its membership in general presents considerable difficulties. As Weber rightly points out, the middle-class element (state employees, professionals, and even tradesmen and shopkeepers) seems at first sight to dominate. But one particularly relevant point needs to be noted: their connection with the traditional rural population and way of life is direct, almost uninterrupted. Codreanu was the son of a schoolteacher and the grandson of a peasant, Motsa the son of a priest and grandson of a peasant. This applies to the leadership at all levels and on the whole to the so-called middle-class element of the Legion.

All this throws considerable doubt on the class membership, let alone on the class identity of the legionaries. It is very likely that we are dealing here with a psychological rather than a social group. Most of its members were climbing up the ladder of social hierarchy in the direction of the middle class. But the point is that they had not yet arrived, they had not yet broken away from their rural traditional background. On the whole they were a marginal group and it was their condition of marginality rather than their class interests and consciousness which determined their political behaviour. What follows is an attempt to demonstrate this point.

The prominent part played by the intelligentsia in the history of the Legion can in itself be taken as a symptom of marginality, of classlessness, as Mannheim would put it. To this general condition can be added a series of more specific ones. First of all, the kind of intelligentsia we are dealing with belonged to an emerging, newly born society without a clear sense of solidarity and identity, and certainly without a stable system of stratification. Furthermore, they belonged to a society in which the upper as well as the urban strata were traditionally associated if not identified with outsiders, Turks, Hungarians, Germans, Greeks and Jews. This says a great deal about the social position, objective or subjective, of Rumanian intelligentsia and of legionary intelligentsia in particular. In reality they could not and did not belong anywhere, and escaped reality by inventing their society and reference group. For example, Codreanu identified himself with the 'people', an idealized community which he never defined except in vague and abstract terms such as 'unity', 'purity', 'Christianity'. It was an unhistorical entity including all Rumanians who had existed in the past and would exist in the future. Even more characteristically, Motsa, after rejecting the corrupt social reality of his time, identified himself with the 'old world', the legendary past of his nation. This is an important point which should occupy a central place in any detailed study of Rumanian fascism. The most one can do here is to point out that the reference group of the legionaries, of the intellectuals in particular, was an imaginary one. It was an ideal society in which the legend of an old traditional Rumanian community loomed large. The predominant utopistic element in this image of society

163

was of a moral religious character, with brotherly unity and love as the basis of communal life.

The only element which linked this image of society to reality was the rural community of the Rumanian village. As has often been said, the legionaries were 'idealists' in that they struggled to maintain and indeed to introduce into Rumanian society of the interwar period the morality and social solidarity of a traditional community and primary group. They were the arch-enemies of secularization, urbanization and industrialization. Moreover, they tried to maintain – in an idealized form, of course – the elements of a pre-market and pre-individualized society. Nobody who lived in Rumania during this period can forget the eerie and anachronistic character of a legionary demonstration. It was something between a political protest, a religious procession and a historical *cortège*. The middle and indeed the core of the demonstration consisted of a well-organized body of young people in uniform – the 'green shirts'. It was normally headed by a group of priests carrying icons and religious flags. Finally, all this was followed and surrounded by men and women in national traditional dress. It is significant that the Captain normally appeared in traditional Moldavian dress, though the green shirt was the official uniform of the Legion.

To all this one should add that the leadership and to a great extent the membership of the Legion was young, a fact which certainly contributed to its idealism and marginality. Particularly significant in this context is the fact that the movement began in student circles. Apart from the *Sturm und Drang* characteristic of their age, the Rumanian students of the period suffered from the anxiety of prospective unemployment.

One can now turn briefly to the mass base of the Legion. As mentioned earlier, in 1937 the electoral support of the Legion represented sixteen per cent of the total voting population. How can one explain this considerable success? Who were its supporters?

Previous attempts to answer such questions have pointed out three factors. First, the legionaries used new electoral methods.

They contacted regions, remote mountain villages, normally neglected by other parties; they also showed considerable skill in making personal contacts with the villagers. Secondly, most of the regions from which they derived their electoral support were poor. Thirdly, some support came from regions with a relatively large Jewish population, though on the whole these regions gave greater support to Cuza's National Christian League. To sum up, the Legion recruited its mass support from the rural population which was either neglected, politically and administratively, or economically poor, or both, as well as from a rural and urban population open in various degrees to antisemitic propaganda.

Though essentially correct, such an interpretation may be misleading in one important respect – the economic status of the Legion's supporters. Poverty does not seem to describe their economic condition adequately. The peasants who joined the Legion and those who voted for it were not the poorest of the poor, not by Rumanian rural standards at any rate. For lack of adequate information I am compelled once more to use impressionistic methods. In a village in the county of Sibiu which I happen to know well, the first converted and the martyr of the organization was a certain Dimitri. When he joined the Legion, Dimitri was in his early twenties and poverty was not the crucial element, for the land holdings of his family were slightly above the average in the village. But Dimitri's father was an isolated figure, mainly because of his quarrelsome character, but also because he was by far the smallest man in the village. One of Dimitri's sisters suffering from a slight physical infirmity had an illegitimate child, an extremely rare event in the village. As a result two other sisters left home and settled down as housemaids in the nearest town. Dimitri was a very religious young man; he used to pray loudly and conspicuously in the village church. This may be an exaggerated portrait of a rural *legionari* but certainly not a wrong one. In most villages, those who joined and supported the Legion were the slightly odd characters, such as the blacksmith and the cobbler, or amongst the peasants those who for one reason or another were living on the fringe of

165

the community. All this reinforces the view put forward in the previous pages: the characteristic traits of Rumanian fascism can only partly be derived from the social class and economic conditions of its supporters. At least as, if not more, relevant is a set of psychological factors, a state of mind, characteristic of individuals and groups suffering in various degrees and in various ways from lack of social integration and purpose.

8 Poland

S. Andreski

The character of the groupings embattled upon the Polish political arena on the eve of the second world war offers interesting material for a comparative analysis of fascism because many of the features which went together in the classic Italian and German cases did appear but in incomplete clusters on different sides of the line dividing the contestants for power.

The régime set up by Pilsudski after his successful coup in May 1926 was a military dictatorship of a relatively limited kind: indeed, much more tolerant than the Spanish régime in 1967 (not to speak of the Greek) as neither parliament nor the opposition parties nor their newspapers were suppressed. True, laws were rammed through by various legalistic subterfuges which violated the spirit if not the letter of the constitution, and by intimidation of the deputies; but the opposition remained vociferous in parliament as well as outside. Opposition newspapers often used to make scurrilous attacks on Pilsudski and his assistants, and although issues would be impounded and legally responsible editors often jailed, the papers continued to appear.

Apart from its lack of totalitarian inclinations, Pilsudski's rule differed from fascism in having no ideology apart from the cult of personality and a vague insistence on the need for order and national strength. Pilsudski had never been a demagogue and was leading no party when he seized power with the help of the officers who had been his subordinates during the wars. The only mass organizations which helped him were certain socialist trade unions who regarded him as a leftist and remembered his

167

past as an activist in the revolutionary fraction of the Polish Socialist Party during the 1905 revolution. Actually the refusal of the railwaymen's union to transport to Warsaw the troops sent against him from Poznan tilted the balance in his favour.

Like Castello Branco in Brazil or Lamizana in Haute Volta – to mention two out of many available examples – Pilsudski could plead with some justification that he had to save the country from the brink of chaos. True, it is by no means proven that things would not have got better without his intervention, and it is certain that his régime had equally grave faults though of a slightly different kind, but the fact does remain that, owing to unbridled demagoguery and factionalism, the country was governed badly, and that parliament was often a scene of un-seemly rows or even brawls. It is also true that deputies (often very ignorant and greedy) interfered with the workings of the administration in a way which aggravated inefficiency and favouritism.

Though undoubted master, Pilsudski refrained from taking up the post of either president or prime minister and until his death remained the Minister of War. The army and foreign policy were his sole real interests and on some issues pertaining to these matters he showed remarkable far-sightedness. For example, he never had doubts about the Nazi danger, and when Hitler came to power he proposed to the French a joint preven-tive war which the latter refused to contemplate. He had no ideas on other aspects of public life; and when asked after the *coup* about his programme, he answered: 'We must bring a bit of order and honesty.' However, despite his personal honesty and indifference to money, his wayward wilfulness and lack of respect for law stimulated rather than impeded the spread of favouritism and corruption. He had absolutely no idea what to do about it beyond complaining that 'a lot of lice have climbed on my back'. In any case soon after his seizure of power his health began to fail, and during the last few years before his death in 1935 he was a feared and irascible invalid who could still appoint the officers of the state but was no longer able to check what they were doing.

So long as the Marshal lived, the régime exhibited no features pertaining specifically to fascism as distinct from other forms of authoritarianism. The ruling circle consisted of Pilsudski's old officers (now mostly ranking as colonels) and chosen top officials. They had no particular views on economic policy beyond a generally conservative orientation. Though only some of them were of aristocratic descent, they all soon acquired fairly close convivial contacts with the landed nobility and to a lesser extent with the wealthy bourgeoisie – which, it must be added, was very small and almost entirely Jewish, except in the western regions where it was mostly German. Although the policy of agrarian reform adopted by the defunct parliamentary governments was not altogether discontinued, the division of big estates proceeded at a slow pace; and the general economic policy was conservative in the sense that no radical reforms were undertaken or even envisaged, and the rulers showed no special concern for the plight of the poor. It would be a mistake, however, to regard the régime as the tool of the bourgeoisie or even of the landowners. The former was too weak and alienated in virtue of its Jewishness, and the latter too ineffectual to govern the country through interposed tools. The predominant vested interest was that of the officer corps and the officialdom with their families. The military component had a clear ascendancy; and one of the most conspicuous results of the *cuartelazo* was the taking over of many of the most important civilian posts by seconded officers – analogously to what has recently happened in Brazil and Greece.

To obtain influence in parliament, and eventually control over it, Pilsudski ordered a pro-government party to be set up, baptized as the Non-Party Bloc of Collaboration with the Government – a name which well indicated its passive nature. Its membership comprised mainly people dependent upon the government for their livelihood – public employees of all grades and aspirants to such posts, with a sprinkling of businessmen hoping for a state contract or licence or a less severe treatment from the tax office. The embryonic ideology consisted of depreciation of the disorderliness of parliamentary rule, insistence on

169

the need for a strong government and army, and persistent reminders that the old Polish kingdom perished through excess of freedom leading to anarchy.

In practice, the most conspicuous activity of the Non-Party Bloc (apart from the allocation of jobs) was public worship of the Marshal. This cult of personality was tied up with a genuine popular reverence for things military, fed by an intense nationalism which saw in the army the sole defence against rapacious neighbours. Although many people resented the insolent bearing of the officers and their interference in politics, they hesitated to criticize this pillar of national existence; and for this reason the Polish pre-war régime enjoyed a larger measure of popular support than do the Latin American militocracies which are regarded by most citizens as tools of foreign economic domination.

To counteract a widespread preconception, I must stress that neither Pilsudski nor his heirs showed antisemitic inclinations. On the contrary the imputations of philosemitism served as the most effective weapons in the campaign waged against him by the National Party. The government had always tried to suppress antisemitic outbreaks – very vigorously when Pilsudski was still alive – and only during the last two years before the war did their resolve on this matter begin to weaken.

Riding on the crest of a boom, Pilsudski's government was not without popularity during the first three years of its existence, and the enlargement of its parliamentary support in the 1928 elections was not entirely due to administrative pressure. A massive recourse to intimidation and fraud became necessary to retain these seats in the following elections fought in the midst of the great depression which hit Poland very hard indeed.

Shortly before he died Pilsudski promulgated in 1934 a new constitution (rather similar to de Gaulle's) which formally transferred many rights and powers from parliament to the president. In itself the constitution was not unsuited to the condition of Poland, and was not completely authoritarian, as the rulers remained under obligation to seek the approval of the electorate. However, it never became much more than a dead letter because (apart from frequent illegal abuses of power) it was supplemented soon after Pilsudski's death by an electoral ordinance which established a system of screening and selecting the candidates to ensure that the government would always win. The new electoral law in fact abolished elections, and created a legal foundation for an authoritarian régime; which, though still less oppressive than the dictatorship of Pérez Jiménez in Venezuela or Perón in Argentina was certainly much more dictatorial than de Gaulle's.

Becoming increasingly irascible and intolerant, Pilsudski ended his days surrounded by a crowd of unintelligent yes-men. At a loss when he died, and searching for something to replace his by then rather tarnished but still persistent charisma, they began to imitate the models which at the time seemed to represent the victorious trend of social evolution: namely, fascist Italy and Nazi Germany.

Pilsudski had certainly been guilty of ordering illegal arrests and ill-treatment of his opponents – probably including a couple of secret murders. Nonetheless, he felt uneasy about doing this, and used force with a great deal of hesitation and with restraint compared to what lay within his power. Encouraged, however, by the example of more 'progressive' states, his successors shed his scruples and set up a concentration camp. It must be added, however, that though evil enough, this camp was no forerunner of Auschwitz: the aim was not extermination but intimidation of political opponents and, at the same opportunity, of economic criminals – mostly Jews whose crime consisted of taking money abroad without permission (which became necessary in the thirties), but whose guilt was only 'known' to the police but could not be proven; for if the latter was the case they would have been sentenced by a court and sent to a normal prison. The inmates were imprisoned without trial on the basis of a decision of a police chief or of a *starosta* – an official similar to the French *préfet* or *sous-préfet*. The stay in the prison camp was usually short – normally not more than six months and often only three weeks – but the treatment was exceedingly cruel and, apart from brutal beatings, involved various forms of chicanery designed to undermine the victim's self-respect, such as limiting the time allowed in the lavatory so as to force him to soil his underwear. The staff consisted of policemen who had a record of admonishments or punishments for assaulting prisoners, and was commanded by a sadistic colonel Kostek-Biernacki.

The imprisoned political opponents represented a wide assortment: Ukrainian nationalists, Polish fascists, peasant leaders, communists, socialists, trade unionists, even conservative journalists guilty of disrespectful remarks about the character of one of the potentates.

The other most important innovation of Prime Minister Slawoj-Skladkowski (a colonel with a degree in medicine but the mentality of a sergeant-major) was the creation of a motorized riot police, whose helmets had the same shape as those of the *Reichswehr*, and who soon had an opportunity of proving their mettle by terrorizing the peasants in southern regions who refused to pay the oppressive taxes.

On the walls of all public buildings the dead marshal began to be flanked by President Moscicki (hitherto a figurehead) and the new Marshal Rydz-Smigly – a very mediocre man who had been Pilsudski's obedient underling. With time the latter moved gradually to the fore as the prime object of a cult of personality which, though meeting less resistance, always remained rather artificial in comparison with the genuine devotion which his many followers had felt for Pilsudski.

Ideologically the pro-government party (now renamed the Camp of National Unity) remained confused, and so disoriented that for a short while some of its organizers even toyed with marxist phraseology. The only sure point (on which a large part of the nation followed it) was a devotion to the army, that is, to militarism. Efforts were made to build up the pro-government youth organizations, but the results were merely quantitative, and amounted to gathering a large number of careerists or indigent students seeking a sojourn in a summer camp with free food and transport. Indoctrination in reverence for the governmental trinity (the dead Marshal, the new one and the President) was intensified and teachers (especially headmasters) culpable of tepidity were dismissed and replaced by more ardent adorers. Nonetheless, these efforts failed on the whole to conjure up fanaticism and mass hysteria, and as far as intensity of feelings was concerned the only analogies to the *Hitler Jugend* or the Rumanian Iron Guard could be found among the opposition youth movements.

Perón's party had also been organized from above, when he was already in the saddle, but in contrast to the 'Camp of National Unity' it had succeeded in stirring up widespread and genuine enthusiasm for 'justicialismo'. Moreover, whereas the Polish government's party consisted almost entirely of white collar state employees to the almost complete exclusion of manual workers, Perón's egalitarian demagogy (made credible by a few measures of real levelling) secured him a mass following among the labourers.

The predilection for regimentation led the rulers to introduce numbers and uniforms for secondary school boys, although the increasingly time-consuming and harsh part-time military training in all educational institutions for boys over sixteen was at least partly dictated by a genuine desire to strengthen national defence. Despite the growing oppressiveness of the régime, the opposition parties continued to operate legally, with the exception of the Communist Party, membership of which was punishable by imprisonment for five years. The trade unions conserved their full independence although they were harassed and their members ran the risk of being beaten by the police during strikes. Outspoken enemies of the régime continued to teach at the universities (which unlike schools had a large autonomy) and vociferously hostile newspapers continued to appear, though under harassment. Even more: in some universities and colleges the strong-arm men of the semi-fascist and fascist opposition youth movements were able to intimidate their pro-government colleagues and even professors, and fought battles with the police which on some occasions lasted several days. On the other hand a citizen could be imprisoned for two years for saying something to an official which could be interpreted as an insult; although the treatment of the public in government offices was very rude.

It was, however, easy to get in and out of the country, or to obtain foreign publications.

The Polish régime was never fully or even half fascist in any acceptable sense of the term: it had not grown out of a movement, it had no doctrine advocating a new social or even political system, its mass organization was created bureaucratically from above, and was never used for street fighting or suppressing strikes or keeping opponents at bay – a job left to the police. It had no equivalent of Hitler's storm-troopers or Mussolini's Blackshirts. None of the leaders was a charismatic demagogue. In career and personality they resembled Argentina's Ongania or Brazil's Castello Branco rather than Hitler, Mussolini or Doriot.

Rather than to Nazi Germany or fascist Italy, pre-war Poland offered more analogies to Franco's Spain; although here too there were a number of important differences – the most obvious being that the Polish dictatorship was much more tolerant of independent organizations and more liberal with regard to the dissemination of ideas and the censorship of the press. Secondly, in Spain the army is regarded as the engine of internal repression, whereas in Poland it enjoyed the genuine affection of the mass of the nation, though not, of course, of ethnic minorities. No contrast could be more striking than between the sullen reactions of the scanty spectators at a military parade in Madrid, and the ovations from large crowds which used to accompany such occasions in Poland. Though opposed to the excessive power and privileges of the officers, even the socialists were not anti-militaristic, as under the circumstances only somebody who favoured a renewed subjugation of Poland by one of its neighbours could have been hostile to the army as such.

The third important difference was that the Polish dictatorship enjoyed no special favours of the Church, which on the whole preferred the opposition National Party and was a bit worried about Pilsudski's socialist past and Jewish friends; whereas the modicum of allegiance which the Spanish military rebels and their landowning allies did manage to find among the masses was due entirely to the Church's blessing of their claim to defend the faith against the godless republicans. To this day pietistic docility is the only part of the ideological support of the Spanish régime which has any motivating force among the common people. In Poland, had the fight been between the socialists and the others, the clerical issue might have become a bone of contention. As it was both the government and its two strongest opponents – the National Party and the People's Party (known abroad under the more descriptive name of Peasants' Party) were not only willing but eager to leave the Church in control of souls, vied with one another in piety, and all welcomed priests into their ranks. Consequently the Church did not have to choose between the main contestants for power and could concentrate its ire on the marxists and the liberal free-thinkers.

The fourth difference between pre-war Poland and Franco's Spain was that the ideological component which could be called fascist (as distinct from militarist or simply authoritarian) was even weaker in the Polish régime, which never had a wing attaining to the programmatic articulation of the *Falange* or the *Opus Dei*. As we shall see in a moment, there existed in Poland at that time a party calling itself *Falanga*, but it was in violent opposition. Furthermore, the Polish rulers have never made any attempts to set up a corporativist economic system, and such measures of economic interventionism as exchange and import controls instituted in the thirties were dictated by a pragmatic concern about the desperate position of the balance of payments.

In comparison with Horthy's Hungary the aristocracy had much less power in Poland, where there was no counterpart to Count Károlyi. Contrary to the opinion generally held abroad, very few of the colonels who ruled Poland were of aristocratic origin. Pilsudski himself was a minor squire, but the ancestry of his successor was so unknown that his enemies whispered that he was the son of a Ukranian peasant woman and an Austrian gendarme. Foreign names like Beck or Bartel, or peasant ones like Koc or Rydz, indicate that their bearers were no aristocrats. Only in the diplomatic service and among cavalry officers did the noblemen predominate. All in all, the Polish régime on the eve of war could be characterized as an authoritarian, highly militaristic, pseudo-fascist bureaucracy.

The most dangerous enemy of the régime – that is, the enemy most capable in the short run of infiltrating the important posts and organizing a *coup* – was the National Party, which started its life under the name of National Democracy, and during the parliamentary era before 1926 offered more analogies to the Indian Congress than to Mussolini's Blackshirts. Its founder Roman Dmowski – like Pilsudski of petty squire ancestry – was a political intellectual like Nehru or Thomas Masaryk rather than an uncouth rabble rouser like Hitler or Doriot; and his writings are on a higher intellectual plane, and in a more educated style, than those of Mussolini or Primo de Rivera, not to speak of the Nazi outpourings. In his outlook and manner of expressing his views he resembled most closely the elders of *Action Française* such as Charles Maurras, but especially Jacques Bainville with whom he shared a fear and dislike of the Germans. He transmitted this attitude to the National Party, including its new fascist wing, which remained throughout its existence warmly pro-French and militantly anti-German, and used to accuse the government (especially when Colonel Beck was Minister of Foreign Affairs) of cowardice or even treason in their negotiations with the western neighbour. Vying with each other in patriotism, the government and the National Party jointly fanned nationalist fervour to such a degree that, regardless of what they thought about Poland's chances of defending itself, the leaders could not imitate Dr Beneš and accede to Hitler's ultimatum.

Apart from general chauvinism, the National Party appealed first to antisemitism, and secondly to the resentment against the privileged bureaucrats, which was particularly strong in the western regions where it combined with the protest against discrimination in favour of other parts of the country. The Party's economic programme was *poujadiste avant la lettre:* protection of small traders and producers against the rapacious bureaucrats and big business which was in the hands of Jews and Germans – which explains the confluence of *poujadisme* and chauvinism. Far from preaching the desirability of dictatorship – hardly a profitable line to take in a country which was already enjoying the benefits of this method of conducting public affairs – the party clamoured for the resurrection of democratic liberties and for honest elections. In fact, the *Führerprinzip* never became the party's official doctrine; nevertheless in its organization and the content of its propaganda, as well as the manner of conducting it, during the thirties the party – and especially its youth movement – fell deeper and deeper under the spell of fascism.

As in most of the world, the great depression of the thirties radicalized all political groupings in Poland; and the sliding of the National Party towards pugilism and subversive preparations was intertwined with the growing oppressiveness of the régime in a relationship of mutual stimulation.

Mussolini had many admirers in Poland both on the government's side and among its enemies; and the attractiveness of his ideas was further enhanced by Hitler's spectacular career and his success in rapidly raising Germany's power and international status. Not that the Polish admirers of Hitler were pro-German. On the contrary, without drawing a rebuke from their elders, the younger leaders of the National Party proclaimed as their goal a re-conquest of all the lands which had ever been ruled by the Polish kings; which on the west meant the present frontier on the Oder and Neisse, with of course East Prussia incorporated. The party emblem was the sword of Boleslav the Valiant who at the beginning of the eleventh century established the frontier of his kingdom beyond the Oder. It is surprising how many people regarded these aims as practicable, particularly as they also included pushing the eastern frontiers of Poland to Pskov and the Black Sea. The last thing which these imperialists expected was that the first part of their programme of territorial expansion would be carried out by Stalin at the price of annexing the eastern territories of pre-war Poland. Their attitude to Hitler was one of admiration for his skill and pluck, coupled with an intense desire to do for Poland what they believed he was doing for Germany: that is, to create a monolithic militarized state which could beat the Germans at their own game. Naturally, this was also the avowed aim of the more extreme splinter group: the Radically National Camp, although in practice this faction played down the issues of foreign policy, and concentrated on baiting and waylaying Jews.

Unfortunately from the viewpoint of the National Party's goals the state comprised large ethnic minorities which added up to over one-third of the population. As far as the Ukrainians, Byelorussians and Lithuanians were concerned, the plan of these Polish double patriots was to apply to them the same medicine which the Germans had tried on the Poles before 1918 – forcible assimilation. Efforts in this direction – consisting of curtailments of non-Polish language schools and publications – were repeatedly made by the administration, but the National Party and its more extreme splinter groups accused the ruling circle of being treasonably timid. As regards the Jews, they regarded a policy of assimilation as undesirable even if it were practicable – which they believed it was not.

Wherever there are large masses of densely settled Jews there exists between them and the *goim* a barrier of endogamy and a certain degree of mistrust and mutual disdain, or at lest condescension, often coupled with expressions of enmity – open on the part of the majority, veiled on the part of the minority. However, in traditional eastern Europe this barrier entailed no questioning of the Jews' right to a place in society. In Poland the idea that it might be possible to get rid of the Jews appeared only at the beginning of the present century, and became widely popular only in the thirties when it was the main plank of the National Party's propaganda; the other contribution of the party to the socio-political climate being an interest in ancestry regardless of the professed religion, which manifested itself most conspicuously in an assiduous search for Jewish grandmothers of prominent political opponents. This preoccupation, it must be added, was suitable only for people of fairly humble descent because it was chiefly among the nobility and the intelligentsia of several generations' standing that Jewish ancestors were to be found. It might be remarked, incidentally, that if one goes by so-called racial traits, it is quite evident that very many central European aristocrats have a much closer genetic relationship with the ancient semites than most of the generals of the Israeli army whose physical appearance is typically Slav. Polish novels contain many references to an 'eagle-like nose' typical of a highly-bred, martial nobleman; and it is clear that this genetic feature is not indigenous to this part of Europe and can only have been imported from the Near East. Almost needless to say, the protagonists of racial purity took no cognizance of such trivia.

Given what could be foreseen at the time, the solution which the National Party proposed for the Jewish problem was as wild as the idea of the frontier on the Oder: namely, a transplantation of the Jews to Palestine. The only Jews of whom the National Party approved were the zionists; and although some of their followers whispered about killing the Jews, the party planners drafted elaborate memoranda on how to organize Jewish emigration, working out how many ships and railway wagons it would require, and how many could travel overland and how many by sea. Some even suggested that Poland should take over the Palestinian Mandate and send troops to carve out a Jewish state. The most common slogan on the placards carried by antisemitic demonstrators was 'Out to Palestine', although in practice the main efforts were directed towards reducing the entry of the Jews into lucrative professions such as medicine and law, keeping them out of the higher posts in the army and civil service, undermining their superior competititive power in business by harassment, and limiting the number of Jewish students at the universities. The official aim of the National Party was to limit the number of Jews to ten per cent of all students (which was the percentage of Jews to the total population), but the hotheads hoped to debar them altogether from higher educational institutions.

As the deepening crisis made *laissez-faire* capitalism appear less and less workable, the National Party gravitated more and more towards the idea of a corporativist economy on the Italian model, but with a strong *poujadiste* streak. The National Party had never been a pretorian guard of capitalism (to use Kautsky's expression), first because the capitalists were either Jews or Germans – and therefore unsuitable allies for a chauvinist

179

party – and secondly, because neither big business (such as there was) nor the estate owners had any need of an additional guard, as they were quite well protected by the arm of the authoritarian state. Consequently, in contrast to the Italian *fasci*, the strong-arm squads of the youth movement were never employed to intimidate the workers or tenants and suppress strikes. Indeed, since breaking the windows of Jewish shops was one of their chief occupations, and since most shopkeepers were Jews, the activities of these militants could at a stretch be called anti-capitalist. Another important difference from Italian fascism (and even more Nazism) was the clericalism of the National Party, which with fair success tried to outbid the government in piety and ultramontane proclamations, and thus to enlist the powerful force of devotionalism on its side.

To assess justly the ideals and the appeal of a corporate state we must divest ourselves of the pejorative emotional resonance which the word 'corporativist' has acquired through being bandied by régimes which lost a war in addition to committing atrocious crimes. The first thing to remember is that until Keynes published his General Theory in 1935 nobody offered a diagnosis of the economic crisis which suggested an effective and reasoned remedy; and that the most successful policy against unemployment at the time was the one pursued under Hitler's aegis by Hjalmar Schacht 'playing by ear'. As *laissez-faire* capitalism was obviously not working, most people agreed that it had to be replaced, the only question in dispute being by what. And here the choice was limited to some form of confiscatory collectivism inspired by marxism on the one side, and on the other some form of regulation by partnership between government and private producers organized in cartels, guilds and corporations. One did not have to be a lunatic or a criminal to opt for the latter solution, particularly if one had property or a good job to lose in the event of a revolution. There is no necessary connection between corporativism and concentration camps; and in any case Mussolini's corporativism was largely (and Hitler's entirely) a sham covering pure despotism. Further-more, although 'corporativist' has become a dirty word, the economic structures of present-day western Europe have evolved in a direction which does not diverge very far from what the academic protagonists of corporativism envisaged in the twenties and early thirties.

Whereas the role of the National Party in society and politics was very different, in the realm of paraphernalia its imitation of the Italian and German models became almost complete. Step by step the increasingly influential youth wing introduced into the old party of black-coated notables brown shirts (though pinker than those of the Nazis), the jackboots, the goose-step and the Nazi salute. Unlike the *fasci* or the SA, however, these cohorts were prevented by the police from carrying weapons. Moreover, in contrast to its latter-day models, the party had no charismatic rabble-rousing leader, although at least one of the younger chiefs was moving into that position. The old intellectual politician Roman Dmowski remained the titular head until his death shortly before the war, but he was quite unfit to lead uniformed storm-troopers.

In western Poland the National Party enjoyed the support of the large majority resentful of Warsaw bureaucrats. As this was the only region where commerce was in the hands of the Gentiles, the local traders liked a party which promised to keep out the Jews; and in any case they were attracted by its *poujadiste* economic programme. Only in these provinces, moreover, were the peasants prosperous and self-respecting instead of feeling underdogs; and consequently, only here were they attracted in mass to a party which tried to integrate them with the artisans, the petty traders and the out-of-office intelligentsia in opposition to the grasping bureaucrats. In central Poland the National Party made some headway among the artisans and the emerging class of Gentile small traders, but not so much among the industrial workers, most of whom adhered to the socialist party. In southern and to a lesser extent central Poland the majority of articulate peasants supported the People's Party. There were many other parties – the Ukrainian nationalists, Jewish socialists, marxist peasants and so on – but none of them had much influence. It must be noted, however, that owing to the

181

government's recourse to fraud and intimidation in the elections, even before the new system of screening candidates was introduced, the returns at the polls did not represent the true measure of popular support which the various parties enjoyed.

The National Party's following among the intelligentsia was largely a question of ins and outs: the well-placed being mostly on the side of the government, whereas students and graduates without connections, and therefore with poor prospects for a good bureaucratic post – but whose piety or non-proletarian background deterred them from socialism – flocked to the youth movement, and prepared to overthrow the government. They were equally attracted to the programme of eliminating Jewish competition for white-collar employment. The underlying condition of these motivations was that the production of diploma holders greatly exceeded the demand – though not necessarily the needs which could not translate themselves into monetary offers.

There were hotheads who found the National Party too moderate – too much under the influence of elderly professors, lawyers and parsons, and perhaps not eager enough to give positions of leadership commensurate with their merits to young firebrands, who consequently broke away and founded a Radically National Camp, which advocated more violent direct action and even terrorism. A small splinter group of similar persuasion called itself *Falanga*, to accentuate its feeling of kinship with its Spanish prototype. Though small in absolute numbers, these factions made a great noise and had a big following among the students. They were accused of a few political assassinations, but their chief activity consisted of organizing student riots and assaults on Jews. They were believed to be collecting weapons. Some of their leaders were put into the government's concentration camp.

The Radically National Camp resembled the Rumanian Iron Guard in its readiness to resort to violence but not in its devotionalism, being in fact much less clerical than the National Party, and in this respect more like the Italian fascists or the Nazis. On the other hand, in the social origins of its members it was much less demotic than either the Iron Guard or the Nazis and more like the French *Cagoulards* or the Spanish *Falange*. As with *Action Française*, their propaganda and activities had fewer populist undertones than those of the Nazis, not to speak of the thoroughly populist Iron Guard.

There was thus a curious constellation of forces on the Polish political arena on the eve of war. The parties expressly vowed to the interests of the poorer classes – the People's Party and the Polish Socialist Party – though in existence and enjoying wide sympathies, were effectively kept down by the police; while the Communist Party was banned and in any case weakened by its subservience to the national enemy, as well as by the extermination of its best leaders during Stalin's purges. The open struggle for power was waged between a pseudo-fascist, militarized bureaucracy and a semi-fascist party of antisemitic and ultramontane chauvinists.

During the last few months before the war the internal quarrels somewhat abated, dampened by the rising wave of unrealistic martial fervour. No doubt the Germans wanted no equivalent of Quisling in Poland, but the fact remains that none of the Polish fascists and semi-fascists turned into one, and many fell resisting the invasion or in the underground army, or perished in the concentration camps. Given their treatment of the conquered, it was not surprising that the Nazis found collaborators (whether for hounding Jews or any other purpose), not on the basis of ideological sympathies but among individuals of generally low moral fibre, lacking any sense of honour, and particularly susceptible to the promptings of cowardice and greed.

9 Finland

A. F. Upton

Finland was one of the European countries where fascism came very close to a successful seizure of power in the early 1930s, though it was her good fortune to survive the danger and preserve a democratic system of government intact, through the strains and stresses of war and defeat, down to the present day. It is probable that the near success of fascism in Finland is closely linked to the fact that in its beginnings it was a natural development of the native nationalist tradition, and owed little or nothing to international fascism, while its later adoption of the outward trappings of fascist orthodoxy added nothing to its strength, and may indeed have weakened it. But it follows that for any understanding of developments in Finland, it is necessary to be aware of the basic features of the history of the Finnish nationalist movement.

From 1809 to 1917, Finland was an autonomous Grand Duchy under the tsar of Russia. It was a predominantly rural society, in which Finnish was the language of the vast majority of labourers, share-croppers, and small independent farmers, but which had been endowed with a native, Swedish-speaking ruling class of landlords, burghers, and officials. During the course of the nineteenth century there had developed a typical romantic-nationalist movement built round the claims of the Finnish language. The political father of Finnish nationalism, Snellman, was deeply indebted to German idealist philosophy, whose ideas and ideals provided the movement with its intellectual backbone, and left the emergent Finnish intelligentsia with a powerful pro-German orientation which it has never lost. As

184

the movement for the development of the Finnish language grew, there was collected a body of folk-poetry, the *Kalevala*, which was to become the Finnish national epic. By an accident of geography the richest finds were made over the frontier in Russian Karelia, and as research developed, further pockets of Finnish-speaking peoples were discovered, scattered over northern Russia as far as the Urals. These discoveries were to leave a fateful, and some would argue, baleful legacy to Finnish nationalism.

The early nationalist movement was naturally directed against the hegemony of the Swedish-speaking minority and their culture, but in the 1890s internal divisions were overshadowed by a change in Russian policy. Hitherto the Russian government had respected the constitutional autonomy of Finland; now they launched a policy of crude russification, involving open violation of the legal and constitutional rights of the country. This inevitably swung the nationalist movement round towards a policy of resistance to Russian aggression and, at a very early stage, there emerged an activist minority, dedicated to underground conspiracy and the use of violence, which ran sometimes parallel, sometimes at odds with the constitutional non-violent resistance of the majority.

Resistance to russification left two abiding characteristic features of Finnish nationalism, of which the first is a hatred of Russia that quickly took on a racialist character. The nationalists saw the Russians as asiatic barbarian oppressors, the hereditary enemies of the Finnish race and culture. Against this enemy, history and divine providence had called the Finnish nation to defend Western and Christian values. In this way the nationalists discovered Finland's place in the great scheme of European history, and her manifest destiny. The second characteristic was the tradition of activism, the taste for extra-legal direct action, for underground conspiracy, and for solutions by violence.

This simple emerging pattern was complicated in the last years of the nineteenth century by the emergence of Finnish socialism, a product of the industrialism that had come to

Finland after 1870. The Finnish workers' movement quickly adopted marxism in its most doctrinaire forms, scorning Bernstein's revisionism, adhering to class-war and revolution. Thus, while the socialists and the bourgeois nationalists shared a common enemy in the tsarist oppressor, so that some co-operation between the movements inevitably developed, as a general rule the socialists rejected all contact with the domestic class-enemy, while as good internationalists they began to seek contacts with the Russian socialist movement. It is true that during the crisis of 1905-6 the socialists and the nationalists managed to work together in forcing liberal reforms on the Russian government, but this co-operation was short-lived, and even renewed Russian oppression after 1907 did not heal the breach between the socialists and the nationalists – their mutual hatred of Russia was no stronger than their distrust of one another.

When war broke out in 1914, all Finns recognized that Russian military defeat might be Finland's opportunity, and the bolder spirits set about preparing for any eventuality. The activist wing of the nationalists, with some socialist support, negotiated with the Germans a scheme for training Finnish volunteers in the German army, who would then become the spearhead of a future Finnish national rising. These were the *Jägers*, of whom there were about two thousand fully trained in Germany by 1917. After the Russian February Revolution, the activists began to plan a revolt, in close collaboration with the German authorities. But the socialists, who in the parliamentary elections of 1916 had won an absolute majority, found themselves in a strong position when parliament was allowed to meet by the Russian provisional government, and lost what interest they had ever had in co-operating with Germany, while their radicals perceived a chance to carry through a revolution that would secure independence of Russia and victory in the class-war at one blow.

In these circumstances tensions built up inside Finland through 1917. They were sharply boosted when first, in fresh parliamentary elections, the socialists lost their majority to the bourgeois parties, and then the Russian October Revolution encouraged

186

the socialist radicals to defy the verdict of the electors, and emulate the bolshevik example. But the socialists were split, and hesitated fatally, while the new bourgeois government declared independence on 6 December, and it was not until late January 1918 that the socialists sought to take over power by an armed *coup*, which precipitated a civil war. In this, the Reds were assisted by Russian weapons and technical advisers, and the Whites by German military aid, and it was the latter who emerged victorious in May 1918, and together with their German allies, indulged in the bloody repression of the vanquished Reds.

They also tried to strike back at Soviet Russia, and to expand the frontiers of the new state by seizing eastern Karelia and the Kola peninsula, at first, under P.E.Svinhufvud as Regent, with German backing, then, under the pro-entente Mannerheim, the White commander in the civil war, with Anglo-French backing. But the Allies could not persuade the Russian Whites to agree to pay the territorial price which the Finns were asking in return for intervention in the Russian civil war. Thus the proposed territorial expansion of the republic was frustrated, and after Mannerheim's defeat in the presidential election of 1919, it was dropped as official policy. But nationalist activists, with the acquiescence of the Finnish government, were allowed to mount two incursions into Karelia in support of anti-Soviet elements there, the last in 1922. But these were defeated. When official Finland made peace with Soviet Russia at Tartu, in October 1920, the best that could be secured was a promise of autonomy for Soviet Karelia, a promise that was to be fulfilled in a manner that was not anticipated. The activists rejected the peace treaty from the outset, while the more moderate Right accepted it grudgingly as an unfortunate necessity. Thus Finland was endowed with one of the most promising ingredients for a fascist movement, a *terra irredenta* in Karelia, whose loss could be blamed on the feebleness of the democratic régime which had negotiated the 'shameful' treaty of Tartu.

The circumstances in which independence had been gained dictated the shape of post-war Finnish politics. Within the

187

Finnish Left, the defeated Red leaders had retired into Russia, where in August 1918 they formed the Finnish Communist Party. The socialists who remained in Finland, and survived the White terror, reformed a Social Democratic Party, still marxist, but of the revisionist brand. This party, which was legal, slowly recovered strength and usually held about sixty seats in the 200-member parliament, but the bourgeois parties mostly continued to treat the social democrats as political outlaws, and would have no open dealings with them, while the communists attacked them bitterly as traitors to the socialist cause.

The Communist Party was regarded from the beginning as an instrument of bolshevik imperialism, a tool of Moscow, and a treasonable conspiracy. It was formally adjudged an illegal organization in Finland, and any of its members who fell into government hands got long terms of imprisonment. But it proved difficult to repress the communists. In the first place they enjoyed a secure base just over the frontier, across which men, money, and propaganda flowed freely. But what was worse was that Soviet Karelia, in a mockery of the provisions of the treaty of Tartu, was indeed given a measure of independence, and became the private colony of the Finnish Communist Party, which they could develop as the nucleus of a future Soviet Finland. It needs no imagination to guess how this situation affected the nationalists in Finland, above all the resentful and frustrated activists.

But in the second place, the communists continued to attract a strong popular following as the true heirs of the defeated Reds, and this enabled them to infiltrate and control the Finnish trade union movement through most of the 1920s, to contest elections through front organizations, publish newspapers, run a youth movement. The first of their front organizations, the Finnish Workers' Party, was dissolved in 1923, only to be replaced by the Workers' and Peasants' Alliance. Through these movements the communists held between twenty and thirty seats in parliament, and controlled many municipalities. This blatant defiance of the clear intention of the law was a further gross provocation to the Right, and did little to encourage respect for the law in general, or for the governments which apparently lacked the power to enforce it. The social democrats, who suffered more directly from the communists than anyone, still felt bound to defend their activities on general democratic principles, exposing themselves to charges of collusion.

The forces of the Right were organized politically in the *Kokoomus* (Coalition) Party. This party had from the beginning adopted an ambiguous attitude to the new republican régime; it had been monarchist in 1918, and still hankered after a strong executive which would be above party politics. The party was fanatically anti-Russian and enjoyed the open support of Finnish big-business. Further, it had the open or implicit support of many of the leaders of the victorious Whites. Svinhufvud was an open supporter, and he had never been reconciled with the parliamentary régime; as late as 1936 he was telling the German ambassador that it had grave deficiencies, and needed at least to be offset by a strong leader at the head of the executive. Similar views were held by the leading military heroes of 1918, like General Walden, organizer of the new Finnish paper industry and a pillar of the *Kokoomus*, whose views were known to echo those of his close friend Mannerheim, though the latter would never deign to be formally associated with a political party. These men, the White grandees of 1918, made no secret of their contempt for party politics, their impatience with the feebleness of the parliamentary republic, their belief that all socialists were traitors and hirelings of Moscow, their conviction that the final reckoning with the bolsheviks was yet to come, and their regret that the job had not been finished properly after 1918. Thus the founding fathers of the new state tended to express rejection of their offspring, because it had failed to follow the paths they had pointed out for it, and the *Kokoomus* Party tended to echo their sentiments. The mood was described by one of them in 1931 as follows:

Out of the game and powerless, embittered and distrustful, the men of 1918 withdrew into their shells. They had a dim perception that what they had won was now being thrown away by a kind of treason. They had no faith in the politics of compromise.

189

This left a very narrow base for the parliamentary régime to operate from. There were the Swedish People's Party, a pressure group dedicated to preserving the rights of the Swedish-speaking minority, the small Progressive Party which represented the liberal bourgeoisie and the intelligentsia, and the Agrarians representing the small independent farmer. Since the anti-parliamentary groups – *Kokoomus* and Communists – controlled between them nearly fifty of the 200 seats, and since the centre parties dare not enter into formal coalition with the social democrats, who had a further sixty seats, the parliamentary situation did not encourage the formation of strong governments. The régime could just survive, basically because there was tacit co-operation between the social democrats and the centre parties. But it was a survival marked by a depressing series of short-lived coalition ministries. In these circumstances it was most creditable that the governments of the 1920s managed to wind up the civil war by a general amnesty, enfranchise the share-croppers and tenant farmers through radical agrarian reform, institute universal compulsory primary education, eradicate illiteracy, raise standards of public health, find new markets for Finnish exports to replace the lost Russian market, and preside over the reconstruction of the Finnish timber and paper industries which was transforming the economy. The achievement is impressive, but its political base remained undeniably precarious and narrow and, as events proved, at the mercy of any serious setback.

Against the background of the parliamentary game which they despised, the forces of the Right entrenched themselves in movements and organizations of a kind different from the orthodox political party, leaving the *Kokoomus* to fly their flag in parliament. The most important of these was the *Suojeluskunta* – Defence Corps – hereafter referred to as the SK. This was a volunteer militia first raised by the activists before 1918, and retained after the war. Although largely armed and financed out of government funds, it was an autonomous organization, whose officers were elected by the membership from the parish level to the national commander-in-chief. It also controlled its own membership, and socialists of any kind were rigidly excluded, so that the SK was in effect a private army at the disposal of the Right, regarding internal security as its first function. In addition the SK gave the Right a nation-wide organizational framework, while its annual congresses provided a platform on which conservative and nationalist views were freely aired. Over wide areas of the country, the local SK and its officials exercised a condominium with the duly constituted organs and officials of the republic.

The second major institutional embodiment of the Finnish Right which developed in the 1920s was the *Akateeminen Karjala-Seura* – the Academic Karelian Society – hereafter referred to as AKS. This began as a student society in the university of Helsinki, founded by activist students who had taken part in the expeditions into Karelia in the immediate post-war period. Its original aim was to stimulate continuing interest in the Karelian question, and to organize relief activities among Karelian refugees, but it quickly grew to be the leading student organization. It was a masonic type of society with a carefully controlled membership, and those admitted were subjected to an examination and had to pledge unconditional obedience to the Society. By 1926 the Society had infiltrated all the student bodies, and in the 1930s could count on about eighty per cent of the vote for its candidates in all student elections. Post-graduate membership was developed, and a nation-wide network of branches established.

AKS became another undoubted power in the land, for the great majority of Finnish-speaking students enrolled, and were subject to the systematic brain-washing and discipline which was the heart of the Society's activity. This was important, because in Finland virtually the whole ruling class is university trained, so that the civil service, the officer corps, the professions, the writers and journalists, the managerial class in industry, and the teachers were predominantly men and women who had subscribed to the ideals of the AKS, and tended to project those ideals on the community at large. Only the minority of socialist students and the Swedish-speaking students stood out against

191

the AKS, so that the pressure for conformity was very strong, and the ideas of AKS became the accepted norm for the educated Finn.

The ideology of AKS was strongly nationalist, and politically reactionary. It stood of course for unyielding resistance to communism at home and abroad, and linked this with its aspirations towards the territorial expansion of Finland at Russia's expense, expressed in the idea of *Suur-Suomi* (Greater Finland). In its more sober forms the idea was that in the inevitable European showdown with communism, Finland would have the chance to annex eastern Karelia. In its more expansive forms it envisaged taking the Kola peninsula, incorporating Estonia and Ingria – the region round Leningrad – and the pockets of Finnish-speaking peoples in northern Russia, which would produce a Finnish great power stretching to the Urals. The Society advocated extreme linguistic and racial nationalism, it was totally hostile to the Swedish-speaking minority, opposed any Scandinavian orientation of Finnish culture or politics, opposed the League of Nations and disarmament, and increasingly came to reject political democracy. Here foreign borrowings became evident in the concept of democracy as a degenerate form of government unsuited to a strong and vigorous nation, and inevitably producing weak and corrupt government. The AKS particularly rejected the party system, since it regarded all parties as corrupt interest groups, while it preached a national unity transcending all internal divisions. A modern Finnish commentator has remarked that 'the Society was born before Nazism and fascism, but it belonged to the same family'. It must be stressed that AKS was never an overtly political movement, and that its activity and influence were confined to the university trained élite, but within that sector of Finnish society AKS was promoting an intellectual and psychological climate favourable to right-wing, authoritarian concepts.

A very different kind of organization which emerged in the 1920s was *Vientirauha* (industrial peace), financed by big business, and dedicated to combating aggressive trade unionism. This organization maintained a roster of volunteer strike-breakers, willing to go anywhere where industrial strife broke out. *Vientirauha* recruited chiefly in Pohjanmaa, the province bordering on the northern part of the gulf of Bothnia, which had been the cradle and power house of the White movement at the beginning of the civil war. The region was dominated by small independent farmers, who had fallen victim in the nineteenth century to the more extreme forms of Lutheran pietism, and mixed this in with a fiery nationalism, and a local tradition of fierce, lawless violence. Socialists were damned as townees, enemies of private landowning, and atheists, and since 1917, as hirelings of Russia. Here it was easy to recruit young sons of the farm, pay them a retainer, and keep them as industrial ever-readies. They needed the cash, and enjoyed the adventure, and paid strike-breaking became an acceptable auxiliary occupation of the region. The first figure-head of Finnish fascism, Vihtori Kosola, was a recruiting agent for *Vientirauha* in Pohjanmaa, who rose to be the area organizer and treasurer of the organization. Kosola was himself a farmer from the region, and he made himself so valuable to his employers that they seem to have overlooked some very curious accounting on his part in 1928.

Looking back over the scene of Finland in the 1920s one can see much that was conducive to the emergence of a fascist type of movement. On the one side, the Right, the self-conscious heirs of the victorious Whites, felt bitterly that somehow they had been cheated of the fruits of victory, that there were accounts still to be settled, and while scorning traditional politics, they built up their strength, especially through the SK, for the day of reckoning that was surely coming. On the other side were the communists, in many ways a mirror image of the Right, openly dedicated to reversing the verdict of the civil war, blatantly building up their forces over the frontier, openly backed by Soviet Russia, brazenly mocking the law by their political and industrial activity inside the country. In these circumstances a renewal of violence was never far away, for in Finland, unlike many parts of Europe, the communist bogey was no figment of the imagination, but a hard and menacing political reality.

Yet, no fascist movement emerged. It is true that one can find

193

plenty of individual approval of Mussolini as a strong man who knew how to deal with communists; the AKS often cited Italy as a model of national regeneration, the *Kokoomus* approved of him. The rise of German Nazism was also noted with approval in many places on the Right, where Weimar Germany was felt to be deplorably weak, and men longed for the re-emergence of a strong Germany that would be a counterpoise to Russia. But this was all, and it seems to illustrate the truth that Finland is stony ground for foreign ideologies in some respects. Isolated by geography and language, given to introspective brooding on their own special problems, the Finns have tended to be scornful of patent solutions for their difficulties imported ready-made from abroad. They do not accept that anyone from outside could teach them much about what directly concerns themselves. Italy was a distant country of which the average Finn had no direct knowledge and little interest. Fascism, as it emerged in Finland, was a home-grown product; what it came to borrow from international fascism were only the superficial trappings.

The economic depression came to Finland early, and was affecting the vital timber trade by 1928, immediately producing a crop of industrial disputes in which the communists and *Vientirauha* clashed forcefully. As unemployment rose there was increasing evidence that the communists would be the immediate beneficiaries of working-class discontent, and their propaganda showed that they sensed that a decisive struggle had begun. The Right reacted by calling on the government to take defensive action, but although the government was willing to respond by new anti-communist legislation, it could not get it through parliament, since any major measures would have to take the form of constitutional amendments, requiring a two-thirds majority, and the social democrats alone, even without the twenty-eight communists in parliament, were enough to block this. In these circumstances, the thoughts of the Right turned naturally towards direct action.

Through the summer of 1929 tension rose steadily, as the communists ran a campaign against the alleged danger of imminent European war directed against the Soviet Union, with processions and mass meetings. They announced that on 1 August they would hold a great peace demonstration in Helsinki, and various organizations of the Right, above all the SK, announced that if the government did not ban the demonstration, they would stop it themselves. The government yielded, and at once became the focus of a communist-inspired campaign over its denial of the basic rights of citizens, pursued through questions in parliament and rallies up and down the country. The extremists on both sides were plainly looking for a showdown, and in November 1929 it began.

The communist youth organization scheduled a week-end school at the town of Lapua, in Pohjanmaa, and a hotbed of right-wing activism, main centre of recruiting for *Vientirauha*, home town of Vihtori Kosola. Although the occasion was perfectly legal, and had police permission, it was in fact a deliberate provocation. Trouble began as soon as the delegates began unloading at Lapua station on 29 November, many wearing red shirts worn outside the trousers, Russian fashion. Some of them, it being the week-end, and this a centre of pietism, held an anti-religious meeting in the street, and were there set upon by local people, beaten up, and stripped of their shirts, the police making no attempt to intervene. When the meetings of the school began, those attending were roughed up, the meetings subjected to constant interruption, with a certain amount of wild shooting around the meeting place, and again the police stood by, until the school broke up in disorder.

In direct response to this, at a meeting on 1 December in Lapua, the so-called Lapua movement was born. Its defenders always claimed that it began as a spontaneous movement of protest by the good citizens of Lapua, that it was the answer of the honest patriotic farmers of Pohjanmaa to the communist threat to their way of life. The evidence, scattered though it is, does not sustain such a theory. From its very inception the Lapua movement had plenty of money and a nation-wide organization behind it. The evidence is that all through 1929 the organized Right in Finland – that is, the *Kokoomus* Party, the big employers' organizations, and the SK – had been preparing

195

something like this, and that the Lapua meeting gave them just the excuse they wanted in just the right place, for in Lapua they could draw on the services of *Vientirauha* and its hirelings for the violent stuff, while at the same time being able to rely on genuine popular local support. The great protest meeting of 1 December has all the marks of a put-up job, and was in fact managed by *Vientirauha*. The chief of *Vientirauha*, Martti Pihkala, himself a prominent member of the Finnish employers' organizations, was busy behind the scenes, Tiitu, one of his local organizers took the chair, and Kosola made the keynote speech.

In this speech, which was enthusiastically endorsed by the meeting, Kosola demanded that all communist activity be effectively repressed, and said that it would never be done properly under the existing system; therefore the time had come for the people to act for themselves. He went on:

> ... it is a waste of time to send delegations ... it would be better to send riflemen to Helsinki ... it may well be that the whole present form of government and the parliamentary system will have to be sacrificed.

He called on the Finnish farmers, the backbone of the nation, to rise up and put an end to the futile posturings of the Helsinki politicians.

Thus Kosola emerged as Finland's strong man, yet it is impossible to believe that he was much more than a puppet. Kosola had no national standing before 1929; though he was locally powerful in Pohjanmaa, he displayed no marked political or oratorical talent, did nothing that would give him a claim to be regarded as a major political figure in his own right – basically he remained what he had been before 1929, the hired agent of *Vientirauha*. He fitted the bill because he made a plausible figurehead for what was supposed to be a farmers' movement, because he could be manipulated, and because when the time came for the real leaders of the Right to take the stage, he could easily be set aside. Even the movement itself in its more euphoric moments did not seriously contemplate that Kosola should take over the running of the country.

The meeting of 1 December was then imitated all over Finland, similar speeches were made, similar resolutions passed, and on 15 March 1930 a congress was held at Lapua to launch a national movement. This set up a national co-ordinating body, *Suomen Lukko* – Finland's Lock, dedicated to the struggle with communism, and aspiring to become a national front of the Right. The first committee had an Agrarian politician and editor, A. Leinonen, as chairman, two bankers, I. Kaitera and I. Koivisto, Martti Pihkala of *Vientirauha*, the big industrialists Walden and Haarla, as well as Kosola and the Lapua leaders. The theme of its programme was the need for direct action, the need to meet force with force. Haarla spoke of a new round in the civil war, and of 'a conflict much bloodier than 1918'. *Suomen Lukko* succeeded in spectacular fashion, almost all the institutions of the Right joined it, including the AKS, and in the course of 1930 it seems to have enjoyed the support of a great majority of non-socialist Finns, and was a genuine popular mass movement. The congress also launched the two key slogans of Finnish fascism, 'Finland awake' and 'we do what we will, others do what they can'.

From the beginning, President Relander and the government sought to appease the Lapuans, and announced that it would bring forward new anti-communist legislation. But the first instalment, a new press law introduced in March, failed to get the necessary two-thirds majority. The response of the Lapuans was immediate and forceful. At the end of March, about seventy men, some of them armed, attacked the printing presses of the Vaasa paper *Työn Ääni*, a left-wing socialist paper, and burned the building. The communists at once raised the matter in parliament, which on 3 April voted by 101 to 91 that legal proceedings should be instituted against those responsible. The narrow margin in this vote shows how far the Right was already prepared to condone direct action; the *Kokoomus* deputies and their press in particular openly welcomed and excused the violence as a proper response to parliament's refusal to pass the press law. A. Palmgren, a *Kokoomus* deputy and head of the Finnish employers' organization, made a speech welcoming the action of the Lapua men, and declared that his organization stood solidly behind them.

When the Vaasa chief of police proceeded to arrest a leading mobster in Lapua, a crowd gathered at once outside the police station and forced his release. But a number of men were brought to trial in Vaasa in April, charged with the attack on *Työn Ääni*. However, from the start of proceedings the court was surrounded by a crowd that rose to over 1500; the leading lawyer for *Työn Ääni* was seized as he left the building on the first day, driven off to Lapua, and not released until he signed a promise to withdraw from the case. The Lapua activists put out a statement signed by over seventy persons including Kosola, claiming that they had organized the attack on the press, and drove down to Vaasa in a triumphant motorcade to present their statement to the local prefect. The accused at the trial were then given nominal sentences and released, while no proceedings were taken against those who had caused the disturbances during the hearings. The perfect at Vaasa now asked the government for the support necessary for restoring order, and when this was refused, resigned; his successor, in order as he claimed to prevent further disturbances, closed down all the local left-wing newspapers.

Thus encouraged, the Lapua movement at once stepped up its pressure on the government, and at a further congress in April decided to organize a farmers' march on Helsinki to demand the full implementation of their programme. But immediate attention concentrated on shutting down the communist press, and when in June the movement threatened to use force against all such papers, the government issued an order to the prefects to close them, although this was clearly illegal. When the government's policy was debated in parliament on 1 July, the Minister of Justice publicly defended his refusal to restrain the illegal behaviour of the Lapua men, and concluded, 'the communists had practiced illegalities under the shelter of the law: now they are being shown how, through illegality, legality is being reinstated'. Parliament endorsed the government's action with a vote of confidence.

But their conversion came too late, for Lapua had decided to get rid of the existing government and put in its own nominees. As soon as the popular success of the movement had become clear, the real leaders of the Right hastened to climb on to the bandwagon, and proceeded to use it to carry out their own take-over of the government. Svinhufvud travelled to Lapua and declared that the movement was a divine blessing on the fatherland, the Speaker of parliament made his pilgrimage to what was fast becoming a holy place and gave his endorsement, and a stream of public figures followed their example. The Lapuans agreed that Svinhufvud should form a government to carry out their programme, and in June they bluntly told the president and ministers to make way. When the ministers demurred, the Lapuans told President Relander that if he did not dismiss them and call on Svinhufvud, the government would be overthrown by force. They were with difficulty persuaded to give him a day or two to consider the matter, after which Relander capitulated. Despite the vote of confidence in parliament on 1 July, the ministry resigned and Svinhufvud became Prime Minister, and at once introduced new anti-communist laws into parliament.

Lapua now turned its attention to this body, and on 5 July, almost certainly with the connivance of the government, armed men broke into the parliament building and kidnapped two communist deputies from a meeting of the constitutional law committee. Svinhufvud, instead of taking steps to assert the authority of parliament, immediately asked for the suspension of the communist deputies, and then arrested them. Even so the social democrats stood firm against the new laws, and with the handful of bourgeois liberals who stood with them could still prevent a two-thirds majority. So Svinhufvud dissolved parliament.

The next step was to ensure that after the elections there would be an adequate majority for the new laws, and the whole campaign turned on this. The government did its part by suppressing the communists, their presses were closed, their leaders put in prison, and their organizations broken up. The rest was left to the Lapuans who were given a free hand to intimidate and terrorize the opposition.

199

Their campaign really opened with the farmers' march on Helsinki, the arrangements for which had been made in Lapua at a meeting on 20–21 June. A delegation was chosen to lead the march and present its demands to the president, and although this delegation contained a handful of farmers to keep up appearances, the bulk of the delegates reflected the real forces behind the movement. There were seven bankers, four priests, three factory owners, two officers, two lawyers, and a police official. The organizers had been in touch with the Italian ambassador, A. Tamaro, who seems to have been enlisted as technical adviser, which is one of the few established examples of direct contact between the Finnish and foreign fascist movements. Once the Svinhufvud government was installed, official assistance was given, two general staff officers were detached to help with the logistics, while the whole organization of the SK was at the movement's disposal. Public figures gave their endorsement of the march and its declared programme, even the aloof Mannerheim came out with a statement of support.

Consequently the march, which had been conceived of originally as a demonstration to force the hand of a reluctant government, was turned into a national festival of the Right. Early in August some 12,000 men, a quarter of them armed, marched through Helsinki and were given a solemn public reception by Relander, Mannerheim, Svinhufvud and the government. President Relander, in his address of welcome, thanked god for the patriotic upsurge which the marchers represented, Svinhufvud assured them that all their demands would be met, and communism in Finland would be stamped out for ever. The marchers then dispersed without further incident.

The summer and autumn of 1930 saw the high peak of Lapua violence, coinciding with the general election campaign. The movement, which became a formal registered organization in September, with Kosola as chairman, was technically a farmers' society dedicated to education and enlightenment; it was not a political party, and did not present candidates in the election. Its energies were concentrated on intimidating the surviving opposition, the social democrats and those few bourgeois progressives who refused to be carried away on the tide of enthusiasm for the movement. The first murders had occurred in July when two radical socialist politicians were killed: in one case, an over-zealous police official who was investigating was called off on orders from Helsinki; in the second, which involved Kosola's son, no legal proceedings were begun for more than a year, and when the murderers were at last brought before a court, they were released after a hearing *in camera*. This travesty of justice proved too much for the then Minister of Justice, who ordered a fresh trial, which resulted in prison sentences for the accused.

But murder was not the characteristic weapon of the Lapuans. They went in for a lot of general violence, breaking up meetings, attacking newspaper offices, forcing local social democratic organs to close down by intimidation. But their speciality was kidnapping. The favourite form was to seize an opposition politician, or a trade union official, or an editor, take them to the Russian frontier, beat them up, and then dump them over the border – this appealed to the Lapuan sense of humour. If the victims were released, or when they managed to get back, provided the Soviet authorities did not proceed against them as spies, they were warned by Lapua to stay out of public life in future. During the summer and autumn of 1930 over a thousand members of local government bodies, social democratic party branches, public agencies, trade unions, staffs of newspapers, even candidates and former members of parliament, including the deputy Speaker, were the victims of abductions, and the authorities did nothing to protect potential victims, or to track down the perpetrators. In October, twenty self-confessed kidnappers went as a delegation to the Ministry of the Interior, including several leading officials of the Lapua movement, one of them a High Court judge, and were assured by the Minister that if they did find themselves before a court, they could count on sympathetic consideration.

It was in face of this rampant intimidation, connived at by the legal authorities, that the election was fought. The opposition rallied round the figure of J. K. Ståhlberg, the first President of the Republic, who emerged from retirement to campaign for the constitution and the law. Ståhlberg immediately became the target of the most venomous Lapua abuse, for nobody could accuse him of being a hireling of Moscow. Inevitably, on 14 October, a group of armed men kidnapped Ståhlberg and his wife, and drove them towards the Russian frontier, clearly intending to leave them on the other side, but at the last moment the kidnappers lost their nerve, and released them. This was going too far even for Svinhufvud's government, and legal proceedings were begun against the attackers, who had made no effort to conceal their identity. The two chief figures were General Wallenius, then Chief of the General Staff, and the secretary of *Suomen Lukko*, and these, with their subordinates, were brought to trial and given prison sentences, but Wallenius was acquitted on appeal.

It was therefore not surprising that the election of 1930 was a triumph for the Right. The *Kokoomus* jumped from 28 to 42 seats, which in Finnish terms is a landslide, but the social democrats, who must have picked up votes from the suppressed communists, hung on to 66 seats, just one short of a blocking third. When the new parliament met, the so-called Lapua laws were rapidly passed, giving strong new emergency powers to the president, sweeping powers for the government to close down offensive associations and publications, and revising the electoral laws so as to disfranchise anyone adjudged to have been a member of an illegal organization. The local electoral boards were given wide discretion to decide who fell into this category. Taken together, the laws were ample for the prevention of communist political activity, and in fact, with their aid, it was almost completely repressed; the Communist Party inside Finland in the 1930s was reduced to a tiny, hunted underground, incapable of any effective political action.

Svinhufvud and the grandees of the Right had now got all they wanted from the Lapua movement, and would have been obliged if it had gracefully retired into the background and left them in control. But they found, as others have before and since, that having gone for a ride on a tiger, it was not so easy to get off again. As soon as the elections were over, Svinhufvud began making speeches about the need to return to legality now that the aims of the movement had been met, but the Lapuans could quote against him speeches of his as late as 28 September, when he had described Lapua violence as 'right, necessary, and therefore to be supported'. They could also cite Mannerheim's appeal of 30 September to all patriotic citizens to give support to the 'selfless, patriotic endeavours, which have been launched into public life through the influence of the Lapua movement'. It was understandable that the Lapuans had acquired a rather high valuation of their own significance.

But for the moment there was no open breach between the Lapuans and the grandees, for there was one more hurdle to be jumped, the presidential election due in early 1931. In this Svinhufvud stood as the candidate of the united Right, with full Lapua support, against Ståhlberg, the choice of the social democrats, and many of the agrarians, on a platform of a return to legality. Although the new electoral law, and continuing intimidation, all worked for Svinhufvud, he was eventually elected by the smallest possible margin in the electoral college, 151 votes to 149, and this may have been swayed by the public intervention of the SK, which sent a delegation to the electoral college declaring that the SK would not tolerate any other choice but Svinhufvud.

With the presidency safe, Svinhufvud truly had no further use for Lapua, and as the established governing authority, began to find its defiance of the laws a nuisance. Svinhufvud was the last man to tolerate sharing authority, but Lapua had got into the habit of claiming to dictate policy to the government. The movement was now working out the next stage in its policy. It had acquired a national journal, *Aktivisti*, and in the pages of this one can trace the evolution of a full fascist programme. Chunks of ill-digested material from foreign fascist books and papers filled its pages, on the domestic front it now demanded the suppression of the social democrats, as the first step towards the abolition of party politics. It also adopted a fully fledged programme of antisemitism, peculiarly absurd in Finland, where

203

Jews are numbered in hundreds and are an utterly insignificant group. But *Aktivisti* claimed that the bolsheviks were financed and directed by international Jewry, and that bolshevism was essentially a Jewish ideology. In the realm of foreign affairs, the movement took up the extreme programme of AKS. In January 1931, *Aktivisti* published an article about the coming European crusade against Russia:

> When it comes – and it surely will come, it must come – then we can really create a greater Finland – then the day will come when Finland's eastern frontier is the Urals, and when Finland, as a great power, will be an important factor in world politics.

Through 1931, Svinhufvud and Lapua drifted apart. Svinhufvud's new government, and in particular its new Minister of the Interior, von Born, made a conscious effort to re-establish legal authority, though progress was slow, since Svinhufvud was keen to avoid any confrontation. The courts continued to show marked partiality to any Lapua defendants who appeared before them, and when, for instance, von Born ordered that the social democrat meeting house in Lapua should be restored to them, after it had been illegally seized by the activists, the Lapua leaders replied publicly, 'the building is closed and is staying closed'. The Minister had to give in, something of a stalemate was developing between the government and Lapua, and once more the movement was contemplating breaking it by resort to violence.

The decisive development was the emergence of General Wallenius, who in 1931, as soon as he was acquitted of the charges arising from the Ståhlberg kidnapping, was elected secretary of the Lapua movement. He found the presiding genius within the movement, now that the respectable backers were increasingly withdrawing, was Minna Craucher, who seems to have been a high-grade prostitute, with convictions for fraud, but a marked talent for persuading monied men to give funds for the cause. Wallenius found that under the Craucher régime, some half-baked plans for a *coup* had been formed, originally timed for November 1931. This sort of thing did not appeal to Wallenius' professional military mind, and he began a thorough shake-up of the movement which involved, as a first step, getting rid of Craucher, with whom a bitter feud developed. Then, once Wallenius was in control, he set about planning a real *coup*, in which the key role would be played by the SK under Lapua direction. When the time came, the Lapua leadership would call on the SK to mobilize and take over the country. At the same time the movement would demand the resignation of the government, and this would be facilitated by the *Kokoomus* ministers resigning at once. Then a government of national unity would be formed, but for this some figurehead was needed, for though Wallenius was willing to become prime minister himself, ideally he wanted Mannerheim to come forward as the supreme leader.

By December 1931, the knowledge of the coming *coup* was so widespread that the social democrats put down a question in parliament. The government replied that it was aware that secret preparations were being made, that money was being raised, and that there had been subversion of the SK and the army, but they were watching events, and did not believe there was any immediate danger. However, in his address to parliament at the beginning of 1932, Svinhufvud referred openly to the danger, and once more appealed for an end to violence and illegality.

The evidence suggests that Wallenius had been thinking of late February 1932 as a date for his *coup*, and it is likely that a meeting of the Lapua leaders in Hämeenlinna, set for the last week in February, was connected with this. Then on 11 February Craucher intervened when she went to the authorities and told them about the projected operation, supplying some convincing supporting evidence. Wallenius' reaction seems to have been to postpone everything, but for some reason, part of the original plan went off on schedule.

The occasion for the rising was to have been a meeting held at Mäntsälä by a leading social democrat, M. Erich. Mäntsälä was well placed for a *coup*, being a small country town close to the capital, a convenient jumping-off place for a march on Helsinki. The local Lapua leaders and the SK had demanded that the authorities should forbid Erich's meeting, and von Born, recognizing a challenge, refused and ordered the police to give the meeting protection. On the evening of 27 February, a crowd of about 400 men, mostly local SK with their weapons, surrounded the meeting place, fired shots, defied police orders to disperse, and then took over the town. As soon as he heard the news, Wallenius hurried down from Pohjanmaa with 200 armed men, and at first clearly tried to persuade the Mäntsälä men that they had mistimed it, but then realized that it was too late to draw back, for already the local SK units were mobilizing and drifting into the town. So he put out a proclamation in the name of the men who had gathered at Mäntsälä, in which they demanded an end to all marxist activity, and the dismissal of von Born. The proclamation concluded:

Marxism must be put down or else we shall first destroy the government and its representatives who are protecting it. The government can send its police to suppress us, but we shall meet them with arms in hand, ready for victory or death.

Thus Wallenius challenged the government to a trial of strength, and the government accepted the challenge. The army commander, General Sihvo, was confident of the loyalty of his troops, and the government ordered him to draw a cordon between Mäntsälä and the capital.

The next day, 29 February, the leaders of the Lapua movement officially endorsed the revolt, and issued an ultimatum to the government in Kosola's name, demanding its immediate resignation and the adoption of new policies – otherwise they would not answer for the consequences. At the same time the leadership moved to Mäntsälä and called their supporters to take arms. But it was at once apparent how they had been caught off-balance, for their plan went off at half-cock. Only part of the SK answered the call, some six thousand assembled at Mäntsälä, and in one or two places – of which Jyväskylä, an important communications centre in the middle of Finland, was the most significant – the local SK took over the functions of government, closed down the local social democratic organs and press, and arrested those who protested – but the general take-over of the provinces that had been planned failed to materialize. Similarly the *Kokoomus* ministers in the government were caught unprepared, and they split; two obediently resigned when Kosola issued his call, but the other two stuck with their colleagues. This helped the government to stand firm, and they answered Kosola by declaring the Mäntsälä gathering an insurrection, and ordering the arrest of the leaders. Svinhufvud, however, seems to have been less keen on a showdown, and was busy trying to negotiate a settlement. During 1 and 2 March he discussed with the rebels the possibility of forming a government under Wallenius and the suppression of the social democrats, to which he personally had no objection, but only if Mannerheim would come forward as a national leader. Mannerheim was willing to see a new government formed, but declined to be personally identified with it. Then his friend Walden was sounded, but he, as always, would go no further than Mannerheim.

So, on 2 March, Svinhufvud threw in his lot with his ministers and resolved on suppression. He issued a proclamation taking over command of all armed forces, including the sk, and ordered all sk members to return home, promising legal immunity for them if they obeyed. Malmberg, the elected commander of the sk, refused to read the order over the radio, so Svinhufvud broadcast it himself, and it seems to have been an impressive performance and gave the death blow to the revolt. He induced Martti Pihkala to go to Jyväskylä and persuade the rebels there to give up, which he did by reading them a stern lecture on discipline and respect for constituted authority. On his return he sent in a bill to the government: 'To suppressing one revolt – 1000 marks.'

The leaders at Mäntsälä now perceived that the game was up. They were faced by a determined government which had retained the allegiance of the army and regained that of the sk, whose planned rising had been a total failure, while Mannerheim and Walden had done a Pontius Pilate act on them, and refused to endorse the movement as they had done in 1930. There was nothing left but to negotiate terms of surrender. This took until

207

6 March, when it was agreed that the rank-and-file could go home, but the outlawed leaders must surrender and stand trial. Thus the revolt ended without bloodshed, and in November 1932 legal proceedings were initiated against the chiefs of the rebellion, though they did not come to an actual public trial until 1934. Then they were adjudged guilty of aiding and abetting an insurrection and given very light prison sentences, two and a half years being the longest. The principals, Wallenius, Kosola, and twenty-three others were released with suspended sentences.

The summer of 1932 saw the Lapua movement give a few dying kicks. On 7 March, Craucher telephoned a newspaper and said that she had valuable testimony to give, but that her life was in danger. The editor warned the police, who afterwards said they had difficulty in finding her. When they did she had been murdered, and the assassin, when brought to trial, was adjudged insane, though he alleged he had been commissioned to do the job. The truth about the Craucher murder has not been established, but the Lapua leaders certainly had strong incentives for silencing her.

There were other incidents; a revolt by the local SK in Sääksjärvi in the summer was serious enough to cause Svinhufvud to use his emergency powers, and in July there was a plot to kidnap several ministers, call out the SK, force Svinhufvud to release the Lapua leaders and let them form a government. The plot was betrayed and hastily cancelled, but one part went off when armed men broke into the house of the Minister of Defence, Lahdensuo. He defended himself with a revolver, and the attackers fled, leaving him unharmed.

It was clear that the government would proceed to suppress the Lapua movement by having it declared an illegal organization, and to forestall this it was decided to form a new, overtly political party. The founding congress was held on 5 June 1932, and it took the name of *Isänmaallinen Kansanliike* – Patriotic National Movement – commonly referred to as the IKL. The programme of the party says quite explicitly that it adheres to the aim of the Lapua movement, and in fact the leadership was simply transferred, though since Kosola was in prison, the chairmanship was to be kept for him on release. But most of the leaders of the new party had in fact been implicated in the Mäntsälä revolt, the most prominent being B. Salmiala, and the priest V. Annala. The IKL developed into a proper fascist party, it adopted a blackshirt uniform, blue-black banners, and organized a uniformed youth movement, the *Sinimustat* – Blue-blacks – who were trained for physical combat. The main planks in the programme remained suppression of the social democrats, anti-semitism, an end to party politics, hostility to the Swedish-language minority, and a chauvinist foreign policy. At first the party fought elections in alliance with the *Kokoomus*, and in their first election, in 1933, they won fourteen seats.

Despite the formal disbanding of the Lapua movement, the forces that had backed it were still strong. They succeeded in having their revenge on General Sihvo, whose firm conduct had done more than anything to defeat them, much to the disgust of many fellow officers. A campaign was mounted questioning his professional competence, and his enemies got the ear of Svinhufvud, who agreed to Sihvo's dismissal, without bothering to consult his ministers. There was a public outcry, and the government had to negotiate Sihvo's resignation and find him a face-saving job as inspector-general.

Even so, in retrospect, it is clear that the Mäntsälä revolt was the beginning of the end for the fascist movement in Finland – it had made its bid for power and failed. The reasons for this failure are partly tactical: the *coup* went off prematurely, and forced the Lapua leadership into hasty improvization. Once the SK failed to rise, and the army stood by the government, there was no chance of a takeover by force. But there were deeper reasons for the failure at Mäntsälä. The movement had been betrayed by its original sponsors. What had guaranteed success in 1930, and was fatal in 1932, was the change in the attitude of the grandees of the Right, the men of 1918, like Mannerheim, Svinhufvud and Walden, men with sufficient stature nationally to make a Lapua régime credible if they chose to endorse it. Their ambiguity and reticence in 1932 killed the revolt, just as

209

their endorsement, making Lapua the legitimate heir of the White movement of 1918, would have saved it. Without the chieftains of 1918, Lapua could not be the truly national movement which it had claimed to be, and had to opt for the alternative role of a political party on the right wing of the *Kokoomus*, and bolster this up by borrowings from the international fascist movement. This is the significance of the transformation into the IKL. The grandees had used the Lapua movement in 1930 when it suited their purposes and helped them to re-establish their authority; they broke it in 1932 when it presumed to challenge the way in which they were exercising it.

In the history of Finnish internal politics, 1932 was a decisive turning point. In December, a new government was formed under professor T.M.Kivimäki, which was the longest lived, and the strongest government in the republic's history. Its advent coincided with the beginnings of economic recovery. Both agricultural and industrial production began to rise, unemployment fell to a tolerable level, and the government, with the aid of orthodox economic and financial programmes, presided competently over the economic revival, so that Finland became the famous country which paid its debts. The government was helped by an advantageous parliamentary position, for after the Mäntsälä affair it stood committed to bringing the fascists under control, and it was clear that only its success in this stood between the social democrats and their probable repression by an anti-parliamentary régime. Therefore, although the *Kokoomus* was in opposition after Mäntsälä, Kivimäki had the tacit support of the social democrats, and his parliamentary position was probably stronger than that of any preceding government.

The threat of violence was still very much present in 1933, an election year in Finland. On one side the IKL was demanding the suppression of the social democrats, on the other the latter were demanding the putting down of the IKL and a drastic reform of the SK. The Kivimäki government was seriously considering taking legal proceedings for the suppression of IKL but finally decided against it, so sporadic violence and brawling between the IKL and the socialists continued to disturb public

210

life; but the government kept it within tolerable limits, in the belief that the situation would gradually improve of itself.

This view proved to be correct, and a major factor was a growing rift between the IKL and the *Kokoomus*. After the 1933 election, in which the IKL got its fourteen seats in parliament, it broke its electoral alliance with the *Kokoomus* Party, and its deputies acted as an independent political group; as they indulged in ever-growing extremist behaviour, based on the worst European models, their respectable bourgeois allies increasingly drew back from defilement. The fourteen deputies caused a sensation early in the new parliament when they all appeared wearing blackshirt uniforms, and proceeded to outrage their fellow deputies by provocative and unparliamentary behaviour, accompanied by an extremism of abuse and vilification in their speeches that caused deep offence. The IKL spokesmen declared that when they took power, the professional politicians would be put out of business, and if necessary behind barbed wire; they affirmed that hatred and violence would continue until the party system was smashed; they told the Minister of Justice, in a parliamentary debate, that he would end his days shovelling dirt (a euphemistic translation) in a concentration camp. Since the general tone of Finnish public life tended to be rather Victorian, particularly in conservative circles, this kind of behaviour was deeply offensive, and it was significant that in 1933 the *Kokoomus* elected as its chairman J. K. Paasikivi, a moderate and realistic politician, who led an active campaign to bring the *Kokoomus* back unambiguously into the constitutional camp. By 1936 his efforts had succeeded, the *Kokoomus*, the voice of big business and finance, had broken completely with the IKL, and ended its flirtation with policies of direct action. It still opposed any move to suppress IKL, still grumbled furiously about the weaknesses of the democratic system, about the failure to re-arm, and still wanted a foreign policy friendly to Hitler's Germany, but it had at last accepted as inevitable the parliamentary republic.

In 1934 the government took two major steps to restrain political extremism, the first of which was a new law against groundless incitement. Under this law, propaganda which brought the government or constitution into contempt or offended morals or common decency, could be suppressed, and with its aid some of the more irresponsible IKL publications were temporarily suspended. The second measure was the so-called 'shirt law', which forbade the wearing of unauthorized uniforms in public, and declared private uniformed organizations illegal. The IKL, and especially its young activists in the *Sinimustat*, persistently defied this law, and further embarrassed the government by becoming involved in a fascist *coup* in Estonia in 1935, so that although the authorities were now displaying a new firmness and determination, the IKL got away with a lot of minor infringements of the law. This may have helped to give them, and others, an exaggerated impression of their real strength, so that the elections of 1936 came as a real shock.

In this election, Finland had its own version of a popular front, an electoral alliance between the social democrats and the agrarians on a programme of safeguarding democracy and social reform. Although the IKL held its fourteen seats, the new allies dominated parliament, and a very reluctant Svinhufvud had to see the Kivimäki government toppled, and a strong coalition of the Left installed. In the following year the new alliance put forward the Agrarian Kallio against Svinhufvud in the presidential election and won. Svinhufvud had to retire into private life. The new régime was now ready to hit back at the fascists; in 1938 they got a court order dissolving the *Sinimustat*, which was promptly re-formed as the Blackshirts. In November 1938, legal proceedings were begun against the IKL itself, on the grounds that it had continually acted illegally and that it was in fact a continuation of the condemned Lapua movement. The case was decided in the High Court in May 1939, when the court ruled that although the IKL had undoubtedly been guilty of illegalities, these were not sufficient to warrant suppression. The government then began appeal proceedings, but these were still pending when war broke out, and were allowed to lapse.

Even so, there is every sign that after 1936 the Finnish fascists were in decline. It is true that there was in Finland a widespread welcome for the revival of German power under Hitler, but this was mostly based on old-fashioned balance-of-power considerations; the business community had a lot of trouble and unpleasantness in arranging trade with Hitler's Germany, and even on the Right it was commonly asserted that good relations with Germany in no way implied acceptance of Hitler's ideology. The most direct echo of Nazism was to be found in the Swedish-language minority, cut off from the IKL by the language issue. There, a few extremists perceived that the Swedish-language Finns might qualify as Aryans, and that in this way Nazism could offer some compensation for their minority status. Men like C.A. Gadolin, with his periodical *Svensk Botten*, became outspoken admirers of Hitler and the Axis, but even within their own community they were a lunatic fringe.

In fact the success of the Kivimäki government, the economic recovery and the democratic victory in the elections of 1936 and 1937, which readmitted the social democrats to a full place in public life, had at last secured and made viable the parliamentary republic. Mannerheim reflected this changed situation by adapting his own position to it; he now became an advocate of national conciliation, and even entered into relations with the social democratic leaders. With the communists still firmly suppressed, Finland in 1939 was a model of prosperity and stability, and it is no surprise that IKL support slumped in the election of 1939, when they were cut down to eight seats in parliament.

When the war came, it dealt the fascists a further cruel blow. For in the Winter War, the long awaited showdown with the bolshevik enemy, Finland's main sources of outside support were democratic Sweden, France, and Britain, while Nazi Germany was virtually the ally of the Soviet Union. Mussolini was friendly, but in no position to help. The Finnish Right, building on the national tradition of pro-Germanism, had always found it easier to put over Hitler as a model than Mussolini, and their sense of betrayal in the Winter War was traumatic. The IKL virtually lapsed into inactivity, and hid itself for shame.

However, with Hitler's triumphant conquests in 1940, and the

213

rapprochement between Finland and Germany which became evident after August 1940, fascist morale began to recover. A symptom of this was the emergence of new fascist groupings, which appeared against the background of a growing debate on Finland's place in the Axis New Order in Europe. They tended to argue that if Finland wanted a worthy place in the New Order, she should adapt her institutions to the prevailing ideologies.

Among these groups there appeared a Finnish National Socialist Party, which was a straightforward copy of the German model, and ran quite a considerable press campaign in the autumn of 1940, but seems to have had a minimal response. Other groups propagated a specifically Scandinavian brand of totalitarianism; such were Teo Snellman's *Vapaa Suomi* – Free Finland – group, and Räikkänen's *Gustav Vasa* movement which projected the great Swedish king as a prototype Hitler. None of these new groups seems to have represented much more than a few enthusiasts grouped round a periodical, their political influence was insignificant, and was commonly dismissed as such in the official press, for the government tended to frown on them as disturbers of national unity.

In October 1940, the IKL organized a congress, inevitably at Lapua, for all groups sympathetic to the New Order in Europe, and succeeded in drawing up a manifesto, calling on the country to prepare itself to take its place in the new Europe then being born. But this attempt to form a common front of totalitarian parties was a feeble gesture, there was no real substance behind it, and the official press brushed it off as empty posturing. Soon after this the IKL lost its freedom of action when, in January 1941, it agreed to enter a new coalition government of national unity. One of the leaders, the Lutheran pastor Annala, became a minister, but there was a price to be paid. The IKL had to agree to stop its attacks on the social democrats and the parliamentary system, which in effect muzzled it, and deprived it of most of its *raison d'être*.

Naturally, when Hitler attacked the Soviet Union in 1941, and Finland joined in, new vistas seemed to open for the fascists. Briefly it appeared as though the dream of *Suur-Suomi* was going to be realized under Hitler's patronage, and much of the energy and propaganda of the IKL concentrated on this theme. Its spokesmen became as bold in their claims as the official censorship would permit, but it was a last moment of triumph, and by 1942 it was clear it had been as illusory as the earlier ones. It is significant that when the Germans were recruiting the Finnish SS Battalion in 1941, although individual members of IKL were involved, the movement as such played no part, and there seems to have been no official contact between it and the German Nazi Party. Indeed, the weakness of Finnish fascism in the 1940s can perhaps best be illustrated by what happened when Ribbentrop flew to Helsinki in June 1944, to stop Finland from making a separate peace with Russia. In the car from the airport he asked the German ambassador if there were not even a few hundred dedicated Finnish fascists who might be used for a pro-German *coup*. The ambassador had to confess that he doubted if there were any at all.

With the provisional peace treaty of September 1944 the development of Finnish fascism came to a full stop, since article eight of the peace treaty requires Finland to dissolve all fascist organizations, and prevent their being re-established. Under this clause, the IKL, the smaller totalitarian groups, the AKS, and above all the SK, were dissolved. It would be rash to assert that the spirit which lay behind these movements has entirely disappeared in Finland even today, but as a political force the movement which came so near to success in the early 1930s is dead.

When we look back on the history of the Finnish fascist movement, it seems clear that it owed its strength to its local, native roots. History and geography had combined to produce a Soviet Russia which embodied both a national and ideological enemy, and also, through the civil war in Finland, forces in the country ready to respond to the double challenge. By contrast with these factors, ideological fascism, a remote and foreign phenomenon, seems to have been of marginal significance. As long as the Lapua movement was solidly based on the tradition of the activists and White Guards of 1918, and could plausibly represent

215

itself as their direct successor, it was powerful, but when, as the IKL, it became more and more openly identified with the ideas and practices of international fascism, its strength ebbed, and even the triumph of Hitler in Europe did not produce any significant revival in Finland. Just as many Finns in the thirties and forties were pro-German without being Nazi, so they could admire the idea of strong anti-communist government without being fascists. The Finnish fascist movement arose as a genuine response to a communist threat that was no figment of the imagination, but a real force with its centre of power tantalizingly close, but untouchable, just over the frontier. But once this menace had manifestly been brought under control, the impulse behind the movement weakened, and the borrowed trappings of international fascism, which the movement came to adopt, were left as an increasingly empty shell, a façade with nothing very substantial behind it.

10 Norway

T. K. Derry

About a fortnight before his execution, the Norwegian fascist leader, Vidkun Quisling, gave the following answer to a private visitor's inquiry about his relations with Hitler. 'You must not misunderstand me if I express myself plainly. I was the leader of a small people in a weak country. In power politics I was dependent upon Germany and Adolf Hitler, but in political ideas I regarded Hitler as my subordinate and my instrument.' Thus Quisling to the very end saw himself in the centre of the scene. And even now history has not reduced him to his true dimensions. In 1940 his name provided a heaven-sent alternative for the clumsy term, 'fifth-columnist': within a week of the German invasion of Norway *The Times* led the way with an item about 'quislings everywhere'. In 1964 a 'Life', in which he was portrayed as a 'prophet without honour', received a degree of attention never accorded to any serious study of Norwegian politics. But to understand fascism in Norway, it is first necessary for us to try to understand Norway.

In the first place, we have to do with a very small people of three millions spread over a territory as large as the British Isles. Parliamentary government dates back to the much venerated constitution set up on 17 May 1814, which is associated with the separation from Denmark in that year; a triumphant nationalism found further expression in the dethronement in 1905 of the House of Bernadotte, which for ninety years had been kings of Norway as well as Sweden. The completely independent Norway of the early twentieth century was, however, a country without any wide political ambitions – neutral in the first world war; an early and enthusiastic member of the League of Nations, where their national hero, Fridtjof Nansen, figured as the spokesman of humanity rather than of any narrowly Norwegian cause; more than content with its position in what was often advertised during the 1930s as the 'peaceful corner of Europe'.

At the same time, it should be noticed that the social and economic structure of this small people, while broadly resembling that of its west European neighbours, had two special features. One was the entire absence of any territorial nobility or even aristocracy, comparable to the great landed families which influenced political development elsewhere, for better or worse. The other was the belated onset of the industrial revolution, for Norway had no coal but abundant sources of hydro-electricity. The growth of machine industry after 1900 brought a rising standard of living to a country which always depended upon imported foodstuffs for its well-being. But it also brought about the uprooting of a part of the rural population, the growth of a navvy class, and some spasms of the social malaise which had been so widely characteristic of English life a hundred years earlier. Accordingly Norway, which lacked so many other prerequisites for fascist movements, was affected very rapidly by the influences of the Russian revolution. In 1918, when the rest of the world was at war, soviets of workers, and in a few cases of soldiers, made a temporary appearance. In 1919–21 the Norwegian Labour Party was the only one in western Europe which adhered firmly to the Comintern.

Against this background we may now attempt to delineate the features of a rather shadowy fascist movement as it existed in Norway down to the second world war. The foreign influences, from which much of its ideology was naturally derived, seem to have been German rather than Italian. Apart from vaguely eulogistic references to Mussolini as a strong man who had put down strikes and established social harmony, a single Oslo newspaper, *Tidens Tegn*, was the only regular source of propaganda favourable to the new developments in a country with which Norway's ties were not particularly close. Germany, on the other hand, had a language and literature with which many

Norwegians were familiar, and an educational system on which theirs was in many respects modelled. Visits of Nazi propagandists to Norway can be traced even before Hitler's accession to power, and the converse is also true – Quisling's leading associates included men who had been frequent visitors to National Socialist Germany.

One example is A.V.Hagelin, who joined Quisling in 1936 and was Minister of the Interior in his wartime régime; he had spent twenty years in business, chiefly in Dresden. Another is his adviser on points of law, a philosopher of rather modest attainments, named Herman Harris Aall. He had steeped his pen in anti-British sentiments as early as the first world war, and by 1939 was in receipt of a considerable subsidy from Berlin for an office in south Sweden, from which he was to spread a very tenuous doctrine which he called social individualism. This has been represented as Admiral Canaris' counterblast to national socialism, designed to sweep through Scandinavia first and afterwards to blow Hitler himself from his perch. But Aall was active in keeping Quisling's name before his German masters, and was in due course promoted by him from the forlorn hope in Sweden to a chair of jurisprudence in Oslo University.

Among native sources of fascism we may name first the disrepute into which parliamentary government for a time fell through its structural weaknesses. Down to the end of the first world war a system of single-member constituencies was used, which in 1918 – the year when events in Russia had roused great expectations among Labour supporters – produced a paradoxical electoral result. With an increase of votes cast in its favour, the Labour Party received one fewer seat than after the previous triennial election. Moreover, their total representation was fifteen, as compared with fifty-one seats secured by the government party (Liberal) for about the same number of votes. The inevitable sequel was the adoption of proportional representation, under which no party secured a majority at any election. In a country where the members of the legislature are strictly representative of their locality; where members of the government, on the other hand, may be chosen by the prime minister from outside the ranks of the legislature (in which they sit and speak but do not vote); and where parliamentary discords are not held in check by any power of dissolution – durable coalitions were hard to construct or maintain. Accordingly, we must picture a series of minority governments, with limited resources in personnel and still more in voting power, struggling to tackle the problems – especially the overwhelming economic problems – of the interwar period.

A programme of direct action had a considerable appeal to the peasants of the big valleys of eastern Norway, who were very hard hit by the fall in prices of farm products, especially the timber from which a third of their profits came. In the 1920s a newly formed Agrarian Party campaigned with much more outspoken bitterness than the conservatives against the growth of trade unionism as a new and highly unwelcome intruder on the rural scene. It championed Norway's ancient claims in Greenland – ultimately disallowed by the Hague Court – with a romantic enthusiasm suggestive of *mare nostrum*. When the party held office in 1931–3, and still more after its fall, when some of its leaders considered the possibility of forming a new government which would try to rule in defiance of the parliamentary majority, its tone was very like that of the openly unconstitutional Lapua movement among the farmers of Finland. It seems significant that the former Agrarian prime minister was to receive a ten-year sentence for collaboration during the German occupation of Norway.

As regards the industrial situation, many of the factors which might stimulate the growth of fascism in Norway were the same as elsewhere. Although the Labour Party definitively broke with Moscow in 1923, when the communist minority set up a party of their own, its aims were still in principle revolutionary. When King Haakon in 1928, because of its electoral success, called upon it to form a minority government, a genuine run on the banks was one main factor in its overthrow after only eighteen days in office. In 1919–31 Norway, like many other countries, suffered from a series of big strikes and lockouts, in which the feelings of the workers were aroused against the 'bourgeois state' by the use of the law to enforce contracts and, more especially, to protect strike-breakers from violence. The bourgeoisie, for its part, never forgot the earlier link between the Labour Party and the Comintern, and believed all the more firmly in the nefarious activities of 'Red Guards' because they were hard to trace.

But in two respects at least, Norwegian society may be regarded as particularly vulnerable. Having been a poor country for so long, she lacked strongly based and highly developed credit institutions: the already mentioned occasion in 1928 was only one of several when the collapse of the currency might easily have been precipitated. At the same time, and partly for the same reason, the forces for the maintenance of law and order were very thin on the ground. In 1931, for example, a single riot (at Menstad) was held by the Minister of Justice to have rendered the State Police for the time being useless. His private calculation was that he had only 620 soldiers with whom if necessary to supplement the Oslo police force; beyond this, he would have to depend on all the uncertainties of a call-up of army conscripts.

The earliest organization, in which some features of fascism made a tentative appearance, was an anti-strike weapon called *Samfundshjelp*, which in 1920 began to solicit support from banks and employers' associations. While its main activity was to protect the public against the withdrawal of essential services, it also acted to some extent as a police reserve and, in one or two towns at least, a part of the membership was recruited and trained as a para-military force. Its presiding genius was a cavalry colonel. But since no threatened marxist *coup* ever caused this organization to demonstrate its true strength, which remains therefore highly conjectural, for the present purpose perhaps the most interesting feature of *Samfundshjelp* was its membership from 1921 to 1930 of the institution in Switzerland sometimes known as the 'international anti-comintern entente'.

From a political standpoint, however, more weight should be attached to the establishment in 1925 of the 'non-party', but definitely anti-marxist, *Fedrelandslag* or League of the Fatherland.

221

Its founders included Christian Michelsen, the Grand Old Man of Norwegian political life, who as Prime Minister twenty years before had successfully broken the tie with Sweden. And its early members included Nansen, who (with the possible exception of his fellow-explorer Amundsen) was the only Norwegian citizen with an international renown. If they had lived longer – they died in 1925 and 1930 respectively – it is possible that the new society's widespread propaganda for stronger government and a united front against the Red Peril would have had important results. In 1930 it had 412 local branches, whose total membership was alleged to exceed 100,000, fed upon a diet of nationalist sentiment, proposals to increase the defence budget, and a general demand for more effective national leadership. But in the later 1930s the movement lost ground, partly at least because its weekly, *ABC* (Anti-Bolshevik Clubs), combined its championship of the corporative state with an undiscriminating enthusiasm for the Hitler régime in Germany.

In March 1931, another ingredient in the ideology of fascism can be traced in Norway in the *Nordisk Folkereisning*, a society which was to preach the superiority of the Nordic race, pointing to the Scandinavian founders of the Russian state as a convincing and significant illustration of the dogma. The movement was virtually stillborn, for within two months its leader obtained office, re-emerging from the tasks of government two years later with schemes for a much larger and more definitely fascist organization. That leader was a Major Vidkun Quisling, who gave a new stamp to an already existing Norwegian fascism.

A brief reference to his earlier career may justify the claim that Quisling was a fascist leader *sui generis*. Four centuries of respectable and unadventurous ancestors; an upbringing in a quiet country vicarage; academic ambitions always crowned with success; patriotic enthusiasm determining the choice of a military career; and a passing-out examination from the military high school with the highest marks achieved in the century or more of its existence. In 1911, at the age of twenty-four, this exceptionally promising officer entered the General Staff, where he was allotted Russia as his special field of study, which in turn gave him three very different openings. In 1918 and in 1920–1 he served for short periods as military attaché in Petrograd and Helsinki, and for a rather longer period in 1927–9 as a Norwegian Legation official looking after British interests in Moscow – for which he received an honorary CBE. In the second place, his familiarity with Russian conditions brought him two appointments under Nansen in his relief work and a third, directly under the League of Nations, for a similar purpose. Finally, for nearly four years (1926–9) Quisling had a private business job in Russia, in connection with a north Russian timber concession operated by a fellow-Norwegian, Frederik Prytz.

But in spite of these promising beginnings, Quisling came to look upon society with the sense of personal grievance which lay at the root of so much fascist leadership. One turning-point was his decision to stay on in Russia in 1923, when he was refused further leave from his duties as an officer of the General Staff. This effectively blocked his military career, with the result that, finding himself temporarily without employment, in the winter of 1924–5 he compromised his political integrity by an attempt to induce politicians of the extreme Left to employ him as an organizer of Red Guards in Norway.

The other turning-point was his experience in 1931–3, when the Agrarian Party, holding office for the first time, short of military connections, attracted by Quisling's racial views, and welcoming his supposed expertise in international relations, appointed him as their Minister of Defence. For this unexpected chance in a position of authority under a parliamentary régime revealed all too clearly that the gifts of absorption and application which had made him a distinguished examinee and a successful attaché were not coupled with gifts of political management, either in his own department of defence or in cabinet discussions or in parliamentary debate. Quisling achieved nothing for his country's defences, which were in a parlous condition; the second of the two prime ministers under whom he served longed to extrude him from his government; and his freely flung accusations of treason made him anathema

223

to the Labour Party whose supposed interests he had once offered to serve. By March 1933, when the Agrarians lost office, he had been proved to be a liability rather than an asset to any democratic political party.

Two months later, Quisling re-emerged at the head of a new party, *Nasjonal Samling*, the National Unity movement, based on the leadership principle – with himself as leader. In considering how this could happen, it is important to bear in mind that the notion of some kind of anti-marxist crusade was congenial to some persons of influence, as had been made clear to Quisling at social gatherings. In such circles the hatred shown by the Labour Party made Quisling something of a hero, especially as the deployment of military and naval units after the Menstad riot was erroneously supposed to have been initiated by him in his capacity as Defence Minister. Moreover, Quisling's propaganda could combine in a kind of cloudy rhetoric a number of ideas of varying appeal.

Mention has already been made of the Nordic race myth, which he seems to have imbibed from Prytz during their business association in Russia. This had been developed in Quisling's book, *Russia and Ourselves*, of which an English translation was published by Hodder and Stoughton in 1932. The curious may find there a full exposition of the anti-communist theme, which he was accustomed to develop in his attacks on Labour. By this time he had also appropriated part of the doctrine of the corporative state, proposing to reduce the power of the Norwegian parliament by superimposing a House of Corporations representative of economic interests. Since 1933 was the year of Hitler's triumph, it is hardly necessary to add that the example of a new era in Germany was freely quoted. But for an English audience it is important to notice that, ever since the death of Nansen three years before, Quisling had built upon his association with Nansen in his Russian relief work – which was never as personal and intimate as he claimed – to represent himself as the heir to that great man's ideas and leadership. He had never dared to suggest this in Nansen's lifetime, and while there may have been some effect on the ignorant, Nansen's friends were outraged.

224

Its original backers looked to *Nasjonal Samling* to establish its influence initially at the polls, and in this it failed signally. The system of proportional representation offered a slender chance to a new party. NS did its best to form electoral alliances, most notably with a direct-action movement among the smaller peasantry, which employed a system of boycotting reminiscent of the Irish Land League in order to prevent forced sales of mortgaged farm property. But the failure of NS was quite over-whelming. In the general election of 1933 they secured 2·2 per cent of votes, which gave them no seats, and next year their participation in local elections yielded only twenty-eight places in the local councils of the entire country. By 1935 the movement had 15,000 members and a network of nine papers (mostly weeklies), but in the following general election their vote showed an absolute numerical decline of 1200 and a percentage reduc-tion of 0·4 per cent. In 1937 the local elections witnessed a final rout, for only seven seats were left in their possession. By this time influential backers had deserted *en masse*, and when the European war broke out two years later Quisling was a dis-credited leader, supported by a handful of personal associates and a minimal following confined to particular districts, and totally lacking the financial resources for any further nation-wide propaganda.

In at least two respects Quisling's failure resembles that of Sir Oswald Mosley. Returning prosperity made the conflict between capital and labour less menacing, so that extreme solutions were no longer called for. At the same time, some inkling of the savageries perpetrated by German fascists against political opponents and the Jews was penetrating into other countries, and made the shortcomings of democracy seem comparatively trivial. The acceptance of a planned economy by all important parliamentary parties was also a stabilizing influence in both countries. But in Norway particular importance attaches to the ending of the long period of political uncertainty in 1935, when the second labour government abandoned the last vestiges of its revolutionary traditions and formed an alliance with the agrarians. Bartering support for farm prices and a tax system

225

which favoured farm interests for acceptance of a not too advanced socialist programme in industrial life, the Labour Party secured a parliamentary majority. This was confirmed by the 1936 election, and when the Germans invaded Norway in 1940 the Labour government was in its seventh uninterrupted year of office.

We must now turn to consider the national characteristics of fascism in wartime Norway. During the seven months of Norwegian neutrality Quisling was almost a one-man fifth column. Having so largely lost his basis of domestic support, he built eagerly upon his earlier, rather tenuous associations with the Germans. His motive at the outset was not, in all probability, purely selfish: it was not irrational for him to believe that the Norwegian government was playing into the hands of the Allies, especially the British, and he may even have imagined quite genuinely that there was some secret agreement for letting them into the country. With that degree of self-justification he contacted in succession Rosenberg, Raeder, and Hitler himself, trying in vain to put over the idea of a political *coup* in Norway, to be engineered by him with German support. The pretext was to be the alleged unconstitutionality of parliament in sitting for a fourth year under a law which it had itself passed substituting quadrennial for triennial elections. But the Germans were more interested in the size and determination of his following, of which he was unable to present a convincing picture.

In the New Year Quisling's visit to Hitler was rewarded by a subsidy, which enabled him to revive his party propaganda. But the German decision to forestall a hypothetical Allied landing by an invasion of Norway was kept a close secret. Six days before it took place, a German staff officer interrogated him in Copenhagen about the state of Norwegian defences; but even then it is unlikely that he was told anything, though he may have guessed a lot. Neither the army commander nor the German minister in Oslo had any instructions to co-ordinate the invasion with a Quisling *coup*. But on the fateful morning of 9 April 1940, the representatives of Raeder and Rosenberg in the Norwegian capital made immediate contact with him, enabling the power vacuum, created by the precipitate withdrawal of the government to avoid capture, to be used to his advantage. With their help Quisling was able by the same evening to broadcast the news that he had formed a government of his party supporters in friendly relations with the Germans. Several of his fellow 'ministers' refused to join him in his act of treachery, but Hitler approved the *fait accompli*. Thus the war situation gave new life to a thoroughly discredited fascist leader and a party which had long been on the verge of extinction.

The immediate consequence was the embitterment of Norwegian feeling by this stab in the back, which predisposed the king and the lawful government to continue what seemed to be a rather hopeless effort of military resistance. After a week the Germans dismissed Quisling from office in a belated and unsuccessful attempt at pacification. At the end of their two months' campaign, with the whole country under their military control, the Germans further explored the possibility of doing a deal with representatives of the regular political parties, while reserving some share of authority for Quisling's NS as the party which was both in ideology and in interest firmly tied to their own fortunes. But in mid-September 1940, when Britain's chances of survival were beginning to improve, the other Norwegian parties escaped from an agreement which they saw would give increasing power to Quisling, and were immediately banned.

For the remaining four and a half years of war *Nasjonal Samling*, with Quisling as its highly publicized Leader, held office under the Germans; at first they were on a kind of probation, but in February 1942 Quisling was given formal authority as Minister-President. Neither the German army commander nor the civilian Reichscommissar, Terboven, regarded him as competent or his party as a worthwhile ally; but as long as Quisling kept within the limits of authority which Hitler thought him fit for, it was too dangerous an undertaking for any German to try once more to dislodge him. Thus within certain limits we can speak of a native fascism let loose in wartime Norway. Yet it must never be forgotten that what we are examining was a strictly subordinate régime, quite unable to achieve the change

227

of status which Quisling most desired, namely, the termination of military occupation through the negotiation of a peace treaty with Germany.

But to find the national characteristics of this fascism is not easy. It was, almost by definition, anti-British and pro-German, but only its anti-Russian gestures appear to have been to any large extent spontaneous. About five thousand Norwegians were recruited for service on the eastern front – about one-eighth of the number of loyalists secretly in training for their own war of liberation – and propaganda about the peril to Europe from the east was fairly well received. The same cannot be said about anti-Jewish propaganda, to which Quisling gave special support in an address at Frankfurt in March 1941. Though at that time he professed to be advocating their removal to a place of settlement outside Europe, the support which he and his party subsequently gave to the rounding-up of the Norwegian Jews for deportation to German concentration camps has always been regarded by the Norwegian people in general as one of the very darkest stains on their record. Many risked their lives in bringing a substantial proportion of Jewish families across the border to safety in Sweden.

It is possible that there was some element of genuine national appeal in the continuous vaunting of the superiority of Nordic man and the leadership principle over the parliamentary systems of the effete democracies. In most social groupings – the Church, the teaching profession, the trade unions, the sports clubs and so forth – the opposition to such ideas was very effective, but there are indications that local government institutions (under the control of Hagelin) were penetrated to a significant extent. The national romanticism fostered by the Agrarian Party had not lost its charm for the inhabitants of remote valleys, who shared Quisling's lifelong passion for the medieval sagas and were not always quick to see the absurdity in such pretences as the identification of his strong-arm men with the *hird* which attended the saga-kings.

Nasjonal Samling rose from a membership of about 7000 in 1939 to a maximum of 43,000 in November 1943, and they

228

represented only the hard core of collaborationism. In Norway as elsewhere, collaborationists, whether accepting a fascist party label or not, were influenced by a variety of non-ideological motives. In a small country, with a long history of subordination to foreign rulers, it was in any case tempting to accept the German 'New Order' in Europe as a fact, without feeling any personal obligation to examine the moral or political principles on which it might rest. A special incentive to do so was provided in some instances by personal disappointment over the failure of Britain to match promises with performance during the two months' campaign in 1940. More often it was provided by a deep-rooted appreciation of German culture, such as was felt by the novelist Hamsun or may be presumed in the scientist Skancke, Quisling's Minister of Education, who had been trained at Karlsruhe. And if collaboration in general meant a secure livelihood in difficult wartime conditions, party member-ship offered a career. Quisling himself had been almost without visible means of support; as 'Minister-President' he pocketed about £30,000 a year. Lesser men of course received lesser rewards, but a career in NS offered profit, power, and a spurious dignity to people normally left in obscurity: cranks, adventurers, social misfits, and occasionally sadists.

Since the picture just given must be broadly applicable to the wartime experience of many occupied territories, it may be desirable to inquire in conclusion whether there are any special features in the Norwegian treatment of the fascist problem when the war ended. Two points may perhaps be made. The trial and execution of Quisling attracted world-wide attention, partly because of the adventitious publicity attaching to his name; partly because of the enigma of his character (did any other major fascist leader end up by offering his services in the Church?); and partly perhaps because it preceded the trials at Nuremberg. Viewed in perspective, he seems a less significant figure than he did then – and by no means a representative Norwegian fascist. The other, possibly less familiar point is the thoroughness of the post-war investigations conducted by the Norwegian courts of law.

About 90,000 persons – more than twice the maximum membership of NS – had their actions during the occupation examined by the police. Of these, twenty-five were eventually executed, mainly for murder, torture, and aggravated acts of delation, Quisling being one of a total of no more than three persons whose death was exacted primarily as the price of high treason. But there were 18,000 prison sentences, of which one-fifth were for more than three years, and another 28,000 persons were fined or deprived of civil rights, which for many of them meant loss of employment. Making every allowance for subsequent acts of amnesty, this is a formidable total for a country of three million inhabitants. To some extent the explanation lies in the marked Norwegian respect for law, which very largely excluded private acts of vengeance but also made it impossible for known illegalities to be glossed over. A deeper explanation may, however, be tentatively suggested.

In 1940–5 the traditions of parliamentarism, nationalism, and neutralism, on which (as was said at the outset) pre-war Norwegian life was based, had all been outraged. Painful experience had shown the hazards to which the independence of a small country is exposed. One of those hazards was the existence of a political movement willing to collaborate with a potential enemy. However slight its native roots, however chequered its earlier history, and however limited its practical achievements as a treasonable institution had been, such a movement was bound to receive a punishment related to the unknown future. Unknown – but for Norwegians today, fascism appears to have been a temporary and rather trivial aberration of alien origins and character, while the consititution of 1814 remains the palladium of their national liberties.

11 Great Britain

R. Skidelsky

1 Introduction

British fascism was the personal creation of Sir Oswald Mosley. There had been a few fascist groups in the 1920s, created to counter the 'leftward' drift of English politics, but they had no significance and were virtually extinct by the early 1930s. Nor is it unlikely that a more powerful fascist movement would have developed in England in the 1930s without Mosley. But it would have been much less significant and much more 'crankish': in all likelihood, a bigger, noisier ancestor of Colin Jordan's present National Socialist Party, feasting exclusively on antisemitism.

For Mosley gave to the British Union of Fascists (BUF) his own prestige which, initially, was considerable, and which, throughout its existence, was to be its greatest single asset; his own seriousness of purpose, and, above all, his own economic policy which had been largely developed in the Labour Party. It was perhaps its possession of modern and relevant economic policy that chiefly distinguished the BUF from its continental counterparts. It was a child of the depression – not of military defeat, or of disappointed national aspirations. It arose because British parliamentary institutions showed themselves incapable, in that period, of coping with the economic problem. It is this fact that necessarily gives this essay its content and form. Mosley's own key role requires, first of all, some consideration of the man and his background. Next I will consider the economic and political problems which British fascism set out to solve. I will then discuss the New Party episode, before turning, more briefly, to the transition to fascism.

231

2 The Man

The salient facts of Mosley's career up to the time of his resignation from the Labour government in May 1930 are as follows. Born in 1896, the eldest son of a wealthy and prominent Staffordshire county family – his grandfather was the original of John Bull – he was educated at Winchester and Sandhurst. One of the earliest volunteers to the Royal Flying Corps, he was invalided out of the war in 1916. Elected MP for Harrow in 1918 on the Coalition Unionist ticket, he crossed the floor in 1920 in protest against the Black and Tans; in 1924 he joined the Labour Party. When Ramsay MacDonald formed his second Labour administration in 1929, Mosley, then thirty-three, was appointed Chancellor of the Duchy of Lancaster with special responsibilities for unemployment.

Certain features of this story help to explain Mosley's attitude to the problems of his time. Unlike Churchill, the young Mosley grew up in an entirely unpolitical atmosphere, comfortably remote from the great political controversies of his childhood – Free Trade versus Protection, Ireland, the 'Labour Question', the People's Budget. His interests were almost entirely sporting, as were those of the great mass of public schoolboys of that era. He entered parliament without the benefit of any political apprenticeship such as might have been afforded by growing up in an intensely political family or through the experience of local politics. It was a new, unexplored world.

It was a world, moreover, for which a training as a professional soldier was not the ideal preparation. Sandhurst, whatever its merits, did not provide an environment conducive to the development of any wide intellectual or philosophic interests such as would have been stimulated by university. It was designed to foster a capacity for leadership and obedience, rather than for compromise and tolerance of other's opinions; the rigid code of personal honour of the army officer was not well-attuned to the jockeying for position and the balancing of interests that characterize the normal operations of parliamentary democracy. The emphasis was on precision of aim and method, rather than on subtlety of analysis and flexibility of approach. In short, Mosley carried with him into parliament an aversion for 'politicking' which he was never able to overcome. He did not understand that pledges were made primarily to win votes and only secondarily to be carried out, that most people entered parliament because it was an acceptable career and not with any particular intention of doing anything, that the MP must necessarily place his own conscience in the service of his party.

Mosley's basic political attitudes were shaped by his experience of war between 1914 and 1918, both in the front line and in Whitehall where he found employment as a temporary civil servant in the Ministry of Munitions. That experience was the experience of the interventionist state. For, during the war, in response to the imperatives of national survival, the government took measures to control the economic life of the nation unthinkable in peacetime. Moreover, its intervention was pragmatic, not doctrinal: the response, in A.J.P.Taylor's words, of 'genius to the challenge of events'. Mosley did not bring to this experience any attachment to conventional, liberal, *laissez-faire* attitudes, any knowledge of the bitter industrial disputes momentarily transcended by the promptings of 'national solidarity', against which to judge and criticize wartime expedients. The interventionist state he took to be the norm, rather than the exception.

The complete contrast afforded by the return to *laissez-faire* in politics and economics, the experience of the 'hard faced' parliament of 1918, and the recrudescence, in accentuated form, of mass unemployment and industrial unrest, forced the young Mosley into hitherto unaccustomed speculation. He had taken Lloyd George's promise to build a land fit for heroes all too seriously, thinking its fulfilment required merely the adaptation of wartime controls of peacetime purposes. The abandonment wholesale of pledges given in the moment of victory, the cynical consignment of those who had survived the bloodbath of Flanders to the unemployment queues, thus provided his first concrete experience of parliamentary democracy. Why, he reasoned, if the state had provided full employment and rising wages in wartime, was it unable to do the same in peacetime?

The search for the solution occupied him for the rest of the decade. It involved him in a study of history and economics; it brought him into contact with Keynes, and others with similar preoccupations. But the point to note is his approach to the matter; first, the definition of the objective; secondly, the search for ways of achieving it. This approach, the product, perhaps, of a still undeveloped intellectual curiosity, did have one very important advantage: it enabled him to see the problem as essentially limited, not as a small part of a much vaster problem calling for grandiose and unobtainable solutions. It was the typical response of the field commander: a limited operation, with a limited goal, an approach that Popper has approvingly dubbed 'piecemeal social engineering'.

Of course, wider questions were not long in obtruding. The world, he saw, was beset with problems; everywhere one turned, one gained a sense of the extraordinary confusion and waste and disorder of human life. Yet at the same time advances in science and technology were giving man an unprecedented opportunity to control his environment, to mould events to his heart's desire. All that seemed to be required to create a prosperous world was the will to do so; the tools were all ready to hand.

This has much in common with Fabian thinking, especially as preached by the Webbs. The difference was that Mosley did not propose a generalized solution. His aim was always to mobilize his forces for a limited campaign: he did not aim at 'total victory' in the sense of a total transformation of society. If war is 'the pursuit of diplomacy by other means' Mosley's war aims never embraced 'unconditional surrender'. The enemy was too strong: the result would inevitably be a costly stalemate. A successful autumn offensive, followed by peace, was the sum of his economic ambitions.

Mosley was thus one of the few people to identify unemployment not only as a problem, but as *the* problem, calling for priority treatment. And he did so, not simply because 'it was there' staring him in the face (it was there for all to see), but because he felt it passionately as a wrong and a disgrace. No doubt this feeling was mixed up with patriotism. It was not *worthy* of a country like his own to allow such a situation to continue: it was a sign of incipient decadence and decline. The power of science, the state, the nation, all cried out against a policy of surrender. The young man's impatience with the bungling of his elders, the aristocrat's sympathy with the sufferings of the poor, the technician's dislike of disorder, and the patriot's love of country, were all mixed together in a combination too explosive to be contained for long within the confines of any single political party.

As a young politician he never saw himself as a party man: he was, in a very real sense, the spokesman of his generation – the generation who felt they had got a raw deal out of the war. This reluctance to think in party terms was facilitated by the unique instability of parties themselves at this time, following the break-up of the Liberal Party, the growth of the Labour Party and Lloyd George's ultimately abortive attempt to form a 'centre' combination from the disparate elements of the Coalition. Mosley's 'understanding' of politics, and, in particular, of the nature of party politics, was thus warped from the outset by these exceptional occurrences. Changing sides was an event sufficiently frequent to be robbed of any special significance. Parties, it seemed, were simply combinations dreamt up by politicians for limited and transient purposes, instruments for political designs, rather than living mass associations, held together by tradition, loyalty, class interest, and common outlook.

Mosley's rather cavalier attitude to party loyalty was determined not only by this experience, but also by certain temperamental traits. People, on the whole, did not interest him, except in the way that they interest a sociologist. Like the Webbs, he used to talk of 'types': so-and-so was a 'new' type, or an 'old' type or a 'fine' type, or a 'pathological' type (which a little later he was apt to identify with a certain kind of socialist). He viewed persons entirely externally, which meant that he had no real insight into their hopes, fears, and needs. They were, perhaps, less 'objects' of study (as to the sociologist), than 'instruments' for his purpose, tools a mechanic uses to fix a car.

This is not to suggest that he consciously manipulated people, simply that he had a rather heartless and unfeeling attitude towards them, which is why he was able to break off associations of long-standing without that emotional disturbance, the dislike of which normally keeps men loyal to persons or groups, in whom they have long ceased to believe, but from whom severance would be too painful. Mosley's approach to individuals had the merits of its defects. Because political associations did not deeply touch his emotions, he remained, and remains today, singularly unpetty. Disagreements with persons never led to rancour on his side. He never impugned their motives, because he never cared much about them. They had disagreed with him, as they were entitled to do: he simply passed on, without regret and without bitterness.

To his associates, on the other hand, Mosley appeared as disturbing, dynamic and exciting. He moved among them arrogant, brilliant, domineering and playful by turns, with an animal vitality that fascinated them and overpowered their doubts.

With this attitude to people and parties, it is not surprising that his notion of democracy was of the referendal kind: the statesman appealing direct to 'the people' over the heads of their particular organizations. He was particularly well-equipped to do this by virtue of his mastery of the public platform. From an early age Mosley's power over people had rested not only on his physical fearlessness, but, even more important, on his eloquence, on his command of biting repartee to silence and wound his opponents. Like Ramsay MacDonald, he came to life emotionally on the platform. He understood crowds as he never understood individuals, was more intimate with them than he was with his closest friends. When he added to his usual incisiveness the moral fervour of the prophet preaching in a great cause, he became one of the great orators of England, and convinced himself that political power lay in the response of a large audience to a stirring speech, rather than in the habitual loyalty and devotion of the party worker – a miscalculation that was to have profound consequences for his career.

As the 1920s unfolded, he came to see himself as a man of

destiny. Many politicians, in their private imaginings, no doubt see themselves cast in a similar role. In almost all cases, reality soon forces a moderation of their aims: either talents or circumstances are inappropriate. In Mosley's case, from the moment of his entry into politics, reality kept pace with his dreams.

His early career was an almost unbelievable success story. He was taken up by the most brilliant (and least stable) politicians of the day: Lloyd George, Birkenhead, Churchill. Beatrice Webb, convinced she had found a 'new type', noted in 1920: 'We have made the acquaintance of the most brilliant man in the House of Commons; here is the perfect politician who is also a perfect gentleman.' The same year he married Cynthia Curzon, daughter of the Foreign Secretary, in the presence of the King and Queen. He always appeared first in those series of political sketches, now out of fashion, entitled 'Prime Ministers of the Future?'

His political gyrations within the orthodox parties produced no more than temporary embarrassments. When he joined the Labour Party, in 1924, seeing in it at last a suitable 'instrument' for the conquest of mass unemployment, he was welcomed like a conquering hero returning home after a successful campaign. Special meetings of welcome were organized; everywhere he and his wife were tumultuously received. After narrowly failing to win Ladywood, Birmingham, from Neville Chamberlain in 1924, he was triumphantly returned for Smethwick in 1926, and his vigorous electioneering in Birmingham clinched the victory of the Labour Party in that hitherto impregnable bastion of Chamberlain Toryism.

Although on the Left of the party, he attracted the attention of Ramsay MacDonald, and in 1928 took his leader on a continental holiday. His reward was a position in the 1929 Labour government; and with his resignation as Chancellor of the Duchy of Lancaster in 1930 he emerged, at the age of thirty-four, into the front rank of politicians. There seemed nothing he could not achieve.

It is not sufficient to 'explain' his later aberrations in terms of nature and nurture. There were 'objective' reasons for the kind

237

of actions he took between 1931 and 1933 which existed quite independently of Mosley's character. In particular there was a problem which there seemed no way of solving within the existing parliamentary system. It is to that problem that I now turn.

3 The Problem

The problem which confronted Britain in the 1920s may be divided into two parts: economic and political. On the one hand, there was the technical problem of how to cure mass unemployment, which for most of the decade averaged about ten per cent of the insured working population, and between 1929 and 1932 reached twenty per cent and more; on the other hand, there was the political problem of how to get any solution adopted and put into practice. We will consider these two aspects in turn.

Broadly speaking, there were three views in the 1920s of how to deal with the economic distress. The 'orthodox' view blamed it on the disorganization of the international monetary system following the war. The path to recovery lay in restoring the pre-war gold standard which by generating confidence in international trading relations would enable London to resume its pre-war role as the world's banker and financier and would help Britain's traditional exports. Inflated domestic incomes and prices were to be brought into line with the restored gold standard parity by deflation. Keynes and other spokesmen for the industrialists, on the other hand, attributed the prolonged unemployment precisely to that policy of deflation. Deflation, Keynes argued, was bad because it reduced entrepreneurs' expectation of profit; which led them to curtail their activity. Keynes switched attention from 'money' to 'real factors'. Stability of the exchange, the prosperity of the City, were indeed desirable, but they should not be purchased, even in the short term, at the expense of industrial health.

This debate was practical rather than theoretical. Whenever a 'theoretically sound' choice existed, Keynes argued, between inflation and deflation, inflation should be preferred 'because it is worse, in an impoverished world, to provoke unemployment

238

than to disappoint the *rentier*'. In short, this policy debate mirrored exactly the conflicting interests of industry and the City, of 'industrial' and 'finance' capital. The fact that in most countries in the 1920s, and especially in the early days of the great depression, 'international' interests were given priority over 'domestic' ones did much to discredit 'international' finance and lend plausibility to the universal fascist charge that 'national' interests were being sacrificed to 'alien' (Jewish) ones.

Socialist economics had no point of contact with this debate. Socialists attributed poverty and unemployment entirely to the maldistribution of income. The scarcity of land and capital, socialists argued, enabled their monopolistic owners (landlords and capitalists) to deprive labour of its share of increasing productivity. The result was that the workers lacked the purchasing power to buy the goods which the capitalists placed on the market, which in turn led to glut, periodic collapse and mass unemployment. The remedy for this 'under-consumption' was the redistribution of income either through penal taxation or nationalization or a combination of both.

The trouble with the socialist view was that it assumed that demand was always sufficient: that the whole problem was one of distributing it in such a way that its increment would accrue to the working class rather than to the owners of capital. It did not see that both entrepreneurs and workers might jointly be victims of monetary policies that disregarded impartially the interests of both. Socialists did not believe in bothering their heads about inflation, deflation, the gold standard, the rate of interest, or trivial matters like that. They were concerned with the fundamentals: once those were taken care of, everything else would follow quite naturally. Indeed as the rate of interest was regarded not as the premium paid to capital, but to private capital, its abolition could confidently be expected once private capital had ceased to exist – which clearly made its study irrelevant. Similarly all problems connected with gold would vanish once the socialist world commonwealth had come into existence.

When, in the Labour Party, Mosley began to study the socialist

239

case for dealing with unemployment, he found it distinctly disappointing. If the alleviation of unemployment had to wait upon the surrender of private capital to the state, then indeed a very long wait was in store. Clearly, there was little prospect of swift advance on that front. On the other hand, the orthodox case pleased him no better. He had absorbed enough of the under-consumptionist theory to make him appreciate that the way back to prosperity did not lie in competitive wage reductions which strove to restore the profitability of industry by reducing the demand upon which industry itself relied to purchase its products. Moreover he was convinced by Keynes' argument that a régime of falling prices meant falling employment. If the curtailment of expenditure diminished employment, then it seemed to follow logically that the expansion of expenditure would increase it.

At this point Mosley was met with the argument that any expansion of credit, by leading to inflation, would force Britain off the newly restored gold standard. Following Keynes he did not regard this as a major disaster. Nevertheless, he did not see why this need ensue, except in the event of speculation against the pound. For with the general under-employment of capacity a price rise, he reasoned, could only follow if demand was expanded haphazardly and indiscriminately. Indeed he argued that the main difference between 'socialist' expansion of credit and a 'capitalist' expansion of credit would be that the latter would be haphazard and indiscriminate, while the former would see to it 'that the new money goes into the right hands'. If subsidies could be given to employment and production in selected industries and selected regions, then, he reasoned, the economy could be 'reflated' selectively, without any general inflation. This reflation would be paid for by an initial period of deficit budgeting. But Mosley did not think that this alone would suffice: a battery of socialist controls, including the nationalization of the banks, the threat of public ownership and the bulk purchase of food and raw materials would probably be required to bring finance and recalcitrant 'capitalists' into line.

This was essentially the programme that Mosley advanced in

240

his pamphlet *Revolution by Reason*, read to the ILP summer school at Easton Lodge in August 1925. It was by no means entirely Mosley's work: already he had with him two able collaborators, John Strachey and Allan Young; he borrowed freely from Keynes and others. Nevertheless it represents an astonishing achievement. The programme in sum was far more than the total of its borrowings. Its striking pragmatism – refusal to be tied down to any particular dogma, determination to make full use of constructive insights wherever these might be found, was the first of Mosley's characteristic contributions. The second was its audacity. Though strongly influenced by Keynes, *Revolution by Reason* went far beyond anything Keynes was then advocating. At that time Keynes was still convinced that unemployment could be substantially cured by reducing the rate of interest. Mosley's love of order and certainty was offended by such an 'open ended' operation, and therefore he welded onto Keynes' reflationary instincts the concept of planning, congenial alike to his socialist audience and his own personality.

In government as Chancellor of the Duchy of Lancaster he was soon sickened by the government's lethargy in face of rapidly mounting unemployment. Nevertheless he realized that there was no political support for the programme of *Revolution by Reason*. Rather than abandon all hope, however, he set about modifying and supplementing his proposals in such a manner that they might win sufficient support to enable their implementation. Since 1925, there had been three main developments relevant to economic policy making. The Liberals had come out, largely under Keynes' inspiration, with a big public-works programme. The Conservatives were, on the other hand, veering rapidly towards protection. Finally, the onset of the world depression had finally discredited the orthodox policy of recovery through a revival of exports.

As a first step, Mosley jettisoned his policy of selective reflation through producers' and consumers' credits, in favour of the Liberal programme of massive government investment. On the other hand, the catastrophic fall of world prices lent strong support to the Conservative demand for protection; for how

could the domestic British market be expanded if British manufacturers were threatened with foreign dumping arising from the
desperate effort of foreign exporters to realize the same price on
a larger quantity of goods? The domestic programme of recovery must be 'insulated' from world price fluctuations. At this
point Mosley was impressed by the free trade argument that
protection, by sheltering industries from competition, would
merely establish inefficient domestic monopolies which far from
expanding their production would merely raise prices by restricting their output. Here Bevin's suggestion that protection be
made conditional upon 'reorganization' was clearly apposite:
the government itself would counteract the sefish monopolistic
inclinations of the sheltered industries by demanding, and taking
steps to ensure, that wages would be progressively raised and
prices lowered as the market for goods expanded. But would not
protection, by making it more difficult for foreigners to buy
British goods, decrease the market for British exports? Mosley
admitted that this was likely, and to meet this objection adopted
the Liberal proposal for expanding the domestic production of
foodstuffs, and the Beaverbrook proposal for grouping foreign
trade increasingly on the Empire. These proposals were largely
hammered out in the course of all-party discussions in the
summer and autumn of 1930 and in sum represent Mosley's
National Programme for dealing with the depression.

Once again, we see the same pirating of others' ideas, irrespective of their source, in the search for a 'constructive' solution;
and the transformation of quite disparate, even contradictory,
strands of thought into a policy at once audacious, consistent,
and apposite to the problem in hand. It was only by the severe
restriction of aim to the solution of a concrete problem that this
conjuring trick could be performed. 'The immediate question
we are concerned with', the New Party statement, *A National
Policy*, declared, 'is not the question of the ultimate form of
Social Organization, but with an emergency in which the whole
structure of industry is threatened.'

Given that it takes a certain kind of mind to reason in this
way, it can scarcely be denied that this approach was not without

242

its merits in the situation which England faced in 1930 and for some years after. Mosley's tragedy was that people's minds remained obstinately fixed on the next hundred years, rather than on the next hundred days. Beatrice Webb, commenting on the New Party policy, observed that it 'falls dead in the No-Man's land between those who wish to keep and those who wish to change the existing order'. Here we have a clear illustration of the difference between two types of political approach: Beatrice Webb thought that the issue facing the country was between two radically different conceptions of society; Mosley thought that the issue was simply how to deal with unemployment. For Beatrice Webb it had to be all or nothing; for Mosley it had to be something in between.

He spent the autumn of 1930 in attempting to form a parliamentary combination from all the parties to support his 'National' policy. When that failed, he broke with the Labour Party and set up the New Party, in March 1931, hoping that as the crisis deepened, it would form a parliamentary rallying point for all those who accepted the 'new' approach to the economic problem. The major parties had failed: the time had come to try something else. But why had they rejected Mosley's 'practical' solution? In order to answer this question it is necessary to say a word about the political divisions of the time. English politics in the inter-war period were dominated by the rivalry of two major ideologies – socialism and *laissez-faire* capitalism, expressed politically and sociologically in the two major parties – the Labour Party and the Conservative Party. The decline of the Liberals was merely a symptom of this growing polarization. As Ramsay Macdonald remarked proudly in 1923: 'There are only two parties in politics today. There is the Capitalist party and the Labour and Socialist party.'

These two creeds were seen as *exclusive alternatives*. The foremost early critics of *laissez-faire* capitalism sought the solution of its dilemmas in a totally new system, rather than in a modification of the existing one. Perhaps the reason for this lies in the intellectual rigidity of *laissez-faire* itself – the fact that it offered a total 'world view', with each element – political, economic, and sociological – dependent on the other, so that it seemed that an attack on any one point must necessarily lead to an attack on every point and eventually to the substitution of a completely new system.

The practical consequence of this intellectual debate was to foist upon politics for fifty years an ideological division that bore almost no relation to the actual issues which governments had to face. I do not want to say anything more about *laissez-faire* except that in my view the fact that its chief antagonist was socialism retarded, rather than hastened, its abandonment. This is contrary to the generally accepted view that although socialism in office achieved little, the existence of the Labour Party forced the capitalist parties into making 'concessions' to the workers in order to ward off the socialist threat. This may have been true as far as welfare measures are concerned. On the other hand, the fact that socialism emerged as *laissez-faire*'s chief intellectual opponent hardened the support for its central economic tenets, on the theory that any concessions in this area were the 'thin end of the wedge' leading inevitably to the full socialist solution. This attitude was to have fateful consequences for the economic evolution of the country, especially by its effect in concealing, under the anti-socialist banner, the real conflict of interest that existed between the industrialists and the City – a conflict that might so easily have been exploited by a reforming government anxious to break up the *laissez-faire* front.

The intellectual extremism of the Labour Party, on the other hand, minimized the effectiveness of its challenge to the existing order. Its central tenets were not only that socialism was the only alternative to the existing order, but also that its coming was guaranteed by history. Indeed, one of MacDonald's chief complaints against Marx was that his economic historicism did not furnish sufficient guarantees for the eventual triumph of socialism; MacDonald preferred to adapt Darwin's evolutionary theory for this purpose. On this view, the Labour Party did not exist primarily to solve concrete problems arising from the day-to-day working of the capitalist system, but to give history a helping hand on its predestined journey. Socialist economics, such as it was, was conspicuously not concerned with the present. It consisted in a generalized critique of capitalism and a generalized statement of what the socialist society would like. This perhaps would not have mattered had the Labour Party been content to hold itself in reserve for the appointed day, leaving parliamentary politics to those who had some commitment to making capitalism work. But it plunged vigorously into parliamentary politics and through a series of accidents, consequent upon the wartime splits in the Liberal Party, found itself in office in both 1924 and 1929, on each occasion without any policy relevant to the existing situation.

The political deadlock arose because neither side was able to secure a decisive political advantage over the other. The minority Labour government of 1929 was manifestly not in a position to pass any socialist legislation, even had it had any to pass. Equally, majority Tory governments were unwilling to pass any anti-socialist legislation for fear of the social repercussions, their memory still fresh with the general strike of 1926. The opportunities for political compromise opened up by this power deadlock were checkmated by the ideological cleavage which we have described. Hence the political situation was 'frozen' on the basis of mass unemployment. Mosley's New Party was an attempt to 'unfreeze' this situation.

4 The Logic of the Situation

The New Party, unlike its successor, the British Union of Fascists, was essentially a parliamentary combination of dissentients, with no very definite long term aims. Besides Sir Oswald and his wife, two other recruits had come in from the Parliamentary Labour Party – John Strachey and Robert Forgan; from the Conservatives, W.E.D.Allen; and just before the dissolution, Major Dudgeon came over from the Liberals. Important non-parliamentary recruits were Cyril Joad, Allan Young, Harold Nicolson and the Sassoon family. An ex-Conservative Minister, Moore-Brabazon, hovered on the brink but finally drew back; Esmond Romilly sold copies of

Action at his preparatory school, an early sign of his political precocity.

It was probably hoped at first that if the Labour government continued for a further two years of aggravating crisis, the party would gather strength at by-elections and through parliamentary accessions till at length it could exercise, without necessarily winning a parliamentary majority, a decisive impact on events. In fact, the financial panic and the formation of the National government which cut the ground from under the New Party's 'national' appeal, destroyed whatever prospects it had of realizing its objective; obliteration at the polls in October 1931 was the penalty. It had started, in Strachey's words, 'as an entirely Utopian appeal for social compromise', but before its final collapse it was starting to move along entirely different lines.

The most interesting statement of the early political purpose of the New Party is contained in an article by C.F. Melville which appeared in the journal *Fortnightly Review* in May 1931. It seems to have been based on interviews with the New Party executive, though not apparently with Mosley himself. The central assumption of the New Party, as related to Melville by 'a prominent member' was:

> The trouble is not that we have a class war so much as that we have a class deadlock. That deadlock must be unlocked. We shall try to do something towards unlocking it.

Melville found strong similarities in the policy, though not in the methods, of the 'German and English movement':

> Both movements are in effect National-Socialist parties which, while appealing to the working masses, attract to themselves the support of industrialists; thereby becoming the protagonists ... of industry versus banking finance.

Thus, Melville thought, 'Sir Oswald Mosley and his associates propose to help both industrial capital and the industrial worker to their mutual benefit . . .', a policy which suggested to him the Mond-Turner conversations of the late 1920s. His prognosis of the New Party's future was not pessimistic:

246

It is obvious that the New Party hopes – and it seems to me to have a good chance of eventually realising this hope, provided it can succeed in reconciling the many aims and as many interests which it represents – to become the principal magnet for a new 'Centrum' in British party politics ... In this sense it cuts right across the old arguments about *Left* and *Right*.

The trouble with having a policy tailor-made to suit the next hundred days is that if the hundred days go by without that policy being adopted, one is liable to seem rather old-fashioned. The dilemma the New Party faced was that it had no immediate prospects of power: yet it had only an 'emergency' programme. Its political appeal depended, far more than its founders realized, on the disappointment engendered by the 'Business as Usual' King's Speech of November 1930. Within six months of that speech the centre of political gravity had shifted elsewhere – not admittedly away from the economic problem in its widest sense – but to a particular facet of it: the financial problem, about which the New Party had nothing special to say. Hence in the summer of 1931 it began to seem increasingly irrelevant to the main issue of the moment. It had shot its bolt.

The New Party's founders were thus forced to think more seriously about the long-term prospects. They all agreed on the imminence of a financial crash. The question that arose, therefore, was: what would happen in the post-crash situation? Once Mosley and Strachey started thinking in these terms, their imaginations went completely to riot. In this, they were by no means unique. Snowden warned the General Council of the TUC in August 1931 that if Britain went off the gold standard there would be millions of unemployed and that the existing distress would seem puny compared to the distress that was sure to follow. There is little doubt that Mosley and Strachey reached similar conclusions: the New Party's opportunity would come in a 'revolutionary situation' with the forces of law and order breaking down against the mounting misery and anger of the unemployed and the ruined. But in that case what would the New Party's position be? There would undoubtedly be other contestants in the field ready to exploit that situation, notably

247

the Communist Party. Was the New Party to side with the forces of law and order? Or with the revolting masses? What attitude was it to take to the Communist Party? These were the questions furiously debated in the New Party Council in the summer of 1931.

When someone is heading towards the Centre it is important to know whether he is coming from the Left or from the Right: in either case he is likely to overshoot the mark somewhat, but in opposite directions. Sir Oswald Mosley was expelled from the Labour Party on 10 March 1931. He therefore started his 'Centrist' career with the organized forces of Labour ranged against him; while the Tories, on the whole, anticipated his return to the Conservative Party. The irony of the situation is that had he been Conservative Chancellor of the Duchy of Lancaster in 1929 he would, in all probability, have found himself moving rapidly to the Left. It was the fact that the party of radical transformation had itself been helpless before the crisis that launched him on his perilous journey towards fascism.

The circumstances of his expulsion from the Labour Party did not hold out much promise of future support from his erstwhile associates. In making his break with Labour Mosley, unlike Joseph Chamberlain or Jacques Doriot in somewhat similar circumstances, had not taken any steps to secure an organized body of local support which he could carry over with him into the new organization. He had failed most signally to gain the support of his constituency Labour executive or indeed done anything to prepare them for his *volte-face*. Of course there had been 'rumours', but his Labour supporters, many of whom hero-worshipped him, put them down to the lies of the capitalist press. Only a week or two before the formation of the New Party he had emphatically denied to his local executive that he contemplated leaving the Labour Party. What perhaps hurt them most was the heartless manner of the break: a short letter, a summons to London, a brief conversation, and a seven-year association ended with hardly a touch of regret. In the upshot, all the constituency parties of the ex-Labour New Party members stayed loyal to the Labour Party, the only hint of a split coming in Stoke-on-Trent where Lady Cynthia Mosley had a strong personal following. The result was that the New Party started life without any grass-roots support to guarantee its continuance: it was a collection of parliamentary exotics and picturesque intellectuals.

The by-election at Ashton-under-Lyne on 30 April 1931 completed Mosley's estrangement from organized Labour. The New Party put up Allan Young to contest this Lancashire cotton constituency following the death of the Labour member, and what there was of the New Party machine went into action in support of his candidature. The Labour Party was a dying force, declared Mosley, soon to be swept aside by the 'New Movement'. Allan Young got sixteen per cent of the votes and the Conservative won the seat. John Strachey has written:

I recollect the figure of Mosley standing on the town hall steps . . . The result of the election had just been announced, and it was seen that the intervention of the New Party had defeated the Labour candidate and elected the Conservative. The crowd consisted of most of the keenest workers in the Labour party in all the neighbouring Lancashire towns . . . The crowd was violently hostile to Mosley. . . . It roared at him, and, as he stood facing it, he said to me, 'That is the crowd that has prevented anyone doing anything in England since the war' . . . At that moment of passion, and of some personal danger, Mosley found himself almost symbolically aligned against the workers. He had realised in action that his programme could only be carried out after the crushing of the workers and their organisations.

Commented an editorial in the Transport and General Workers' *Record*:

The Ashton-under-Lyne election shows that whatever Mosleyism may mean in theory, in practice it means helping the Tories to get back into power. The workers can get all they want by being loyal to their own Movement, and giving the Mosley party and all other political Judases a wide berth.

In fact, the commentators were quite wrong about the effect of the New Party's intervention: it harmed the Tories, not the Labour Party. As Mosley remarked to Harold Nicolson about this time: 'The main response we are getting, and which is very

encouraging, comes from the younger Conservative group. . . .'
On either interpretation, though, the chances of the New Party
being able to hold the Centre looked distinctly unpromising.
Either the mounting hostility of organized Labour would drive
it to the Right, or the nature of its grass-roots recruitment would
have the same effect.

Throughout the early summer the New Party wrangled about
its future political alignment. In miniature, this debate echoed
similar cleavages in both the Nazi and Italian fascist parties in
their early days – in the Nazi Party, 1925–6, between Gregor
Strasser and Goebbels on the Left and the Munich headquarters
on the Right, in Italy between Mussolini and the *squadristi*. In
both cases the Right won, though initially at any rate splits were
avoided.

The issue facing the New Party has been described by John
Strachey as follows:

The position of social compromise was becoming untenable. It was
clear that the inexorable facts of the situation would very soon drive
the New Party either to the Left, as a party of working-class revolt,
or to the Right, as a party of ruling-class reaction. . . .

In other words, Strachey agreed with Mosley that a revolutionary situation was approaching: the only question was: on
which side was the New Party to be?

On neither side, was Mosley's answer. It was to come down on the
supine Government and the disorderly workers and knock their
heads together.

Mosley indeed faced a painful dilemma. As he saw it, either
he would come to power by breaking the power of communism
in a revolutionary situation, or he would not come to power at
all (for he admitted that should circumstances revert to normality, there would be no future for the Modern Movement).
His technician's mind had never been attracted by the marxist
philosophy. In a revolutionary situation his task, as he saw it,
would be to limit the damage, not join forces with those who
proposed a complete transformation of society. He had no wish

250

completely to transform society: merely to solve the economic problem. Yet any expectation of a revolutionary situation undoubtedly forced an unpleasant choice. For the development of sufficient anti-communist feeling to sweep him into power presupposed a considerable development of communist strength, with a parallel anti-fascist radicalization of the trade union and labour movement (as in the militant *Reichsbanner* organization of German social democracy). In those circumstances, Mosley would find ranged against him the whole force of the organized working class, minus what working-class support he might pick up from the unemployed. Now he might come into power in this situation, but it would hardly be from the 'Centrist' position of social compromise. In short, on any theory of deepening economic and social crisis, a choice was inescapable between the Right and the Left.

The first encounter in this ideological battle within the New Party took place over the youth movement. The New Party was regarded by Labour activists as a disloyal and traitorous offshoot of the Labour Party, and the implacable hatred that is always reserved for traitors to the cause pursued the New Party from the start. For the Left can always live with the Right, but it cannot tolerate the *soi-disant* Left. Mussolini had hoped to fight 'many a good fight still' with the proletariat, but he later had to admit that the proletariat had remained in the hands of his enemies. The hostility of Labour took the form of systematic attempts by Labour and Communist militants to break up New Party meetings. Mosley was genuinely alarmed at the danger to his wife, Cynthia, who deputized for him, when he was ill with pleurisy, at the first New Party meetings.

Arising out of the disturbances at Ashton, he decided to form a squad of 'Biff Boys', as they were soon dubbed, to steward his meetings, and at the same time to start a para-military club organization to train young recruits in judo and fisticuffs. Appropriately, a famous boxer, 'Kid' Lewis, was put in charge of the 'physical force' side of the movement. There was as yet no uniform, but the New Party members wore orange marigolds in their buttonholes to distinguish them from their opponents.

The explanation given for these somewhat alarming developments was the need to protect meetings from 'Red violence'.

At a private meeting of the New Party in London on 14 May 1931, Mosley spoke of organizing a 'powerful' body of young men to give physical support to his programme. 'We shall use no sticks, no knives and no bombs but we shall rely on the good old English fist in time of need.' To a reporter of the *Birmingham Gazette* he remarked:

We have already experienced organized violence from our opponents. Twice during my wife's tour of England . . . her meetings were smashed up by an organized mob. That is not going to happen again. . . . We are going to defend the right of free speech in this country. . . .

The left wing of the New Party was extremely worried about the growth of this 'Youth Movement'. The whole organization was conceived on too big a scale for its purpose to be simply that of keeping order at public meetings. Mosley

had to admit to us [John Strachey recalls] that this force was to be used in the revolutionary situation which we all agreed (and this is perhaps the one point on which we still do agree) must sooner or later come upon Great Britain. But on which side was our army to be used?

Mosley himself was in no doubt. On 10 June Allan Young repudiated 'the idea that we should meet communist force with fascist force. He is deeply opposed to the Youth Movement, which, to his mind, is either meaningless or else means disciplined force.'

For a little while longer Mosley was restrained from converting the Youth Movement into a fully fledged private army on the SA model. Jack Jones, at that time a New Party speaker, even managed to persuade him to keep his 'bodyguard' out of sight when he addressed meetings in Scotland in September. 'Kid' Lewis and his boys were regarded by local audiences as definitely 'provocative'.

However, on 21 September, Mosley got the excuse he was waiting for. He and his bodyguard were stoned at a great open air meeting in Glasgow, with a crowd estimated by *The Times* at 40,000. Mosley's speech itself consisted of a straightforward exposition of New Party policy, but with a strong anti-socialist bias. 'They could not make the working-classes of Britain wait', Mosley said 'until every Hottentot in Africa had joined the ILP.' The socialist opposition to the National government, he went on, had reduced the Commons to the state of a girls' school in hysterics. All the press reports agreed that the opposition had been organized beforehand. The whole speech was punctuated by booing and the singing of the Red Flag. Mosley afterwards told a reporter that there were four hundred organized interrupters in the crowd. 'Some were Communists and others members of the Council for the Defence of Free Speech. . . .' As he and his entourage made their way through the crowd after the meeting, they were attacked with stones and razors and it was only the police who saved them from serious injury.

Back in London a meeting of the New Party Council was hurriedly summoned. 'Tom [Mosley] says that this forces us to be fascist and that we need no longer hesitate to create our trained and disciplined force.' They then discussed uniforms. Harold Nicolson, in one last effort to preserve English middle-class respectability, suggested grey flannel trousers and shirts, and this was, for the moment, accepted. It took another year for the Greyshirts to become the Blackshirts.

Strachey and Young had already resigned, but before that event, a week-end school was held at the Mosleys' country house at Denham, which well illustrates the split-personality of the New Party, as well as its comic-opera aspect. Strachey delivered a 'good old-fashioned Marxian speech' which was applauded by Allan Young, Cyril Joad and others. A young man called Peter Winkworth read a paper on 'The Attic State' in which he argued that the ideas of the New Party were based on Hellenism rather than Hitlerism. Joad, in an obvious reference to the 'Biff Boys', dubbed the Hellenites as 'men with the heads of athletes on the bodies of thinkers', to which Mosley riposted that the Labour movement suffered from having the 'heads of communists on the hearts of social democrats'.

Cynthia Mosley [wrote Jack Jones] looks troubled, so does Mrs Strachey. Harold Nicolson smokes his pipe diplomatically, and later

253

speaks like a diplomat. . . . Dr Robert Forgan, MP, speaks non-committally – for they are all his friends. . . . Mr Box [the New Party Chief Agent] stands in the background with a smile on his face as he watches Allan Young squirming impatiently whilst Mosley is speaking soulfully of the Corporate State of the future. . . . Denham is a charming little place in which to differ.

But sterner business was at hand.

The actual breaking-point [Strachey recalls] came upon that touchstone of the modern world, our attitude to Soviet Russia. I was asked to write a memorandum defining the New Party's attitude to Soviet Russia. I wrote an unequivocally pro-Russia document. Mosley equally unequivocally rejected it, and gave, quite frankly, his real reason for doing so. If the New Party adopted a pro-Russian attitude, all hopes of support from the Conservatives and capitalists would be gone.

Mosley put a rather different interpretation on Strachey's memorandum. In an explanatory letter to New Party members, he argued that acceptance of Strachey's memorandum would have meant the reversal of the New Party's policy of investment at home and co-operation with the Dominions, in favour of 'an economic and military alliance with Russia which would admittedly antagonise nearly every other nation in the world'. It represented the 'extreme dogma' of international socialism. 'It is difficult to conceive that anyone but a communist could possibly support on the public platform such an extraordinary proposition.'

Following the rejection of the memorandum Strachey and Young resigned from the New Party on 24 July 1931, and Cyril Joad followed two days later. Mosley expressed relief that the party was now free of the 'incubus of socialism'.

The real significance of the resignations was not that the Right had triumphed in this particular instance, for there is little doubt that Strachey's policy was indeed the 'very midsummer of madness' as Neville Chamberlain was later to remark in another connection; rather that the Left had been eliminated from the New Party's counsels. The 'pathological element', as Mosley liked to dub Strachey and Young, having disappeared, there

254

were now only the 'diplomatic' Harold Nicolson and the 'non-committal' Robert Forgan to restrain his plunge into fascism.

Strachey was right to suppose that the adoption of his memorandum would cut off the supply of funds from the 'capitalists'. Mosley was at that time being financed by Sir William Morris (later Lord Nuffield), who contributed £50,000, and other industrialists; he was attracting 'the young Conservative group'; he was angling for the support of Lord Rothermere, 'colloguing' with disaffected leaders of the old gangs like Churchill, Beaverbrook and Lloyd George for some kind of 'National' parliamentary combination to oppose MacBaldwinism; all this would have been irretrievably jeopardized by Strachey's proposals.

Yet the New Party had started life angling for the support of the Right as well as the support of the Left. Deprived of the support of the Left it was stuck with the Right. The alliance of worker and industrialist in a common cause was a non-starter: at best what was left was a Tory paternalist scheme for improving social conditions with Lord Nuffield's money; at worst, an incipient fascist movement, which would gain more dubious adherents than the naive, if well-meaning, car manufacturer.

In parliamentary terms, then, there was no future for the New Party. As an experiment in 'centrism' it had failed both ideologically and electorally. The BUF, its successor, was an attempt to substitute a grass-roots centrism for a parliamentary one. Yet this fresh attempt to achieve an ideological neutrality was vitiated by Mosley's belief in the inevitability of collapse and revolution. For it is in the nature of the revolutionary situation that it forces people to 'take sides'; to choose not between old gangs and new movements but, in Mosley's own words, between 'the arch protagonists – communism and fascism'.

Once Mosley and Strachey saw themselves on opposite sides of the barricades, the weak thread of centrism that held them together immediately snapped. Each sought what associations he could, unaware, perhaps, of where they would lead him. They both sought to mobilize for the great day. Thus, in the end, they were both prisoners of the very world they had tried to escape:

the world of ideological politics, with the difference that this version offered the prospect of a bloody breakthrough.

5 The Laws of History

After October 1931, the New Party ceased to exist as a political force: all its twenty-four candidates had been defeated in the General Election and Mosley himself was out of parliament. At the end of 1931 the party's high-brow weekly, *Action*, edited by Harold Nicolson, was discontinued; in April 1932, the central organization was formally wound up. However, the 'Nupa' clubs – the Greyshirts – were kept going and they were to be the basis of the British Union of Fascists, founded in October 1932, which thus started off as a para-military organization. In January 1932 Mosley had left for Italy to study the 'new movements'. Harold Nicolson, still trying desperately to preserve the illusion of ideological neutrality, had persuaded him to add Moscow to his itinerary, but Mosley did not have to go that far. In Rome he found what he was looking for.

The question that remains to be considered is: how did Mosley come to convince himself that economic collapse was inevitable? For there is no doubt that, like the communists, he thought that this was the final crisis of the old order. It is true that he did not express this conviction in the 'scientific' terminology of marxism. Indeed its basis was quite different. Marxists believed that the inherent contradictions of capitalism would eventually lead to its collapse; admittedly the success of the communist revolution would depend on the 'revolutionary consciousness' of the proletariat; but the collapse itself was guaranteed by laws of historical development quite independent of human volition. Mosley himself did not subscribe to any grandiose historicism of this kind. He believed that economic collapse would be caused quite simply by the bungling of the politicians. He saw no prospect of an end to that bungling until the new movement had triumphed.

It is true that in order to reach this conclusion Mosley exaggerated the economic problem out of all perspective. In his

256

book, *The Greater Britain*, published simultaneously with the foundation of the BUF, he tried to 'prove' that the export trade was doomed to go on declining. This implication had carefully been avoided in the New Party policy statement. Subsequent editions of *The Greater Britain* attempted, with conspicuous lack of success, to square this apocalyptic vision with the undoubted fact of recovery from the depression. It is no doubt extremely irritating for a man of destiny slowly to realize that his services are not required, at least, not to the strains of *Götterdämmerung*; for the expert mechanic, who has spent years acquiring exactly the right tools for the job, suddenly to see the car come to life at the press of the self-starter and drive away – even if only on three cylinders. That was indeed Mosley's fate. Without having done anything particular to deserve it, the National government found itself with a moderate boom on its hands; and could complacently congratulate itself on having proved the alarmists utterly wrong.

In a sense Mosley was right: had it been up to the National government to pull the country out of its mess, it would most likely have bungled the job. As Malcolm Muggeridge says, its creative capacities had been fully exhausted by the very act of its coming into existence; the forced devaluation of the currency which it had been formed to prevent completed its remedial functions. In this sense, it is fair to say that the recovery was unexpected, and that Mosley was right in thinking that politicians of the calibre of MacDonald and Baldwin would never have been able to achieve it had it depended upon them. But the unexpected occurs so frequently in history that one should not even think of it as unexpected. There are no laws of probability, much less of necessity, that can be applied to a historical situation. There are simply choices – which is quite a different thing. But most politicians like Mosley 'strengthen' the choice they are offering with terrifying prophecies of doom if it is not accepted; prophecies which are invariably and necessarily ill-founded, even if they prove justified, which in this case they did not. As an article in *Time and Tide* shrewdly remarked of Mosley early in 1931: 'He would rather cramp circumstance by fitting it into his plan and personality than acknowledge his plan too small for circumstance.'

But Mosley's call for a new movement to end the bungling was not simply a protest against the continuance in power of MacDonald and Baldwin. It was a protest against a whole system of politics and government, a call for a new 'type' of man, willing to accept major reponsibility and competent to exercise it. Behind this call lay the conviction that an age of modern and unprecedented change and transformation could not afford the luxury of a system of government designed for more leisurely times, when politicians were not expected to be executives and when blunders were not likely to have fatal consequences.

Parliamentarians he saw as talkers, not doers. Even if they entered the Commons with an urge to do something, this was rapidly drained away by the corroding and deadening atmosphere of the House, with its mechanical and time-wasting ritual, the attractions of the bar and smoke-room, the endless 'politicking'. (This echoed much left-wing criticism.) In this atmosphere MPs quickly lost all sense of duty to their constituents, so that in practice the 'will of the people' was constantly frustrated – an outcome which Mosley saw as the reverse of democracy. 'Nothing', he wrote in the *Star* on 19 December 1930, 'could be so anti-democratic as a system of government like our present one which ensures that nothing should ever be done.'

Even more fundamentally, the 'democratic' notion of committee responsibility and the bargaining of interests, with which he contrasted the fascist leadership principle, inhibited rapid action. 'The present system', Mosley concluded in a speech at the Albert Hall in 1934, 'produces a type of man to whom action and decision are impossible even if he had the power.'

Even when members were disgruntled with the performance of the old gang leaders, the whip of party discipline was too painful ever to enable dissatisfaction to emerge into open revolt. His experience in 1930, when those rebellious members who supported his policy shrank from the decisive step of breaking with their parties to follow him, convinced him that party discipline would retain its stranglehold to the end. 'The power of the party machine', he wrote in *The Greater Britain*, 'has crushed all attempts to secure a natural alignment in British politics.'

The inertia and complacency of the MPs was one factor: the other was that the ideas of the parties to which they belonged were completely out of date. The conservatives wanted to preserve things exactly as they were; the socialists had a completely inappropriate solution which in any case they were not prepared to implement. About Ramsay MacDonald's Labour administration he asked: 'What would we think of a Salvation Army that took to its heels on the Day of Judgment?' The communists at least were logical: they wanted a revolution and were prepared to use revolutionary means to achieve it. In short, the conservatives were stupid and the socialists were cowards. Either way, they were incapable of taking the measures required.

Finally – and this is perhaps the most important point in Mosley's analysis of the political system – 'both political parties ... stand bound by the great vested interests of "Right" and "Left" which created them'. Neither would co-operate for any constructive purpose. The result was paralysis at the centre of government – 'indecision, compromise, and blether'. 'Somebody must be trusted', Mosley wrote, 'or nothing will ever be done.'

6 Conclusion

I have not attempted to carry this account of the origins of British fascism beyond 1932; nor have I attempted to analyse its appeal in terms of social groups or psychological types. What I have tried to do is to show why the BUF came into existence. The method I have used is to describe the intellectual and political pilgrimage of Sir Oswald Mosley.

Essentially the explanation falls into two halves. First, there was the realization that unemployment was the major economic and social problem of the inter-war years, and the attempt to find a solution to it. Second, there was the political problem of how to get that solution adopted.

Sir Oswald Mosley brought to the unemployment problem a mind unfettered by past controversies and devoid of philosophic curiosity; a political understanding limited to the experience of the interventionist state; an independent, critical judgment and capacity for hard work; a belief in himself as a man of destiny; and a compulsive will to action and achievement. He felt unemployment to be both *unnecessary* and a *betrayal* of the sacrifices of the war generation.

The result was a series of plans between 1925 and 1931 which stamp him as one of the major creative minds in modern English politics. The fact that his constructive efforts were directed towards a limited problem should not obscure the greatness of his achievement. Mosley was not propounding a 'world view': neither was Keynes. Both started with a limited problem which the *laissez-faire* system could not solve; and both ended up as prophets of regulated capitalism. Keynes' breakthrough in terms of ideas is paralleled by Mosley's breakthrough in terms of policies: only he, in the words of Taylor, 'rose to the height of the challenge'.

Mosley's success in devising good policies was matched by his failure to get them carried out. It was the maddening inability to get anything done that drove him to political extremism. There was, in fact, no 'leverage' in the English political system for the kind of non-sectarian approach that Mosley was advocating. In retrospect I think it is obvious that the 'unfreezing' of the ideological and political stalemate of the late nineteenth century was bound to take a long time. Had Mosley had a maturer sense of history and a more realistic estimate of the politically possible, he would, I think, have realized this at the time, as did many others who shared his impatience and frustration. As it was he convinced himself that eloquence alone could achieve a rapid breakthrough. Of course, he postulated that eloquence would only be effective in a situation of economic collapse; but ensnared by the logic of his own analysis, overimpressed by the incompetence of the politicians and the trend of events in central Europe, and bursting with impatience to get to grips with the problem, he convinced himself that that collapse was inevitable. Thus, like the communists, he ended up utterly dependent upon the *deus ex machina* of economic catastrophe to bring him to power: and like them, paid the penalty of those who put their faith in the laws of history.

12 France

G.Warner

In view of the breadth and complexity of French fascism, it is essential to begin an essay which cannot claim to be an exhaustive treatment of the subject with a brief statement of its limitations. These are: a restriction to the decade 1934–44 and the exclusion of all but passing references to the *Action Française* movement. Given the scope of most of the essays in this symposium, the first limitation is a reasonable one. The period dealt with is, at any rate, the one in which fascism was an issue of major political importance in France – something which it had not been before and has not been since, except perhaps during the years 1958–62. The deliberate exclusion of the *Action Française*, on the other hand, may seem capricious to the point of wilful distortion. It can only be justified by the fact that recent scholarship has subjected the movement to an exhaustive examination which not only cannot be improved upon here, but which has also tended to reinforce the view that the *Action Française*, while undoubtedly influenced by fascism, was not a fascist movement. This is perhaps most clearly seen in the field of doctrine. Fascism, whatever its achievements, at least professed to be a revolutionary creed, dedicated to the destruction of the old order and the creation of a new one. The *Action Française*, on the other hand, was almost self-consciously reactionary, looking back to some mythical past untainted by the ideas unleashed upon Europe and the world by the French Revolution. Fascism sought to exploit these ideas for its own ends; the *Action Française* rejected them completely.

The year 1934 is an obvious starting point for an essay on

French fascism. On 6 February of that year there took place in Paris a bloody riot in which 15 people were killed and 1,435 injured, 328 of them seriously. The Left saw the riot as a fascist plot to overthrow the republic and, although the immediate result of the disorders was the replacement of Edouard Daladier's left-wing government by Gaston Doumergue's right-wing one, the long-term consequence was the rallying of all the left-wing forces, including the communists, into the Popular Front, which was to triumph in the elections of April-May 1936. The period which runs from 6 February 1934 to May 1936 constitutes the first of what I believe to be three fairly distinct phases in the history of French fascism during the decade covered by this essay.

Recent research has not substantiated the charge that the riot of 6 February 1934 was a plot – fascist or otherwise – to overthrow the republic. Rather it was a particularly violent explosion of the latent anti-parliamentarianism of the Parisian middle class, brought about by a succession of impotent governments – there had been no less than six since the elections of spring 1932 – and by a particularly unsavoury financial scandal, the so-called Stavisky affair, in which members of the ruling Radical Party were involved.

What prompted the charge that the riot was a fascist conspiracy was the fact that it was organized and in large part carried out by a number of right-wing para-military organizations known as the Leagues. Only one of these movements, Marcel Bucard's *Francistes*, openly proclaimed that it was fascist. Bucard had had an audience with Mussolini, was to represent France at the international fascist congress in Montreux in December 1934, and drew over half a million lire in subsidies from the Italian press attaché in Paris between May 1934 and April 1940. But Bucard's movement was small. According to the parliamentary committee of inquiry into the 6 February riot, it had only twelve to fifteen hundred members and it was never a significant political force.

Apart from the *Action Française*, the major Leagues involved in the riot were the *Jeunesses Patriotes*, the *Solidarité Française*

263

and the *Croix de Feu*. The *Jeunesses Patriotes*, led by the Paris deputy Pierre Taittinger, were founded in 1924 in another period when right-wing Parisians were up in arms against the impotence and financial incompetence of left-wing governments. It was anti-left, particularly anti-communist, but not much else. It had about 90,000 members in all, 6,000 of them in Paris. The *Solidarité Française* was an even more confusing organization. Founded in 1933 on the initiative of the talcum powder tycoon and political crank, François Coty, it was said to have 180,000 members in 1934, but this is almost certainly an exaggeration. Coty claimed to be a Bonapartist, but he was ailing and effective control of the movement was in the hands of a man called Jean Renaud, who told the parliamentary committee of inquiry into the riot that he 'would bray like an ass' if anyone told him he was a Bonapartist. One of the *Solidarité Française* slogans was 'France for the French' – it was violently antisemitic – but this did not stop it from recruiting among the unemployed north African population of the Paris slums. Indeed, the influx of these *sidis*, as the north Africans were known, led left-wing wits to dub the movement the *Sidilarité Française*.

Much more important was the *Croix de Feu*. Although it played a relatively unheroic role on 6 February, it was the *Croix de Feu* which captured the headlines in the following months and came to symbolize the fascist threat in left-wing eyes. When it was founded in 1927, the *Croix de Feu* was an organization for ex-servicemen who had been cited at least once for gallantry on the field of battle. Although patronized by the ubiquitous François Coty, it seems to have been genuinely apolitical at first. In 1929 it widened its ranks by admitting men who, while they had not been cited for gallantry, had served at least six months in the trenches. It was also in 1929 that Lieutenant-Colonel Count Casimir de la Rocque joined the organization. After service in Morocco, on the western front, on Marshal Foch's staff and in Poland, he retired from the army in 1926 and got an executive post with the *Compagnie Générale d'Electricité*. To judge from the memoirs of Paul Chopine, who was a member of the *Croix de Feu* before de la Rocque joined it, and who subsequently broke with the organization, the Colonel immediately began to take over the movement, a process which was completed by 1932. He also widened its membership still further by creating the *Volontaires Nationaux*, who did not have to be ex-servicemen at all. By the end of 1933, these 'national volunteers' formed about a third of the movement's total membership of 58,000. Most important of all, de la Rocque turned the *Croix de Feu* into an overtly political movement which supported the right in the 1932 elections. According to Chopine, who is admittedly a biased source, de la Rocque's motives were purely self-seeking.

As I have already said, the *Croix de Feu* came to symbolize the fascist threat in France after 6 February 1934. How and why is clear from the following account of the movement's activities in mid-1935, written by the *Manchester Guardian*'s brilliant Paris correspondent, Alexander Werth.

Giant rallies and mobilization exercises began to be held in various parts of France [Werth wrote] and the behaviour of the *Croix de Feu* became rather alarming. . . . [De la Rocque] swore that the *Croix de Feu* had been 'on their guard' during the cabinet crisis [of May-June] and that there would have been some fun (*il y aurait eu du sport*) if . . . Daladier had been included in the new government . . . and, becoming bolder and bolder, the Colonel proclaimed that 'he did not care a hang for legality', and that the *Croix de Feu* would 'take command' at the appropriate moment. The most impressive rally . . . took place at Algiers, complete with thirty aeroplanes belonging to the *Croix de Feu* organization; and there were also many other rallies mostly held on the estate of some wealthy patron, without warning and with 'lightning speed' . . . On several occasions the roads leading to these 'secret rallies' were policed by *Croix de Feu* men.

In spite of its cars and aeroplanes, however, the *Croix de Feu* was never a mass movement. Its total membership never exceeded a few hundred thousand and most members seem to have been of middle or upper-middle class origin. Its success was due, I believe, to three main causes: its discipline, which was very effective and which made it somehow 'respectable'; the vague nature of its programme, which gave it a wider appeal

265

than some of the other right-wing groups; and, most important of all, its position as the number one target of the Popular Front. Right-wingers frequently complained after the 1936 elections that, by its activities, the *Croix de Feu* had helped the Popular Front to power. Equally, the *Croix de Feu* would hardly have become the threat it apparently was without the constant attacks launched upon it by the Popular Front.

But was it fascist? The rallies, the para-military exercises, the open contempt for parliamentary and democratic procedures were certainly reminiscent of fascism. In so far as it had one, the *Croix de Feu*'s programme clearly owed much to the same source. Five points stand out from a statement of principles published in the movement's newspaper, *Le Flambeau*, on 19 October 1935 and reproduced in Chopine's memoirs: (1) Elimination of foreign influences upon the economy and the establishment of an autarchic economic system based upon France and her colonial empire; (2) reorganization of professional associations and the enactment of a corporative labour law; (3) reinforcement of the executive at the expense of the legislature; (4) rearmament; (5) anti-communism.

One genuine fascist, however, would have taken Colonel de la Rocque's protestations that his movement was not fascist at their face value. This was Signor Landini, the press attaché at the Italian embassy in Paris and one of the main contacts between the Italian government and French extremist political groups. In August 1935, when, it should be remembered, the *Croix de Feu* was at the height of its power, one of the younger and more militant members told him that he did not think the movement could seize power before the beginning of 1937. 'I observed that it was dangerous to wait until 1937,' Landini wrote. 'It reminded me of the sign outside some popular barbers' shops: "A free shave – tomorrow." During the delay, and without having clearly defined aims before them, the troops will stagnate and go soft.' The *Croix de Feu* militant replied that the French were patient and that 'the troops' had faith in de la Rocque. Landini, however, reckoned that 'for the most part, they are only too glad to put off action until the Greek Kalends,

266

and imagine that they are heroes in the meantime'. Italian contempt for the *Croix de Feu* is reflected in the fact that there is no evidence of any financial support for the movement.

The very fact that the Popular Front came to power meant that de la Rocque had failed and his movement went into decline thereafter. One of the first things the new government did was to ban the *Croix de Feu*, together with the *Solidarité Française* and the *Jeunesses Patriotes*. De la Rocque's reaction was to transform his movement into a straightforward political party, the *Parti Social Français*, but it was never the force that the *Croix de Feu* had been, and its leader's personal reputation suffered a serious setback in the autumn of 1937 when a former right-wing prime minister, André Tardieu, accused him of having received subsidies from the government's 'secret funds' in the movement's early days.

With the success of the Popular Front and de la Rocque's eclipse, the stage was set for the second of the three phases which I mentioned at the beginning of this essay. On the surface, it was marked by the rise and fall of Jacques Doriot's *Parti Populaire Français*, but its real manifestation was the far more sinister conspiracy of the *Comité Secret d'Action Révolutionnaire*, more commonly known as the *Cagoule*, or 'Hood'. There was a world of difference between the aristocratic de la Rocque and his middle-class rallies and the working class Doriot with his Marseilles gangsters; even more between the phoney conspiracies invented by the Left before the 1936 elections and the very real one hatched by the *cagoulards*. The difference was due quite simply to the fact that the Popular Front was in power. It is not easy to appreciate just how French *bien-pensants* viewed the situation in June 1936, with France's first socialist prime minister – and a Jew into the bargain – 70 Communist deputies instead of 12 in the old Chamber, and no less than two million workers occupying the factories in a wave of sit-in strikes just to prove that they were the masters now. Nevertheless, some idea of the atmosphere can be gained from the following quotation from the diary of the Abbé Desgranges, a right-wing but by no means an extremist deputy.

267

Many foreigners have left Paris in a hurry [Desgranges noted on 13 June]. They believe in imminent revolution. . . . A state of anxiety and dejection weighs upon the Parisians you meet on the *Métro* and in the buses. Some envisage the collapse of the franc and even the taking over and looting of private houses, with the hoarding of money and flight to the provinces or abroad as a result. [One of my friends], in a state of considerable anxiety, asks me whether I think he ought to leave his family in Paris.

Extreme situations call for extreme remedies and Jacques Doriot's *Parti Populaire Français*, which was founded in that very summer of 1936, looked to some like the answer. Doriot was an ex-communist and therefore knew the enemy. He had broken with the party soon after the riot of 6 February 1934 by advocating a united front with the socialists before it became the official party line. The party's adoption of the united front tactic coincided with his own expulsion, which left him something of a rebel without a cause. His machine in the Paris suburb of Saint-Denis just secured his re-election to the Chamber of Deputies in 1936 and his new party, the PPF, soon developed into what has been described as 'an authentic fascism', with its emphasis upon the leadership principle and its opposition, not only to communism, but also to capitalism and democracy. In March 1937 it claimed a membership of 137,000 and, in sharp contrast to the movements described above, two-thirds were said to be working class.

The Doriot party suffered a severe setback at the end of 1938 when several of its leading members resigned. Their motives were mixed. Pierre Pucheu, a young technocrat who later became Darlan's Minister of the Interior at Vichy, subsequently wrote that he left the PPF when he found out that it was being subsidized from abroad. Anti-capitalists resented the support the movement was getting from big business and nationalists were disgusted at Doriot's appeasement-minded attitude at the time of Munich. The party did not again become a force to be reckoned with until the German occupation.

Unlike the PPF, the *Comité Secret d'Action Révolutionnaire* was a clandestine organization. It was founded in 1936 by a

47-year-old consultant naval engineer and company director, Eugène Deloncle. He had been a member of the *Action Française* and most of his supporters were dissident members of that movement or of the *Croix de Feu* who felt that their erstwhile colleagues were not doing enough to combat the communist threat. The *Action Française* treated its dissidents with contempt and it was one of its leaders, Maurice Pujo, who jokingly dubbed the members of the CSAR '*cagoulards*', or 'hooded men'.

The CSAR was run on strictly military lines. Like the French army, its high command was divided into four bureaux: overall direction, intelligence, operations and logistics. The basic unit was the cell, which contained between ten and twenty men. Larger units were the unity, the battalion, the regiment, the brigade and the division. Deloncle claimed that he could raise 12,000 men in Paris alone, but this figure is almost certainly an exaggeration and I have seen no reliable estimates of the organization's total membership. Some of the provincial branches enjoyed considerable autonomy, as well as such picturesque designations as 'The Children of the Auvergne' and 'The Knights of the Sword'. The CSAR bore all the marks of a secret society. Cell members knew only their immediate superiors and knew nothing about other cells. Each recruit had to swear a solemn oath of allegiance and serve a probationary period during which he was under constant observation. Discipline was rigid and disloyalty was punishable by death after a court martial. There are, moreover, cases on record of *cagoulards* who were executed in this way.

The CSAR's aim was freely admitted by Deloncle to be the establishment of a dictatorship in France that would forestall what he considered to be the imminent threat of a communist *coup*. The seizure of power had been planned down to the last detail. When the conspiracy was uncovered, the police found plans of access, via the Paris sewers, to the Elysée Palace, the Chamber of Deputies and the ministries of foreign affairs, war, public works, the interior and the navy. Detailed information had been collected concerning the capital's water and power

269

supplies and plans had been drawn up to dislocate communications between Paris and the provinces by sabotaging the railways. There was even a list of prominent Popular Front politicians to be seized as hostages.

If the CSAR was short on numbers, it made up for it in firepower. In raids upon the organization's arms dumps, the police discovered 12,000 grenades, 34 machine-guns, 135 Schmeisser sub-machine-guns, 95 Beretta carbines, 149 army rifles, 151 hunting guns, 50,000 rounds of ammunition, 375 lbs of explosive, 330 thunder-flashes, 1,000 chemical detonators, 4 time-bombs and 4,000 assorted revolvers and pistols. This arsenal came from a variety of sources – notably Italy and Nationalist Spain – in exchange for services rendered. On one occasion, however, with the help of a member of the staff of the Iraqi embassy in Paris, three *cagoulards* managed to pose for a day as the Iraqi ambassador and two senior civil servants. They summoned a representative of a German armaments firm and calmly ordered a quantity of arms and ammunition in the name of the Iraqi government, to be delivered to an address in Geneva.

'Your *Duce* is and will remain our master,' a leading *cagoulard* told Colonel Emanuele Santo of the Italian secret service in August 1937. 'We entirely agree with your *Duce* in considering that fascism is a norm of political life, not only Italian but European. . . . The fascist régime must be copied and applied in France. That, in essence, is our programme.' It is doubtful, of course, whether Mussolini really wanted a fascist France; it would have deprived him of one of the more convenient scapegoats for Italy's frustrations. In any case, he must have realized that the prospect of the CSAR's actually seizing power was extremely remote. The organization was, however, extremely useful for sowing confusion in the ranks of the French body politic and for performing certain unpleasant services. It was *cagoulards*, for example, who brutally murdered two Italian anti-fascist émigrés, the Rosselli brothers, in June 1937 on the instructions of the Italian secret service.

It would be an interesting, but irrelevant, story to tell how the French authorities got on to the track of the CSAR. It suffices to say that the socialist Minister of the Interior, Marx Dormoy, who paid for his zeal with his life during the German occupation, disclosed the existence of the conspiracy to the public in November 1937. The notorious slowness of the French judicial machine meant that it was June 1939 before seventy-one of the CSAR's members were actually sent for trial. But the war broke out in September and the government rashly agreed to amnesty them if they enlisted in the armed forces. Most did so and were thus enabled to continue their activities after the collapse of 1940.

French fascism was somewhat in the doldrums after the break-up of the CSAR and the resignations from Doriot's PPF. This was mainly due, I believe, to the fact that fascism's number one enemy, the Popular Front, had crumbled from within. At the end of 1938, Daladier, the villain of 6 February 1934 and one of the architects of the Popular Front, was presiding over a government which was showing itself to be increasingly right-wing and authoritarian in temper. Having smashed a general strike in November 1938, the government took plenary powers and, in July 1939, postponed the elections scheduled for 1940 by two years and enacted, among other things, a 'family code' designed to boost the sagging birth-rate. Further indications of what may be called the Daladier government's 'proto-fascism' were its banning of the communist party as a result of the Nazi-Soviet pact and the establishment of France's first concentration camps to house communists and others opposed to the war.

It is impossible to say how far this process would have gone, of course, because the French collapse of May-June 1940 completely transformed the entire situation. Indeed, it inaugurated the third phase of fascism in France during the decade 1934–44: that of fascism in power. But while such a régime as Vichy would never have come into existence without the German victory and occupation, it would be a mistake to bracket it with some of the other Quisling-type régimes of Axis-occupied Europe. There was genuine popular support for Vichy at first, not only because it seemed a good idea to back what looked like the winner, but

271

also because there was widespread disillusionment and disgust with the régime deemed responsible for the defeat itself: namely, the Third Republic.

To describe the Vichy régime as 'fascism in power' may seem at best something of an exaggeration and at worst the communist party line, but although Marshal Pétain was no Hitler or Mussolini and although his so-called 'national revolution' gained a great deal of its inspiration from authentic French traditions going back far beyond 1922, there were undoubtedly strong elements of fascism in much of what Vichy said and did. There was, for example, much talk of the need to 'align' the French political, economic and social system with those of the victorious Axis powers. As the Deputy Prime Minister in the Pétain government, Pierre Laval, brutally put it to a private meeting of members of parliament on 6 July 1940, 'One of two things can happen: either you agree to what we are asking and align yourselves on the German and Italian constitutions, or Hitler will force you to do so.' But he would have agreed with the sentiments expressed in Pétain's broadcast message in October that 'the new order cannot be a slavish imitation of foreign experiences. Some of these experiences have their purpose and attraction, but each people must conceive a system which is adapted to their climate and their genius. The new order is a French necessity.' In other words, the French hoped – to use current political terminology – that the European new order created by the Axis victory would be polycentric: there would be 'different roads to fascism'.

But the basic unity was still there. Nowhere is this more evident than in some of the legislation which constituted Vichy's 'national revolution'. In October 1940 the first anti-Jewish statute was enacted. It excluded Jews, who were defined on the same basis as in the Nuremberg decrees, from the public service and from a number of other professions. This legislation was extended in June 1941. Although racial persecution never reached the height it attained in Germany and German-occupied territory in eastern Europe, it existed and was justified in similar terms. On the economic front, the government borrowed wholesale from Mussolini's corporatist state. Organizing committees to run industry were set up as early as August 1940. In November all trade unions and employers' associations were abolished and in October 1941 a 'labour charter' was introduced which laid down that each industry should be run by 'mixed social committees' consisting of both employers and employees. Strikes and lock-outs were declared illegal. Agriculture was reorganized on corporatist lines in December 1940. But all this legislation, allegedly designed to soften the excesses of capitalism and abolish the class war, was really so much window dressing. Real control of the economy rested in the hands of the government throughout the Vichy period and it preferred to act through the employers, frequently appointing to the industrial organizing committees members of the very employers' organizations it had supposedly abolished. Only the trade unions were effectively dissolved; that was real enough.

By the end of 1941, the 'national revolution' was a transparent failure. This was not only because of its dishonesty, but because the premise upon which it was based – French partnership in an Axis new order in Europe – was becoming increasingly invalid. In the first place, it was clear that Germany and Italy were not interested in partnership with France, but only in exploiting her. Secondly, after the entry of the Soviet Union and the United States into the war, the prospect of an Axis victory grew steadily more remote. From the positive task of building a new France, the Vichy government gradually turned to the negative one of preserving what already existed. From the point of view of this essay, the most interesting aspect of events during the last two years of the Vichy régime is the growing struggle between the French government on the one hand and those who may be called the 'hard core fascists', who refused to admit either the possibility or the consequences of an Axis defeat, on the other.

These 'hard core fascists' were based in Paris. It should be remembered that, under the terms of the Franco-German armistice of June 1940, France was divided into an occupied and unoccupied zone. Paris, which was in the occupied zone, remained the capital of the country, even though the French government was at Vichy in the unoccupied zone. In theory, the French government's writ ran across both zones, but in practice German interference was more persistent in the occupied zone. The difference survived, albeit in an attenuated form, even after the occupation of the rest of France following the allied landings in north Africa in November 1942. Throughout the war, the military commander in France, the German embassy and the ss had their headquarters in Paris. It was only natural, therefore, that the ultra-collaborationist groups, frequently with the encouragement of the German authorities, should establish their headquarters in the capital too.

One important group was led by Marcel Déat, who had left the socialist party in 1933 to form a new party which became known as the 'neo-socialists'. Although he told the Italian press attaché as early as 1934 that 'he considered that a corporatist régime like [Italy's] could and should be established in France', there was little in Déat's conduct before 1940 to suggest that he was a fascist, although he gradually became an out-and-out appeaser and wrote the notorious 'Die for Danzig?' article in his newspaper, *L'Oeuvre*, in April 1939. It was the French collapse of 1940 which turned him into a supporter of Hitler's New Order and, acting with the zeal of the converted, he was attacking the Vichy government for its lack of enthusiasm for collaboration with Germany as early as the autumn of that year. In February 1941 he founded the *Rassemblement National Populaire*, which was intended to form the nucleus of a single collaborationist party. One of its early supporters was Eugène Deloncle, the former *cagoulard* leader, but the alliance between the two men did not last for long. Deloncle tried to take over the RNP and, when Déat was the victim of an assassination attempt in August 1941, he was convinced that Deloncle was responsible. Deloncle finally left the RNP in October 1941 and gradually evolved to an anti-German position. His conspiratorial nature prevented him from leaving it at that, however, and he was soon in contact with anti-Nazi elements in the German intelligence service. He was shot by Gestapo agents who came to question him in 1943.

Déat's great rival was Jacques Doriot of the PPF. While Déat condemned Marshal Pétain and the 'national revolution' from an early date, Doriot was in his own words 'one of the Marshal's men'. It was not until the end of 1941 that he too began to adopt an attitude of hostility towards Vichy.

Various minor collaborationist groups and parties tended to gravitate around either Déat's RNP or Doriot's PPF, but it proved impossible to unite these two major formations. Although both sides sought doctrinal reasons for their disagreement, it was probably due more to the differing backgrounds and personalities of the two leaders. About the only thing they did manage to agree upon was the establishment in July 1941 of the *Légion des Volontaires Français contre le Bolchevisme* which was to fight alongside the Germans on the eastern front.

In addition to their quarrel with the Vichy government's policy, Déat and Doriot had a personal grievance against Pierre Laval, who was the effective head of the government during the last two years of the régime. For reasons which do not concern us here, Laval had been dismissed by Pétain in December 1940 and, although he disagreed with their views, he was not above using the services of Déat and Doriot to help him return to power, an objective which he achieved in April 1942. He refused, however, to reward either by appointing him to his government and this, not surprisingly, gave rise to considerable bad feeling. Doriot's supporters, in particular, began to suggest that their leader might prove more successful in dealing with the Germans than Laval himself. Laval was greatly alarmed by this talk, for he suspected that the SS, who had recently expanded their activities in France, were backing Doriot. In December 1942, after the allied landings in north Africa and the occupation of the rest of France, Laval asked the Germans for permission to dissolve the PPF and combine it with Déat's RNP in a new *parti unique* under his leadership. The Germans refused. This decision was in line with their traditional policy. Beyond a few SS fanatics, no one in the German government seriously considered making Doriot head of the French government in place of Laval, but to keep the threat of a rival government in Paris in front of its nose was a highly effective way of making Vichy toe the line.

By the summer of 1943, however, when the French resistance was becoming a serious threat, when the middle and lower ranks of the French police and administration were ever more actively sabotaging German interests and when there was a constant flow of rumours to the effect that Pétain was about to dismiss Laval once more, the Germans began to take the view that some of the 'hard core fascists' should join the Vichy government to stiffen its backbone. Not surprisingly, they were supported in this by the 'hard core fascists' themselves, some of whom sent a lengthy memorandum to the German authorities in September 1943 in which they outlined their proposals for a 'French recovery'. Laval did his best to block any suggestion that he should take these people into his government. If he did this without a prior clarification of relations with the German government, he told the German diplomatic representative in Paris in October, it 'would completely discredit the government with the French administration and police . . .' If Hitler would make it clear, both to the French people and to Marshal Pétain, 'that Germany was making a tangible contribution to the establishment of a new Europe', it would create the necessary climate of opinion for their appointment. Laval had tried, without success, to wrest just such a commitment from Hitler for the best part of a year and he must have realized that the *Führer* had no intention of giving it. But a final clumsy attempt by Pétain to get rid of him in November 1943 led to a German ultimatum ordering the Marshal 'to entrust . . . M.Laval with the task of the immediate reconstruction of the French cabinet in a way which is acceptable to the German government and which will guarantee collaboration'. Laval could either accept this commission or resign. As he considered himself indispensable, he accepted. After various negotiations which need not detain us, a number of 'hard core fascists' entered the government, including the ex-*cagoulard* Joseph Darnand as Secretary-General for the Maintenance of Order and Marcel Déat as Minister of Labour and National Solidarity.

Laval's last battle with the 'hard core fascists' was in July 1944, when they presented Marshal Pétain with a manifesto bemoaning the government's impotence and calling for action.

Gestures and acts must be accomplished [the manifesto proclaimed]. These gestures and acts will give the country the impression that, at long last, the government knows what it wants. These gestures and acts will show it that strength, faith and intelligence are on the government's side and not on that of its enemies. Thousands of public servants and millions of Frenchmen will rally to authority when it is displayed.

The fact that such rubbish could be written in all seriousness a month after D-day shows the extent to which the signatories, who included both Déat and Doriot, had lost touch with reality. At a cabinet meeting on 12 July, Laval carried the day with his argument that there was no alternative to his policy of neutrality in the struggle that was now raging on French soil. He was bitterly critical of those of his ministers who had had the temerity to put their names to the manifesto, particularly Déat who stayed away from the meeting. 'Either Déat stops his activities, or he resigns, or he replaces me,' he cried. 'I can no longer work with him. If he comes to power, it will be catastrophic. Civil war will be precipitated.'

Unfortunately, as such power that it still possessed slipped from the Vichy government's grasp, extremists on both sides were already precipitating the very civil war which Laval feared. The *Milice*, the élite corps of Darnand's police force, were already engaged in a bitter conflict with the resistance. The situation might have deteriorated still further had not the allied advance been so rapid. By the beginning of September 1944, the Germans had more or less completely withdrawn from France and the Vichy government, against its will, had gone with them. Marshal Pétain and Laval refused to co-operate any further with their captors, but Déat, Darnand, Doriot and others had no such scruples. Déat and Darnand joined the 'French governmental committee for the defence of national interests' which was presided over by Fernand de Brinon, the former Vichy

277

ambassador to the German authorities in Paris. Doriot, unable even at this stage to resolve his differences with Déat, presided over a rival 'French liberation committee' which enjoyed the support of Himmler, Goebbels and perhaps even Hitler himself. With this kind of backing, it was only a matter of time before Doriot was recognized as the head of the French émigré movement. On 22 February 1945 he set out in triumph to receive the 'surrender' of his rivals. *En route*, his car was strafed by an aircraft – accounts differ as to whether it was Allied or German – and he was killed.

If one were asked to sum up the essence of French fascism during the decade 1934–44, one could do no better than quote the 21-point programme of Joseph Darnand's *Milice*. It is set out in the form of a diptych, with one side recording what the movement was against the and other what it was for: a kind of catalogue of vices and virtues. Here it is in full:

1   Against the forgetting of crimes; for the punishment of the guilty.
2   Against scepticism; for faith.
3   Against apathy; for enthusiasm.
4   Against bourgeois selfishness; for human solidarity.
5   Against individualism; for the community spirit.
6   Against futile freedom; for the real freedoms.
7   Against equality; for rank.
8   Against influence; for merit.
9   Against routine; for the spirit of initiative.
10   Against tradition; for worth.
11   Against democracy; for authority.
12   Against anarchy; for discipline.
13   Against demagogy; for truth.
14   Against the tutelage of money; for the primacy of work.
15   Against the trust; for the profession.
16   Against international capitalism; for French corporatism.
17   Against the proletarian condition; for social justice.
18   Against Gaullist dissidence; for French unity.
19   Against Bolshevism; for nationalism.
20   Against the Jewish leprosy; for French purity.
21   Against freemasonry; for Christian civilization.

The woolly mindedness, the barbaric sentiments, the contradictions and, above all, the yawning gap between aspiration and achievement express the tragedy of French, and perhaps of all, fascism.

13 Spain

Hugh Thomas

For over twenty years, from 1939 to 1962, the Spanish national radio repeated several times a day the well-worn record of the falangist hymn. A few ageing listeners doubtless muttered the words: 'Face to the sun, wearing the tunic, which yesterday you embroidered; Death will take me radiant, I shall never see you again; arise conquering battalions, awake here is Spain beginning: Spain – One; Spain – Great; Spain – Free; Spain Arise.' Even today at the entry of every Spanish village, and on the walls of nearly every church, there is to be seen not only the falangist symbol of yoke and arrows, but very often the, on the face of it rather mysterious, words: *José Antonio Presente:* that is, 'let us commemorate the founder of the movement, José Antonio Primo de Rivera who is here in spirit'. The Unions of Spain continue to be organized as 'Vertical Syndicates'.

The question therefore is whether in discussing fascism in Spain we are considering a system of government which is not only still fascist and has always been so but one which, by the nature of things (the international acceptance gained by Franco over the last ten years, the undoubted rise in the standard of living of the Spanish people), represents the cream of European fascism, the most successful fascist state, the fascist state where appeasement has actually worked? Such indeed would seem to be the case if we were to take our judgments from current political and intellectual leaders, such as Mr Fred Lee, the Colonial Secretary, and the editor of the *New Statesman*; both these gentlemen have encouraged us in vigorous terms to stand up against 'fascist Spain'.* However the situation is rather more

* Over Gibraltar in 1966.

peculiar than this would suggest, for none other than the secretary general of the Spanish Communist Party, Santiago Carrillo, recently has explained that Francoism has lost many of its fascist characteristics.

This remark may very well suggest not that Mr Fred Lee is wrong but that we are about to witness yet one more of those sudden friendships between the two most prominent enemies of the open society, a totalitarian rightism and communism, which, from the Ribbentrop-Molotov pact to the alliances between Cuban communists and Batista, have often been heralded by remarks such as that. But on the other hand there is one other voice which, in deciding frankly whether, in the title of this essay, we are talking about a corpse or a healthy cad in the prime of life, I think we should hear: the voice of those who ever since the early days of the founding of the Spanish fascist movement, the *Falange*, thirty-five years or so ago, have remained, in the face of war, of the execution of their comrades and of the persistent frustrations of their dearest hopes, fascists of the first line. These men would assure you that fascism has never had its day in Spain; that General Franco's present intrigues with the Bourbon family are the last line in a long list of betrayals of the ideas for which so many fascist martyrs fell: fascism has been deformed in Spain under Franco, by the Church and by the capitalists, they would tell you, and to prove it they have begun, with the infinite diffidence born of twenty years' subservience, to dig out forgotten letters and other documents which suggest that their founder, José Antonio Primo de Rivera, actually condemned General Franco's rising.

There is just one more preliminary point which I should note: I have been using the word *Falange* as if synonymous with fascism, fascist with falangist. Such a use of words would not seem right to any Spanish falangist. To them, this somewhat peripheral point is of importance; strictly, they would tell us, there has never been a fascist party in Spain; José Antonio refused to go or be represented at the so-called Fascist International of Montreux in 1934. Nevertheless, I am prosposing to ignore such purists and to assume that if Nazism in Germany and fascism in Italy are to be regarded as brother movements, the Spanish fascists of the *Falange* are younger brothers still.

Brothers, but by the nature of different circumstances with not only different goals, but different opportunities. Spain about the year 1920 seemed economically and socially a country of stagnation. Of course there had been some changes: whereas throughout most of the nineteenth century and indeed in 1910, 66 per cent of the active population of Spain worked on the land, in 1920, after the first world war, the figure had dropped to 57 per cent. There had been a steady movement into Barcelona throughout the nineteenth century: the population went up from 100,000 to over a million between 1800 and 1900. Still, Barcelona was the only town in Spain which had so increased. Madrid, Saragossa and Bilbao, the only other large cities, had grown far less – hence, doubtless, their relative political tranquillity in comparison with Barcelona.

Thus, except for Barcelona there were not to be found in Spain the huge overblown cities of the industrial north where a rootless proletariat sought charismatic leaders to lead them, in times of unemployment, out of misery into struggle, national or international. There was unemployment, but this was more the chronic unemployment of the landless labourers in the south, or chronic under-employment of the tenant farmer in the centre or smallholder in the north-west. Barcelona, as I say, was a different matter, where a high percentage, perhaps fifteen per cent of the population, were immigrants from the south; and there and, as far as can be seen, for that reason, was the home not of fascism, but of the large anarchist-federalist movement, as well as of occasional demagogues like Lerroux.

By 1920 or so this movement was far the strongest movement in Spain, perhaps over a million strong, dedicated to the overthrow of existing society, relying on violence (the propaganda of the deed), though owing as much to Proudhon the federalist as to Bakunin, and something also to Georges Sorel, the propagandist of violence, a skeleton to be found in the genealogy of most fascist movements. Sorel's part in anarchist theory lay not so much in the propaganda of the deed, which derived from rural banditry in Spain and terrorism in Russia, but the revolutionary general strike, conceived as a sudden thunderbolt which in the right 'objective conditions' was expected to paralyse industrial capitalism, and usher in the millenium.

It can be reasonably argued that anarchism, with the accompanying terrorism and repression in Barcelona was, with the colonial war in Morocco, the main cause of paralysis in the old constitutional monarchical system, making easy the establishment in power of Spain's first twentieth century military dictator, General Primo de Rivera – the father, critically (as will be seen), of the founder of the *Falange*. The reasons for the anarchist failure on the other hand to crush industrial capitalism by violence were of course various, but most important was the fact that industry played so small a part in Spanish society. Paralyse industry and in 1920 you paralysed only twenty per cent of the nation. The service sector of the economy was then as large as the industrial.

In any discussion of fascism in Spain, the seven-year dictatorship of General Primo de Rivera must have a place, if a small one. King Alfonso XIII referred to him as 'my Mussolini', and that indeed did resemble this general's relationship with the monarch. The same, however, might have been said of any *maire du palais* or grand vizier. Nor was Primo de Rivera in temperament a fascist. Henry Buckley has described how, as a young man walking home after dinner in Madrid, he saw ahead of him a somewhat weary figure, but his back still erect, swathed in a cloak, returning alone on foot along the Gran Via in winter: it was the dictator. Primo de Rivera had no concern about personal security, he was relatively magnanimous, fairly merciful by the standards of the second half of the twentieth century, and, if he banned the press and silenced or even exiled intellectuals, his dictatorship was more agreeable to live under than most of his type. The key to his time of power was that world terms of trade favoured expansion; it was as easy to be in power in the late twenties as in the late fifties; his policy of cheap money was for a long time successful and under him the standard of living

283

leapt up in a situation of relative political stability: *per capita* income in Spain under Primo was as high as it ever was until 1959–60: a fundamental fact explaining why the middle class afterwards looked back towards his time as a golden one.

Yet he cannot be quite dismissed as a mere military dictator, with none of the trappings of fascism. If fascism implies a charismatic leader, Primo had more appeal than Franco. If the cynical manipulation of the press is fascist, Primo's regime was fascist. One shudders to imagine what he would have done with radio or television. Although Primo's own efforts to found a national movement of his own were not successful he hardly needed to do so, since his power depended on the army: and, in a sense, the Spanish officers, who are really a rather pretentious political party more than a corps of warriors, have always made a mass fascist party unnecessary; in the education of officers, their oaths to the flag, their contempt for civilian politicians, their sense of divine mission to incarnate the unity of the country (as opposed to its fragmentation into federal units), their tradition of political action, can be observed the outlines of a permanent authoritarian though not totalitarian movement. Not accidentally, perhaps, did José Antonio de Primo de Rivera, in one of his last letters, remark that in the last resort it has always been a platoon of soldiers who have saved Spain.

But to return for a moment to his father, the dictator. His economic and labour policy had some of the elements of Mussolini's: a much publicized programme of public works, road building, large industrial fairs, great projects designed to catch the eye: in this Primo had little to learn from Mussolini. His treatment of the Spanish socialists is also of interest: that party in the twenties was by no means yet a dogmatic social democratic one. The Spanish socialists had narrowly escaped being engulfed in the communist international; though in the event only a small group split off to found the Communist Party. Throughout the twenties the socialists collaborated effectively with Primo as a party and as a union, Largo Caballero becoming the government labour chief, in effect Minister of Labour. The chances were that had Primo lasted longer the Spanish socialists would have developed into something similar to the official state-sponsored unions found in Sweden.

With a growing intellectual revolt, with the world depression and the disillusion, even of the army, with Primo's personal rule, the King dismissed his Mussolini in early 1930; a year later he was dismissed himself, less by an adverse vote than by the evident reluctance of the traditional forces of order in Spain – the army and the Church – to regard the principle of monarchy as relevant to Spain's political predicament.

The fall of the monarchy began the period of intense political activity and disputation which resulted in the civil war. Of this period three general points might be made: first, Spain was experiencing the side effects of the depression, share prices slumped, and the country was for the first time since the Napoleonic wars sharing in a Europe-wide phenomenon of the first magnitude. Second, the political instability was not simply a matter of hastily changing parties such as characterized for instance the Fourth Republic in France, but of discord over the whole range of political habits and traditions of the country. New parties sprang up persistently, such old parties as there were (such as the Socialists or the corrupt Radicals) changed, during these five years, their philosophy of politics. New leaders appeared suddenly and established themselves as potential saviours of the country with a few strong speeches. Third, this political instability persisted against a background of social stagnation, the old order being scarcely altered even by the socialist-liberal reforming government, the fundamental land problem being left virtually unaltered by the agrarian reform.

It was natural that when common economic problems and increasingly internationalized political movements were dragging Spain closer towards the rest of Europe that there should spring up some kind of fascist party in the country: in fact there were to be several. But all of them, it must be said, throughout these five years were so small and so unimportant as barely to deserve more than the traditional footnote in history. The first such party – it scarcely deserves the name – to emerge briefly was

285

founded by Ramino Ledesma, the poor son of a Castilian school-master who founded a newspaper for himself and a few student friends about 1930; he affected Hitler's coif, though his political views sound vaguely like those of the younger Hitler, or perhaps Strasser. Anything new, from Soviet Russia to Mussolini, was to be praised, the old condemned. After about a year of fruitless activity, he joined forces with another young Castilian, Onésimo Redondo, symptomatically a native of the old capital of Castile, Valladolid, who with slightly more articulate dreams of military grandeur, had a certain success among the sugarbeet growers of that district (of whom he was a paid organizer): odd cannon fodder, it is surely not too ribald to think, for restoring the Spain of the Catholic kings, for sugarbeet growers are in all countries the most privileged of farmers, depending on tariffs to prevent their expensive product from being priced into waste by Caribbean producers.

These two young men grumbled on for two years in almost total obscurity, attempting without success to resolve the delicate problem of how a new Spain organized on Nazi lines might restore the Catholic kings without, however, benefiting the Church.

They were not alone. With a worthy, reforming but none too politically adept government in power, there were others, some young men, some old, who in articles or speeches were bent on discrediting liberal myths. Some visited Rome and observed from a distance the mighty figure of Mussolini on his famous balcony. Unlike Harold Nicolson, then editor of the English proto-fascist newspaper, this sight had not filled them with disgust; on the contrary: one of them, Ernesto Giménez Caballero returned to announce what remains to my mind the most engaging of fascist slogans: 'We are going to exalt national sentiment with insanity, with paroxysms, with whatever need be. Better a nation of imbeciles than international sanity.'

But there were more formidable critics of liberalism than this gentleman (who today occupies the post of Spanish ambassador to Paraguay). On the one hand, such prestigious intellectuals as Ortega and Unamuno, both of whom had been in the lead of the movement to overthrow the monarchy, and now, caught up by their own romanticism and in the case of Ortega by a belief in the role of an élite – any élite – in regenerating the nation, had decided by 1933 that the Republic was not what they had hoped it would be. They became busy with manifestos for vague parties-above-parties, poetic documents never completed. On the other hand there was a whole school of upper-class monarchists, some army officers dispossessed by the Republic's mild scheme for reducing the size of the army, some grandees worried about the effects of the diminutive agrarian reform, who with verve and energy (notably lacking in their defence of the king when he was on the throne) embarked, almost immediately he had left it, on fund-raising and conspiracy designed to restore him, though explicitly not on terms of constitutional monarchy. What type of partyless monarchy would be established was always obscure. Some of these men gave money to poor Ledesma, on the grounds that any trouble-maker was better than none. These Alfonsists – they wished of course to restore Alfonso XIII – were also able in opposition to do something which they had utterly failed to do in power: namely, to make common cause with their old enemies of three civil wars in the nineteenth century, the Carlists.

Carlism in Spain is far from being simply a quarrel over what colours should figure in the national flag, large though that important matter does actually loom; I have in my possession an invitation to a Mass to commemorate the solemn enthronement of the Sacred Heart of Jesus to be celebrated in the barracks of a Carlist regiment in the civil war of 1936, on All Saints Day 1936, and in the year 103 of the struggle of Traditional Spain against liberalism, masonry and Judaism. The simple passion for a monarchy without parties backed by a pastoral nation of happy smallholders, which appears at first sight to be the Carlist ideal (along with the enthronement of a monarch dedicated to non-democratic principles) was thus sustained in the thirties, as it had been during the civil wars of the nineteenth century, with a vague but powerful antisemitism, none the less strong because the Spanish Jews had almost all been deported in the sixteenth century: it could be represented that what was wrong with the

287

modern world was the existence of a powerful Jewish conspiracy of masonic bankers, with headquarters in Zurich and branches in Moscow (it was not known in Pamplona that such prominent Jewish bolsheviks as Trotsky, Radek and Zinoviev were hardly in a position of power), and also in Madrid and Barcelona: though there were few Jews, there were several ministers who were masons and many Spaniards of the Right ignorantly looked on these harmless aprons as being as dangerous as the hammer and sickle. The forged *Protocols of the Elders of Zion* had also been published in Spain and believed there as elsewhere.

Carlism, it must be admitted, had been going through a difficult stage since the late nineteenth century, but in the early thirties, faced with the new challenge of an anti-clerical government, unity at least was restored, an all too constitutional pretender happily died and was succeeded as the claimant by his uncle who actually fought in the Carlist wars of the seventies; training for some kind of military anti-republican action began as early as 1932. A temporarily retired colonel travelled through the valleys of Navarre with army training manuals and from 1934 onwards a few Carlists were trained in Italy. Do not ignore the Carlists in your estimate of fascism in Spain then or even now; even with the *Falange* itself, relations were to be close. The man who ultimately trained *them*, Colonel Rada, was a Carlist. The Carlists also had a youth movement which in many places closely worked with the fascists.

Two other forces should be mentioned: one a professional élite with precise views, the other a large and amorphous political movement. The first was a group of young officers in the army, the *Unión Militar Española* specifically designed to overthrow the Republic, and establish presumably a military dictatorship, of order and authority; the other was the large semi-Christian Democratic political party, the CEDA, which sprang from a group of parties inspired by the powerful lay Catholic body Catholic Action. These Christians were a large middle-class party with naturally many people of all sorts of policies adhering to them, and most of their leaders aimed at revising from a democratic standpoint the anti-clerical clauses which the Republic had unwisely fitted in to the constitution. The trouble was that in the kaleidoscopic and imitative atmosphere of elections in the thirties, the young, carefully chosen leader, Gil Robles, did sound more and more fascistic in his speeches; he had visited Austria and had been rather impressed by the ill-starred experiments of the unhappy Dr Dollfuss. Sometimes this came out in his speeches. On a more superficial level, his followers chose to call him *Jefe*, leader, in an obvious imitation of the *Führer*, plastered huge pictures of him over the hoardings depicting him as a man of destiny, and demanded for him the 'ministry of war and all the power'. Actually, as it turned out, Gil Robles was far from a man of destiny, and in power (which he obtained in 1935) he behaved in a generally democratic fashion, refusing to use his opportunity to establish himself on a permanent and illegal basis.

Now out of all these forces or pressures General Franco, with his brother-in-law Serrano Súñer, was eventually to forge the united movement which won the war and still, after a fashion, runs Spain today. Lots of little streams, some too small to be noticed, others quite appealing in a way, gradually united and lost their individuality in a large dull sluggish and gloomy river, carrying the movement across the wearisome plains of Spanish history since 1939. Franco, it should be said, was in the early 1930s known only as a successful young general, with somewhat contradictory though severe views; Serrano Súñer, significantly, was a young lawyer who succeeded in being elected to parliament and who later led the vociferous and militant Christian Democratic youth movement.

This process of unification began, as we have already seen, with the merger of Ledesma's little group of so-called national syndicalists with Redondo's *juntas offensivas* – the united movement being known as the JONS. This had little success. Then in 1934 a new figure appeared on the scene: José Antonio Primo de Rivera, son of the dictator. He is at this distance of time an appealing figure. A little older than some of the other people we have been talking about – he was fully thirty – he had lived, like most of his countrymen, without much political life during his father's dictatorship. With his father he had the ambiguous relationship that one might expect where the father was a good-living philanderer and the son severe, though high minded, and somewhat humourless. After his father's death, Primo de Rivera *fils* entered politics as a somewhat unorthodox monarchist determined to avenge his father's memory. Since almost everyone had betrayed his father before the end, young Primo de Rivera found himself up against the entire established range of political parties. He gathered around him a group of *señoritos*, young men of middle-class family bent on cutting some sort of heroic dash, some aristocrats, no one of working-class origin. For a time he too received money from wealthy monarchist bankers, though otherwise he drifted between 1931 and 1933 in a generally fascist direction, hailing the capture of power by Hitler in January 1933 as a 'victory achieved by irreproachable democratic means'. In late 1933 he, an air ace named Ruiz de Alda and a professor, Garcia Valdescas, formed a little party which they named the *Falange Española*, the Spanish phalanx. José Antonio's speech on the occasion deserves quotation:

Finally the liberal state came to offer us economic slavery, saying to the workers with tragic sarcasm, 'You are free to work as you wish: no one can compel you to accept specified conditions . . . as *free* citizens you are not obliged to accept them, if you do not want to; but as *poor* citizens, if you do not accept them you will die of hunger surrounded of course by the utmost liberality'.

Why therefore was José Antonio not a socialist? Because socialism, a 'legitimate reaction against liberal slavery, went astray, since it resulted in the material interpretation of life and history; second, in a sense of reprisal; and third in the proclamation of the dogma of class struggle'.

What precisely would José Antonio put in place of these unsuccessful schools of political economy? This is more difficult to say: in his founding speech and afterwards we hear much of the fatherland, as a 'total unity', a transcendent synthesis with its own goals to fulfil: 'When one has a permanent sense of life and of history that very sense gives solutions beyond the concrete, just as love may tell us when we ought to scold and when we ought to embrace, without true love having to set up a minimum programme of embraces and reproaches.' After more rhetoric of this nature, José Antonio tells us that the Spaniards, despite regional differences, should 'feel in harmony with an irrevocable sense of destiny'; political parties should disappear. No one was ever born a member of a political party; on the other hand we are all born members of a family; we are all neighbours in a municipality; 'we all labour in the exercise of a profession'. So society would so far as possible be organized politically on the basis of professions, families, municipalities. And then:

there must be no shrinking from violence. For who has said (while speaking of everything save violence) that the supreme value in the hierarchy of values is amiability? Who has said that when our feelings are insulted we are obliged to be accommodating, instead of acting like men? It is very correct that argument should be the first instrument of communication. But no other argument is admissible, than that of fists and pistols when justice or the fatherland is attacked.

Of course these arguments, if they can be so called, were bound to seem fairly unappealing to the working class: and to them José Antonio had a special word:

Let no one imagine that we recruit men in order to offer rewards; let no one imagine that we join together in the defence of privileges. I should like to have this microphone before me to carry into every working class home to say; Yes, we wear a tie; yes, you may say of us that we are *señoritos*. But we urge a spirit of struggle for things that cannot concern us as *señoritos*; we come to struggle for a totalitarian state that can reach the humble as well as the powerful with its benefits. We are thus, for so always have been the *señoritos* of Spain. In this manner they have achieved the true status of *señores* because in distant lands and in our fatherland itself, they have learned to suffer death and to carry out hard missions precisely for reasons in which as *señoritos* they have no interest at all.

And then Primo de Rivera allowed an echo of Shelley into his thoughts:

There are some who think that in order to unite men's wills against the march of revolution, it is proper to offer superficially gratifying solutions; they think it necessary to hide everything which could

291

awaken an emotion. What a mistake! People have never been moved by anyone save the poets, and woe to him who, before the poetry which destroys, does not know how to raise the poetry which promises ... In a poetic movement we shall raise this fervent feeling for Spain ... our Spain will not emerge from elections, nor is our goal there. The atmosphere there is tired and murky, like a tavern at the end of a night of dissipation ... Our place is outside under the cloudless heavens, weapons in our hands, with the stars above us. Let the others go on with their merrymaking. We outside, in tense fervent and certain vigilance, already feel the dawn breaking in our hearts.

Such was José Antonio Primo de Rivera. He himself actually secured election in the 1933 *Cortes*, chiefly on his family name, and early in 1934 Ledesma and Redondo of the JONS, attracted by him as a leader, joined with him, so that a new united movement was launched known as the *Falange Española de las JONS*. With a now right-wing parliament and government its activities were circumscribed. Primo de Rivera never saw eye-to-eye with Ledesma, who in turn from a puritanical standpoint began to look on Primo de Rivera as a tool of rich interests. And indeed the question of money for the party was naturally a main preoccupation. In 1934–5 the *Falange*'s activities were confined to running a broadsheet, training on Sundays in blue shirts in the Casa de Campo – where José Antonio would maintain the poetic spirit by reading Kipling's *If* through a megaphone; and there might be occasional raids (along with Carlist youth) into working-class districts, and more often and most important street fights between student friends of the *Falange* and socialist students. An atmosphere of gun law dominated the University of Madrid during this time; the first martyr of the *Falange* was a student killed by a socialist while selling the *Falange* newspaper in early 1934.

It would seem that on the eve of the elections of 1935 the party had about 8000–10,000 members, nearly half in Madrid and Valladolid, another 2500 in the Seville-Cádiz area, and the rest scattered, though there were almost none in the anarchist fief of Barcelona and none among the Basque Nationalist districts or in Carlist Navarre. There was a very small feminine section organized by José Antonio's sister Pilar. The *Falange* had a workers' organization too, though the reason for this was apparently that a recent subsidy had been agreed with the Monarchist Party who had stipulated that forty-five per cent of the funds should be spent on an anti-marxist syndicalist workers' organization. This body gathered a few dozen members in Madrid, mostly taxi drivers and waiters (significantly so, it certainly seems). Apart from the sugarbeet-men in Valladolid, the overwhelming majority of workers who became attached to the *Falange* before the civil war seem to have beeen employed in services, and particularly among those such as waiters or taxi drivers who performed an essential task to the old master class. However, this effort at syndicalism before the civil war really made no headway.

Between 1934 and 1936, José Antonio's party seemed often in sight of disintegration. The movement remained mostly lower-middle class or middle class in nature. Students were notably the largest single support; about four ex-communist students joined in, but on the whole there was no major desertion from the parties of the Left. José Antonio once approached the right-wing socialist leader Prieto to take over the leadership of the movement, on the model of Mosley in England perhaps, but this offer was courteously rejected. Imitation seemed the keynote: even the falangist hymn 'Face to the Sun' was a plagiarism of a poem by the Cuban Martí. On the simple level of street-fighting there was a little contact between anarchist gunmen and the *Falange*; both hated the socialists more than anyone else, and there may even have been in Madrid some possibility of other contact. The gunmen in the *Falange* argued for a more militant attitude, and José Antonio himself, though, as I have said, he did not shrink in theory from violence, was somewhat opposed to it in practice. Another with whom José Antonio had some contact was his father's old Finance Minister, Calvo Sotelo, almost the only economically informed politician on the Right, who returned from exile in 1934 as a monarchist leader. Partly due to José Antonio's scorn for Calvo's desertion of his father, this move also failed to develop into anything. Franco, to whom José Antonio wrote about the time of the socialist insurrection of Asturias, calling on him to rally to the cause of a new Spain, does not seem to have answered the letter.

In early 1935 Ledesma was finally expelled by José Antonio from the united movement and he faded away into the Post Office. José Antonio reigned alone inside the political system which he hoped to overthrow, living privately in the world of the *haute bourgeoisie*, dressing up in blue uniform on Sundays, having lost (after a visit to Germany) his past admiration of Nazism and refusing any overt connection with Mussolini. The party's propagandists ceased referring to it as fascist, José Antonio spoke more and more of each nation's need to develop its own party of destiny and, now that Ledesma was out of the way, the Church could be talked of as an inescapable aspect of the national soul. The party remained immature and its most capable historian, Stanley Payne, has estimated that sixty to seventy per cent of Falangists were under twenty-one years of age in 1936.

The elections of 1936 radically altered the position. The *Falange* first sought to join the right-wing National Front, with the Catholics and monarchists, but negotiations broke down and they entered the lists alone: they failed to win a seat, their leader himself being defeated. With the victory of the Left, parliament remained a battleground but only one of several. The army re-entered Spanish politics immediately. Generals got together to plan a right-wing revolution, carefully negotiating with the in-creasing militant Carlists, and reaching by mid-summer a broad understanding with most politicians of the Right. The Catholic Party lost momentum, having failed to win the election and, at the same moment as the socialist youth movement went over to the communists, the Catholic Youth under Serrano Súñer entered into a common understanding with the *Falange*. The rising tide of violence following the elections, partly brought on by the release of left-wing political prisoners, secured that in the *Falange* the gunmen, anxious to step up the pace of violence, gained an increasing hold. José Antonio was unable fully to control his followers, and in the spring he and other *Falange* leaders were imprisoned on charges of disturbing the peace and permanently held. This was counter-productive. Bereft of leaders, the falangists of different districts followed their own whims, shooting at socialists in some cases almost unthinkingly, communicating only occasionally with José Antonio. The officers who were engaged in planning the overthrow of the Republic took no heed of the falangists, and timed the rising without in many cases informing them. José Antonio himself seems to have given a somewhat grudging if contradictory support to the rising in a letter to General Mola at the end of June, written from Alicante jail.

The rising occurred on 18–19 July 1936 and in the event was in some places successful, in others not. Nowhere save in Valladolid did the *Falange* play much part in the fighting or the planning. The civil war began as basically a struggle between the army and the workers' organizations. In places where the workers won, the *Falange* were however imprisoned and many shot, some with trials, some without. These included nearly all the leaders. Ruiz de Alda, the aviator who had founded the *Falange* with José Antonio, was shot in the Model Prison in Madrid; Redondo was killed by socialist militia in Castile; Ledesma was shot in Madrid. José Antonio himself was tried on a charge of helping to prepare the revolt against the Republic and found guilty, and was shot by a firing squad. The falangist movement seemed to have been eliminated completely.

In the areas where the generals won, however, there remained a few unimportant local falangist leaders. They and their followers took a certain role in the repression of the Left though no more than either the army or the orthodox Right: significantly, perhaps, the poet Lorca hid for several weeks in the house of a falangist in Granada before being taken out and shot on the orders of the Catholic deputy for the city. Deeply imbrued in the massacres though they were, the *Falange* are believed on occasion to have raised doubts as to their desirability.

Soon, as the war continued, the remains of the *Falange* began to develop a new authority; the generals who were running the war found some sort of political organization to gear the country to the war effort quite useful. All the older parties were discredited. Indeed, the Catholic Party ceased to function altogether, and its members began to join the *Falange* in swarms. Once it became clear that there were obvious advantages in this course, membership grew at a quite phenomenal rate. New members – new shirts – swamped the surviving old shirts. Even ex-members of the anarchist movement or the socialists hastened to put on the blue shirts of the *Falange*. The *Falange* itself operated as much as a recruiting organization as a political party. Able-bodied men were swiftly drafted to the fronts in falangist units which for a time operated independently within the army, as did the brave and merciless Carlists. The few party leaders who had survived the holocaust of the first weeks of the war held a series of meetings, principally designed to keep the place of leader open for José Antonio when he should return. But of course he could not do so, a fact not admitted for a long time. None of his successors could compare with him as leader. Nevertheless, disturbed by the apparently conservative aspirations of the military leaders of the rebellion, they opened negotiations to achieve a measure of unity with, bizarrely, the Carlists, whose political leaders were also disturbed, though for other reasons, by Franco. Franco meantime, as a result of a series of meetings with his fellow generals, had assumed the post of both Head of State and Head of government on 1 October 1936 without consultation with either the *Falange* or the Carlists.

By the spring of 1937, the now vast but amorphous *Falange Española* had as its temporary boss an ex-mechanic without formal education and no oratorical power, named Hedilla. He had been the party leader in the Castilian port of Santander. His semi-proletarian origin commended itself to some, such as the German ambassador who (without much encouragement from Berlin) hoped to see the development in Spain of a serious copy of the Nazi movement. The Germans offered to Franco to send one of their political agents to assist in this. The offer was refused. Franco clearly had his own ideas. In early 1937 Serrano Súñer escaped from a Republican prison; he met Franco and

worked out a scheme for the unification of all the political parties
on the generals' side in the war. Franco himself would be national
head. The problem was to foist this on the *Falange* and the
Carlists. The latter's political leader had already been exiled.
The falangist leaders were carefully duped into the appearance
of a conspiracy against Franco, Hedilla and others were
arrested by the army, Hedilla was hastily tried and condemned
to be shot (an unfair sentence later commuted: Hedilla was freed
in 1942), and Franco and Serrano took over, the one as nominal
head, the other as organizer. The Carlists, under the stress of
war, accepted without a murmur, and since then, April 1937, the
one political movement in Spain has been the monstrously
named *Falange Tradicionalista y de las Juntas de Ofensiva
Nacional-Sindicalista*, or FET, the state party, through which
General Franco has ever since maintained military rule in Spain.

It is not my intention to trace the history of this organization
throughout this period but I should of course attempt to estimate
how far it can indeed be referred to as fascist.

Despite the act of formal unification of the parties supporting
Franco in the war, each of the groups so swallowed up persisted
in its ultimate aspirations and to each General Franco gave
encouragement; the monarchists were assured that the monarchy
would be restored; the remaining old shirts of the *Falange* were
told that a totalitarian state would eventually be set up. The
German ambassador pointed out that in late 1937 'one is as apt
to hear the opinion in Spain that "Franco is entirely the creature
of the Falange" as that "Franco has sold himself entirely to the
reactionaries" or "Franco is a proven monarchist" or he is
completely under the influence of the Church.' Everything was
postponed indefinitely; no great new constitution was set up.
Gestures were made to all sorts of groups. 'How do you find
the New Spain', another German diplomat was asked. 'When
I find it I shall tell you', was the answer.

In the government, nearly all the ministers were either monarchists, generals or technicians. The exception was Serrano
Súñer, who not being one of them never had the confidence of
the old shirts, and played his own and his brother-in-law's power

297

game with great success. The propaganda ministry was admittedly handed over to the *Falange* and their most brilliant speaker Ridreujo sought to make clear from that position the future totalitarian lines of the state. At the beginning of the world war Spain was favoured with passionate anti-democratizing, anti-semitism, and various revolutionary dreams in the style of José Antonio. But the ministries of justice and education were given to ex-Carlists. These ministries did their task efficiently: in 1938 they ensured that education in Spain would be completely run by the Church, that all other religions would be banned, that civil marriage would be illegal and so on. The Jesuits triumphantly came back.

These gestures of course brought the Church to back the régime but it also meant that the régime would be persistently Catholic. The Church, whose members had suffered so severely at the hands of the anarchists in the early days, had anyway always favoured the rebellion; they had contributed much of the mythology of the nationalist side: it was they who had referred to Franco as carrying out a crusade; they who had endorsed the claim that St Teresa had appeared to stop the Republican militia on the road to Avila; who had approved Franco's retention of St Teresa's hand by his bedside; or who had agreed that it would be appropriate for the Virgin of the Pillar to be made a captain-general. The bishops had signed a letter addressed to the bishops of the whole world approving the saintliness of the crusade. True, the archbishop of Santiago had complained of the bloodletting and the bishop of Pamplona had criticized the murders in his province. But in general the Church had been the most invaluable ally of the victors; indeed they had been the victors and they were handsomely rewarded by the Generalissimo who himself began in the war to show a piety not previously much marked, and kept it up afterwards, acknowledging an obeisance only to God and to history, certainly not to the philosophy of José Antonio.

Much is said of clerical fascists but this would be to overdo it; in Spain the Church emerged from the war so badly hit, so bitter against the defeated that little would be heard of the social side of the Church's role for almost a generation. Those embarrassing pictures of bishops doing the fascist salute were hastily put away. Better the old world of privilege than the new dawn of fascism. Though the fascists might in Spain acknowledge a role for the Church, the Church made no such gesture to fascism. The Church was conservative and that for the time being was that.

But what of the party, the FET, itself? Surely this had some meaning? It was certainly organized. But there was no exclusiveness. Everyone with any post in government was automatically a member of the party, so was anyone who had ever been in a Republican jail. There were party *locales* in every village and suburb of Spain but they became quite simply a large national movement of place-hunters. The National Council of the FET was named by the *Caudillo*, who carefully balanced membership to avoid difficulties for himself. Even the women's section had almost 600,000 members, or five per cent of the entire female population. This was a well-meaning and not ineffective group of social workers while the war was on. Afterwards, membership disintegrated. In the FET proper, disintegration began even earlier. Carlists ceased to take it seriously almost at the beginning. The generals saw to it that no para-military SA type of body was set up. A general, Muñoz Grandes, was made the secretary-general of the FET, and was answerable only to Franco. The falangist ex-combatants were utterly harmless as an organization. Prominent falangists were kept happy with jobs of various kinds: the surviving senior member of the movement who had spent much of the war in a Republican prison, Fernández Cuesta, was sent off after a spell as a minister to be ambassador to Argentina.

The old shirts did not actually surrender without further controversy. A labour charter partly under Italian inspiration had been devised to give a progressive front to the military dictatorship. Many people, Franco included, felt at times that for safety's sake the workers ought to be given a better deal after the war. Interminable arguments attended the presentation of various drafts. A ministry of syndical organization was set up. Beneath it there were regulated vertical syndicates in which the labour force would be organized. A vertical syndicate is a union which is run from the top. Over the years syndicates have become the most typical of the institutions of Francoism – a vast, cynical bureaucracy, a state management body for the effective deployment of labour. Some benefits – social insurance, higher wages, education courses (technical and even liberal) – have been obtained. But they have not secured their pretentious goal: the abolition of the class struggle. Nor have they abolished either strikes or dismissals. There has been some development in recent years; the lower officers are now elected. They are on bad terms with the Ministry of Labour and their whole future is ambiguous. But the leaders have remained nominated by the cabinet, that is by Franco.

Thus the new Spain of General Franco was certainly not the new country of which the early fascists spoke so lyrically. Francoism doubtless bears a relation to fascism, as did the rule by Primo de Rivera. But Francoism derives essentially from the fact that the country ended the civil war with two emotions; infinite fatigue and a desire for vengeance: hardly the best attributes for the construction of a new society. Falangists have played a part in one or other of Franco's cabinets, or state boards such as the State Investment Institute (INI), but as individuals not as ideologues; since 1957 even as individuals they have vanished. Some old shirts live on as local bosses; typical among them is Girón, Minister of Labour for sixteen years, who owns and runs most of the resort of Marbella. Doubtless from his splendid villa on that sunny coast he remembers with a touch of sentiment his early days as a heroic gunman in Valladolid. From time to time José Antonio is commemorated in some splendid gathering, and indeed his body is occasionally shifted from one resting place to another. But there is little more. Brutal of course this régime has often been, cynical, opportunistic, emptily rhetorical, but these things were devised long before the fascists; authoritarian it is too, though, at least not now in what would seem to be a transitional stage into something new, not totalitarian. We still hear the mingled appeals to past glories accompanied by demands for regeneration; but one should not be

300

deluded by semi- or ex-fascists with important places in the propaganda machinery into believing that they are talking about substantial things. Nor has General Franco any pretension to charisma; his speeches have been short and rare; his régime has been a military rather than a fascist one, and for this reason I have not seen fit to lay before you more than a few vague hints of its consistency. A semi-fascist pressure group has persisted but of little power: on the twentieth anniversary of José Antonio's death an old shirt spoke on the national radio:

Jose Antonio . . . Are you satisfied with us? I do not think so. You watch us from your place, from your 20th of November [his death date] with a profound sense of melancholy and scorn. You could not be satisfied with this mediocre sensual life . . . this pursuit of riches . . .

Even more appropriate would such a sermon be in 1968. The future of course is obscure, and maybe a fascist party in the future will play a less insignificant role in the Spanish life of the future than has the Italian fascist movement since 1945. At all events that is a matter which will not become clear until after General Franco has ceased to improvise for ever, and has gone to test for himself the truth of one of José Antonio Primo de Rivera's most famous dictums: 'Paradise is not rest. Paradise is against rest. In paradise one cannot lie down. One must hold oneself up like the angels. Paradise is difficult, erect and implacable.'

14 Portugal

H. Martins

1 Integralismo Lusitano

The extreme Right in a relatively modern sense may be dated in Portugal to 1914. It was in the spring of that year that the first journal of the new 'counter-revolutionary' movement, the *Integralismo Lusitano*, started publication. Until then the only cohesive, politically organized body radically opposed to the dominant 'demo-liberal' élite was a vestigial hereditary grouping known as the 'legitimist party'. This shadowy organization was made up largely of aristocratic families owing allegiance to the exiled *miguelista* branch of the House of Braganza. The *miguelistas* may be regarded as the Portuguese counterpart of the Spanish Carlists, in terms of historical origins, social bases and ideological content. In both cases dynastic and ideological issues had converged in the 1830s and in both cases the traditionalist strata had emerged as losers in bitter civil wars with groups which included the modernizing élites. Both Carlists and Miguelists shared similar values, beliefs and symbols of an authoritarian, anti-parliamentary, corporatist and ultramontane kind. They may be regarded as typologically similar, but some crucial contrasting features should be noted.

The Miguelists lacked a regional base comparable to that of the Carlists which, whilst making them a more comprehensive national movement, prevented them from surviving in a massive, semi-organized fashion. The fairly continuous 'counter-revolutionary' intellectual tradition sustained by Spanish Carlism is also lacking in Portugal: in the Portuguese case there is a much more marked conceptual and historical discontinuity between the reactionary ideological effervescence of the 1830s and the renovation of ideological traditionalism of the late nineteenth and early twentieth centuries.

The *integralistas* only discovered the Legitimist Party and the intellectual counter-revolutionary forerunners of their movement in Portugal after they had elaborated their ideologies. But the sense of discontinuity they felt was not – as they argued – simply due to the permeation of the Portuguese élite by the rhetoric of 'demo-liberalism'. As the comparison with Carlism shows, it was also partly due to the lack of a distinctive ecological 'constituency' or regional base for the early nineteenth-century type of ideological traditionalism. It can also be explained in terms of an intellectual and stylistic dependence on France much closer among the Portuguese politico-cultural élite than among its Spanish counterpart. From the 1850s onwards, all branches of 'high' culture and all ideological tendencies were geared to French sources. The engineers and financiers of *Fontismo* in the 1850s sought to modernize the country on the lines of Saint-Simonian strategy. In the case of the Left, Proudhonian socialism, neo-Comtist positivism and radical anticlericalism were most prominent; in the right-wing groups, social catholicism and literary nationalism of the Barrès type acted as major influences so that *Action Française* found many disciples among both the integralists and the Catholic intellectuals. It was only to be expected that the intellectual vacuum left by the demise of Miguelism would be filled by an ideology of the extreme Right originating from France. It is not surprising that *Action Française* met this diffuse demand for an intellectualization of traditionalist tendencies; in fact the example and system of beliefs of 'Maurrassism' reached Portugal through a variety of channels more or less independently, which testified to the manifold pathways linking the innovating milieus of the Portuguese élite to their politico-cultural metropolis.

It is futile to discuss whether *Integralismo Lusitano* was a 'nationalist' movement which modelled itself in all its principles and policies on *Action Française*. Despite a good deal of mimicry

303

even of points of detail and the undoubted fact that personal contact with the French movement triggered off the formation of the Portuguese integralist movement, *Integralismo Lusitano* acquired a lively momentum and dialectic of its own, however parasitically Maurrassian its fundamental ideas. But in this sense it certainly did not break with the 'gallicization' or 'cosmopolitism' which it bitterly attacked in its political and ideological adversaries.

One may perhaps regard the counter-revolutionary ideologies or movements we have been reviewing as falling into two types. One type is exemplified by Carlism and Miguelism, and the other by *Action Française* and its kindred movements. They are both corporatist, monarchist, anti-parliamentary, repudiating both the French Revolution and the Reformation. But the second type is not merely chronologically later than the former: Carlism for instance survived as a vital force even beyond the peak influence achieved by 'Maurrassism'. Rather it is conceptually more modern, to the extent for example that it capitalizes on the symbols of 'nation' and 'race', advocates or practises the institutionalization of violence, and transcends regional particularism and clerical tutelage. The timing and sequence of the crystallization of the ideologies of these counter-revolutions is extremely important. Thus in Spain the *Acción Española* and *Falange* crystallized more or less at the same time in the early 1930s. In Portugal the Maurrassian-type ideology of *Integralismo Lusitano* emerged in 1914 and was zealously propagated for two decades; it succeeded in capturing important segments of several generations of university students. At the time when Italian fascist and Nazi models assumed 'world-historical' importance, those most predisposed to learn from and emulate them had all been grounded in the teachings and intellectual style of *Integralismo*. In fact the leaders of Portuguese 'national syndicalism', a movement which in a sense aimed at a much more rapid and extensive 'fascisization' than has ever been attained in Portugal, had been members of the *integralista* movement from the earliest days. Thus Portuguese 'national-syndicalism' did not represent the emergence of new political leaders or more generally of new political resources, but rather a continuation and an intensification of pre-existing ones; in any case its brief life of less than two years (1932–4) prevented it from differentiating itself too sharply from its *integralista* matrix. To some extent the success of *Integralismo*, and the critical circumstance that it flourished for a decade or more before full-fledged 'totalitarian' models gained wide appeal, pre-empted the ground from other influences and paradigms of the extreme Right.

Integralismo Lusitano was not alone in mediating the influence of *Action Française*. One other strategically located milieu in which 'the Marx of the Right' found close readers and admirers was the *Centro Académico de Democracia Crista* (CADC) at the University of Coimbra. Founded in 1901, this student society sought to reinvigorate the sluggish intellectual life of the Portuguese Catholic élite and, after the proclamation of the Republic, to develop strategies of adaptation to the prevailing anticlericalism. Although the doctrines of the French 'social Catholics' and of the conservative sociology known as the school of Le Play or *science sociale* were also closely studied, Maurras seems to have exerted a strange fascination. The title of 'Christian democracy' showed a willingness to court the new symbols of political legitimation which was somewhat belied by the obviously crucial role of Maurras' loathing for 'demo-liberalism', which strongly influenced the formation of the most famous members of this association and especially of Dr Salazar during his undergraduate career and after. Although there was a certain amount of overlapping between the doctrines and cadres of the two movements, there was also a certain degree of tension, particularly after the creation of the *Centro Católico*, a Catholic party which was neutral on the monarchist-republican issue (1915). But *Integralismo* is a much better known movement, thanks to its more formally political character and to the fact that its members have been much more articulate in self-documentation and collective autobiography. The integralists form the only political movement which has been allowed to define its own historical identity under the 'New State': this may lead to an over-estimation of their role in the political and ideological

305

struggles of the Republic (1910–26) compared to the more diffuse permeation of reactionary values and beliefs through more informal, less salient agencies such as the CADC. On the other hand, since both groups shared a number of key ideological themes (authoritarianism, corporatism and nationalism) and zealously maintained their ideological independence from other monarchist or Catholic organizations, they represented very similar alternatives outside the political system then operating.

The intellectuals who launched the first publications of *Integralismo* in 1914 and the public lectures in 1915 which brought their ideology to the attention of a wider public were drawn mostly from graduates from the law faculty of the University of Coimbra. They were thus a 'new' movement both in the initial strangeness of their political rhetoric against the reified values of 'liberty' and 'progress' and in their age-composition which averaged about twenty-five. Quite self-consciously they felt they owed little to the teachings of their professors and, as far as direct ideological impact is concerned, they were right: the traditionalism of some student subcultures played a more important role. This traditionalism did not necessarily have a manifest political content: indeed a number of the 'integralists' were not originally monarchists or hyper-Catholic as undergraduates but shared common literary and artistic tastes. Traditionalism as an aesthetic or a mode of sensibility preceded traditionalism as an ideology and political programme, in the individual cases of some 'integralists', in the larger scene of the Portuguese élite, and in a longer historical perspective – for the 'literary nationalism' of the generation of 1890 foreshadowed the specifically political crisis of liberal democracy in Portugal.

Both the 'integralist' movement and the CADC show the structural importance of academic peer groups in the political behaviour of the Portuguese élite. The basic leadership of *Integralismo* was constituted on this basis and has sustained its identity over four decades. The most famous or notorious academic peer group still occupies key positions: Salazar and his close friends of Coimbra and the CADC, the Cardinal Patriarch head of the Portuguese Church (Dr Cerejeira), the leader of the 'nationalist' sector of the officer corps (General Santos Costa) and a former Minister and political auxiliary of the dictator (Prof. Mario de Figueiredo). The fact that the last three to some extent owe their own positions to the former professor of finance does not mean that they do not enjoy limited autonomy in their roles, for it is precisely within the armed forces and the Church that the potential for organizational autonomy in political or quasi-political action is greatest. Nor does the fact that in both cases – of *Integralismo* and the CADC – the leading groups arose within the University of Coimbra necessarily mean that in terms of student recruitment, academic staff and political culture the University was much more reactionary than the others. The new universities at Lisbon and Oporto were not legally incorporated until 1910, and Coimbra retained the monopoly of legal training for a while longer, so that it is not surprising that the intellectual leadership of the extreme Right should have originated there.

The integralists soon became notorious for their verbal violence and their romanticism of physical violence, which they derived from Maurras and Sorel. Their political style earned them the reputation of 'Jacobins of the Right', and even their 'integral monarchism', by a curious conceptual shift around the term 'integral', came to be presented as a 'total remodelling of Portuguese society'. Attempts to identify the intellectual leadership of extremist movements as characteristically stemming from the *Lumpenintelligenz*, the intellectual proletariat, uprooted or socially marginal 'café intellectuals', do not fit the Portuguese situation with respect either to the integralists or to any other political movement, since such categories have never been structurally important. In terms of social origin, university education and careers, the integralist leaders were not atypical of the Portuguese élite. A number of the most distinguished and influential were from landowning families, in two or three cases owning fairly large estates in the latifundia region of the Alentejo, and were thus able in part to finance the movement's organizational, journalistic and conspiratorial activities. As university graduates their élite status was ratified and in that capacity those without sufficient private means followed the usual bureaucratic or teaching careers. If anything, the data on their social origins would tend to support a class hypothesis which would impute counter-revolutionary ideology to landed interests (whether of large-scale owners or middle-income farmers). They certainly gave voice to eulogies of rural values and virtues and the country's pastoral vocation, the agrarian symbols of their poetry and rhetoric. But the arcadia motif was not exclusively theirs. In the Portuguese literary, moral and historical imagination it involved a much wider and deeper shift of sensibility dating at least from the 1890s, shared by republicans, anti-clericals and 'demo-liberals', but which the integralists politicized in a very specific direction.

As in the case of *Action Française*, the ideas of *Integralismo* hardly deserve a full-fledged exposition. The vigour of the negations, the force of the attacks on 'demo-liberalism' and its logical postulates (individualism, popular sovereignty) and its alleged corollaries (collectivism), were most salient at the time; in the end the integralists abundantly showed at all critical moments that they would rather have a régime of personal power and a highly centralized authoritarian state than risk the return of parliamentary democracy by pressing for their maximum positive programme of monarchy, a decentralized polity (with extensive municipal, provincial and regional autonomies) and corporatism. The integralists even imported the special vocabulary of opprobrium of *Action Française* (the 'anti-nation', the 'internal foreigners', etc.) and its antisemitism. Although antisemitism was never very central to the doctrine or propaganda of *Integralismo*, it persisted right through the decades when its historical meaning was unfolded in genocide. It is because of this integralist antisemitism that one finds antisemitic statements in the official newspaper of the *União Nacional* well after the second world war; for the régime's publicists have almost all had an integralist formation, directly or indirectly. This ideological antisemitism has never had any practical implications in terms of discrimination or persecution, but its retention almost as a fetish testifies to the persistence of ideological themes.

As is invariably the case in Portugal, ideological controversy generated by *Integralismo* shifted to the arena of historical self-interpretation. The integralists had to move into this field not only because of general cultural imperatives but because of the very logic of their nationalist ideology. Since they repudiated virtually the entire nineteenth century *en bloc*, they – and especially their most gifted and influential intellectual leader, Antonio Sardinha (1889–1925) – sought to define the 'eternal essence', the traditional heritage of Portugal, in terms of symbolic events and figures embodying messianic, pastoral and hierarchical values. This reconstitution of the past in a reactionary nationalistic perspective was aptly characterized by sympathetic commentators as a 'futurism of the past'.

As an organization, *Integralismo Lusitano* was not geared either to the parliamentary opposition (by definition) or to the seizure of power. Its strength always lay with youth, especially students and young officers. The integralists co-operated in nearly every monarchist rising against the Republic, and after 1917 were involved in a number of army conspiracies which were not simply aimed at monarchical restoration. The most formative political experience they enjoyed prior to the general rising of May 1926 was the republican dictatorship of Sidonio Pais (1917–18). The integralists by and large supported this régime and through their sympathetic advice helped to steer its highly opportunistic and improvised policies in an authoritarian-corporatist direction. Sidonio Pais came very close to becoming a charismatic leader with a genuine gift for demagogy and the manipulation of masses, much more so than his successors after 1926. It should be noted that the corporatist experiment evolved by Sidonio with integralist advice and cooperation preceded those of fascist Italy or Primo de Rivera, which are sometimes regarded as prototypes of the corporative republic defined by the Portuguese Constitution of 1933.

Between 1918 and 1926, although weakened by schisms – including the setting up of a separate integralist organization, the *Acção Realista* (1923–7) – the integralists waged a dual campaign against the Republic and against what they regarded as the 'demo-liberal' prejudices of the constitutional monarchists.

309

They were helped to some extent by the settlement of the dynastic issue whereby the claims of the last constitutional king of Portugal passed to a prince of the exiled miguelist branch, which in a sense could be construed as a moral victory for the absolutist or traditionalist values which that branch had for so long embodied. The military dictatorship initiated in May 1926 was warmly welcomed by them: their role lay in unremitting struggle against residual 'demo-liberal' beliefs or reflexes within the officer corps, which in its younger elements had long been a major target for the integralists' propagandistic and proselytizing activities. Since one sector of the officer corps favoured a presidential republic rather than an authoritarian state, the integralists sought to discredit this model of political reorganization. The two key speeches made by Salazar in 1930 marked a turning point for the dictatorship and for the integralists since they envisaged an authoritarian corporate order. The integralist 'old guard' retained its monarchical aspirations and a concern for the purity and completeness of the doctrine which prevented it from simply joining the new government party. However, a considerable number of the younger integralists joined the new régime and their participation was crucial for the régime's consolidation, especially in its early stages.

Looking back at the integralist movement one can identify five clusters of integralists (not necessarily mutually exclusive) from the standpoint of their relation to international fascism and the new state's own ideological options:

(1) The integralist 'old guard' who have never ceased to press for monarchical restoration, and have always maintained a certain critical independence. Partly because their ideological orientations crystallized in a pre-fascist era, they have at times been in formal opposition to the régime.

(2) What one may call integralist-fascists who, especially after 1923, adopted certain fascist styles of political vocabulary and valuations. Unlike the integralist 'old guard', they were often pro-Nazi during the second world war and after. However, they never transcended certain premises of integralism such as monarchism.

310

(3) The national-syndicalists, who were most concerned with developing and sustaining a charismatic leadership, a mass movement and an armed militia for the Portuguese régime. They stressed the need for systematic violence as an instrument of a revolutionary process, and freely used 'bourgeoisie' and 'capitalism' as major negative symbols in an attempt to mobilize the working class for the régime. After the termination of the movement in 1934, some of the ex-Blueshirts continued to serve the new state and occasional journalistic outlets have been found for this kind of fascist discourse in a limited and sporadic way. A few, such as their former leader, Rolão Preto, have worked for the opposition.

(4) A fairly large number of the younger integralists, who were recruited for the new régime, especially after Salazar's appointment as minister and virtual financial dictator in 1928. These we may call the new state integralists, although some have ceased to be integralists in any sense in the course of their political careers within the régime. These integralists served the new state in the building up of the corporate order, in ministerial, diplomatic and top administrative roles, and in activities of all kinds. In the early years of the régime when its character was slowly being defined, the 'shared understandings' that came from similar ideological backgrounds considerably eased and quickened the institutionalization of the new state. It is difficult to see how the political recruitment and integration necessary for the 'civilianization' of the military dictatorship could have been accomplished without pre-formed cadres and a shared universe of discourse. To be sure there was no revolutionary party or mass movement, nor a single complex of symbols; but there was a quasi-group of scattered but 'available' cadres, and a set of ideological themes (corporatism, authoritarianism) common to a number of politico-cultural circles which could be and were tapped for the new state. Such key men of the régime as Teotónio Pereira and Marcelo Caetano, two possible candidates for the succession to Salazar, both came from integralist backgrounds.

(5) Finally we may distinguish what for want of a better term

we shall call the 'neo-integralists'. This group has not added anything to the received body of integralist doctrine, but has sought to present it in a topical context. It represents the intellectual wing of the monarchist 'opposition', if one excludes the apparently small minority of liberal monarchists proper.

The persistence of integralism over a span of fifty years shows that this doctrine has embedded itself among the Portuguese élites as a kind of permanent subculture, transmitted from generation to generation, almost like a hereditary sect.

2 Salazar and the New State

The 28 May 1926 rising involved a momentary near-unanimity in the officer corps against the 'corruption' and 'degradation' of the parliamentary republic. Since the armed forces comprised both monarchist and republican officers, and monarchist risings had rarely achieved anything near success, one permanent task of the ruling junta was to avoid any action that might be interpreted as aimed at a restoration. Although this tacit rule was never seriously questioned within the army, almost nothing else was shared by the officer corps as a whole. The 'meaning' of '28 May' was in doubt from the beginning. At first the rising was welcomed by virtually all the minority political parties (from the conservatives to the socialists) as a means of breaking the electoral machine with which the Democratic Party had managed to win nearly every election for sixteen years and so gain control of the allocation of political patronage. This illusion was gradually dispelled as administrative sanctions, imprisonment and deportation of leaders extinguished the political parties without actually outlawing them. The working-class organizations, the trade union confederation, the anarchists, anarcho-syndicalists and communists were fairly neutral: despite increasing persecution, the 'revolutionary' parties attempted to divorce themselves from 'bourgeois political quarrels'. But eventually, by 1932, they had ceased to exist as legal organizations.

Although the 28 May rising was bloodless, fresh risings to overthrow or redefine the military dictatorship were not. The revolt of February 1927 in Oporto, which was supported by left-wing civilians, was quite costly by the standards of Portuguese 'revolutions' since 1910: one hundred and sixty dead, several hundred wounded. Subsequent risings against the military dictatorship in 1928 and 1931 in Lisbon, Oporto and the Atlantic islands added to the bloodshed engendered directly or indirectly by the 1926 rising. Within the framework of the military dictatorship itself there were a number of small abortive *coups*, any number of plots and conspiracies which never saw the light of day, and threatened insurrections which did not materialize because the political or administrative demands of the rebellious troops or officers were conceded.

The monarchist-republican issue, if not carefully handled, could destroy the unity of the armed forces. The logic of the situation led to the emergence of a Catholic, General Carmona, as formal head of the military government and subsequently – as a result of 'popular' election – as President of the Republic. General Carmona never became more than 'first among equals', for power within the military establishment never concentrated on any section or leader. In a sense Carmona balanced the monarchist and republican factions: no monarchist general became premier during the military dictatorship, but other key posts (Interior, War) were given to them in compensation.

During the 'pure' military dictatorship (1926-8) the armed forces purged the politico-administrative apparatus and replaced civilian officials by officers. Though low pay had been a major grievance of the officers against the Republican politicians, pay was not increased directly – instead, officers received additional salaries on account of their plurality of posts. Partly because of inexperience, partly because of a sense of political weakness which led to over-expenditure, the military government only worsened the precarious state of public finances inherited from the liberal Republic. In order to forestall the bankruptcy of the state, the government sought a foreign loan; in the event the only willing source turned out to be the League of Nations, whose conditions the military government found unacceptable, probably as much out of domestic political weakness as out of a sense of patriotic dignity. It was thus forced to accept Dr Salazar as finance expert with veto power over all public expenditure.

The expert was successful in his budgetary, monetary and credit reforms. With the backing of the army new taxation could be enforced, and this together with the veto on expenditure proved amply sufficient to balance the budget, liquidate the floating debt, stabilize the currency, etc. 'Financial saviours', however, have rarely been able to translate their skills and achievements into durable political gains – much less to use them as the leverage to supreme personal power. Between 1928 and 1930 Dr Salazar was able to establish himself not only as a 'technician' but also as a political leader. By 1930 already he had greater political power than anyone else, even though he remained nominally only the Minister of Finance until his accession as President of the Council of Ministers in 1932.

Between 1928 and 1932 a curious process of interaction between the government and its political constituency took place whereby the new political order was gradually defined. Various options were discussed at the time, including an indefinite continuation of the military dictatorship, with civilians only as experts and not as political leaders, perhaps with plebiscites for a periodic popular legitimation of the régime; or a return to 'constitutional normality' which by definition appeared to entail a modified form of the parliamentary republic, a 'presidential' but not illiberal or undemocratic régime. Both alternatives had supporters within the army even up to 1933, when it was already obviously too late, short of an armed revolt, to alter the new course towards a 'constitutionalization' of the régime in the shape of an authoritarian state largely administered by civilians.

The earliest public attempt to define the institutional form of the dictatorship as an authoritarian corporate republic was made by Salazar in major speeches in 1930. The first official political organization to be set up after 1926 was the *União Nacional*, founded in 1930 and absorbing unofficial pro-dictatorship organizations such as the 28 May League. Owing to the ideological expectations created by such movements as integralism and the 'social Catholics', the new doctrine found a ready echo. Hence Salazar could say without too much exaggeration, 'We have a doctrine of our own and we are a force'. These political assets had not just appeared *ex nihilo*, as some accounts suggest.

The success of the political campaign waged by Salazar and his supporters, and the urgent need to mark a clear transition from the military dictatorship and engage the enthusiasm aroused by nationalist ideals led to a very rapid flow of fundamental legislation. Between 1932 and 1934 the legal foundations of the 'new state' were laid, in particular the political constitution ratified in 1933, which incorporated retrospectively the Colonial Act of 1930, and the National Labour Statute, also promulgated in 1933. These constitutional or quasi-constitutional provisions remain in operation, substantially unchanged, to the present day. Only the Concordat with the Vatican ranks in importance; it was only signed in 1940, although its provisions were foreshadowed in the constitution.

The 1933 constitution, although heralded as 'the first Corporative Constitution in the world' was in content a partial compromise with 'demo-liberal' forms. However, it was made clear at the time, and abundantly repeated since, that the spirit or ethos of the constitution was thoroughly 'anti-liberal, anti-parliamentary, anti-democratic'. The constitution has undergone few substantial revisions, all in an authoritarian direction, although not as far as the régime's more coherent supporters would have wished.

Although the drafters of the constitution seriously considered whether to establish solely a corporative chamber, they settled for a 'political' chamber with members formally elected on the basis of geographical constituencies, as well as a corporative chamber. The powers of the corporative chamber have been steadily increased and in 1959, when direct suffrage for the Presidency of the Republic was abolished, they were upgraded significantly by making the chamber a substantial part of the electoral college that formally chooses the President.

Elections – whether for the National Assembly or until 1959 for the Presidency of the Republic – are of course conditioned

315

by the franchise. Measured by the franchise or by the actual number or votes cast (in relation to the total potential electorate or the total adult population), the political system does not show a high degree of political development. Literacy, sex and property restrictions limit the size of the electorate. But even so the régime has been unwilling or unable to invest resources in mobilizing the limited electorate. Although normally (in fact with only one exception) all presidential elections won over ninety per cent support for the régime's candidate, the size of the electorate has not increased significantly in thirty years: between 1933 and 1965, it remained at about a million and a quarter, even though the illiteracy rate was halved in the same period, and the population increased by two million (to over nine million). To some extent the consistency of votes cast over thirty years reflects the weakness of the party organization, which is unable to 'deliver' more than this number of votes. This weakness is further corroborated by the high proportion of potential electors in the public sector (teachers, civil servants), who are amenable to direct pressures of an administrative character quite apart from other sanctions and inducements. The ratio of electorate to total population is reminiscent more of classical representative oligarchies or limited democracies than of plebiscitarian, authoritarian, totalitarian and democratic régimes.

Until the end of the second world war no opposition candidates presented themselves at elections to either the Presidency or the National Assembly. After 1945 opposition candidates stood at all presidential elections until 1959, when direct suffrage was terminated, and at elections for deputies. However the standard pattern has been for opposition candidates to withdraw before polling day on account of the numerous and vexatious restrictions on fair electioneering. Only one presidential candidate and a handful of candidates to the National Assembly have failed to withdraw in this manner. As the régime controls the electoral roll and counts its own votes – quite apart from police terror and army intervention – this has seemed the only possible mode of protest. By abolishing direct suffrage for the Presidency in the wake of General Delgado's electoral campaign, the régime in a sense closed the limited electoral period opened in 1945 as a concession to the then prevalent 'anti-fascist' climate.

The 'duality' of roles between the Presidency of the Republic and the Presidency of the Council of Ministers – although designed to match the factual circumstance of General Carmona's pre-emption of the former role – has not been resolved. The implicit rule appears to be that the Head of State shall be a high-ranking officer of the armed forces, while effective power lies with the Prime Minister. On Carmona's death it was widely expected that Salazar would become head of state as well as premier but this somewhat ambiguous demand was not met.

The constitution is a typical document of the new state in that the maximum demands of no group are fully met. Thus the constitution maintains the principle of territorial as well as occupational representation, direct suffrage for the Presidency of the Republic (until 1959), duality between the Head of State and the Head of the Government, formal and regular 'elections', etc. The Concordat did not make Portugal a confessional state, did not re-establish the Catholic Church, abolish divorce, or even restore to the Church properties expropriated in 1911, although it was basically a satisfactory settlement for the Church. All in all, the liberal aspects of the constitution are substantially inoperative but potentially threatening to those with vested interests in the maintenance of the régime.

Probably no aspect of the new state received more attention – at least until the colonial issues of the 1950s and 1960s – than the corporative organization. By defining itself as 'corporative' the régime sought to obviate more direct political classifications and identifications. As with other conceptualizations, however, it sought to identify itself in a cautionary manner by claiming that its corporatism was suffused by Christian values, that it was a *corporatisme d'association* rather than a *corporatisme d'état*, and that it was integral at least in so far as it intended to include 'moral' and 'cultural' as well as purely 'economic' corporations.

317

The corporate character of the polity is enshrined in the constitution and elaborated in the National Labour Statute promulgated in 1933. Relying on the Italian fascist Labour Charter for some of its major formulations, this labour code defined a corporate organization for the industrial sector and for agricultural employers. As only a quarter of the population lived in urban centres with a population of ten thousand or more in 1940 the working agricultural population was only tenuously 'integrated' in this organizational scheme. In the 1960s only one-fifth of the agricultural population belonged to the quasi-corporate *Casas do Povo*. In essence, therefore, the corporate scheme controls the industrial working class, which at the time of the Labour Statute was not much larger than about one hundred thousand. Like all such schemes it declares strikes illegal (they had only been legal in Portugal from 1910 to 1926), makes certain labour associations compulsory, restricts freedom of internal government in such associations and closely defines its powers in dealing with employers' corporative organizations (*Gremios*). The labour organizations, the *sindicatos*, have never been more than instruments of government policy, which dictates the timing and terms of labour contracts.

The labour movement, or what remained of the free labour movement, responded to the promulgation of the new Labour Statute early in 1934 with the most effective general strike yet seen in the country. This strictly labour protest involved both anarchosyndicalist and communist workers. The strike was put down by the police and the army. Since then only the Communist Party has been able to survive as a political organization with a solid base in the working class. Low-cost housing, social welfare measures and benefits distributed by the corporate order have neither significantly affected the distribution of income nor at certain periods counteracted a fall in the real income of industrial workers. The moral and political alienation of the industrial working class has remained, it seems, complete. This has inevitably affected those involved in the labour world, such as Catholic Action groups, especially the Catholic Worker Youth Organization.

3 National Syndicalism

Salazar's rise to the head of the first civilian government since 1926 raised again with urgency the question of legitimate political action and the agencies of political participation. In the first place, ever since Salazar's major speeches of 1930 had won him the support of 'nationalist' opinion (both diehard integralists and those uncommitted to 'integral monarchy' but sharing a basically similar outlook), this movement of opinion had been gaining strength. Numerous associations, student or youth organizations, had been founded and were supported by those eager to participate fully in the building up of the new state and to act as the shock troops of the 'National Revolution'. University students were deeply divided politically, with integralists and communists as the main forces of the Right and Left – although we must remember that less than 7,000 students were engaged in higher education in 1926. Outside the two major cities of Lisbon and Oporto republican *caciques* and cliques retained a good deal of local, diffuse influence not easily counteracted by the police or army. Hence the need was felt for more subtle, flexible, extra-legal agencies to crush these forms of opposition and resistance, and keep alive the moral enthusiasm of nationalist youth.

Secondly, the 'civilianization' of the government and public administration, which included the replacement of military officers as civil governors of the majority of Portugal's eighteen districts, opened up opportunities for political action over and above the formal processes of administration and legislation. Lastly, the new foreign models of fascist movements constantly suggested the need for militias and/or a new type of party-state. In fact throughout the 1920s militia-type organizations of the extreme Right had sprung up repeatedly, without overmuch success, as part of the process of 'fascistization' of the younger integralists. Now that the political character of the new régime had, it seemed, been clearly defined, it seemed to some of its supporters that the time had come to establish the organizational requisites of its existence, since the *União*

Nacional had not developed into anything like a totalitarian party.

In 1932 there thus emerged the Blueshirt or National Syndicalist movement, initially conceived as a vehicle of the 'National Revolution', the basis of a militia at the disposal of the Leader (Salazar, of course). The Blueshirt leaders were integralists, in fact two of the 1914 founders of integralism, but specifically those who had been most concerned with 'social questions', labour problems and integralist propaganda among the working class. At first the new movement gained strength and was able to claim fifty thousand paid-up members and about eighteen periodicals, including a daily newspaper *Revolução*, published in Lisbon (which, interestingly enough, had started as the journal of the nationalist student association in Lisbon). It had the support of several hundred army officers, and claimed to draw members from the working class and industrialists as well as from the liberal professions.

However, as the movement gained momentum its relationship to the régime became increasingly problematical. The previous militia-type or would-be totalitarian organizations which had been formed 'spontaneously' in support of the régime had failed to grow significantly in numbers, so that the régime was able simply to ignore them. This case was different: the scale and thrust of the national syndicalists, the widespread feeling that it was unfolding the logic of the situation and that it enjoyed official sympathy, were sufficient to demonstrate that the government would have to take positive action. Official pressure was brought to bear on the movement, especially on its upper ranks, and restrictions were placed on its propaganda. The movement's leader, Rolão Preto, had been a friend of Salazar and it may well be that he collaborated with the proclaimed 'National Revolution': but he was eventually (June 1934) eliminated from the new political order and exiled. Soon after, in August 1934, barely two years after the movement's entry into the political arena, the purged executive committee of the national syndicalists decided to terminate its existence and called upon its members to join the *União Nacional*.

Such a brief life and smooth dissolution offers a contrast to similar crises in fascist or fascistoid régimes (e.g. the Brazilian 'New State', which was a curiously parallel case in other respects). In effect, the movement's social composition was as élitist as that of any other Portuguese political organization despite the movement's efforts to obtain working class support and its use of 'capitalism' and 'bourgeois' as negative symbols. The dissolution of national syndicalism was a deeply disillusioning experience for some of its members, especially the two leaders Rolão Preto and Monsaraz who stayed in opposition ever after, the former even supporting General Delgado's presidential campaign in 1958. Despite the overt smoothness with which the movement abolished itself, rumours of a conspiracy were soon abroad. The government took extensive precautionary measures, keeping the army and police in a high state of readiness. In the event, partly because of the visible loyalty of the armed forces to the régime, the *coup d'état* in Lisbon was a pathetic affair which the police was able to crush in a few hours. But despite the small numbers involved, the composition of the rebels – industrial workers, military officers, national syndicalists and anarcho-syndicalists – is noteworthy. It was the kind of grouping that is not intrinsically incapable of success, as Bolivian experience shows, but it was highly unusual in terms of recent Portuguese political history.

Quite apart from its organizational relationship to the new state, the national syndicalist movement was highly ambiguous in its latent meanings and definitions of the situation. For some of its members at any rate the main aim was to re-establish a full-blooded military dictatorship and the pure rule of force or perhaps institutionalized violence. For others, the main aim lay in the establishment of a militia-type of organization for the permanent repression of opposition and resistance. On another dimension some emphasized the rhetoric of anti-capitalism, others the importance of property values. But most members would perhaps have agreed on the need for charismatic leadership, for a mass movement and for cadres to ensure the institutionalization of a régime based on personal power. These three

321

demands were not and have not been met by the régime: leadership is not charismatic in the usual sense associated with historic fascist régimes, political support is not mobilized on a large scale, and the mechanisms of political recruitment and succession have not been elaborated.

4 The 'fascistization' of the régime

Although in his post-mortem on the September 1935 rising Salazar once more rejected the idea of a militia as a necessary agency of the 'National Revolution', such a militia did come into being the year after. The main intervening factor was of course the Spanish Civil War. But the new para-military organization, the *Legiao Portuguesa*, was not dissolved after the end of the second world war (as some supporters of the régime expected) and is still in being. The year 1936 in effect saw the creation of organizations and the enactment of laws which definitely mark a new level of 'fascistization' of the régime, or at least a stage of political development which goes beyond the traditionalistic, conventionally authoritarian, Christian corporate polity which was perhaps the initial 'project' of the régime (and which is its dominant international stereotype). Thus, alongside the *Legiao Portuguesa* was created a compulsory youth organization, the *Mocidade Portuguesa*, initially embracing the entire school and university population but in practice limited to certain age groups; political loyalty tests were instituted, the civil service and universities were purged, the repressive apparatus was modernized, and a cultural policy and propaganda agency was set up. Although some of these policies have been modified and some of the underlying ideological enthusiasm has waned, the organizational complex remains and cannot simply be regarded as a temporary aberration brought about by a wartime situation or as an artificial superstructure masking a pre-fascist or simply authoritarian core or essence.

Almost as soon as the Spanish civil war started the Portuguese government more or less cast in its lot with the rebel forces and decided to support them by all means short of actual participation in the war. This decision – the most important foreign policy decision taken since Portugal's entry into the first world war – seems to have been based on the calculation that whether by Spanish intervention or contagion the new state would not survive a republican victory: thus aid to the rebels would not create risks of retribution, since the régime would be lost anyway if the rebels were defeated. The risks inherent in a nationalist victory, the possibility that a victorious army aiming at a unitary state might seek to complete peninsular unity were obviously discounted, and the usual reliance on the British alliance may have allayed such fears. The American Minister in Lisbon was not exaggerating when he wrote in a dispatch to his government in August 1936 that the Portuguese government had since the beginning of the Spanish civil war regarded the rebels' success 'as a matter almost of life and death'.

From the earliest days of the civil war the Portuguese government and officially supported private organizations gave every facility to the rebels. Transit through ports and railways was particularly important in the earlier stages until Atlantic ports became available to the nationalists, but continued to be used afterwards. All such facilities were of course denied to the republican government. Miscellaneous help was also offered in the form of funds given by Portuguese industrialists, money collected from sympathizers, communications facilities (broadcasting stations), etc. Portuguese diplomacy worked strenuously in support of the insurgents' cause. Finally, direct military support was also given not only in the form of arms and ammunition (partly sabotaged by pro-republican workers, as readers of Malraux's *Espoir* may recall) but of volunteers – the *viriatos* who fought on land and air with the Francoist forces. The number of *viriatos* has been estimated at twenty thousand and the number of their dead at up to eight thousand.

One should not stress unduly the stigmata of the thirties in such organizations as the *Legião* and the *Mocidade*, their uniforms, the Roman salute, the terminology and organizational detail, and a number of the formulae (e.g. 'rotten pacifism'). What matters more in appraising the character of the régime as a whole is the persistence of these organizations and even the grafting of new tasks (civil defence and 'counter-insurgency' training for the Legion, student welfare for the *Mocidade*), the granting of additional legal powers and facilities for political purposes (such as those granted to the *Mocidade* in 1966) long after the external stimuli and paradigms had lapsed. These phenomena do seem to go beyond mere organizational inertia or displacement of goals within such organizations. They do at least illustrate a characteristic behaviour pattern of the régime: the tenacity with which it holds on to its key symbols and the resilience with which it revives dormant organizations after periods of international discredit (as in the case of corporate institutions).

Although the external danger perceived by the régime and its supporters in the Spanish civil war triggered off the creation of the *Legião* and the *Mocidade* ('fascistization from without'), this paramount factor should not lead us to neglect 'fascistization from below', especially in the case of the Legion which existed *de facto* before it was recognized *de jure*. Even in the case of the *Mocidade*, set up by a decree-law, something was learnt from previous 'spontaneous' nationalist student organizations. To be sure, these pressures from below did not stem from the masses properly so-called, but rather from or under the leadership of élite segments: as we have noted, all political movements within the régime are largely homogeneous in such crucial social characteristics as education and occupation. Socially displaced or marginal strata, *lumpen*-elements, etc. were absent from the Portuguese social structure, at any rate in the critical quantities required for significant mass movements.

The Legion was perhaps the most spontaneously created organization of the régime. After the outbreak of the Spanish civil war the pressure from volunteers to participate in the 'anti-bolshevik' struggle was such that a militia came into being and was eventually officially recognized and regulated, with a membership of twenty thousand. As a para-military body it is trained by reserve officers, with air and naval 'brigades', and has been entrusted with the organization of civil defence. As a political organization it was formally committed to a 'heroic ethic' and a 'revolutionary mystique', to the 'defence of the spiritual patrimony of the Nation' as well as to the 'defence of the corporate order'. Originally membership of the Legion was virtually compulsory in certain kinds of public employment, but this practice no longer holds good. The Legion sometimes acts quite openly in the terrorization of opponents of the régime, although its public salience has decreased since the end of the second world war. There is no doubt that it might act as a reserve force of the régime: forewarned of a *coup d'état*, a number of ministers took refuge at the headquarters of the Legion during the late 1950s.

The greenshirt *Mocidade Portuguesa* (and its parallel organization for girls) aimed at 'total integration', but is now compulsory only for children aged seven to fourteen. Its task include para-military training, especially in the older age groups, working closely with the *Legião*. It provides a nationalistic education and a 'corporative' formation. A special effort has been made in recent years to attract university students to the *Mocidade* centres at universities, a trend which has been reinforced by student para-political rebelliousness. As with other phases of the corporate régime, social welfare benefits and facilities are tied to membership of the organization in schools and universities. The leaders of both the *Legião* and the *Mocidade* are usually either military officers or important political leaders of the régime; in either category such posts are often stages in outstanding political careers.

The oldest repressive mechanism of the régime is censorship, instituted shortly after the rising of May 1926 and maintained ever since except for brief and partial relaxations since 1945 (officially thirty days before polling day at each general election). Censorship is most strictly and efficiently applied to periodical publications, as well as to other media such as the theatre, cinema, radio and television, although the greatly increased availability of transistor radios in the late 1950s somewhat restricted the efficacy of such controls. It is noteworthy that this type of censorship applies to parish magazines, Catholic news-papers proper, etc., so that a separate formal Catholic com-munications system immune from official controls does not exist. In addition to continual censorship, periodical publications can be and often are suppressed, as happened particularly in the late 1930s. Paradoxically it is possible to regard the majority of Portuguese daily newspapers as more or less vaguely 'Republi-can' (although not the ones with the largest circulation); how-ever, such a classification is largely notional, with little practical impact on editorial policy even during the official semi-free electoral period.

Books are not subject to pre-publication censorship on the same basis as periodicals; however, they can be withdrawn on police orders, and their authors and publishers are liable to various types of negative sanctions. It is fear of such sanctions as much as direct administrative orders that has prevented a number of works from seeing the light of day, such as the long awaited critical study of Portuguese historiography by the finest Portuguese mind of this century, Antonio Sergio (who has played in Portuguese intellectual life a role of similar significance to that of Croce in Italy). To be sure, national historiography is a highly sensitive area for a régime much of whose ideology is embedded in historical legitimations and imagery, and prior to 1926 Sergio had been a brilliantly successful critic of the integralists' conceptions of Portuguese history.

From 1926 to 1935 political repression had taken place on a somewhat *ad hoc* and extra-legal basis. This was partly because armed rebellion or conspiracy was the main agency of opposition (outside the working class) under the military dictatorship; thus military justice was often applied and penalties against rebellious officers were on the whole surprisingly mild, in many cases con-sisting almost solely of deportation to the colonies. Moreover, until about 1935 the régime had not defined its political character beyond corporate authoritarianism and had sought to absorb and co-opt as much as possible of the 'centre' opposition rather than proscribe it: for example, there had been no significant purge of senior civil servants. But about 1935 the régime stepped up its political demands and started to build up a relatively complex and technically sophisticated repressive apparatus which it has preserved and perfected to the present day, and to develop (curiously enough, particularly since 1945 at the peak of democratic hopes) a system of political justice.

In 1935 and 1936 decree-laws were enacted which turned the entire field of state employment into the preserve of the politically loyal. Loyalty oaths were required of all members of the civil service proper, the teaching profession, officials of the corporate apparatus, etc. Penalties were placed outside the scope of normal administrative law and reserved to the Council of Ministers. Given the size and relative importance of the public sector such measures automatically 'controlled' something like half the working population with secondary school or university education, apart from such other sanctions as the political police could enforce. In a curious way the régime had visibly returned to the political system it had claimed to destroy: the exchange of public posts for political support, only this time with direct coercion and permanent political monopoly built in. Although such measures only affected the public sector of employment, leading private employers followed suit: banks and the larger industrial companies demanded similar loyalty qualifications, such as membership of the *Legião Portuguesa*, from their managerial and clerical employees.

The political police was reorganized partly with the advice and training of Nazi specialists and over the years has been built up into a remarkably efficient apparatus with an allegedly far-flung network of informers. After 1945 its operations were eased by the creation of a system of political justice. Political crimes which until then had been tried by a special military court became the prerogative of special tribunals, the *Tribunais Plenarios Criminais* in Lisbon and Oporto, with a special magistracy and procedures. Special penalties are applicable to political crimes as determined by decree-laws of 1945, 1949 and 1956. Political crimes are in principle subject to life imprisonment, counter to the constitution and Portuguese legal tradition. The same decrees grant the political police (PIDE) a wide range

327

of powers to control voluntary associations, search residences, ban meetings, and control the frontiers. From 1936 to 1956 a major concentration camp was in operation in the Cape Verde Islands. Currently political prisoners are housed in the more lugubrious civilian prisons. Severity of treatment in the past was determined by class and ideology (with working-class communists the worst treated) but there has apparently been some equalization.

The repressive apparatus includes a number of other police organizations, all currently described as 'para-military' (*corporaçoes militarizadas*), including the *Guarda Nacional Republicana* (to control rural disturbances) and the *Policia de Segurança Publica* (to break up meetings and demonstrations). The *Legião Portuguesa* is no longer used as an organized body for police purposes. All these police or militia organizations, with the exception of the PSP, are led by army officers and manned by officers with military rank, so that at any given time several hundred army officers are seconded for those purposes – leading the PIDE, the GNR, the *Guarda Fiscal*, the *Legião*, etc.

The division and partial militarization of police forces is by no means unique to this type of régime – it may be found in a number of Latin American countries with rather different historical backgrounds. One consequence of the 'investment' in these police forces in the Portuguese case is to diminish dependence on the army for the more routine tasks of political repression. It is doubtful whether even the better equipped of these forces would be able or willing to resist an army *coup* against the régime, but on two relatively recent occasions ministers and even Dr Salazar took refuge in the headquarters of the *Legião* and the *Guarda Nacional Republicana* on threat of rebellions. The military officers involved in the abortive Beja rebellion of January 1961 were tried by court martial and thus escaped the much heavier sentences they would probably have received from the political tribunals: this may represent a degree of continuing army autonomy.

The Portuguese régime, if one restricts oneself to non-colonial issues, has never attained the scale of political murder and mass imprisonments of its neighbour. However, the relative complexity and sophistication of its repressive apparatus, the degree to which it has been called upon over several decades to deal with multiple types of protest and rebellion (peasant, rural labourer, industrial strikes, mass urban demonstrations, university student strikes, military and civilian plots and *coups d'état*), and its differentiated system of political justice indicate that such 'mildness' represents neither organizational deficiency nor low incidence of protest. For the alienated sectors of the élite and the underlying population the acuity of the terror appears ever present. It is noteworthy that in France in recent years of all the emigrants the Portuguese workers are regarded as the most resistant to unionization.

In fact the Portuguese case provides an object lesson in the economy of terror. There can be an optimum coefficient of terror comprehensive in impact, embracing the totality of the population, without the extermination of large numbers, but with maximum visibility or publicity as well as cruelty. The Portuguese régime has achieved such an optimum: with a small number of political murders and arrests (between 1948 and 1959 the annual rate of political 'cases' registered by the PIDE with the political tribunals fluctuated between 700 and 2000) it has succeeded in politically atomizing the underlying population and paralyzing the élite opposition. Part of its success lies in the unremitting character of the repression, with no wide swings between 'excesses' and 'liberalizations'.

5 Economic policies

Ever since 1928 the principles of a balanced budget and monetary stability have enjoyed the status of categorical imperatives for the régime. Orthodox public finance in the shape of mandatory balanced budgets has been written into the constitution (an example followed by the Brazilian constitution after the military coup of 1964). Such prosaic achievements as monetary and price stability, a strong and stable currency, the forever balanced budget have been reified in the régime's domestic and international

329

propaganda as charismatic titles of the leader and defining features of the régime. Such economic policies have made for rigidity, lessened the régime's freedom of manoeuvre and virtually necessitated its characteristic slow and gradual tempo and style. But as far as international systems of communication are concerned they have been almost pure gain for the régime as they have minimized the visibility of its internal tensions and concealed its relative economic backwardness. Currently, by indulging in the rhetoric of economic growth rates, the régime is shifting its legitimation base; by making political obligation conditional on satisfactory economic growth (now forecast as 6·5 per cent per annum in the next few years), it is entering into a much more precarious arena. How the original principle of budgetary and monetary stability can be permanently and immutably combined with rapid economic growth is something which the régime will have to demonstrate.

Such economic growth as has been achieved stems from industrialization. The régime has been unable or unwilling to transform agrarian structures or induce new patterns of entrepreneurial behaviour in the primary sector, especially in the southern latifundia. Although the support of the big landowners has always been an important factor in the régime, it must be remembered that – unlike in most Latin American countries – agriculture has never provided a major portion of income from exports, as compared to remittances from emigrants (until the great depression), foreign earnings of the colonies, and recently tourism. Nor is agriculture able to achieve self-sufficiency in food production: the famous 'wheat campaign' launched in 1928 to avoid repetitions of the bread shortages which had been a factor in industrial and political strife during the Republic of 1910–26 did not have permanently satisfactory results. But until the 1950s agriculture was the major source of domestic taxable income and this was a key determinant of the relationship between the régime and agricultural interests. The very process of industrialization focuses attention on the blockages within the industrial sector: it will be interesting to see how far calculations of political rationality and economic growth mingle in determining the régime's attitudes to landed interests, given the general crisis of agriculture and the increasing proletarianization of the agricultural population.

Professor K. Organski has argued that fascism should be viewed as a model of development, as a tacit partnership between agricultural and industrial élites to carry out industrialization, but to impose its costs primarily on the industrial working class. In general terms, this is borne out by the 'syncratic' or unified character of the régime as far as propertied interests are concerned – financial, landed, industrial and commercial. But the banking world is of peculiar importance. For financial interests greatly outweighed industrial ones before the 1950s and have played an important role in industrialization since; they must be regarded as a somewhat autonomous segment of economic interests.

The major industrialization drive in Portugal coincides with the growth of European economic integration, the Common Market and the European Economic Community. It is possible that the more backward and internationally vulnerable the economy (not to mention more obvious geopolitical circumstances), the more industrialization is to be explained in terms of the rewards and threats of the larger European milieu, especially when both agricultural and industrial interests are equally threatened. Moreover, as semi-official Portuguese economists have pointed out, since resources can no longer be extracted from a highly deprived working class or peasantry, while the régime lacks the political capacity to extract even potentially available resources from the upper income brackets, only foreign capital remains as a source of investment capital. The logic of the situation, compounded by the demands of the colonial wars (defence and security account for forty to forty-five per cent of budget expenditure), has made the government relinquish its time-worn autarkic policies. In 1966 foreign capital provided twenty-five per cent of total private investment.

It seems fairly clear that the régime envisages full European economic integration as a long-term aim. In the meantime the régime seeks to perpetuate its politico-ideological framework – a 'second corporative drive' was started in 1956 to continue and complete the corporate state-building of 1933 – and to maintain the colonial empire. Thus, in abstract terms, it is possible to envisage the régime today as an 'industrializing' or 'modernizing' dictatorship. But this would remain an exceedingly partial and schematic characterization unless one took into account such other factors as domestic repression with the same basic symbols and themes as before the second world war, three colonial wars waged simultaneously (in Guinea, Angola and Mozambique), and a neo-corporatist resurgence.

The 'colonial empire' or 'overseas provinces', as they have alternately been called, were not salient in pre-1926 ideologies, even among the integralists. Owning the third largest colonial empire in the world, in the first instance the new state sought to make it pay its way (Colonial Act 1930). At that time it was not seriously considered as a major outlet for Portuguese emigration (then flowing at a rate of thirty thousand a year, according to the official figures, which of course do not take into account illegal emigration). Later it was defined as a source of raw materials for the industries of the 'mother country' (1936). An attempt was made to develop an 'imperial consciousness' through various official policies, but with only a modicum of success. After the second world war emigration to the colonies was encouraged and promoted more systematically, contemporaneous with the growing moral and political crisis of 'colonialism'. After momentary demoralization at the outbreak of the Angolan war in 1961, this emigration policy was more vigorously pursued than ever, both because of the obvious need to police the colony and in order to dampen international criticism.

The concomitance of incipient industrialization and the waging of colonial wars by this small, weak and poor country in a conjuncture of general, especially African, decolonization, carried through or supported by its NATO, Iberian and Brazilian associates, appears paradoxical. Some of the historical roots of the present paradox clearly antedate the régime. The geographic contours of the present Portuguese colonial empire date from 1890, the year of the British ultimatum which determined the limits of possible Portuguese expansion in Africa and imposed the criterion of effective occupation as against historical titles of possession. The profound trauma of '1890' and the crisis of the intelligentsia it brought about are in many ways comparable to the Spanish crisis of 1898. But whereas in the Spanish case the loss of possessions held for centuries was a very real one, the Portuguese only lost some of the legal historical claims and titles in their vast portfolio and no portion of territory which they had continuously held for any length of time. The effects on national self-evaluation were fairly similar, but it is characteristic of the Portuguese mentality that the whole crisis was played against a background of remote, obscure, but profuse historical claims. But after 1890 the Portuguese still gradually came to occupy their large African territories and obtain the rank of third largest colonial power in the world.

The strains stemming from the consciousness of a great national past and low contemporary status by every accepted scale of international comparison might have found some alternative resolution (other than the wave of suicides amongst the élite which Unamuno deemed a sure sign of the loss of will to live in the country), but in the event the empire became a generally accepted symbol to achieve status. It is curious that while at community and association level (municipal or federal, corporatist or co-operativist) a partly inherited ideology of the small scale was sustained by the present régime, no corresponding ideology of the virtues of the small nation ever developed. Of the small nations which could be construed as models to imitate, Belgium was preferred to Switzerland, for instance; nor did their anti-bourgeois ethos prevent the integralists from making a similar choice. Pro-imperial ideology involved two types of considerations: the 'weak' argument that Portugal, albeit small and poor, could be 'great' with the empire; and the 'strong' argument that Portugal could not long subsist as an independent state without its colonies. Both theses have enjoyed wide currency to the present day. But since 1945 the régime has preferred to shift the burden of its imperial inheritance from such *Realpolitik* arguments, which involve an appeal to reason and fact, to mythicized historical self-images, singularizing its colonial past and present, presenting it as unique, *sui generis*, incomparable or even exemplary. In this manner the régime has tried to obviate the moral bankruptcy of 'colonialism' and the concomitant power alignments but it has been obliged to stretch to the utmost the limits of credibility and to license certain myths which it would not have condoned in the climate of opinion of the 1930s. The construction of this ideology of 'anticolonial colonialism', claiming unique virtues for the Portuguese dispositions and experience in cultural contact and cross-racial relations, is greatly indebted to the work of Gilberto Freyre. Both in his books, which have helped to form a Brazilian sense of national identity, and in a number of special essays Freyre has argued that the Portuguese colonial experience is set apart from any other by such factors as the influence of Franciscan ideals, the practice of miscegenation or what he calls 'luso-tropical civilization'. On the whole the régime has found it politic to take over a number of Freyre's themes in its propaganda and to some extent it has utilized them internally in its broad strategy.

It is worth noting that at no time has anything like a moral and political critique of imperialism developed in Portugal. Discussions at various times of national crisis (for example, whether the colonies should be sold in part or in whole) remained at an instrumental or utilitarian level. Conversely, a systematic official racist ideology has not developed, although there were signs of it in the 1930s. Since the liberal intelligentsia shares some of the basic presuppositions about the Portuguese colonial experience, the régime has had little reason to fear a moral undermining of its colonial policies. The extreme Left, to be sure, does not share this magical self-image of a uniquely tolerant colonialism but it has not been able or willing to do much to transform such widely shared and satisfying myths.

One result has been that close students of the subject, without necessarily surrendering to the myth of utter Portuguese singularity, have sought to conceptualize its partially original characteristics in some fashion as 'uneconomic imperialism', 'metaphysical colonialism' and most fittingly by Perry Anderson as

334

'ultra-colonialism' – at once the most extreme and most primitive form of colonialism. In fact until quite recently such economic gains as accrued from colonial possessions came largely from shipment facilities, export of labour, and other 'parasitic' or indirect forms of exploitation. Latterly a policy of autarky has been relinquished in order to bring foreign capital into the exploitation of colonial resources, both because Portuguese capital is scarce and unwilling to enter into such ventures and because domestic funds are needed for the colonial war on three fronts – a somewhat paradoxical development for a colonialism which has notoriously been fearful of foreign alignments, dependency or even mere contact.

The outbreak of the colonial war in 1961 very nearly toppled the régime since it was added to unremitting multiple economic, social and political strains. The generals' plot of April 1961 was apparently directed towards a more 'liberal' solution of the colonial question. With Salazar's 'decision to stay' and the transformation of the colonial war into one of attrition, the régime was once more able to demonstrate its ability to surmount both domestic and foreign crises. With the unquestioning commitment to colonial war at a manageable rate of expenditure of both physical and human resources, the régime entered a new stabilization period in the 1960s, following the crises of 1958–63. Since the maintenance of the colonial order is regarded as the overriding priority, the régime is able to compensate for its moral atrophy by appeal to reactionary nationalism and to subordinate economic growth to such 'higher' political goals – once more *politique d'abord*. The colonial war thus provides the régime with the moral equivalent of full-scale ideological renewal and manifest 'refascistization'. By placing such political aims and reactionary nationalism in the forefront in a context of war, in a sense the régime can deny with relative safety that 'socio-economic growth' is the overwhelmingly decisive, privileged 'moment' of Portuguese development and justify the postponement of rewards now that backwardness can no longer be regarded as either virtuous or an *adiaphoron*. Thus, in the Portuguese case, fascism cannot be regarded purely as a stage of

335

industrialization; but must be related to manifold other determinants, including the fast rising imports of foreign capital, which stand in contrast to its earlier economic nationalism and that of kindred régimes.

Portuguese fascism has from a methodological standpoint both peculiar advantages and disadvantages. It has a very long history (or even pre-history, according to how we interpret the earlier years of military dictatorship). It is still in being, formally and (it would be difficult to deny) substantially as well. Personal and organizational continuity may exaggerate the permanent character of the régime. On the other hand the belatedness of industrialization and urbanization in its history, as well as its dependence on foreign resources and the international conjuncture, render it difficult to impute permanency to the régime in the quasi-teleological fashion of some analytical models of fascism. An appraisal of the Portuguese régime today can transcend neither certain ambiguities which only its demise will be able to dissipate nor the absence of a satisfactory conceptual scheme which encompasses all the significant 'fascistizations and fascisms'.

15 Fascism in Contemporary Europe

Christopher Seton-Watson

In 1946 Alfred Rosenberg, soon after being condemned to death at Nuremberg, declared, 'Within fifteen years we will begin to be talked about again, and within twenty nazism will again be a force.' Twenty years takes us to 1966. Has there in fact been a 're-emergence of fascism'? The communists tell us there has; many Germanophobes are ready to agree. Undeniably there has been a revival of the extreme Right in western Europe over the last twenty years. Given the starting point of 1945, it could hardly have been otherwise. It is less clear that there has been a significant revival of fascism. Indiscriminate use of the label 'fascist' in contemporary political controversy adds greatly to the difficulty of defining and identifying the true phenomenon.

It is first of all important to distinguish between what might be called the fascist hard core and the numerous parties and political groupings of the extreme Right which have emerged in western Europe over the past twenty years.* The hard core is overtly fascist and consists mainly of survivors from the fascist era; it is small and has so far been of negligible political importance. The parties of the extreme Right, though not overtly fascist, undeniably contain fascist elements. According to some observers, they are essentially fascist beneath their democratic camouflage; they constitute the mass of the fascist iceberg of

---

* The present essay is limited to western Europe for evident reasons. However, neither Spain nor Portugal will be discussed, as they form the object of specific essays in this symposium.

which the hard core is the visible tip. As one of the most articulate of contemporary fascists, Maurice Bardèche, has written in his *Qu'est ce que le fascisme?* (published in 1961):

It is a strange phenomenon: the fascist writer, the fascist intellectual, are creatures not to be found; the régime which accepts the fascist label is non-existent ... On the other hand there are fascist groups, and they do not conceal it; there are young fascists, and they proclaim it; there are fascist officers, and men tremble at the discovery; finally there is a fascist spirit, and above all there are thousands of men who are fascist without knowing it.

The preceding essays in this volume have attempted to define European fascism in the interwar years. They show that it was a complex and confusing phenomenon. That is no less true of European fascism today.

The hard core consists of conspiratorial, semi-clandestine extremists, gathering in small groups to indulge their nostalgic memories, occasionally resorting to small-scale violence. They are now past middle age and their efforts to recruit from the postwar generation have so far had limited success. Bardèche describes them in the first postwar years as 'these bands of lost soldiers who recognized each other in the murk of injustice and hatred ... nourishing themselves on duplicated propaganda sheets and singing the songs of Hitler's armies'. They are survivors from the 'heroic' fascist age, who keep their faith alive by refusing to accept the verdict of history. As Giorgio Almirante, one of the leaders of the Italian neo-fascists, has put it, 'The fortune of arms was never the final judgment on statesmen, their ideals and philosophies.' Colin Jordan, the British National Socialist, expressed the same view, with characteristic aggressiveness, in 1962:

If the creed was right before its military defeat, it is no less right since that defeat ... Christianity was no less unpopular seventeen years after the death of its founder than is national socialism today. Hitler was right; you can't kill national socialism.

Against such faith no rational arguments can prevail.

The fascist hard core keeps itself alive by continuous intellectual rebellion against the facts of the contemporary world.

338

It rejects *in toto* the Europe of the postwar years, with its 'hypocritical and impotent democratic régimes', its 'propaganda of anti-fascism' and its myth of the heroic anti-fascist resistance. A major aim is the rehabilitation of the fallen fascist régimes, their leaders and their soldiers. Bardèche himself went to prison in 1948 for defending the memory of the 'victims of Nuremberg injustice'. For him, as for his fellow-believers, the accepted facts of Hitler's crimes are merely the fictions of 'atrocity campaigns'; the destruction of Dresden and Hiroshima surpassed anything that Hitler perpetrated, and the atrocities of the Russians rivalled those of the Germans.

Any estimate of the size of these hard-core groups must be speculative. A report by the West German Ministry of Interior in 1964 calculated their numbers in Germany at 112, and their membership at 27,000 (compared with 78,000 ten years before). Others, probably less numerous, are to be found in most west European countries. They have their international contacts and they speak the same language across the fontiers. From time to time they meet and talk of common action to create a united fascist Europe. It is conceivable that, given another cataclysm on the 1914–18 scale, they could one day become as significant as the small groups of extremists who sowed the seeds of post-1918 fascism within the apparently stable society of pre-1914 Europe. Today their importance lies in the fact that most of their ideas and aspirations are to be found, in a less pathological and uninhibited form, among the parties of the extreme Right.

Both Italy and Germany have provided examples of such parties since 1945. The first to appear was *Uomo Qualunque* (Party of the Common Man), which reached its peak early in 1956. From its right wing was born at the end of that year the *Movimento Sociale Italiano* (MSI). In Germany the *Sozialistische Reichspartei* (SRP) was founded in 1949 under ex-Nazi leadership and in 1951 polled eleven per cent of the votes in the *Land* election of Lower Saxony. Next year it was declared 'inimical to the constitution' and banned. Its successor, the *Deutsche Reichspartei*, merged in November 1964 in a new *Nationaldemokratische Partei Deutschlands* (NPD) which flourishes today. All these parties proclaimed themselves democratic and denied any intention of seizing power by unconstitutional means. They differed from the fascist hard core in assuming, to a greater or lesser degree, a respectable image, and in trying to adapt themselves to the political realities of the day. Their aim today is to recapture a mass following for the extreme Right by exploitation of all discontents and resentments, and by continuous denigration of existing democratic governments and of the parties composing them. In the NPD at least half of the present executive committee were active members of the Nazi Party. The MSI similarly has among its leaders men who remained loyal to Mussolini even in the final phase of the Italian Social Republic of 1944–5. The MSI has declared that its policy is 'neither restoration nor renunciation', that it wishes to preserve only those aspects of fascism that are adaptable to contemporary conditions and capable of winning the support of the post-fascist generation. Its problem, like that of the NPD, is how to give sufficient satisfaction to the hard core without either inviting repression by the law, as did the SRP, or alienating the younger voters. Dissension over this question of tactics led in the spring of 1967 to a crisis in the NPD leadership, which ended in the victory of the radical von Thadden over the moderate Thielen. Similar conflicts have occurred within the MSI.

In France the pattern of revival of the extreme Right has been less simple than in Germany or Italy. The French extreme Right has more sources of inspiration than the German or Italian, and some of them have roots deep in the past. *Action Française*, Bonapartism and the Catholic counter-revolution all have their followers today. On to these national roots were grafted foreign fascist models between 1934 and 1945. The products were so hybrid that it is necessary to speak of French fascisms rather than fascism. The first chance of renewed life for the French extreme Right, after the enforced silence that followed the liberation, came with the emergence of de Gaulle's *Rassemblement du Peuple Français* (RPF). This movement had acquired a membership of a million by 1948 and in 1951 won 120 seats in the National Assembly. Paradoxically, though its leader was the

340

incarnation of resistance to Vichy and Hitler, RPF attracted by its denunciation of the 'system' of the Fourth Republic, its call for a strong state and its quasi-fascist style of organization and propaganda, many survivors of the pre-war extreme Right and many Vichy supporters. The RPF would have been fascist without de Gaulle, declared Bardèche. By 1953 the RPF had been abandoned by its founder and was close to disintegration. Its successor was Poujade's *Union de Défense des Commerçants et Artisans* (UDCA), which after polling two and a half million votes in the general election of 1956, went like its predecessor into decline. It was the Algerian crisis of 1954–8 that restored the power of the extreme Right.

All its heterogeneous elements, Catholic reactionaries, Bonapartists, survivors of the *Cagoule*, admirers of the Vichy state, rallied to the defence of *Algérie Française* and plotted, sometimes in collaboration, more often in rivalry, to overthrow the detested 'system'. Amongst them were a few organizations that were overtly fascist. One, *Jeune Nation*, was founded in 1950 by the Sidos brothers, sons of a collaborator executed after the liberation. It stood for a popular authoritarian state, both national and social; it was virulently antisemitic and used the Celtic cross as its emblem, to symbolize its aim 'to unite the very remote past of our people with the hope of a greater future'. In 1954 Biaggi founded a *Parti Patriotique Révolutionnaire* which found widespread support among students and ex-servicemen, especially in Algiers, and claimed ten thousand members within three years. But the majority of the enemies of the Fourth Republic were not fascist. From the crisis of 1958 one section of the extreme Right, the Gaullists, emerged triumphant, to become the establishment of the Fifth Republic. Many non-Gaullists accepted the Gaullist triumph. Others soon turned against de Gaulle, accusing him of betraying the Algerian cause and 'smothering the revolution'. A few plotted to overthrow the Fifth Republic as they had helped to overthrow the Fourth. De Gaulle destroyed them. Since the failure of the military insurrection of April 1961 the anti-Gaullist extreme Right, which includes a fascist hard core, has been fragmented and impotent.

All these parties and movements attracted at least temporary fascist support. In most of their programmes and pronouncements traces of fascist ideas and phrases can be found. In a few of them fascists have played a leading role. The German and Italian parties clearly resemble their Nazi and fascist predecessors in the rallies they stage, the demagogic oratory in which they indulge, and the undertone of violence implicit in their methods of organization. All contain some of what might be called the 'elements' of fascism. These elements have been identified in the preceding essays of this volume. Between the wars different fascist movements combined them in differing proportions, hence the different characteristics of particular national fascisms. No one element singly can constitute a fascist movement; fascism is the product of a fusion of several. Since 1945 no such fusion has taken place. Nevertheless all the same elements are present in contemporary Europe.

Five may usefully be distinguished: nationalism, racialism, militarism, anti-communism and anti-democracy (often with an anti-capitalist flavour). Nationalism is the basic component of fascism. Where national grievances are deeply felt, where patriotic sentiments have been exasperated or bruised, where irredentist aspirations flourish, there is fertile soil for fascism. It can feed also on imperialist nostalgia and the resentments of decolonization. Irredentism is most powerful in Germany. Ten million refugees from the east settled in Western Germany after the war. In Schleswig-Holstein they at one time constituted forty per cent of the population, in Lower Saxony thirty per cent, in Bavaria twenty per cent. Two and a half million still belong to *Landsmannschaften*, each representing a different ex-German area, which publish periodicals, organize rallies and keep the old feelings of kinship alive. The Sudeten Germans from pre-war Czechoslovakia are among the most active. The NPD draws a significantly large proportion of its support from the areas where the refugees are most numerous. More generally the NPD's appeal to frustrated national pride has been both persistent and successful. It calls for a restoration of national dignity and an end to 'twenty years of self-accusation' and 'one-sided attempts to redeem the past by war crimes tribunals'. It is time, the party declares, to rehabilitate the German soldier and stop 'the glorification of treason' (i.e. of anti-nazism). The NPD appeals also to anti-American feelings by calling for a check to the Americanization of German culture and by pointing to the extravagance and alien ways of the foreign armies stationed on German soil. Germans are urged to stop feeling like 'moral pariahs' and to realize that 'once again we are somebody in the world'.

In Italy the MSI has made the same appeals for rehabilitation of the fascist past and restoration of the nation's dignity, combined with denigration of the resistance. In its early years it thrived on resentment at the harsh peace treaty of 1947 and on accusations against successive democratic governments of 'servility' to the foreigner. Italy also has its refugees from Istria and the eastern Adriatic, and repatriates from ex-Italian Africa: few in total numbers, but receptive to the nationalist appeal. While the fate of Trieste was still unsettled, a favourite theme of the extreme Right was denunciation of the 'insidious Slavs' and their protectors in the foreign, especially British, forces of occupation. The MSI still polls a significantly higher proportion of votes in Trieste than in the rest of Italy. Since Trieste returned to Italy in 1954, Italian nationalists have turned their attention to South Tyrol, which has also become an irresistible magnet for the fascist hard core. In Austria the nationalists exploit the grievances of their compatriots south of the Brenner. In south Tyrol Austrian fascists, with German fascist support, fight Italian fascists, and violence in the form of sabotage, terrorism, assassination and even military operations by 'commandos' has occurred on both sides. In Belgium militant Flemish nationalism still gives life to quasi-military combat groups, continuing the tradition of the interwar Rexist movement. Algeria was the clearest example of all. The *colons* and *pieds noirs*, threatened by Muslim Algerian nationalism and in growing fear of a sell-out by democratic governments in Paris, steadily drifted into violence, with nationalist students and schoolboys leading the way. Racial frontiers create tension, fever and hysteria, and extremist

343

movements find in them their natural habitat. And all too often, as happened in France, the nationalist fever spreads inwards from the periphery to the centre and infects the whole body politic.

Racialism in Europe between the wars took mainly the form of antisemitism. Overt antisemitism has been rarer since 1945, but it is by no means dead. Many countries have seen sporadic outbursts of swastika-daubing, attacks on synagogues and desecration of Jewish graves. These are favourite activities for the bolder spirits of the hard core. There have also been provocative marches through Jewish districts, in the East End of London in 1949 and in the Rome 'Ghetto' in 1962. Sir Oswald Mosley, the Italian neo-fascists, Bardèche and many others have denied being antisemitic. Nevertheless the old spirit often breaks through. Many sections of the European extreme Right, for example, expressed their horror at the trial and execution of Eichmann, and Poujadists and leaders of the NPD frequently indulge in euphemistic denunciation of international bankers or the hidden power of 'parasitic, predatory super-capital'.

Contemporary racialism, however, tends to take an anti-coloured rather than an antisemitic form. The 'Keep Britain White' slogan and the Smethwick situation have their parallels elsewhere in Europe. In Germany the NPD has delighted in denigrating 'dirty, indisciplined, criminal' foreign workers (of whom there are a million from southern Europe, the Middle East and North Africa in West Germany today), in insisting on priority in employment for Germans and in warning of the danger of contamination of the German race. Algerian immigrants have aroused similar reactions in France. The chairman of NPD, von Thadden, has extolled Ian Smith as 'the guardian of peace and freedom', and admiration for South African *apartheid* and for the Portuguese, 'fighting the battle of civilization in Angola', is not confined to the fascist hard core. Xenophobia is a general feature of NPD pronouncements, which call for an end to wasteful spending of public funds on foreigners, whether in the form of reparations to Israel or of overseas development aid.

Militarism in the past has often been the precursor of fascism.

The function performed by members of the *Freikorps* in Germany in the 1920s, or the *Arditi* in Italy, or the veterans of the Croat Guards Regiments of the Habsburg Army in Yugoslavia, are well known. It has been said of Sir Oswald Mosley that his approach to politics in the 1920s was that of the ex-serviceman. Europe today is full of ex-servicemen. Twelve hundred associations exist in Germany alone, loosely united in the *Verband Deutscher Soldaten*, in whose activities heroic commanders from the last war have played an important role. Rehabilitation of the German soldier and welfare of the ex-serviceman are their main (and legitimate) aims. The most interesting is *Hilfsorganisation auf Gegenseitigkeit der Waffen-SS* (HIAG), the veterans' association of the SS, which has international connections. Two hardcore organizations, *Nation Europa* and *Jeune Europe*, are led by ex-SS men and make it their business to keep the SS legionaries of all Europe in touch and summon them from time to time for reunions. In Italy a naval war hero, Prince Valerio Borghese, who remained faithful to Mussolini to the end, has played a part in the neo-fascist movement. The MSI has made deliberate appeals to the spirit and pride of the crack divisions of the Italian army and to the veterans (*i ragazzi*) of the western Desert and Alamein. The NPD's equally deliberate appeal has had some success with serving soldiers of the *Bundeswehr*. In France veterans of Indo-China, often active in ex-service associations, played a key role in the Algerian insurrections of 1958–61.

The psychology of élite or shock troops has much in common with that of fascism. *Arditi*, SS, French paratroopers or foreign *légionnaires* share many characteristics: the cult of the superman, of the hero and of death, the mysticism of sacrifice, the sense of being people apart from the common herd, the abnormal emphasis on *esprit de corps* and *camaraderie*, the devotion to commanders whose exploits become legendary, the contempt for the plodding infantryman or the office-bound staff officer, for the conscript or the conventional civilian. All these traits were found in interwar fascist movements at their most youthful and militant stage. Contemporary fascists are well aware of this. Colin Jordan said in 1962, 'The ss man is our model.'

All the leading military rebels of Algeria had served in Indo-China and been moulded by that traumatic experience. They returned to France in 1954 with the conviction that their defeat had been political, not military; that the nation had abandoned them in a distant land and the democratic politicians had stabbed them in the back. Their experience over the next four years in Algeria, where they believed they were fighting the next round of the third world war against the universal enemy, communism, completed their sense of alienation from the parliamentary Fourth Republic, and led them to identify themselves with the cause of *Algérie Française*, where beat the heart of 'true' France. Fighting in Algeria strengthened their conviction that strong purposeful government was essential to victory, and that war must be total, fought in the minds of civilians as much as on the ground, against the internal as much as the external enemy. Such beliefs drew them into a political position that was close to fascism. When the politicians once again seemed on the point of selling out in 1958, they stood by and watched while the *colons* seized power in Algiers. It was in great part the army that canalized the insurrection into Gaullist channels. But de Gaulle, too, failed to satisfy the extremists. When he showed that he was prepared to compromise with the 'system' and with the old degenerate France, a few officers and élite regiments staged a military insurrection in April 1961. It was the paratroopers and Foreign Legion which provided the force on that occasion; the conscripts of the ordinary regiments remained passive and declined to follow the rebels' lead. The failure of the insurrection drove the irreconcilables of the *Organization Armée Secrete* (OAS) into nihilistic terrorism, which made them the heroes of the fascist hard core throughout Europe.

Anti-communism also is a basic component of fascism. All fascists demand, if not the suppression, at least the isolation and harassment of communist parties. Their anti-communism often extends to socialists. On this point the parties of the extreme Right share the hard core's views. Both in Italy and in Germany

346

they have attacked their ruling Christian Democratic governments for allying themselves with the socialists rather than leaning
upon the 'healthy' national forces of the Right. In 1953 and
again in 1960 it seemed that Italian governments were about to
comply with their wishes, but in 1962 the opposite policy of the
apertura a sinistra was adopted. 'They are playing the communists' game' was the MSI's comment. In Germany the attitude of
NPD to the 'grand coalition' of Christian Democrats and Social
Democrats has been identical.

Anti-communism links up in Germany with irredentism. The
NPD's proclaimed goal is to liberate Eastern Germany from
communism and roll the iron curtain back. But such sentiments
are not confined to Germany. One of the most striking aspects
of the extreme Right in Europe since 1945 has been the new
emphasis on European unity, on 'nationalism within a greater
Europe'. The idea of the 'new order' has perhaps been Hitler's
most lasting legacy. It is a favourite theme of the hard core.
The very names of its organizations and publications show this:
European Social Movement, *Ordine Nuovo*, European New
Order, *Jeune Europe, L'Europe Réelle, Nation Europa*. In 1962
Mosley, von Thadden, Jean Thiriart, the Belgian fascist, and
others met at Venice to found a 'National Party of Europe'. The
title of Bardèche's periodical is *Défense de L'Occident*. In his
words, 'only its [fascism's] mission of the Defence of the West
has remained in the memory, and this is still the chief meaning
of the fascist idea'. The MSI talks of 'Europe from Brest to
Bucharest', the NPD of 'Germany first, then Europe; Germany
for the Germans, Europe for the Europeans'. 'Neither Moscow
nor Washington' is the ideal of both the hard core and the
NPD; a regenerate and truly independent Europe which will
constitute a third force in the world. 'History will prove that the
idea of a united Europe originated with the *Waffen-SS* volunteers', declared a high official of HIAG at an SS reunion in
Germany in 1965. Not long before Biaggi had declared, 'The
paratroopers will create the real Europe.' On the basis of
European unity the anti-communists, the racialists, the nationalists and the militarists can find common ground.

The fifth element of fascism, anti-democracy, is the least precise. It can take several forms. In its simplest and commonest it is merely a yearning for strong government and a state above parties and factions, a deep contempt for parliamentary government and a passion for order and discipline. A second variety may be loosely labelled 'Poujadism'. Its detractors called Poujade's UDCA a 'grocers' party'. Poujade himself, when he founded it in 1953, was a humble stationer from St Céré in south-west France. Starting with a flamboyant refusal to pay his taxes, and skilfully exploiting his personal demagogic talent, he built up a mass movement composed predominantly of small shopkeepers, peasants and artisans. Its greatest strength lay in the economically declining south and south-west (unlike the RPF which appealed primarily to the modern and dynamic sectors of the French economy). Its programme was almost entirely negative; against the supermarkets, against the bankers, against big business, against privilege and élites of all kinds and, in political terms, against parliament and the democratic parties, especially of the Left. It was the party of that section of the middle class that earned its living from obsolescent businesses and farms, and felt itself threatened by the pace of modernization. It shared the traditional French radical fear of *les gros*, which included the trade unions and the organized working-class. Closely associated with it was a peasant defence movement under Vichyite leadership. In its use of strong-armed thugs and rowdyism at political meetings it imitated its predecessor, the RPF. Middle-aged grocers do not by themselves constitute a fascist movement; they are more concerned with order and stability than with revolution. Nevertheless in times of crisis, especially in times of weak democratic government, they can find common ground with fascists and with other sections of the extreme Right with more positive programmes. The Poujadists gladly joined in exploiting the 'scandals' and corruption of the Fourth Republic, and added their voice for strong government, the restoration of national greatness and a halt to decolonization. The antisemitic and xenophobic note was clearly evident in their pronouncements, and the movement had its contacts with the Algerian *colons.* Some of Poujade's lieutenants (e.g. Ortiz and Lefèvre) played an active part in the insurrection of 1958.

The other striking example of a Poujadist movement was *Uomo Qualunque,* which for a brief moment in 1945-6 captured the support and votes of the small men of Italy, together with the nostalgic and the defeated in the civil war of 1943-5. UQ's main strength lay in the south, the most backward region economically. The MSI has drawn its support from much the same sectors of the population. In Germany, too, NPD has shown that it has Poujadist elements. In its party programme it calls for a struggle against the corrupting aspects of the affluent society. Indeed there is a provincial puritanical side to Poujadism: in France, as in Italy and in Germany, the extreme Right protests against the degeneracy and 'public licentiousness' of cosmopolitan Paris or Rome or Bonn. Over half the NPD's supporters are small and medium-sized businessmen and farmers, living often in areas that were old Nazi strongholds. It wins votes in small and medium-sized towns rather than in large cities. Significantly it has so far made no attempt to fight elections in such areas as North Rhine-Westphalia (which includes the Ruhr) nor in west Berlin. Like the Poujadists and MSI, it is from the backward regions that it draws its main strength.

The second variation of anti-democracy (also with an anti-capitalist flavour) is corporatism: an even less precise concept than Poujadism, but one that, for all its nebulousness, has had a persistent appeal for fascists and the near-fascist extreme Right. The corporatists dream of an 'organic' or 'national-social' state, within which capital and labour, family, profession and local community will be harmoniously integrated in the 'superior interests of the nation'. Such ideas were current in Algiers both before and after the *coup* of 1958. Bardèche writes of 'socialism' as the ideal, with capital and labour joined in one *fascio.* Mussolini, he declares, died of caesarism, having abandoned the original fascist ideal. Similarly the MSI corporatists led by Almirante hark back to the 'origins' of 1919, as elaborated in the eighteen points of Mussolini's radical Verona Manifesto of 1944. True corporatism, says

349

Bardèche, will be Europe's third force between capitalism and marxism.

Nationalism, racialism, militarism, anti-communism, anti-democracy: none of these are fascist in origin nor exclusively fascist today. Neither the fascist hard core nor the parties of the extreme Right have a monopoly of aspirations to roll back the iron curtain, or build a united Europe, or restore national dignity, or establish strong government, or create an 'organic' state, or secure justice for ex-servicemen, shopkeepers or refugees. The five elements considered above do nevertheless form the bare bones of fascism. What has been lacking in Europe since 1945 has been the breath to give the bare bones life. Fascism between the wars thrived on passions more than on ideas; it threw up charismatic leaders of great power, it recruited massive paramilitary formations and gloried in physical violence, it captured the idealism of youth and persuaded millions in many countries that it had the answer to the world's problems. Since the second war nothing similar has occurred. Only in Algeria between 1954 and 1961 has anything that could remotely be called fascism won the hearts of the (European) masses, and even there it met disaster when it failed to move metropolitan France. The fascist hard core survives, but few outside its ranks regard it as other than a pathological relic of a previous age. Even the parties of the extreme Right have had a limited appeal. The MSI has polled between 4·7 per cent and 5·9 per cent of the votes in Italy's three general elections since 1953. At the last French presidential election in 1965 the candidate of the extreme Right, Tixier-Vignancourt, ex-junior minister under Vichy and defender of the OAS rebels, polled five per cent. In Germany the NPD polled only two per cent (658,000 votes) in the national election of September 1965; but in the *Land* elections of 1966–7 it registered between 5·8 per cent and 8·8 per cent in Schleswig-Holstein, Rhineland-Palatinate, Lower Saxony, Hesse, Bremen and Bavaria. Under the German electoral law, which requires a party to win five per cent of the votes in any one district (*Kreis*) before it is entitled to representation, the NPD is now represented in six of the eleven *Land* parliaments, but not in the fedral *Bundestag*. In the summer of 1967 it claimed 32,000 members. It still has not reached the peak attained by SRP in 1951. In general the extreme Right seems still to be on the defensive, to be the repository of many varied discontents and resentments, but to offer no positive alternative for the future.

How may such relative lack of success be explained? Three connected factors suggest themselves: first, the new affluence in western Europe; second, the provision in the shape of US power of security from communist aggression or subversion; third, western Europe's good fortune, for a substantial part of the past twenty years, in enjoying stable and effective government.

The first factor needs little elaboration. The connection between mass unemployment and the rise of fascism is well-known, Germany in the 1930s being the outstanding example. Full employment and steady economic growth are the surest antidotes to mass political extremism.

The US presence after 1945 relieved European governments of the temptation to resort to desperate measures for the containment or repression of communism, and so enabled them to resist pressure from the extreme Right which otherwise could have destroyed democracy. It is surely not a coincidence that the recent weakening of US influence in Europe, thanks to de Gaulle's nationalist erosion of NATO and the US preoccupation with Vietnam, has been accompanied by a revival of German nationalist sentiment and the growth of the NPD.

As regards stable and effective government, Germany and Italy owed much to Adenauer and De Gasperi during the first crucial postwar years. Their tough treatment of communism gave the extreme Right few openings to exploit, yet their restraint and resistance to extreme measures allowed the democratic foundations to set firm. The MSI immediately profited from the uncertainty that followed De Gasperi's death in 1954, and will certainly profit again if the present Christian Democratic-Socialist coalition fails to provide stability. Similarly the recent progress of NPD has been stimulated by loss of confidence

351

in democratic government from Bonn after the removal of Adenauer's strong guiding hand.

The clearest example of the opportunity that weak democratic government gives to right-wing extremism was provided by France between 1954 and 1958. De Gaulle has restored strong government to France and in so doing has dried up the main potential source of French fascism. However severe the critics may be of de Gaulle's nationalist policies and authoritarian practice of government, he cannot be portrayed as a fascist. Even at the height of the crisis of the Fourth Republic, he gave no encouragement to those who wished to seize power by force, but instead strove to find a democratic solution to a revolutionary situation. If he gave the appearance in opposition of a man of the extreme Right when leading the RPF, since his return to power he has proved himself a man of the Centre. Never has he indulged in fascist glorification of violence, nor attempted to reinforce his personal authority with totalitarian institutions. De Gaulle's strength lies in large part in his ability to satisfy right-wing aspirations for strong government while preserving the essentials of a free society. Had there been a de Gaulle in Italy in 1918–22, it is questionable whether fascism would ever have come to power.

A comprehensive analysis of contemporary fascism, if space allowed, would require examination of such other factors as the influence of the Catholic Church (which has in the main supported Christian democracy since 1945, whereas after 1918 it preferred the extreme Right), the political role of industry and big business (which financed fascism between the wars in certain notorious instances, but does not seem to have been so tempted since 1945) and the attitude of the post-fascist generation (ultranationalist organizations powerfully influenced the youth of Algiers, and the MSI has found some support among Italian students; recently, for the first time since the war, nationalism appears to be attracting sections of German youth). On such matters information is scanty. For an interim judgment on the prospects of fascism, it is perhaps best to turn to fascists. 'Fascism', says Bardèche, 'is impossible to define outside periods

of crisis . . . Where there is no occasion for heroism, it perishes
. . . It is the party of the nation in wrath: that wrath is indispensable to fascism. It is the very blood that irrigates fascism.' In
1963 Mosley attributed Hitler's success to 'the great unemployment following the great inflation'. A year later he asked himself, 'What are our chances?', and replied, 'None until the
crisis'.

Chronological Tables

Italy (Chapter 3)

1919	23 March	Foundation of the first *fascio di combattimento* at Milan.
	12 September	D'Annunzio's occupation of Fiume.
1922	28 October	'March on Rome'.
1923	23 July	Electoral law passed, guaranteeing two-thirds of seats to party with relative majority.
1924	6 April	Elections.
	10 June	Matteotti kidnapped and murdered.
1925	3 January	Mussolini's acceptance of responsibility for all past fascist actions.
	2 October	Palazzo Vidoni pact between the industrialists' association (*Confindustria*) and the fascist syndicates.
	24 December	Law extending powers of the head of the government, giving him full executive responsibility.
1926	31 January	Decrees given the power of laws.
	3 April	Right to strike abolished; collective contracts reserved to the fascist syndicates.
	25 November	Law for the defence of the state; creation of a special tribunal for political crimes.
1927	15 January	Churchill's visit to Mussolini.
	21 December	Exchange rate fixed at 'quota 90' (L.92·45 to £1).
1929	11 February	Lateran pacts, including the Concordat.
1932	30 October	*Decennale* celebrations.
1933	23 January	Creation of IRI.
1934	14 June	Meeting of Mussolini and Hitler at Venice.
	10 November	Council of Corporations inaugurated at Rome.
1935	5 October	Invasion of Abyssinia.
1936	21 October	Rome-Berlin 'Axis'.
1938	14 July	Publication of the *Manifesto della Razza*, first antisemitic measures.

1939	19 January	Creation of the *Camera dei Fasci e delle Corporazioni*, replacing parliament.
	7 April	Invasion of Albania.
	22 May	Pact of Steel signed.
1940	10 June	Italy enters the second world war.
1943	25 July	Grand Council of Fascism votes Mussolini out of power.
	8 September	Armistice declared; Nazis take over the country.
	23 September	Mussolini announces the creation of the fascist social republic (Republic of Salò) over Munich radio.
1945	28 April	Mussolini executed by partisans at Dongo.

Germany (Chapter 4)

1889	20 April	Hitler born in Braunau in Austria. Educated in Linz. Moves to Vienna.
1918	7–8 November	Bavarian monarchy overthrown.
	9 November	German Kaiser abdicates; Germany becomes a republic.
1919	5 January	Drexler founds 'German Workers' Party' in Munich.
	28 June	Treaty of Versailles signed.
	12 September	Hitler attends his first meeting of the German Workers' Party.
1920	24 February	Hitler – now a leading speaker in the German Workers' Party – reads out its new programme. The party also becomes known as the National Socialist German Workers' Party (NSDAP or Nazis).
	13 March	Kapp *putsch* in Berlin. New right-wing government in Bavaria.
1923	10–11 January	Germany declared to have defaulted on reparations payments. French and Belgian troops occupy the Ruhr. German currency, already badly inflated, collapses completely. Germans answer with passive resistance in the Ruhr.
	26 September	Stresemann, the German Chancellor, announces end of passive resistance. State of emergency declared in Bavaria.

355

1923	8–9 November	Hitler's first bid for power in the abortive Munich *putsch*. Nazi Party dissolved by order.
1924	1 April	Hitler sentenced to five years fortress arrest.
	20 December	Hitler released under general amnesty.
1925	27 February	Nazi Party refounded.
1929	7 June	Young plan fixing German reparations payments announced in Paris.
	3 October	Stresemann dies.
1930	14 September	German elections return 107 Nazi deputies to Reichstag in Berlin.
1932	10 April	Election of Reich President sees Hitler beaten by Hindenburg but obtaining 13,417,460 votes.
	31 July	General election: 230 Nazi deputies elected.
	6 November	New general election; Nazis lose votes and fall in numbers to 196 members of *Reichstag*.
1933	30 January	Hitler appointed Chancellor of Germany.
	28 February	Decree for the Protection of the People and the State, suspending guarantees of individual rights and giving government the power to make arbitrary arrests.
	5 March	General election gives Nazis 288 seats and 43·9% of vote.
	23 March	Enabling law giving Hitler the right to govern by decree.
	2 May	Trade unions abolished.
	14 July	Germany a one-party state.
	14 October	Germany leaves the League of Nations.
1934	30 January	German State (i.e. *Länder*) parliaments abolished.
	29–30 June	Purge of the SA. Röhm and others murdered.
1935	16 March	Germany announces compulsory military service.
	15 September	Nuremberg laws discriminating against Jews.
1936	7 March	Hitler occupies demilitarized zone in the Rhineland.
	17 June	Himmler appointed chief of police forces in the Reich.
	September	Hitler proclaims four-year plan.
	25 October	Rome-Berlin collaboration agreement.
	23 November	German-Japanese anti-comintern agreement signed.

1938	12 March	German invasion of Austria.
	30 September	Munich agreement over partition of Czechoslovakia.
1939	14 March	Germans seize Prague.
	23 August	Nazi-Soviet Pact signed.
	1 September	Germany invades Poland.
1940	10 May	German invasion of France and Low Countries.
	June	Fall of France.
1941	22 June	Germany invades Soviet Russia.
	Summer	Decision to begin mass extermination of Jews.
	11 December	Germany declares war on USA.
1945	30 April	Hitler commits suicide in Berlin.

Austria (Chapter 5)

1918	12 November	Republic of Austria proclaimed.
1919	10 September	Treaty of St Germain accepted by Parliament.
1920	10 October	Klagenfurt plebiscite; southern Carinthia, claimed by Yugoslavia, remains Austrian.
1921	14–16 December	Ödenburg (Sopron) plebiscite; capital of Burgenland (transferred to Austria) remains Hungarian.
1927	15 July	Armed clashes in Vienna between police and socialist demonstrators; over 100 killed.
1929	7 December	Austrian constitution revised.
1930	18 May	'Korneuburg Oath' of Heimwehr movement.
	September	Starhemberg elected leader of Heimwehr; joins Cabinet.
	9 November	Last general election; Social Democrats strongest single party (42 per cent of total vote).
1931	March	Customs union with Germany projected.
	13 September	Heimwehr putsch under Pfrimer.
1932	24 April	Last provincial elections; Nazi vote increases.
1933	4 March	Parliament suspended by Dollfuss.
	26 May	Austrian Communist Party banned.
	19 June	Austrian NSDAP banned.
	11 September	Dollfuss proclaims authoritarian state.
1934	12 February	Heimwehr and government forces attack socialists; Social Democratic Party, trade unions, etc., banned.

1934	17 March	'Rome Protocols' on co-operation and consultation between Italy, Hungary and Austria signed.
	25 July	Dollfuss killed in Nazi *putsch*, succeeded by Schuschnigg.
1936	20 March	'Rome Protocols' reaffirmed.
	14 May	Starhemberg dropped from Government.
	11 July	'July Agreement' between Austria and Germany.
1938	11–13 March	Schuschnigg resigns under German pressure, succeeded by Seyss-Inquart; *Anschluss* proclaimed.

Hungary (Chapter 6)

1918	31 October	Democratic revolution. Independence Party, Radicals, and Social Democrats form coalition government under Mihály Károlyi.
1919	21 March	Coalition of Communists and Left Social Democrats proclaims 'Hungarian Councils' Republic' – Bela Kun's dictatorship emerges.
	29 May	Nationalist anti-revolutionary government formed in Szeged.
	1 August	Communist-Socialist government resigns. Trade union leaders form government.
	3 August	Rumanian army enters Budapest.
	7 August	Right-wing rising replaces trade unionist government. I. Friedrich Prime Minister.
	19 August	Szeged government resigns and joins forces with I. Friedrich.
	16 November	Rumanian troops evacuate Budapest. Adml. Horthy and 'National Army' enter capital of Hungary.
	23 November	K. Huszár forms coalition government.
	5 December	Decree on internments legalizes 'white terror'.
1920	25 January	Elections for national assembly.
	17 February	Two editors of a social-democratic daily murdered.
	1 March	Adml. Horthy elected Regent by National Assembly.
	4 June	Hungarian treaty of peace signed at Trianon Palace, Versailles.
	19 July	Count Paul Teleki nominated Prime Minister.

1921	26 March	Charles IV's first attempt to regain Hungarian throne fails.
	13 April	Count Paul Teleki resigns. Count István Bethlen new Prime Minister.
	20 October	King Charles' second attempt fails.
1922	2 February	Prime Minister Bethlen forms 'united' government party.
	2 March	Secret ballot in rural constituencies abolished.
	May–June	General elections produce big majority for government party.
1923	May	Count Bethlen starts negotiations on international loan.
	2 August	Captain Gömbös leaves government party and forms 'Racialist Party'.
1924	May–July	Hungary under League of Nations financial control obtains stabilization loans. Reconstruction law adopted by Parliament.
1926	11 November	Law re-establishes Upper House of Parliament.
	December	General elections. Racialist Party defeated.
1927	2 April	Italo-Hungarian friendship pact signed in Rome.
1928	6 September	G. Gömbös rejoins government party.
1929	September–October	Strikes and demonstrations of unemployed workers – G. Gömbös Minister of Defence.
1930	15 May	League of Nations control of Hungarian finances terminated.
1931	June–July	General elections. Bethlen victorious.
	14 July	Financial crisis.
	19 August	Regent accepts Count Bethlen's resignation – Count Gyula Károlyi Prime Minister; 'austerity' programme.
1932	1 October	Gyula Gömbös replaces G. Károlyi as Prime Minister.
1933	17 July	Gömbös visits Hitler in Berlin.
1934	17 March	Mussolini, Gömbös and Dollfuss conclude 'Rome Protocol'.
1935	March–April	General elections managed by Gömbös. Bethlen resigns from government party.
1936	23 March	Second Rome Protocol signed.
	6 October	Death of Gömbös in Munich – K. Darányi Prime Minister.
1937	1 July	Law on extension of the powers of the Regent.

1938	5 March	Speech of Darányi in Györ announcing measures against Jews and economic (rearmament) plans.
	13 May	Darányi replaced by B. Imrédy as Prime Minister.
	22 August	Horthy visits Hitler – F. Szálasi condemned to three years in prison.
	2 November	First Vienna award redrafts Hungarian-Slovakian frontier.
1939	13 January	Hungary signs Anti-Comintern Pact.
	12 February	B. Imrédy forced to resign. Count Paul Teleki Prime Minister.
	15 March	Hungarian army occupies the Carpatho-Ukraine.
	11 April	Hungary withdraws from League of Nations.
	5 May	Promulgation of the so-called 'second Jewish law'.
	29 May	General election produces strong national-socialist opposition group.
1940	30 August	Second Vienna award allots north-east Transylvania to Hungary.
	20 November	Hungary adheres to the Three-Power Pact.
	12 December	Hungary and Yugoslavia sign friendship treaty.
1941	3 April	Suicide of Count P. Teleki. L. Bárdossy Prime Minister. German troops cross Hungarian territory for attack on Yugoslavia.
	12 April	Hungarian army enters the Bachka (Vojvodina).
	27 June	Hungary declares war on the Soviet Union.
	6 December	Great Britain declares war on Hungary.
	13 December	Hungary at war with the USA.
1942	January	Massacre of civilians in the Bachka by army and gendarmerie units.
	7 March	Bárdossy dismissed by Horthy; Miklós Kállay Prime Minister.
1943	January	Second Hungarian Army destroyed at Voronesh (Soviet Russia).
	September	Secret armistice negotiations between Hungary and Great Britain.
1944	18 March	German army invades and occupies Hungary. Gestapo begins arrest of anti-German politicians.

1944	22 March	Hitler imposes D. Sztójay as Prime Minister on Horthy.
	May	Mass deportations of Jews begins.
	July	Horthy stops deportations; reorganizes government.
	29 August	Horthy dismisses Sztójay; Gen. Lakatos Prime Minister. All political parties to suspend their activities.
	15 October	Horthy announces armistice with Soviet Russia – German troops move on Budapest.
	16 October	Horthy arrested by Germans. F. Szálasy forms government.
	20 December	Anti-German left-wing coalition government formed in Soviet-occupied Debrecen. Siege of Budapest begins. (Siege ends 11 February 1945.)

Rumania (Chapter 7)

1919	Corneliu Zelia Codreanu becomes a student at the University of Jassy where he meets the nationalistic demagogue Professor A. J. Cuza.
1920–3	C. Z. Codreanu initiates and takes part in nationalistic student movements in all four Rumanian universities.
1923	C. Z. Codreanu and A. J. Cuza form together a political party, 'The League of the National Christian Defence', which in 1926 wins six seats in the Rumanian parliament.
1927	The foundation of the Legion of the Archangel Michael, which is the political organ of the Iron Guard movement and the first independent political party led by Codreanu.
1932	The Legion wins five seats in parliament. Its first dissolution as a political party.
1937	The Legion, under the name of 'All for the Fatherland', wins sixty seats in Parliament representing more than sixteen per cent of the electorate.
1938	The Legion is dissolved again and in 1939, the year of martyrdom, more than 1200 Legionaries, including Codreanu, are exterminated.

| 1940–1 | The surviving elements of the Iron Guard under the leadership of Horia Sima join the coalition Government headed by General Antonescu. As a result of the abortive *putsch* of January 1941 they are eliminated from the government, and the leadership is decimated. |

Poland (Chapter 8)

1918	Resurrection of independent Polish state.
1920	Russo-Polish War.
1921–6	Parliamentary government.
1926	Pilsudski seizes power.
1935	Pilsudski dies.
1939	German invasion.

Finland (Chapter 9)

1917 December	Finland declares independence.
1918 January	Socialists attempt to seize power. Civil war follows.
May	Victory of the Whites, followed by severe repression of the Reds.
August	Foundation of Finnish Communist Party with programme of renewed revolution.
1919	Establishment of parliamentary republic.
1920	Peace treaty of Tartu with Soviet Russia.
1921–2 Winter	Defeat of final attempt by Finnish activists to invade Soviet Karelia.
1928	Communist-led dock-strike. Beginning of economic depression.
1929 Autumn	Lapua movement launched.
1930 March	Attack on communist press at Vaasa, increasing Lapua violence.
June–July	Formation of Svinhufvud government under Lapua pressure. Diet fails to pass anti-communist laws. Communist deputies arrested. Diet dissolved.
August	Peasant march on Helsinki.
October	General election: two-thirds majority to Right. Communist Party suppressed.
1931	Svinhufvud elected President of the Republic with Lapua support. As return to legality demanded, Lapua plans *coup d'état*.

1932	February	Mäntsälä revolt suppressed. Lapua movement transformed into IKL.
1933		General election: IKL wins 14 seats out of 200. IKL modelling itself increasingly on foreign fascist parties.
1936		General election: IKL holds its seats. Victory for Agrarian-Social Democratic alliance.
1938		Legal proceedings against IKL with view to suppression.
1939		High Court refuses to suppress IKL, but at election representation cut to eight.
	November	War with Russia.
1941	January	IKL enters coalition government.
	June	Finland joins attack on Soviet Russia.
1944	September	Armistice with USSR: one condition that fascist organizations be suppressed. IKL dissolved.

Norway (Chapter 10)

1919–21	Labour Party adheres to Comintern. Major strikes.
1920, 1925	Establishment of strike-breaking and anti-marxist organizations.
1928	Nineteen-day minority Labour government.
1931–3	Agrarian Party in office, with Quisling as Minister of Defence.
1933–7	Successive electoral failures of Quisling's 'National Unity' movement.
1935–40	Labour Party in power, supported by Agrarians: solid majority.
1940 9–15 April	German invasion, enabling Quisling to seize temporary power as self-proclaimed Premier.
25 September	Quisling ministers placed in office provisionally by German authorities.
1942 1 February	Quisling installed as Minister-President under German Reichscommissar.
1945 24 October	Quisling executed for high treason.

Great Britain

1896	Oswald Mosley born.
1914–18	16th Lancers, Royal Flying Corps, and temporary civil servant.
1918	Elected Coalition Unionist MP for Harrow.

1920		Married Lady Cynthia Curzon. Crossed floor as Independent in protest against the Black and Tans. Beginning of postwar mass unemployment.
1922–3		Re-elected for Harrow as an Independent.
1924		Joined Labour Party. Lost to Neville Chamberlain at Ladywood, Birmingham, in the general election of October 1924.
1925		Great Britain returns to the gold standard. Keynes wrote *The Economic Consequences of Mr Churchill*. Mosley wrote *Revolution by Reason*.
1926		Returned as MP for Smethwick.
1927		Elected to National Executive Committee of Labour Party.
1929	7 June	Chancellor of the Duchy of Lancaster in MacDonald's second Labour Government.
	29 October	Wall Street crash: beginning of the great depression.
1930	23 January	Mosley Memorandum sent to MacDonald.
	21 May	Mosley resigned as Chancellor of the Duchy.
	7 December	*Mosley Manifesto*.
1931	March	New Party formed; *A National Policy*.
	30 April	Ashton-under-Lyne by-election.
	24 July	Strachey and Young resigned from New Party.
	24 August	MacDonald formed the National Government.
	24 September	Great Britain forced off the gold standard.
	27 October	General election: New Party failed to win any seat of the twenty-four contested, Mosley losing at Stoke-on-Trent.
1932	January	Mosley visited Rome.
	April	New Party dissolved.
	1 October	British Union of Fascists established. Economic recovery started in Great Britain.

France (Chapter 12)

1934	6 February	Right-wing riot in Paris; Daladier government resigns on following day.
	27 July	Signature of 'unity of action' pact between the Socialist and Communist Parties – first major step towards formation of the Popular Front.

1935	14 July	Big Popular Front demonstration in Paris; *Croix de Feu* counter-demonstration.
1936	26 April– 3 May	Elections to the Chamber of Deputies resulting in a Popular Front majority.
	19 June	*Croix de Feu, Jeunesses Patriotes* and *Solidarité Française* dissolved by government decree.
	June	Jacques Doriot founds *Parti Populaire Français*.
1937	24 November	Marx Dormoy, Minister of the Interior, announces existence of a plot against the security of the state (the *cagoulard* conspiracy).
1938	9 April	Edouard Daladier forms government without socialist participation – this marks effective end of Popular Front.
	September	Munich agreement; resignations from PPF.
	30 November	Daladier government breaks general strike.
1939	30 July	Daladier government postpones elections until 1 June 1942 and enacts 'family code'.
	3 September	France declares war against Germany.
	26 September	Daladier government dissolves Communist Party.
1940	10 May	German attack in the west.
	17 June	Marshal Pétain forms government and asks for an armistice.
	10 July	French National Assembly meeting at Vichy rescinds constitution of the Third Republic and votes full powers to Marshal Pétain.
	18 October	Promulgation of first anti-Jewish measures.
1941	February	Marcel Déat founds *Rassemblement National Populaire*.
	26 October	Promulgation of 'Labour Charter'.
1942	11 November	Germans invade unoccupied zone of France.
1943	4 December	German ultimatum to Pétain, as a result of which Marcel Déat and Joseph Darnand enter the government.
1944	6 June	Allies invade Normandy.
	15 August	Allies invade southern France.
	August	Germans forcibly evacuate Vichy government to Belfort in eastern France; de Gaulle government takes over in liberated France.

1944 September — Germans forcibly evacuate Vichy government to Sigmaringen in Germany; formation of 'French governmental committee for the defence of national interests', which includes de Brinon, Déat and Darnand.

1945 6 January — Doriot forms 'French liberation committee'.

22 February — Doriot killed while on way to receive adhesion of Déat, Darnand and de Brinon to 'French liberation committee'.

7 May — Germany's unconditional surrender.

Spain (Chapter 13)

1898		Spanish-American war: loss of Cuba.
1917		General strike.
1923		Pronunciamiento of General Primo de Rivera.
1930		Fall of General Primo de Rivera.
1931		Abdication of King Alfonso XIII.
1931		Foundation of *La Conquista del Estado* by Ramiro Ledesma Ramos.
1931		Foundation of JONS by Onésimo Redondo and Ledesma Ramos.
1933		Foundation of FE (*Falange Española*) by José Antonio Primo de Rivera.
1933		Election of José Antonio Primo de Rivera as member of the Cortes.
1934		Merger of JONS in *FE de las JONS.*
1934		Asturias revolution.
1936	February	Popular Front wins election.
	March	Imprisonment of José Antonio Primo de Rivera.
	July	Military revolt and beginning of civil war. Death of Onésimo Redondo.
	August	Death of Ruiz de Alda.
	October	Franco proclaimed head of government.
	November	Death of José Antonio Primo de Rivera and of Ledesma Ramos.
1937	April	*L'affaire* Hedilla. Merger of Carlists and *Falange Española de las JONS.* Arrest of Hedilla and followers.
1938	January	Franco's first formal cabinet.
1939	April	End of the civil war.

1940	Serrano Súñer Foreign Minister.
1942	Dismissal of Serrano Súñer.
1948	Referendum declares Spain a monarchy.
1953	First bases agreement with USA.
1963	Bases agreement renewed.
1966	New constitution.

Portugal (Chapter 14)

1910	Manuel II deposed, Republic proclaimed.
1911	First Portuguese Republican constitution: President elected by Senate and Chamber of Deputies; universal suffrage.
1917–18	Short military dictatorship of Sidonio Pais, until his assassination.
1926	Military *coup*: dictatorship of Gomes da Costa, Carmona and Cabecadas.
1928	Salazar enters government as Finance Minister.
1930	Creation of the National Union (*União Nacional*), the only authorized party. Proclamation of the Colonial Act, which transforms the Overseas Provinces into colonies.
1932	Salazar becomes President of the Council of Ministers, while retaining his post as Finance Minister.
1933	Proclamation of the constitution, the basic document instituting the corporate state or *Estado Novo*. National Statute of Labour, reorganizing and integrating the trade unions within the corporate state.
1935	General Carmona re-elected to the Presidency of the Republic, with Salazar as President of the Council of Ministers.
1936	Creation of the Portuguese youth movement (*Mocidade Portuguesa*). Creation of the Portuguese Legion (*Legiao Portuguesa*), complementary to the youth movement, organizing adults above the age of eighteen.
1940	Concordat with the Vatican.
1945	Powers of the political police (PIDE) legally defined.

1949	Portugal enters NATO. Presidential election: opposition candidate, General Norton de Matos, withdraws before poll in protest against pre-electoral irregularities.
1951	Death of General Carmona. Opposition candidate for presidency, Admiral Quintão Meireles, withdraws before election; official candidate, General Craveiro Lopes, elected.
1958	Presidential elections: official candidate, Admiral Americo Tomaz, elected, but opposition candidate, General Humberto Delgado, former Portuguese representative in NATO, polls officially twenty-three per cent of votes.
1959	Decree law that henceforth president to be elected by an Electoral College and not by direct suffrage.
1961	Angolan nationalist movement begins armed insurrection. Portuguese territories of Goa, Damao and Diu annexed by India.
1962	Nationalist guerrillas begin insurrection in Portuguese Guinea. Student unrest and strikes in universities of Lisbon and Coimbra.
1965	Colonial war begins in Mozambique. General Delgado, in exile since 1958, murdered in Spain.

Bibliography

Italy

The bibliography on Italian fascism is vast. The author has found the following of use for the present essay. On the origins of fascism:

ALATRI, P. *Le origini del fascismo* (Rome 1962).

Il fascismo e i partiti politici (Bologna 1921, reprinted 1966).

PROCACCI, G. 'Appunti in tema di crisi dello Stato liberale e di origini del fascismo,' *Studi Storici*, V, 2 (1965).

'ROSSI, A.' (A. TASCA). *The rise of Italian fascism* (London 1938).

SALVATORELLI, L. *Nazionalfascismo* (Turin 1923).

I also wish to acknowledge my debt to G. Di Meo, who is engaged on exhaustive researches on the early *fascio*, and to A. Lyttleton, who is writing a history of Italy from 1922 to 1929.

On the fascist régime:

AQUARONE, A. *L'organizzazione dello stato totalitario* (Turin 1965).

CHABOD, F. *History of Italian fascism* (London 1963).

DEAKIN, F.W. *The brutal friendship. Mussolini, Hitler and the fall of Italian fascism* (London 1962).

SALVATORELLI, L. and MIRA, G. *Storia d'Italia nel periodo fascista* (Turin 1956).

SALVEMINI, G. *The fascist dictatorship in Italy* (London 1928).

SALVEMINI, G. *Under the axe of fascism* (London 1936).

UNGARI, P. *Alfredo Rocco e l'ideologia giuridica del fascismo* (Brescia 1963).

WISKEMANN, E. *The Rome-Berlin Axis. A history of the relations between Hitler and Mussolini* (London 1949).

The most exhaustive biography of Mussolini so far has only covered the early years:

DE FELICE, R. *Mussolini*, 2 vols (Turin 1965–6).

Of considerable interest, however, are the following biographies:

FERMI, L. *Mussolini* (Chicago 1961).

KIRKPATRICK, I. *Mussolini: study of a demagogue* (London 1964).

MEGARO, G. *Mussolini in the making* (London 1938).

Germany

ALLEN, W.S. *The Nazi Seizure of Power. The Experience of a single German Town. 1930–1935* (London 1966).

BRACHER, K.D. *Die Auflösung der Weimarer Republik* (Villingen 1964).

BRACHER, K.D., SAUER, W. and SCHULZ, G. *Die Nationalsozialistische Machtergreifung* (Cologne and Oppladen 1960).

BROSZAT, M. *Der Nationalsozialismus* (Stuttgart 1961).

BUCHHEIM, H. *Das Dritte Reich* (Munich 1958).

BUCHHEIM, H., BROSZAT, M., JACOBSON, H.A. and KRAUSNICK, H. *Anatomie des SS-Staates.* 2 vols (Freiburg-im-Breisgau 1965).

BULLOCK, A. *Hitler, a study in Tyranny* (2nd ed. London 1962).

FRANZ-WILLING, G. *Die Hitlerbewegung. Der Ursprung 1919–1922* (Hamburg 1962).

MASER, W. *Die Fruhgeschichte der NSDAP* (Frankfurt/M 1965).

MOSSE, G.L. *The Crisis of German Ideology* (London 1966).

NEUMANN, F. *Behemoth. The structure and practice of National Socialism* (New York 1944).

NOLTE, E. *Three Faces of Fascism* (London 1965).

PULZER, P.G.J. *The rise of political anti-semitism in Germany and Austria* (New York 1964).

SCHOENBAUM, D. *Hitler's Social Revolution: Class and Status in Nazi Germany, 1933–1939* (New York 1966).

SCHWEIZER, A.A. *Big Business in the Third Reich* (Indiana 1964).

The Third Reich. Published under the auspices of the International Council for Philosophy and Humanistic Studies and with the assistance of UNESCO (London 1955).

ZEMAN, Z.A.B. *Nazi Propaganda* (London 1964).

For more comprehensive bibliographical information on the history of national socialism the reader is referred to the catalogues issued by the Wiener Library in London and to the bibliographies published in the *Vierteljahrshefte für Zeitgeschichte* in Munich.

Austria

ANDICS, H. *Der Staat, den keiner wollte* (Vienna 1962).

Documents on German Foreign Policy, series C, vol. 5 (London 1966).

Heimatschutz in Österreich (Vienna 1935).

HOFMANN, J. *Der Pfrimer-Putsch* (Graz 1965).

JEDLICKA, L. 'The Austrian Heimwehr,' *Journal of Contemporary History*, vol. 1, no. 1 (1966).

JEDLICKA, L. 'Zur Vorgeschichte des Korneuburger Eides,' *Österreich in Geschichte und Literatur* (April 1963).

KEREKES, L. 'Die "weisse Allianz" ,' *Österreichische Osthefte*, vol. 7, no. 5 (1965).

KEREKES, L. *Abenddämmerung einer Demokratie. Mussolini, Gömbös und die Heimwehr* (Vienna 1966).

LOCHNER, L. (ed.), *The Goebbels Diaries* (London 1948).

MASER, W. *Die Frühgeschichte der NSDAP* (Berlin 1965).

MOSSE, G. L. 'The genesis of fascism,' *Journal of Contemporary History*, vol. 1, no. 1 (1966).

NEUBACHER, H. *Sonderauftrag Südost 1940–1945* (Göttingen 1956).

NOLTE, E. *Three faces of fascism* (London 1965).

PICKER, H. *Hitler's table talk* (London 1952).

PULZER, P.G.J. *The rise of political antisemitism in Germany and Austria* (New York 1964).

SCHILLING, A. *Dr Walter Riehl und die Geschichte des National-sozialismus* (Leipzig 1933).

SETON-WATSON, H. 'Fascism, Right and Left,' *Journal of Contemporary History*, vol. 1, no. 1 (1966).

STADLER, K.R. *Österreich 1938–1945 im Spiegel der NS-Akten* (Vienna-Munich 1966).

STADLER, K.R. *The birth of the Austrian Republic 1918–1921* (Leiden 1966).

STARHEMBERG, E.R. *Between Hitler and Mussolini* (London 1942).

SWEET, P.R. 'Mussolini and Dollfuss, an Episode in Fascist Diplomacy,' in J. Braunthal, *The tragedy of Austria* (London 1948).

WANDRUSZKA, A. 'Österreichs politische Struktur' in H.Benedikt, *Geschichte der Republik Österreich* (Vienna 1954).

Hungary

BIBÓ, I. *A Harmadik Út* (The Third Way – Essays in History and Politics), introd. by Z.Szabó (London 1960).

DARVAS, J. *Város az Ingoványon* (The City on the Swamp) (Budapest 1945).

DEÁK, I. 'Hungary' in *The European Right*, ed. H.Rogger and E. Weber (London 1965).

HORTHY, H. *Memoirs* (London 1965).

IGNOTUS, P. 'Radical Writers in Hungary,' *Journal of Contemporary History*, vol. 1, no. 2 (1966).

KÁLLAY, N. *Hungarian Premier* (New York 1954).

KÁROLYI, M. *Memoirs* (London 1956).

LÉVAI, J. *Black Book on the Martyrdom of Hungarian Jewry*, Zürich (Hungarian edition: Budapest 1946).

LÉVAI, J. *L'Église ne s'est pas tue – Dossier Hongrois 1940–1945* (Paris 1966).

MACARTNEY, C.A. *October Fifteenth – A History of Modern Hungary 1929–1945*, 2 vols, 2nd ed (Edinburgh 1961).

MACARTNEY, C.A. and PALMER, A.W. *Independent Eastern Europe – A History* (London 1962).

NEMES, D. *Az Ellenforradalom Története Magyarországon 1919–1921* (History of the Counter-revolution in Hungary) (Budapest 1962). An implicit but devastating criticism of this sort of 'simpliste' historiography can be found in T.Pethö's essay 'A király nélküli királyság és a tenger nélküli tengernagy korszaka' (The epoch of the kingdom without a king and of the admiral without a sea – Characteristic traits of the ruling class of the Horthy-epoch), published in the *Magyar Hirek Kincses Kalendáriuma* (Budapest 1966, pp. 87–98).

SETON-WATSON, H. *The East European Revolution* (London 1950).

SETON-WATSON, H. *Eastern Europe between the Wars* (Camb. 1946).

SULYOK, D. *A Magyar Tragédia* (The Hungarian Tragedy), (Newark 1954).

SZABÓ, A. and PAMLÉNYI, E. (ed.), *A határban a halál kaszál ... Fejezetek Prónay Pál feljegyzéseiböl* (Death scything nearby. ... Chapters from the notes of Pál Prónay). With an intr. study by the editors (Budapest 1963).

SZINAI, M. and SZÜCS, L. (ed.), *The Confidential Papers of Admiral Horthy* (Budapest 1965). See especially the following documents:

No. 15. Minutes of the first cabinet meeting convened during the Gömbös administration.

No. 16. Draft letter of M.Horthy to PM G.Gömbös ... on race protection (1933).

No. 30. Memorandum of Count I.Bethlen *et al.* to M.Horthy on the policy of the Imrédy government.

No. 35. Letter of PM Paul Teleki to M.Horthy on his controversy with the Chief-of-Staff (1 Sept. 1940) – see also Appendix no. 1.

No. 39*a*. Farewell letter of PM Teleki to M.Horthy before his suicide (3 April 1941).

No. 40. Letter of M.Horthy to A.Hitler on the suicide of Paul Teleki and the military mesaures taken ... by Hungary against Jugoslavia (3 April 1941).

No. 52. Memorandum of the MPS of the National Socialist Party, Federation of Hungarian Renewal, to M.Horthy on the policy of the Kállay administration. Signed by B.Imrédy, L. Baky and 31 other MPS (5 May 1943).

No. 62. Rescript of M.Horthy to PM D.Sztójay on the 'mitigation of certain exaggerations' in the 'solution' of the Jewish problem and on the dismissal of L.Baky and L.Endre (early June 1944?).

No. 64. Memorandum of Count I.Bethlen on the necessity of dismissing the Sztójay administration (end of June 1944).

Rumania

CODREANU, C.Z. *Pentru Legionari* (For the Legionari) (Bucharest 1936).

MOTSA, L. *Cranii de Lemn* (Wooden Skulls) (Sibiu 1936).

PAPANACE, C. *Martiri Legionari* (Rome 1952).

PATRASCANU, L. *Sous trois dictatures* (Paris 1946).

PROST, H. *Destin de la Roumanie* (Paris 1954).

ROBERTS, H. *Rumania* (New Haven 1951).

WEBER, E. 'The men of the Archangel,' *Journal of Contemporary History*, vol. 1, no. 1 (1966).

WEBER, E. 'Romania' in E. Weber and H. Rogger (eds), *The European Right* (London 1965).

Poland

No objective analysis of Polish politics between the wars and its social background exists. This is not a topic on which one can truthfully write in present-day Poland, while the exiled writers view the recent past with a romantic nostalgia, and are anxious to avoid mentioning anything which might throw a bad light on the country, as if an entire nation could be judged by the behaviour of its politicians, or as if one could not find plenty of disreputable deeds in every country's history. Anyway a sociological analysis of this picturesque society and culture – full of extraordinary contrasts and contradictions – remains to be done.

A competent account of the framework of events can be found in Hans Roos, *A History of Poland 1916–1945* (London), where further bibliography is given.

Although it deals only in part with Poland, Hugh Seton-Watson, *Eastern Europe Between the Wars* (Cambridge 1946) offers the best general account of the interplay between its economy, social structure and politics. An analysis of the causes of anti-semitism, which explains a number of points made in the present article, can be found in S. Andreski, *Elements of Comparative Sociology* (London 1964), chap. 21.

Norway and Finland

As the information about Norwegian fascism is widely scattered and in Norwegian, Dr Derry has preferred not to offer a bibliography which could be of little use to most readers. Students who wish to read further on the subject can contact Dr Derry at Nils Lauritssóns vei 27, Oslo 8, Norway.

Almost all works on Finland are in Finnish or Swedish, and students interested in pursuing the subject further can get in touch with Mr Upton. However, one work in English should be mentioned: M. Rintala, *Three Generations: the Extreme Right in Finnish Politics* (Bloomington 1962).

Great Britain

JONES, J. *Unfinished Journey* (London 1937).

KEYNES, J. M. *Essays in Persuasion* (London 1931).

MOSLEY, O. *The Greater Britain* (London 1932).

MOSLEY, O. *Revolution by Reason* (n.p., 1925).

A National Policy. An account of the Emergency Programme advanced by Sir Oswald Mosley, drafted by Allan Young, John Strachey, W.J. Brown, and Aneurin Bevan, March, 1931.

NICOLSON, H. *Diaries and Letters 1930–1939* (London 1966).

STRACHEY, J. *The Menace of Fascism* (London 1933).

TAYLOR, A. J. P. *English History 1914–1945* (Oxford 1965).

For a good modern account of the British Union of Fascists, see C. Cross, *The Fascists in Britain* (London 1961).

France

The following bibliography does not pretend to be in any way exhaustive. It merely lists the published sources which have proved most useful to me in the preparation of my essay.

ALLARDYCE, G. 'The Political Transition of Jacques Doriot,' *Journal of Contemporary History*, vol. 1, no. 1 (1966).

ARON, R. *Histoire de Vichy* (Paris 1954).

BELOFF, M. 'The Sixth of February,' in James Joll (ed.), *The Decline of the Third Republic* (St Antony's Papers No. 5) (London 1959).

BRISSAUD, A. *La Dernière Année de Vichy* (Paris 1965).

CHOPINE, P. *Six Ans chez les Croix de Feu* (Paris 1935).

COTTA, M. *La Collaboration, 1940–44* (Paris 1964).

DESGRANGES, A. *Journal d'un Prêtre Député, 1936–40* (Paris-Geneva 1960).

LIEBMANN, L. 'Entre le mythe et la légende: l'"anti-capitalisme" de Vichy,' *Revue de l'Institut de Sociologie* (1964, vol. I).

MICHEL, H. *Vichy Année 40* (Paris 1966).

NOGUÈRES, L. *La Dernìère Etape: Sigmaringen* (Paris 1956).

PICKLES, D. *France Between the Republics* (London n.d.).

PLUMYÈNE, J. and LASIERRA, R. *Les Fascismes Français, 1922–63* (Paris 1963).

RÉMOND, R. *La Droite en France*, 2nd ed. (Paris 1963).

ROCQUE, E. and G. DE LA. *La Rocque tel qu'il était* (Paris 1962).

'SAINT-PAULIEN' (M.-Y. SICARD), *Histoire de la Collaboration* (Paris 1964).

SOUCY, R. 'The Nature of Fascism in France,' *Journal of Contemporary History*, vol. 1, no. 1, (1966).

TOURNOUX, J.-R. *L'Histoire Secrète* (Paris 1962).

TRACOU, J. *Le Maréchal aux Liens* (Paris 1948).

'VARENNES, CLAUDE' (G. ALBERTINI). *Le Destin de Marcel Déat* (Paris 1949).

WARNER, G. *Pierre Laval* (London 1968).

WARNER, G. 'The Stavisky Affair and the Riots of February 6th, 1934,' *History Today*, June 1958.

WARNER, G. 'The Cagoulard Conspiracy,' *History Today*, July 1960.

WERTH, A. *France in Ferment* (London 1934).

WERTH, A. *The Destiny of France* (London 1937).

WERTH, A. *France and Munich* (London 1939).

Spain

The best general study of Spanish fascism is Stanley Payne's *Falange*, in particular the French edition of the book (Ruedo Ibérico 1964).

Useful studies illuminating one or other aspect of the movement before the civil war are: F.Ximénez de Sandoval's life of José Antonio: *José Antonio (Biografía Apasionada)*, Barcelona 1941; the short history of the *Falange* by F.Bravo Martínez, *Historia de la Falange Española de la JONS* (Madrid 1940); D.Jato's *La Rebelión de los Estudiantes* (Madrid 1953); and the study of the beginnings of the movement in Seville, by Julián Pemartín and Sancho Dávila, *Hacia la Historia de la Falange: Primera Contribución de Sevilla* (Jerez 1938).

Useful material can also be found in general studies, such as those of G.Brenan, *The Spanish Labyrinth* (Cambridge 1943), and Raymond Carr, *Spain 1808–1939* (Oxford 1966); on the civil war, Hugh Thomas, *The Spanish civil war* (London 1961), Gabriel Jackson, *The Spanish Republic and the Civil War* (Princeton 1966) and P. Broué and E. Jémime, *La Revolution de la Guerre d'Espagne* (Paris 1961). There are no good studies of Franco's Spain however; the most useful are those by A. Whitaker, *Spain, The Uncertain Ally* (Council on Foreign Relations 1961); and B. Welles' *The Gentle Anarchy* (London 1965). Recent biographies of Franco by Brian Crozier and R. Hills do not add much.

Portugal

AINSLIE, R. *The unholy alliance* (London 1962).

ANDERSON, P. *Le Portugal et la fin de l'ultra-colonialisme* (Paris 1964).

CAETANO, M. *O sistema corporativo* (Lisbon 1937).

DUFFY, J. *Portuguese Africa* (London 1962).

FERRO, A. *Salazar. Portugal and her leader* (Lisbon 1939).

FIGUEIREDO, A. *Portugal and its empire: the truth* (London 1961).

FRYER, P. and MACGOWAN PINHEIRO, P. *Oldest ally. A portrait of Salazar's Portugal* (London 1961).

MENDEZ FONSECA, M. *El fracaso del salazarismo* (Caracas 1963).

OLIVEIRA, A. DE. 'Salazar's Portugal' in *Angola: a symposium* (London 1962).

OLIVEIRA SALAZAR, A. DE. *Discursos (1923–34)*, (Coimbra 1935).

OLIVEIRA SALAZAR, A. DE. *Doctrine and Action. Internal and foreign policy of the New Portugal, 1928–1939* (London 1939).

OLIVEIRA SALAZAR, A. DE. *El pensamiento de la Revolución Nacional* (Buenos Aires 1938).

PEQUITO REBELO, J. A. *Pela dedução a Monarquia* (Lisbon 1922).

PINTO DE MESQUITA, S. *O espírito corporativo* (Barcelos 1936).

PROENÇA, R. *Acerca do integralismo lusitano* (Seara Nova 1964).

ROLÃO PRETO, F. *A monarquia é a restauração da inteligência* (Lisbon 1920).

SARAIVA, A. J. 'Portugal,' *International Socialist Journal*, II, 7 (1962).

XAVIER PINTADO, V. *Structure and growth of the Portuguese economy* (New York 1964).

Fascism in Contemporary Europe

The best source of information in English on the political underworld of the fascist hard core is the Wiener Library Bulletin.

The most comprehensive work that has yet appeared, covering both hard core and parties of the extreme Right, is: ANGELO DEL BOCA and MARIO GIOVANA, *I 'figli del sole'* (Milan 1965). Most of the same ground is covered, less thoroughly, in: DENNIS EISENBERG, *The Re-emergence of Fascism* (London 1967). Unfortunately, though Eisenberg's book contains much information, it is selected and presented uncritically, and few references to sources are given.

M. BARDÈCHE, *Qu'est ce que le fascisme?* (Paris 1961), is an illuminating and beautifully written apologia by a contemporary fascist intellectual.

On fascism and the Extreme Right in France:

RÉMOND, R. *The Right Wing in France, from 1815 to De Gaulle* (Philadelphia 1966).

HOFFMANN, STANLEY. *Le mouvement Poujade*, Cahiers de la Fondation Nationale des Sciences Politiques, No. 81 (Paris 1956).

PLUMYÈNE, J. and LASIERRA, R. *Les Fascismes Français 1923–63* (Paris 1963).
GIRARDET, R. (ed.) *La Crise militaire française 1945–62* (Paris 1964).

On Germany:
Wiener Library Bulletin, New Series, Nos. 4 and 6 (1966–7): two informative articles on NPD.
MONTAGU, IVOR *Germany's New Nazis* (Panther Books 1967) (published after this essay was written).

Index

Contributors

S. ANDRESKI, M.Sc.(Econ.), Ph.D.(Lond.), Professor of Sociology, Reading University.

Z. BARBU, Ph.D.(Glas.), D.Phil.(Cluj), Professor of Sociology, Sussex University.

T. K. DERRY, M.A., D.Phil.(Oxon.), author of *A Short History of Norway*.

J. ERÖS, D.Phil.(Heidel.), Ph.D.(Manc.), Senior Lecturer in Political Institutions, Keele University.

H. MARTINS, Department of Sociology, Pennsylvania University.

A. J. NICHOLLS, M.A., B.Phil.(Oxon.), Fellow of St Antony's College, Oxford.

CHRISTOPHER SETON-WATSON, M.C., M.A., Tutor, Lecturer in Politics, Vice-Provost, Oriel College, Oxford.

R. J. A. SKIDELSKY, Research Fellow, Nuffield College, Oxford.

K. R. STADLER, B.A.(Brist.), M.A.(Lond.), Senior Lecturer, Department of History, Nottingham University.

HUGH THOMAS, M.A.(Cambridge), Professor of History, Reading University.

H. R. TREVOR-ROPER, M.A.(Oxon.), Regius Professor of Modern History, Oxford University.

A. F. UPTON, M.A.(Oxon.), A.M.(Duke), Lecturer in Modern History, St Andrews University.

G. WARNER, B.A.(Cambridge), Lecturer in Politics, Reading University.

S. J. WOOLF, M.A., D.Phil.(Oxon.), Reader in Italian History, Reading University.